Macroeconomic Policies of Developed Democracies

This book synthesizes and extends modern political-economic theory to show how varying interest and institutional structures and shared exposure to similar economic challenges interact to explain commonalities and divergences in the postwar evolution of macroeconomic policies in developed democracies. Where more participatory institutions enhanced governmental responsiveness to inequality and economic hardship, transfers grew more dramatically. Where more fractionalized governments retarded fiscal-policy adjustment rates, debt responses to spending growth, shocks, and other conditions were greatly magnified. These differently rising costs of transfers and debt spurred anti-inflationary policy shifts that amplified fiscal problems and proved more costly where monetary conservatives confronted less coordinated, public-sector-led rather than more coordinated, traded-sector-led wage-price bargainers. The book shows how such multiple interactions among political-economic institutions and interests induce differing policy choices and effects across democracies; how to model such complexly interactive propositions empirically compactly and substantively revealingly; how such arguments and models explain the evolution of developed democracies' macroeconomic policies from postwar commitments to full employment and social insurance to more recent conservative monetary, fiscal, and other "reforms"; and how political conflicts over such policy and institutional choices always were and still remain primarily about distribution, and only subsidiarily about efficiency, whatever partisan protagonists may claim.

Robert J. Franzese, Jr., is an assistant professor in the Department of Political Science, a faculty associate of the Center for Political Studies of the Institute for Social Research, and a faculty affiliate and advisory board member of the Center for European Studies of the International Institute at the University of Michigan, Ann Arbor.

Cambridge Studies in Comparative Politics

General Editor

Margaret Levi *University of Washington, Seattle*

Associate Editors

Robert H. Bates *Harvard University*
Peter Hall *Harvard University*
Stephen Hanson *University of Washington, Seattle*
Peter Lang *Duke University*
Helen Milner *Columbia University*
Frances Rosenbluth *Yale University*
Susan Stokes *University of Chicago*
Sidney Tarrow *Cornell University*

Other books in the series

The list continues on the page following the index.

Macroeconomic Policies of Developed Democracies

ROBERT J. FRANZESE, JR.
The University of Michigan

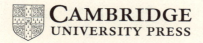

CAMBRIDGE
UNIVERSITY PRESS

PUBLISHED BY THE PRESS SYNDICATE OF THE UNIVERSITY OF CAMBRIDGE
The Pitt Building, Trumpington Street, Cambridge, United Kingdom

CAMBRIDGE UNIVERSITY PRESS
The Edinburgh Building, Cambridge CB2 2RU, UK
40 West 20th Street, New York, NY 10011-4211, USA
477 Williamstown Road, Port Melbourne, VIC 3207, Australia
Ruiz de Alarcón 13, 28014 Madrid, Spain
Dock House, The Waterfront, Cape Town 8001, South Africa

http://www.cambridge.org

© Cambridge University Press 2002

First published 2002

Printed in the United Kingdom at the University Press, Cambridge

Typeface Janson Text Roman 10/13 pt.   *System* QuarkXPress [BTS]

A catalog record for this book is available from the British Library.

Library of Congress Cataloging in Publication data
Franzese, Robert J. 1969–
    Macroeconomic policies of developed democracies / Robert J. Franzese.
        p.   cm. – (Cambridge studies in comparative politics)
    Includes bibliographical references and index.
    ISBN 0-521-80294-6 – ISBN 0-521-00441-1 (pbk.)
    1. Economic policy.   2. Comparative economics.   3. Democracy.
I. Title.   II. Series.
HD87 .F715   2001
339.5–dc21
                                                             2001035033

ISBN   0 521 80294 6   hardback
ISBN   0 521 00441 1   paperback

For my family, with all my love:

To my mom, Pierina Franzese, my first and still my best teacher; I would never have begun and could never have completed this project without her loving guidance and encouragement from start to finish.

To my dad, Robert J. Franzese, whose industrious example I have always tried to follow but have seldom equaled; I would have completed this project years ago had I managed that.

And to my sisters, Tonie, Roberta, and Rachel, whose loving support (and teasing) made this project's long gestation bearable by keeping it all in perspective and perhaps (though not likely) prevented me from becoming a *total* geek.

Contents

Tables and Figures

Tables

Figures

Tables and Figures

Tables and Figures

Preface

The most striking and strikingly common features of the postwar history of macroeconomic policy in developed democracies were the sharp upward trends in transfer payments and attendant increases in total fiscal activity, the dramatically rising public debt–to-GDP ratios since the stagflationary 1970s, and the strong shifts toward antiinflationary monetary policies and institutions that followed. Policy and outcome differences, however, were at least as notable. Transfers share of GDP nearly septupled in the Netherlands while less than doubling in Germany. Irish, Italian, and Belgian government debt rocketed past 100% of GDP, while remaining more subdued in the United Kingdom and generally declining in Australia. Inflation, drifting higher through the 1960s and spiking twice in the 1970s, eventually subsided everywhere, but at differing paces and to differing degrees, while the unemployment costs of that policy shift varied even more radically.

This book applies and extends modern political-economic theory to explain the commonalities and differences in this evolution of macro-economic policies and outcomes across 21± developed democracies over the 50± years since World War II. Through this explanation, the book elaborates a theoretical view of comparative political economy in which *similar* policy-making challenges and *universal* tensions between the allocations of political and economic resources in liberal-market democracies induce *different* policies and outcomes because the domestic and international political-economic institutions, interest structures, and conditions within which public and private actors operate and to which they respond differ across countries and over time. Moreover, the policy and outcome effects of interests, institutions, and conditions are generally complex, because each factor tends to *interact* with the rest in shaping the incentives of strategic political-economic actors. Thus, most broadly, policy and outcome commonalities arose because similarly democratic governments had similarly conflicting goals, felt similarly incongruent political and economic pressures, and faced similar international and domestic policy challenges. Yet differences also emerge because the shared pressures and challenges create different incentives for strategic actors operating under differing structures of international and domestic political-economic institutions and interests, and, in particular, these institutions, interests, and conditions typically *interact* to shape public and private actors' incentives, and thus their choices, and so political-economic outcomes.

To be sure, the broad claim that differing political-economic institutions induce different policy and outcome responses to similar stimuli is a core tenet of comparative and international political economy and hardly new, although many of the specific propositions I forward in that regard are novel. That institutions have complex effects because they interact among themselves and with the structure of interests and other impetuses in the political economy to shape the incentives of strategic public and private actors is also an increasingly emphasized theme in political economy, although, again, the implications of this view are clarified here and many of the specific interactions illuminated are entirely novel. The book's broader and newer contributions, though, arise from how it links (semi)formal theoretical explorations of such strategic interactions to empirical specifications of statistical models that more directly reflect such interactive propositions, and those empirical specifications to the substantive illustration of the strong historical-comparative support for such carefully specified propositions. That chain yields, I believe, theoretical, methodological, and substantive payoffs.

Theoretically, I take a more formal approach than is common in work stressing institutional interactions, which clarifies certain interactive effects others have intuited and uncovers some new ones, and a more holistic approach than is common in most other studies that attempt some degree of formal analytic precision, which underscores the importance of institutional interactions more usually suppressed in such work. Chapter 2, for example, affirms that more participatory democracy induces greater government responsiveness to its whole citizenry, but clarifies how this implies that electoral and other institutions that impact participation interact with underlying income inequality to determine the *effective* democratic impetus toward transfers. Similarly, Chapter 3 clarifies that the impact of governmental institutions that create more policy-making veto actors is to retard policy adjustment rates and that this implies that fractionalization of governments magnifies the long-run fiscal effects of *all* other political-economic conditions. And Chapter 4 demonstrates that the impact of conservative monetary policy on nominal (e.g., inflation) and real (e.g., unemployment) outcomes varies with the broader structure of interests in the political economy and, especially, with the institutions and structure of wage-price bargaining. Most challenging to conventional wisdom, that study reveals that recent conservative "reforms" of monetary policy-making institutions often had relatively small antiinflationary benefits but sizable real (equilibrium) costs.

Methodologically, the book shows how empirical specifications that more precisely reflect theoretically predicted effects can provide strong evidentiary leverage on such complexly interactive and dynamic theoretical propositions, even from the very limited data available to comparative political economists, and in tractable and intuitive ways from which we can learn. For example, while a standard multiplicative interaction term suffices to capture the proposition that proparticipatory institutions enhance government responsiveness to inequality, the proposition that fractionalized governments retard policy adjustment implies the long-run effects of *all* other variables depend on fractionalization and so may seem to require many interactive terms. Chapter 3 demonstrates, however, that a single conditional (interactive) temporal-correlation parameter encapsulates that proposition more directly, efficiently, and intuitively than would the great many (and therefore inestimable) individual interaction terms. The proposition that the nominal effects of monetary conservatism depend on the broader structure of interests in the entire political economy can likewise be modeled remarkably compactly, intuitively, and powerfully with one single parameter reflecting the degree to which autonomous central banks can resist democratic governments' desires to respond to political-economic pressures. And, in each of these cases, the limited comparative-historical evidence available supports such carefully specified interactive predictions very strongly.

Substantively, in applying this interactive view of comparative political economy to the study of transfers, debt, and monetary policy, and in empirically evaluating the emergent propositions, the book also offers a theoretically guided, aggregate empirical history of the postwar evolution of macroeconomic policy in developed democracies. That historiography demonstrates that (1) this evolution has increased the political-economic difficulties for democratic management of the macroeconomy by exacerbating the distributional conflicts inherent in the policies to which governments have committed while undermining those policies' more universally desired roles in fostering economic efficiency and growth; so (2), in response, democratic policy makers increasingly turned sequentially through emphases on fiscal policies to monetary policies to various political-economic institutional and structural "reforms," aiming to rebuild broad coalitions behind their purported efficiency-improving effects; but (3) these "reforms," whatever their efficiency effects, and despite frequent claims to the contrary by many politicians and some academics, retain strong distributional effects; and so (4) the familiar, traditional conflicts of macro-political-economy between right and left – efficiency-equity, growth-distribution, inflation-unemployment – that used to occur primarily over policies conducted within the framework of the postwar policy commitments are reproduced in modern battles over putative "reforms" of that framework, that is, in conflicts over the institutional rules within which democratic struggle over macroeconomic policy and the structure of free-market competition will continue. Figuratively, even as the battleground changes, the battles remain remarkably familiar: "reform" is often just another word for "redistribution."

All data used in this book and many supplementary tables, figures, and analyses are available from the author's web page, currently located at <http://www-personal.umich.edu/~franzese>.

Acknowledgments

I proceed chronologically here to relate the book's development and to thank properly the many mentors, colleagues, and friends whose valuable advice immensely improved the final product (even if I have not always managed to incorporate it fully). All remaining inadequacies are entirely mine and, indeed, are all the more inexcusable considering the wealth of intellectual input received.

I began developing these arguments as a graduate student in the Departments of Government and Economics at Harvard University, September 1990 to June 1996. I received financial support in those studies from a Harvard Graduate Student Fellowship (1990–1); a National Science Foundation Graduate Student Fellowship (1991–4); grants from the NSF, the Wissenschaftszentrum-Berlin, and Harvard's Center for European Studies for research travel (summer 1993); a fellowship from the NSF-funded Harvard-MIT Research Training Group in Positive Political Economy (RTGPPE) (1994–5); and a Mellon Foundation Dissertation Completion Fellowship (1995–6). Since then, the Political Science Department, the Center for Political Studies of the Institute for Social Research, and the Rackham Graduate School at the University of Michigan, Ann Arbor, have funded my work and paid my salary, except for a fruitful stint from January to June 2000 during which I visited the Political Science Department at the University of California, Los Angeles. I also have deepest gratitude for several organizations, especially the Lee Iacocca Foundation, whose undergraduate scholarships enabled me to attend Cornell University to major in government and in economics. I am very grateful to these generous benefactors for having opened so many doors for me and hope they may continue to be able to open doors for many more in the future.

My debts of intellectual gratitude are no smaller. I began in June and completed in August 1993 the first draft paper to contain the germs of arguments more fully developed later exploring the political-economic implications of monetary institutional "reform" toward credible conservatism. That project, begun at the Wissenschaftszentrum-Berlin under David Soskice's invaluable tutelage, undergirds Chapter 4. Upon returning, I discovered that Peter Hall, one of my dissertation advisors, was developing related arguments. His earliest work on the topic appeared in the *Financial Times* and *German Politics and Society* in 1994. I later discovered that Torben Iversen, another advisor, was also working on another aspect of these issues. Although our projects began separately and retain important differences, discussions with Peter and Torben certainly helped shape and improve my own arguments. Especially valuable to me were the time and effort Peter and I spent developing the shared portions of our arguments and relating them to European Monetary Union. Various aspects of these arguments, and some extensions as they evolved, appear in Hall and Franzese 1998; Franzese and Hall 2000; Franzese 1999a,b, 2000a, 2001. However, none brings all the theory and evidence together and relates it to the broader political economy of postwar macroeconomic policy in developed democracies as does Chapter 4, which represents my current, fullest view and also contains much new material.

Exploration of developed democracies' turn to monetary conservatism led me to the "explosion" of public debt, which seemed to have reduced fiscal-policy maneuverability and efficacy and so helped spur that policy shift. I wrote the seeds of Chapter 3, exploring the political-economic sources of public-debt growth, as an RTGPPE fellow in the 1994–5 academic year, gratefully receiving Jim Alt's and Alberto Alesina's expert advice and guidance, and the helpful comments of discussant Jaume Ventura. I have presented various aspects and iterations of this project (Franzese 1998a and precursors) in many other venues and developed one aspect more thoroughly in Franzese 2000b. Again, only Chapter 3 brings it all together and relates it to the comparative democratic management of the macroeconomy, and it also contains much that is wholly new.

Studying the growth of public indebtedness led, in turn, to the growth of government fiscal activity more generally. Chapter 2, which explores the political-economic sources of differential public-transfers growth, the main engine of total fiscal growth, originated in a paper presented to the RTGPPE in 1995, which received valuable input in those early stages from that forum and from my committee. In revisions for presentations to the

Acknowledgments

1998 American Political Science Association (APSA) Meetings (Franzese 1998b) and in various other venues, Chris Achen's and Nancy Burns's sound advice improved the current product greatly.

Finally, Ken Kollman's careful reading of the introduction saved me from several sophomoric gaffs persisting from its original version, written in summer 1996, and suggested how to set the stage more effectively for the rest of the book. Seven anonymous reviewers at three university presses (Cambridge, Princeton, and Michigan) also deserve grateful acknowledgment, especially in this regard.

I could not possibly manage to thank all the generous intellects whose input – advice, data, criticism, kind encouragement – made this manuscript possible and better, but I am pleased to try, hoping that those I unwittingly neglect will forgive me. First, to my dissertation committee chair, Jim Alt, and committee member and graduate-student faculty-advisor, Peter Hall, I am eternally grateful and indebted beyond hope of repayment for past and continuing guidance and for specific comments and advice regarding this manuscript. Committee members Torben Iversen and Alberto Alesina likewise have my deepest gratitude for help and guidance on several parts of the book.

In addition to advice early and throughout from David Soskice, Peter Hall, and Torben Iversen, Chapter 4 greatly benefited from comments on various aspects of the broader project from Chris Achen, Bob Barsky, Neal Beck, Greg Caldiera, Steve Casper, Pradeep Chhibber, Alex Cukierman, Tom Cusack, Jakob De Haan, John Freeman, Geoff Garrett, Jim Granato, Jon Hanson, John Huber, Vince Hutchings, Paul Huth, Bill Keech, Ken Kollman, Barbara Koremenos, Ann Lin, Susanne Lohmann, Sylvia Maxfield, Walter Mebane, Bob Pahre, Torsten Persson, Jonas Pontusson, Jim Poterba, Michael Ross, Jasjeet Sekhon, Mariano Tommasi, Andrés Velasco, Michael Wallerstein, and Nick Winter.

Chapter 3, its precursors, and relatives received valuable input from Jim Alt and Alberto Alesina as mentioned, and also benefited from very insightful discussants: Jaume Ventura at RTGPPE, Michael Wallerstein at APSA 1997, and Antonio Merlo at the Rochester-Northwestern Wallis Institute Political Economy Conference. Mark Hallerberg, John Huber, Louisa Lambertini, John Londregan, Torsten Persson, Rolf Strauch, George Tsebelis, and Jürgen Von Hagen, and participants at the Wallis Conference and the Institutions and Fiscal Policy Conference at the Zentrum für Europäische Integrationsforschung (Bonn), both in 1998, also offered comments that vastly improved the final product.

Chapter 2 and precursors received valuable input from my committee and from Chris Achen and Nancy Burns as mentioned, and also benefited from the comments of discussants Steve Ansolabahere (RTGPPE in 1995), Torben Iversen and Thomas Cusack (1996 APSA), Carles Boix and Michael Thies (1998 APSA), and Bill Clark (2000 APSA). Jeff Lewis, Tom Romer, John Huber, Nolan McCarty, Helen Milner, and others also offered very helpful comments at presentations at Columbia and Princeton in October 1998.

Finally, over these ten years, a host of helpful souls have aided in ways not yet detailed (providing data, criticizing, commending, provoking thought, etc.). Adding those whom the preceding discussion neglects produces the following daunting list of intellectual creditors: Chris Afendulis, Alberto Alesina, Jim Alt, Steve Ansolabahere, Bob Bates, Neal Beck, Ken Benoit, Bill Bernhard, Carles Boix, Nancy Burns, Randy Calvert, Steve Casper, Kelly Chang, Pradeep Chhibber, Bill Clark, Mary Corcoran, Alex Cukierman, Tom Cusack, Sheldon Danziger, Don Davis, Jakob De Haan, Avinash Dixit, Alan Drazen, Jim Ellis, Sven Feldman, Mo Fiorina, John Freeman, Jeff Frieden, Geoff Garrett, Roberta Gatti, Miriam Golden, Jim Granato, Tim Groseclose, Peter Hall, Mark Hallerberg, Will Heller, John Huber, Torben Iversen, Amaney Jamal, Kenneth Janda, Cindy Kam, Bill Keech, Lane Kenworthy, Gary King, Hans-Dieter Klingemann, Ken Kollman, Barbara Koremenos, Peter Lange, David Leblang, Jeff Lewis, Susanne Lohmann, John Londregan, Bryan Loynd, Nolan McCarty, Greg Mankiw, Catherine Matraves, Sylvia Maxfield, Walter Mebane, Antonio Merlo, Helen Milner, Irfan Nooruddin, Harvey Palmer, Brad Palmquist, Sofia Perez, Roberto Perotti, Torsten Persson, Jonas Pontusson, Keith Poole, Jim Poterba, Tom Romer, Jeff Sachs, Ken Scheve, Ken Shepsle, Curt Signorino, Jasjeet Sekhon, Beth Simmons, Renée Smith, David Soskice, Rolf Strauch, Duane Swank, Guido Tabellini, Kathleen Thelen, Michael Thies, Ashley Timmer, Mariano Tomasi, Dan Triesman, George Tsebelis, Andrés Velasco, Jürgen Von Hagen, Michael Wallerstein, Chris Way, Ann Wren, and Vincent Wright, and seven anonymous reviewers. My deepest gratitude to all of these and my apologies to those I have inadvertently slighted.

1

Introduction

1.1. Overview

The most striking features of the postwar history of macroeconomic policy in developed democracies[1] are the dramatic and considerably common upward trend of transfer payments, the attendant increase in total fiscal activity, the sharp post-oil-crisis rise in public debt, and the strong shift toward antiinflationary monetary policy that followed. Upon closer examination, however, the differences in policies and outcomes across countries and over time are at least as striking.

For example, the average share of gross domestic product (GDP) devoted to transfer payments in 21 developed democracies more than tripled from 6% (±) to 20% (±) from the 1950s to the 1990s, yet transfers septupled in the Netherlands while less than doubling in Germany. Driven heavily by this transfers growth, the 21-country average of total fiscal activity, government revenues plus expenditures as a share of GDP, almost doubled from 40% to 70% in the same period. This growth eventually

---

[1] *Developed democracies*, here and throughout, are the relatively wealthy, capitalist, and democratic countries: the United States, Japan, (West) Germany, France, Italy, the United Kingdom, Canada, Austria, Belgium, Denmark, Finland, Greece (excluding an autocratic period in the late sixties and early seventies), Ireland, the Netherlands, Norway, Portugal and Spain (since their democratic transitions in the late seventies), Sweden, Switzerland, Australia, and New Zealand. The chosen sample reflects that the arguments considered in this book typically presuppose relatively free-market capitalism and relatively liberal democracy to be undisputed among relevant political-economic actors. The theoretically important aspect of that presupposition is that decision makers do not seriously consider continued democracy or free-market capitalism themselves to be at risk depending on their actions. *Developed democracies* are occasionally abbreviated as the "OECD" because they are that organization's prominent membership, but this is merely a convenient empirical (not theoretical) grouping.

1

spurred public debt accumulation, but, again, debt burdens exploded in some places while remaining far more moderate in others. The average debt-to-GDP ratio fell from 38% in the 1950s to 25% in the mid-1970s before rising to 63% by the mid-1990s, yet debt rocketed past 100% of GDP in Belgium, Ireland, and Italy while remaining much more moderate in the United Kingdom and mostly declining in Australia over this period. Finally, as rising transfer and debt liabilities reduced fiscal efficacy and maneuverability, governments commonly turned to monetary and other institutional "reforms" aiming to restrain inflation. Again, however, they did so to varying degree and with varying effects. From 1980 to the 1990s, inflation fell everywhere, from 13% to 3% on average, but less so or more slowly in some places and more dramatically elsewhere, while the accompanying unemployment and growth effects varied even more radically.

This book draws from, synthesizes, and extends current political-economic theory to explain these policy and outcome developments, both the commonalities and the differences. It emphasizes that and shows how international and domestic political-economic institutions, structures of interests, and conditions *interact* to shape different incentives for strategic political-economic actors from the largely common challenges they face; it demonstrates that careful incorporation of such interactive theoretical propositions into empirical specifications allows the limited data available to provide leverage; and it shows the comparative-historical record to support such well-specified, highly interactive propositions strongly.

The commonalities, for their part, are readily explained. In every capitalist democracy, postwar governments committed to some degree of political provision of social insurance, public goods, and macroeconomic management. Over the ensuing decades, however, policy makers faced political-economic challenges in which the broader goals underlying these commitments – to foster capitalist efficiency and growth and to alleviate their distributional consequences – often conflicted because, in short, democracy and capitalism allocate political and economic influence differently. The differing allocation of political and economic power, ultimately of votes and wealth, produced popular pressure on policy makers everywhere to make trade-offs between their competing goals that typically expanded the public role in the economy. Thus, summarizing drastically, the commonalities arose because similarly democratic governments with similarly conflicting policy goals faced similarly incongruent distributions of political and economic influence and similar domestic and international policy challenges.

These shared challenges and universal tensions, however, also induced strikingly different policies and outcomes across countries and over time. Again summarizing drastically, these differences arose because the incentives for political-economic actors that emerge from their similarly conflicting goals and the similar distributions of influence on them differ according to multiple interactions among the domestic and international institutions, structures of interests, and conditions within which they interact and to which they respond.

In elaborating the theoretical bases and demonstrating empirical support for these broad claims, the book makes five specific contributions.

First, most narrowly, Chapters 2–4 offer self-contained studies of the politics and economics of macroeconomic policy making and outcomes in developed democracies. Chapters 2 and 3 address fiscal-policy, public transfers and debt respectively, and Chapter 4 analyzes monetary policy and wage-price regulation. Chapter 2 stresses that electoral institutions and party systems that foster more participatory democracy enhance government responsiveness to income disparity, resulting in more swiftly expanding transfer payments where conditions produced greater pre-transfer inequality. Chapter 3 emphasizes that party systems and governmental institutions that create more policy-making veto actors retard fiscal-policy adjustments to political-economic challenges, inducing, for example, greater post-oil-crises increases in public debt where governmental fractionalization was larger. Chapter 4, lastly, shows that the anti-inflationary effects of the ensuing monetary-policy shift depended on the structure of interests in the broader political economy and the degree to which conservative central banks or responsive governments controlled monetary policy, and it demonstrates that the real (e.g., employment) costs of that policy shift depended on the interaction of the monetary authorities' degree of credible conservatism with wage-price bargainers' sectoral composition and degree of coordination.

Second, more broadly, the book elaborates through these studies a theoretical view of comparative political economy in which universal tensions between liberal democracy and free-market capitalism, arising from their differing distributions of political (votes) and economic (wealth) influence, induce strategic public policy makers and private actors to respond differently to similar challenges because the varying international and domestic political-economic institutions, structures of interests, and conditions within which they act and to which they respond *interact* to shape their incentives differently. That is, differences in how governments resolved their conflicting goals in responding to similar pressures arose from variations in the broad configuration of political-economic institutions and interests, as well as from any differences in the specific policy challenges, they faced. And, in particular, the effects of these political-economic conditions, institutions, and interests are generally complex because they tend to interact to induce differing public policies and private choices and, thus, outcomes.

Third, methodologically, in establishing the historical support for these claims, the book demonstrates powerful, yet tractable and intuitive, empirical techniques for gaining evidentiary leverage on such complexly interactive and dynamic theoretical propositions from the limited data available to comparative political economists. These methods stress foremost the careful incorporation of theoretically predicted interactive effects into the empirical specifications. For example, while a standard multiplicative interaction term suffices to capture Chapter 2's core new proposition, that institutions that foster more participatory democracy enhance government responsiveness to underlying inequality, Chapter 3's emphasized proposition, that fractionalized governments retard fiscal-policy adjustment rates, implies that the long-run effects of *all* other variables depend on governmental fractionalization. The chapter shows how a conditional (interactive) temporal-correlation parameter suffices to encapsulate all these interactive effects more compactly, powerfully, and intuitively than would the great many (and thus inestimable) individual interactions that are implied. Chapter 4's propositions that the nominal (inflation) effects of monetary conservatism vary with the broader structure of interests across the political economy, and that the real (e.g., output) effects of monetary conservatism and the structure of wage-price bargaining depend on each, likewise imply multiple interactive effects. Nonlinear models and linear models with nonlinear regressors, respectively, can again capture these many interactions compactly, powerfully, and intuitively. On the nominal side, for example, a single parameter reflecting the degree to which conservative central banks as opposed to politically responsive governments control monetary policy encompasses all the theoretically implied interactions. Dynamics, too, receive careful attention, especially regarding transfers and debt policy where the evidence strongly suggests distinct and important short-run momentum-like and long-run equilibrium-like relationships. Lastly, the empirical work also stresses intuitively revealing presentation, making extensive use of graphical hypotheticals – some types of which may be new to and have broader application in the field – to illustrate the substantive import of the statistical support for the theoretical propositions and to facilitate evaluation of the relative weight of various political-economic factors in explaining the historical record.

Fourth, in applying this interactive view of comparative political economy to studies of transfers, debt, and monetary policy, and evaluating the propositions that emerge, the book offers a theoretically guided aggregate empirical history of the postwar evolution of macroeconomic policy in developed democracies.

Fifth, in accomplishing these tasks, the book argues most substantively that (1) this evolution has involved increasing political-economic difficulties for democratic management of the macroeconomy, exacerbating the distributional conflicts inherent in the policies to which governments had committed while undermining their more universally desired role in fostering economic efficiency and growth; so (2), in response, democratic policy makers increasingly turned sequentially through emphases on fiscal and then monetary policies toward various political and economic structural and institutional "reforms" intended to rebuild broad coalitions behind their purported efficiency-improving effects; but (3) these "reforms," whatever their efficiency effects, and despite frequent claims to the contrary by many politicians and some academics, retain important distributional implications; and so (4) the familiar, traditional macro-political-economic conflicts between right and left – efficiency versus equity, growth versus distribution, inflation versus unemployment – which used to occur primarily over policies conducted within the framework of the postwar commitments, are now reproduced in modern battles over putative "reforms" of that framework, that is, in conflicts over the institutional rules within which democratic struggle over macroeconomic policy and free-market competition will continue.

The rest of the chapter completes this introduction thus. Section 1.2 describes the commitments to political provision of social insurance, public goods, and macroeconomic management that all developed democracies made to some degree in the postwar era, and the tensions among those commitments created by the differing allocation of political and economic influence in capitalist democracy. Section 1.3 offers a brief empirical tour of the extent and evolution of these commitments – documenting trends in total government-size generally, and in public transfers, debt, and employment specifically, and concurrent trends in macroeconomic performance (unemployment, inflation, and growth) – and presages some of the arguments and findings in subsequent chapters that explain these developments. Section 1.4 outlines a *cycle of political economy* framework within which explanations for these developments are derived theoretically and examined empirically. That framework underscores the book's core interactive and dynamic contentions, that similar political-economic challenges induce different policy choices and outcomes across countries and over time according to multiple interactions among the political-economic institutions, interests, and conditions within which democratic policy makers and private actors operate and to which they respond. Section 1.5 overviews some of the political and economic consequences of the trade-offs between the public-policy agendas embodied in the commitments. That is, it discusses some of the ways the problematic *policy* developments affect the political and economic *outcomes* about which citizens, and therefore policy makers and scholars, ultimately care. The section previews the argument, elaborated and empirically substantiated in the book, that modern political struggles over institutional-structural "reforms" reflect rather than replace familiar left-right conflicts over policies. Section 1.6 relates the arguments and evidence offered here to other recent contributions in comparative and international political economy, and guides the reader through the consummation of these agendas in the rest of the book.

1.2. The Democratic Commitments to Government Involvement in the Macroeconomy

Political scientists have long noted that, in the postwar era, governments in all developed democracies committed themselves, to greater or lesser degrees, to three economic policy agendas: (1) some provision of social insurance for disability, illness, old age, and unemployment; (2) some provision of "public" goods and services (often beyond the standard public goods of economic theory); and (3) some public management of the macroeconomy and the macroeconomic cycle through fiscal, monetary, and wage-price management policy.[2]

---

[2] For alternative expressions of this "postwar settlement" on the "class compromise" inherent in the "Keynesian welfare state," see, e.g., Shonfield 1965; Cameron 1978; Cameron and McDermott 1995; Esping-Andersen 1985, 1990; Katzenstein 1985; Hall 1986; Lindblom 1977; Offe 1984; Rose 1984; Wilensky 1975.

The terms of this postwar commitment were perhaps most explicitly stated in the United Kingdom. The 1942 Beveridge Report to Parliament advocated universal social security and fully publicly funded health care (the National Health Service), was largely achieved under Aneurin Bevan's leadership (1946–8), and has not been seriously challenged since, until recently. Concurrently, the 1944 White Paper on Employment Policy, also largely unchallenged until recently, confirmed bipartisan acceptance of political responsibility for macroeconomic management: "The Government accepts as one of their primary aims and responsibilities the maintenance of a high and stable level of employment after the war" (quoted from Hall 1986). Although often more implicit elsewhere, some degree of such commitment to social-insurance, public-goods, and macroeconomic-management provision was evident, and broadly unchallenged, in all developed democracies, until recently.

1.2.1. The Postwar-Settlement, Neoclassical, and Class-Compromise Views

Classic contributions to comparative political economy refer to these commitments and the policies and policy-making institutions that arose to fulfill them variously as the "postwar settlement," "class compromise," or "Keynesian welfare state." Each phrase refers to essentially the same constellation of policies and policy-making structures but also carries an implicit statement of its political and economic purposes and, thereby, of its political-economic underpinnings. Doing great injustices to each view, their cores may be distilled thus.

In the postwar-settlement view, these commitments arose from immediate postwar struggles over government's appropriate role in the economy, wherein key interest groups fought to set public-private boundaries that would maintain and augment their advantages. It thus stresses the commitments' political roles in setting the ground rules under which legitimate democratic contestation of, and distributional conflict over, government action in the economy would continue. From this view, macroeconomic policy and outcome variations stem primarily from cross-national differences in the organization of key interests and the institutions of governmental politics (e.g., the organization of labor and employers; the electoral, party, and governmental systems) and the position of the country in the global economy. Aspects of this view figure prominently in, for example, Katzenstein's *Small States in World Markets*

(1985), Hall's *Governing the Economy* (1986), and Gourevitch's *Politics in Hard Times* (1986).

The neoclassical view emphasizes instead the economic roles of the policy commitments, focusing on the common interest of political-economic actors in a system that fosters "efficiency"-enhancing public economic action. However, the view also stresses that democratic governments will not automatically undertake even highly "efficient" actions. Rather, it acknowledges that political economies contain divisions that spur the more purely distributional or otherwise political battles highlighted in the postwar-settlement view. Indeed, from this view, precisely this political contestation over distributional effects jeopardizes the commitments' aggregate "efficiency." Such concerns – that democracy relatively empowers those underprivileged economically and educationally by free-market outcomes and may thereby endanger capitalism itself – have a long (traceable, e.g., to Aristotle), varied (including, e.g., Mill and Marx in broad agreement), and distinguished (e.g., Tocqueville, Hamilton) intellectual pedigree:

The egalitarian threats of mass society and democratic mass politics . . . would necessarily lead to tyranny and "class legislation" by the propertyless, uneducated majority. (J. S. Mill, quoted in Offe 1984: 179)

[Democracy is] a political form that . . . exacerbate[s] social contradictions by withdrawing political guarantees from the socially dominant and giving political power to the subordinate. (Karl Marx, quoted in Offe 1984: 179)

Current scholars emphasize democratic dangers to capitalist "efficiency" rather than to capitalism itself, sometimes explicitly considering the presumed efficiency costs of the postwar commitments to be the price at which they reduce such dangers to free-market capitalism. From this view, *varying* macroeconomic policy and outcome deviations from a presumed-common optimum stem from differing organizational advantages of "special" interests (Olson 1965, 1982) and other characteristics of electoral and governmental politics that weigh citizen inputs to democratic policy making differently than the market weighs their inputs to aggregate economic outcomes: for example, the division of voters into electoral districts, or the obstruction of policy-making decisiveness from multiple veto-actors within government. This view most animates the public-choice school as, for example, in Buchanan and Wagner's *Democracy in Deficit* (1977) and Meltzer and Richard's "A Rational Theory of the Size of Government" (1981).

From the class-compromise view, the set of policies and policy-making structures that support the three commitments serves to co-opt the working class sufficiently to enable capitalist accumulation to continue relatively unmolested under democracy. The core conflict, from this view, involves bringing the necessary productive results of capitalism into manageable disagreement with its inevitable consequence of relative working-class impoverishment. Key to the evolution of macroeconomic policies and outcomes from this view, then, are the political and economic strength of capital and labor, and the alliances each are able to make within the party system. Aspects of this view are prominent in, for example, Esping-Andersen's *Politics against Markets* (1985) and *Three Worlds of Welfare Capitalism* (1990) and Offe's *Contradictions of the Welfare State* (1984).

This book takes each of these classic views as stressing different but equally real aspects of the commitments to political provision of social insurance, public goods, and macroeconomic management. These commitments did and do serve as the accepted boundaries for the continuing democratic struggle between conflicting interests in society. They did avert working-class radicalization,[3] and conflicts between their goals of fostering capitalist growth and efficiency and of alleviating their inegalitarian consequences do remain fundamental. And the differing distributions of political and economic influence in capitalist democracy did and do make achievement of the neoclassical conception of "efficient" macroeconomic management politically problematic.

1.2.2. Emerging Challenges

The set of policies and policy-making institutions that implement these commitments has felt considerable strain in recent years. Popular and academic presses everywhere now teem with cries for governments to redress burgeoning social-insurance systems and public indebtedness and for related public-policy "reforms." For example, in recent annual reports on key political issues written by local experts in twenty-eight democracies (*European Journal of Political Research*, 1992–8), virtually every entry

---

[3] Modern readers should not forget that European fascism rose partly in response to grounded fears of radical communism and that these fears continued to drive foreign and, somewhat, domestic policies through at least the early postwar period.

mentions one or more of these issues as a – or often as *the* – major political issue in the country.[4]

Not coincidentally, seemingly inexorable growth of government, higher
unemployment, and slower real growth accompanied the rising discontent.
In the most dramatic cases, transfers exceeded 25% of GDP in Belgium,
Finland, the Netherlands, and Sweden; public debt surpassed 100% of
GDP in Belgium, Italy, and Ireland; and public employment accounted for
over 30% of total in Denmark, Norway, and Sweden. Meanwhile, double-
digit unemployment became common, and sustained real per-capita
growth surpassing 3% seemed only a fond memory in most countries.
In this context, recent lamentations (or celebrations) of "crises" in the
Keynesian welfare state (KWS) are understandable (if not necessarily justified). This book seeks to explain prominent aspects of this varying public-
sector growth and macroeconomic-performance decline and to explore
their political-economic consequences for the continued viability and
utility of these policy commitments.

Broadly, these "crises" have roots in two related contradictions, which
a synthesis of the classic views will illuminate. As the class-compromise
view emphasizes, in implementing the KWS, governments sought simultaneously to address two core needs of democratic-capitalist society:

> The strategic intention of Keynesian economic policy is to promote growth and
> full employment, the strategic intention of the welfare state to protect those
> affected by the risks and contingencies of industrial society and to create a measure
> of social equality. The latter strategy becomes feasible only to the extent that the
> first is successful, thereby providing the resources necessary for welfare policies
> and limiting the extent to which claims are made on these resources. (Offe 1984:
> 198–9)

Thus, policy makers sought to buttress and to facilitate capitalist development but also to alleviate its distributional consequences. As Offe notes,
only success in the former goal can sustain pursuit of the latter; but, as he
also notes,[5] the two goals frequently proved inimical:

1. The Keynesian welfare state is a victim of its own success. By (partly) elimi-
nating and smoothing crises [i.e., economic downturns], it has inhibited the posi-

---

[4] Only issues surrounding the European Union, the new democracies in Eastern Europe,
and various corruption scandals are near as prominent over this period.

[5] He attributes these arguments to "conservative economic policy ideologues" but notes that
they are "equally, if reluctantly, acknowledged by practice and partly by theories of the left"
(nor does he challenge them himself).

tive function that crises used to perform in the capitalist process of "creative destruction."

2. The Keynesian welfare state involves the unintended but undeniable consequence of undermining both the incentives to invest and the incentives to work.

3. There is no equilibrating mechanism or "stop-rule" that would facilitate adjustments of the extensions of social policy so as to eliminate its self-contradictory consequences; the logic of democratic party competition and the social democratic alliance with unions remains undisciplined by "economic reason." (Offe 1984: 199)

The first two points are the core contradiction from a class-compromise view. Capitalist development cannot continue (politically) without government involvement in alleviating the risks of macroeconomic fluctuations and in sufficiently co-opting workers (i.e., without the KWS), yet successful alleviation and co-optation undermine the incentives that drive capitalist development, which, in turn, is necessary to fund the KWS. The postwar-settlement and neoclassical views more clearly explicate the third point and its relation to the first two.

As in Meltzer and Richard (1978, 1981) most directly, the neoclassical view identifies the fundamental problem in the democratic implementation of KWS policies as arising from the differential distribution of influence in the political and economic arenas. Democracy, in principle, distributes political influence uniformly: one person, one vote. In the economic arena, however, the unit of influence is wealth, which capitalism tends to distribute with right skew (many poor and middle class, fewer wealthy and some very rich). Therefore, when democratic policy makers must make trade-offs between their goals of fostering capitalist development and of alleviating its distributional consequences, as they frequently must, they will tend to overemphasize redistribution relative to growth and "efficiency." From this view, then, capitalist democracy creates a natural tendency toward government "over-"activity in the economy.

What actually results from this *potential* conflict between the distributions of electoral and monetary influence, though, is an empirical issue. If, for example, control of investment capacity more than compensates for the fewer votes of the wealthy, the effects just described would reverse. Also, as others in this school stress, "rationally ignorant" voters[6] will find

---

[6] *Rationally ignorant voters* recognize as minuscule the probability of one individual's vote altering an electoral outcome and thus the expected benefits of casting an informed vote, so they do not expend effort becoming informed.

accurate cost-benefit evaluation of government activities difficult because budgets are complex (Buchanan and Wagner 1977) and because the value of public goods is inherently difficult to gauge (Downs 1960). If the latter consideration dominates, or if the spending-side dominates the revenue-side complexity of budgets, then democratic governments will do too little. Thus, political-economic analysis must go beyond mere counting of votes to assess *effective* political weight, considering the cognitive challenges for voters and other potential sources of political influence (e.g., economic resources, institutional organization) that may counteract or reinforce electoral numbers.

Moreover, as the postwar-settlement view best highlights, interests that cut across class divisions can also employ political means. For example, when terms-of-trade or technological shifts threaten particular economic sectors, the goals of fostering growth and reducing inequality can again conflict.[7] Capital and labor in the afflicted sector will likely press policy makers for subsidies, protection, or other redress for their losses. Accommodating such demands may accord with governments' distributional goals, but, by hindering capital and labor reallocation to maximize gains from trade or technological improvement, it would also retard growth. Again, political influence will not generally be distributed such that democratic policy makers will make trade-offs that reflect the unweighted sum of their citizen's interests. Following Olson (1965), for example, the group seeking compensation for trade losses is much smaller than that which would pay for them (consumers and taxpayers) and so could likely bring more effective political force behind gaining subsidies than their relative numbers alone would suggest.[8] Again, the analysis of *effective* political

---

[7] Some limited subsidy mechanism might even be economically efficient as social insurance against uncertainty over returns to investment subject to such risks. Even so, a trade-off would exist between the distributional goal and the need for insurance on the one hand and gains from trade and technological progress on the other hand. The different distribution of political and economic power and the different ways in which each translates into political influence would imply that democratic policy makers will not generally make such trade-offs "efficiently."

[8] The preceding paragraphs may seem contradictory. The first argues that, as poor outnumber rich, democratic governments will overemphasize distributional relative to efficiency goals. The second claims, contrarily, that the smaller group will influence policy more. The first seems to ignore Olson's "logic of collective action," but the types of policies and the absolute and relative sizes of the groups involved differ importantly. Broad redistribution distinguishes only rich from poor. Both groups are "very large" from an Olsonian view, so neither can coordinate much more effectively than the other. The other policies distinguish one sector from the rest, and a sector is much smaller, especially on the

influence must go beyond raw numbers to consider organization and other political resources. Chapters 2 and 3 attempt some inroads into the empiricism necessary to address these issues.

Thus, the postwar-settlement and neoclassical views both suggest possible tendencies toward overprovision and overmanagement in the evolution of the democratic commitments to social insurance, public goods, and macroeconomic regulation. This, as the class-compromise view elucidates, suggests a universal tendency toward "crises" – that is, increasing difficulties in rectifying the equality- and growth-fostering goals of these commitments. Indeed, the extreme sizes to which some public sectors grew and the rising predominance of public-sector "reform" as a political issue provide prima facie evidence of such tendencies. However, not every developed democracy accumulated equally massive debt, nor does each face the same difficulties in macroeconomic management, nor does each have equally burgeoning transfer systems. Yet, although no two countries confront the same set of difficulties, times and places where at least one of these elements does not seem critically overextended are exceedingly rare. That is, at different times in different places, the universal pressures manifest as different "crises."

Subsequent chapters offer and empirically evaluate explanations for these phenomena. Broadly, the different distribution of economic and political resources fundamentally drives the deviation of democratic governments' policies from those that would maximize unweighted sums of their citizens' interests. Because international and domestic structures of institutions and interests differ over time and across countries, however, public policy makers and private actors respond to these common pressures differently, producing *differing* deviations from textbook "optima," even when facing similar political-economic challenges. For example, plurality laws in parliamentary systems tend to produce single-party governments of oscillating partisanship, rendering stable and consistent policies difficult to maintain over time. Conversely, proportional-parliamentary systems tend to produce multiparty coalition governments of less variable partisanship, facilitating policy stability but also tending to produce sluggish policy responses to economic challenges. (Note that, as often found

employer side, than the economy and so should manage to coordinate much more effectively. Plus, losses from freer trade are concentrated, individually large, certain, and current while gains are diffuse, uncertain, and future. Gains and losses from broad redistributive policies tend, contrarily, to be more certain and current, and of more-equal relative magnitude.

in this book, neither institutional structure is unambiguously superior; rather, each has differing strengths and weaknesses.)

1.3. The Evolution of the Policy Commitments and of Macroeconomic Performance

1.3.1. Overall Government Activity in the Economy

Figures 1.1–3 begin broadly, graphing the postwar evolution of total public activity in the macroeconomy in 21 developed democracies, respectively plotting consolidated central-government revenue plus expenditure as a share of GDP[9] annually within each country, by each country's postwar average with standard deviation and interextrema ranges, and by each year's cross-country average and variation. As seen, public economic activity was large and expanded dramatically in most times and places.

Figure 1.1 reveals, for example, that roughly half the economy circulated through government by 1990 in France, Belgium, Denmark, Ireland, the Netherlands, Norway, Portugal, Sweden, and New Zealand. In six others – Germany, Italy, the United Kingdom, Austria, Finland, and Greece – public budgets circulated more than a third of GDP by 1990. Only the United States, Japan, Canada, Spain, Switzerland, and Australia kept their total public flows below 60% of GDP. From 1950 to 1990, government size tripled in Sweden and doubled or more in most other countries, including many that began the postwar era with smaller governments, although some retrenchment is now visible. A fairly common pattern of roughly stable sizes until the seventies, swift expansion in that stagflationary decade, slower growth through the eighties, and some retrenchment since then is apparent. Yet, variation in government size and in the pattern and pace of its growth is at least as striking.

Figure 1.2 highlights the tremendous cross-country variation. Differences across countries' postwar averages alone encompass 50%[10] of the total country-time variation seen in Figure 1.1. French, Belgian, or Dutch governments, for example, averaged about four times the Swiss and over

---

[9] IMF, *International Financial Statistics*, 6/96 CD-ROM, extended by tape and print editions where possible. "Consolidated central government" excludes subnational governments but includes separate national public agencies. Analogous graphs of revenues or expenditures alone are available on the author's web page <http://www-personal.umich.edu/~franzese>.

[10] I.e., $R^2 \approx .539$ from regressions of revenues plus expenditures on the complete set of country indicators.

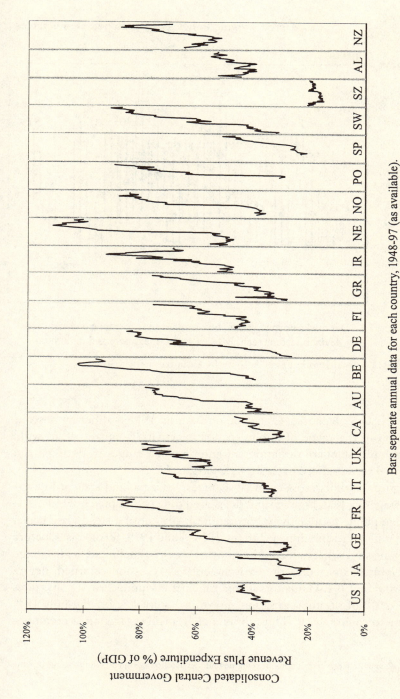

Figure 1.1 Total Public Fiscal Activity by Country-Year

Bars separate annual data for each country, 1948-97 (as available).

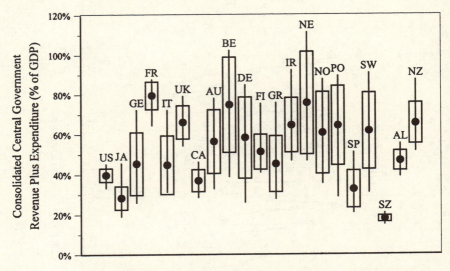

Dot marks postwar mean; box extends plus to minus one standard
deviation from mean; lines extend to maximum and minumum.

Figure 1.2   Total Public Fiscal Activity by Country

twice the U.S., Japanese, Canadian, or Spanish. Widely differing postwar
variation in the scope of public economic activity is equally clear, with,
for example, standard deviation and interextrema ranges in Portugal and
Austria dwarfing those in Australia and Canada.

Figure 1.3 plots cross-country averages, extrema, and standard deviation ranges by year, highlighting the shared time path espied in Figure 1.1.
Average public fiscal activity hovered near 40% until a steady rise began
in the mid-sixties; it jumped with the 1973–4 and 1979–80 oil crises, before
flattening somewhat in the mid-eighties. Some retrenchment begins in the
late eighties, aborted in the early nineties as recession returned, before
renewing by 1994. While this shared time path is quite clear, it constitutes
only 32%[11] of the total variation shown in Figure 1.1, leaving fully 18%
unique to country-year. Thus, differences remain as striking as common-

---

[11] I.e., $R^2 \approx .321$ from regressions of revenues plus expenditures on the complete set of time
indicators.

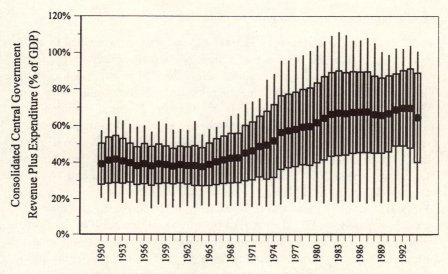

Dot marks 21-country mean; box extends plus to minus one standard deviation from mean; lines extend to maximum and minumum.

Figure 1.3 Total Public Fiscal Activity by Year

ality, with rising variance (and skew, with a few governments remaining much smaller than others) readily apparent.

To sum, the overall public economy clearly exhibited some common tendency to expand considerably in the postwar era, as synthesis of the classic views suggested. As Chapters 2–4 demonstrate in more detail, common patterns at this broad level arose because governments faced similar economic conditions and political pressures in implementing their shared commitments to social insurance, public goods, and macroeconomic management. Still, wide variation in where, when, and to what extent government economic activity grew remains to be explained. Some of the variation obviously stems from differences in the political-economic challenges faced; but, in exploring three prominent components of this expansion, Chapters 2–4 find the differing structures of political-economic institutions and interests, and key interactions among them, were also central. The next subsection details empirical developments in these components: public transfers, debt, and employment.

1.3.2. Aspects of the Size and Growth of Government

1.3.2.1. Transfer Payments

If total government grew swiftly in most countries, Figure 1.4 reveals that transfers grew absolutely meteorically virtually everywhere.[12] For example, in less than 40 years, transfers share of GDP more than sextupled in Finland and the Netherlands, more than quadrupled in the United States, Japan, Greece, Norway, Portugal, and Sweden, and more than doubled everywhere else except Germany (where it rose by over 50%). Indeed, all 21 countries now redistribute over 10% of GDP; three exceed 25%: Finland, the Netherlands, and Sweden; and five more exceed 20%: France, Austria, Belgium, Denmark, and Norway. Contrarily, in the early fifties, nine – the United States, Japan, Canada, Finland, Greece, Ireland, Norway, Switzerland, and Portugal – redistributed less than 5%. The sizable redistribution characteristic of developed democracies and the dramatic and common upward trends depicted in Figures 1.4–6 give further prima facie suggestion that the different distributions of political and economic influence in capitalist democracy create certain universal pressures toward large and expanding government activity in the economy. The rapid redistributive growth also renders recent widespread cries for transfer-system "reform" unsurprising (without implying that outcry is warranted). However, variation across time and countries is again as noteworthy.

The common trend illustrated in Figure 1.5 accounts for 48% of the total variation, but widening diversity and skew across countries over time are as apparent. Standard deviation ranges in the eighties double those in the sixties, and a few countries began to amass much larger transfers than others in the seventies. Moreover, cross-country variation in postwar average transfers share (Figure 1.6) is nearly as large (43% of the total) as the shared time path. For example, Belgium averaged over three times the share of GDP transferred that Portugal averaged and over twice the U.S., Japanese, Canadian, or Australian average. Variations in transfer system size over this period also differed greatly; the Dutch transferred as little as 5.5% and as much as 28.3% of GDP, a 22.8% range, and the Finns from 4.4% to 25.4% (range, 21%); Australian and Japanese transfers ranged only from 5.1% to 11.3% and 2.8% to 12.1% (ranges, 8.2%, 9.3%), respectively.

---

[12] OECD, *National Accounts, vol. 2: Detailed Tables*, 1996 disk, extended by print editions where possible. "Transfer payments" sum items 30–32 (social-security benefits, welfare, and pensions) of "Table 6: Accounts for General Government." "General Government" includes national and subnational governments and separate public agencies.

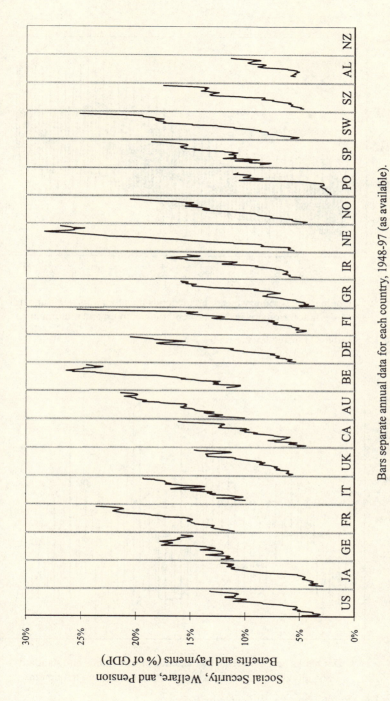

Figure 1.4 Public Transfer Payments by Country-Year

Bars separate annual data for each country, 1948-97 (as available).

19

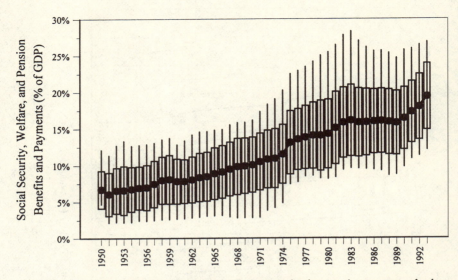

Dot marks 21-country mean; box extends plus to minus one standard
deviation from mean; lines extend to maximum and minumum.

Figure 1.5   Public Transfer Payments by Year

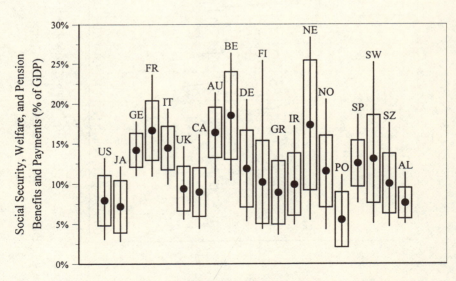

Dot marks postwar mean; box extends plus to minus one standard
deviation from mean; lines extend to maximum and minumum.

Figure 1.6   Public Transfer Payments by Country

20

Introduction

Chapter 2 seeks to explain these widely varying sizes and growth rates of redistributive states and their shared upward trend. The commonalities are largely economic and demographic in origin; higher unemployment and inequality, lower inflation,[13] older populations, and, especially, slower growth increased the costs of the democratic commitments to social insurance. As the previous section would suggest, all democratic governments found reducing transfers generosity to redress these increased costs very difficult because net beneficiaries of progressive transfer systems outnumbered net contributors and also because older citizens, having already paid for others' generous transfers, were now reluctant to accept reductions in theirs. Thus, over the postwar era, all democracies experienced swift growth in and now have large transfer systems.

Part of the explanation for the striking variation in transfers growth stems simply from differences in these economic and demographic conditions, but as much arises from differing structures of political-economic institutions and interests, and interactions thereof, across these country-times. Stronger blue-collar organization, for example, fostered larger redistributive states, as did greater risks to individuals' income streams produced by rising volatility in income distribution. Election year politics and government partisanship also played predictable roles.

Most interesting, though, was how transfer systems responded differently to income inequality in different polities. The right skew of income distribution in all capitalist societies (i.e., many more poor and middle class than rich) implies that net beneficiaries of broadly proportional and progressive transfer systems outnumber net contributors, perhaps creating popular pressure for redistribution. However, what matters democratically is the distribution of income relative to that of political influence: specifically, the *mean income in the population* relative to income of the person at the *median of political influence*. Because relative wealth correlates positively with political participation,[14] more-participatory democracies generally exhibit greater skew between the population's mean income and the income of the median-influence citizen for any given societal income distribution. Thus, governments in democracies whose institutions fostered greater, broader citizen participation responded to (increases in)

---

[13] Evidence indicates that transfer systems less than fully adjust for inflation in the short run. Thus, reduced inflation actually increases the real costs of transfers.
[14] Some other conditions, which Chapter 2 explains, and which the evidence suggests hold, are also necessary.

21

income disparity with more generous (increases in) transfers than did those in less-participatory democracies. In short, the interaction of the structure of interests, as reflected in the income distribution, with political institutions, specifically those that affect participation, produced greater or lesser transfers growth across different country-times.

Chapter 2 then demonstrates that the dramatic (but varying) transfers growth drove the (also varying) general-government growth and that the latter, in turn, tended to drive proportionate deficits. Specifically, the estimates suggest that governments typically expanded total spending to absorb transfers shocks fully – not reducing other spending to counteract those shocks – but that they gradually redressed expenditure shocks by reducing other expenditures excluding transfers. Thus, transfers growth drove general-government growth. The estimates also reveal that only about two-thirds of spending increases, in transfers or elsewhere, was typically met over the intermediate term by corresponding revenue increases. Thus, government growth, in turn, tended to drive public-debt growth.

Finally, Chapter 2 notes that, while these burgeoning transfer systems did generally alleviate the distributional disparities arising from unfettered capitalist competition, they also tended to reduce labor market flexibility, exacerbating (especially long-term) unemployment problems. Thus, recent political battles over "reforms" of transfer systems involve familiar left-right issues quite directly. Greater social-insurance generosity tends to increase unemployment, as critics argue, but also reduces the economic hardships of those unemployed, as critics forget.

1.3.2.2. Public Debt With sharp rises in transfers and other spending, the widespread and rapid public-debt growth documented in Figure 1.7 is unsurprising.[15] More unexpected perhaps is that debt-to-GDP ratios

---

[15] The data are gross debt of consolidated central government, taken from IMF, *International Financial Statistics*, 6/96 CD-ROM, extended where possible from tape and print editions and by country-specific regressions on OECD data for net and gross debt of general government (from OECD, *National Accounts, vol. 2: Detailed Tables*, 1996 disk, extended from print editions). Regression of each on the other two extends all three series, yet none is ideal. The IMF data neglect subnational debt, which is substantial in some places. The OECD gross and net series double-count in some places by including debts from one level of government to another. The net-debt series also has very limited coverage. The book employs the IMF data because they cover the largest sample by far and because the arguments to be explored regarding debt determination generally refer to central government. Nonetheless, correlations across series are comfortably high (see Chapter 3).

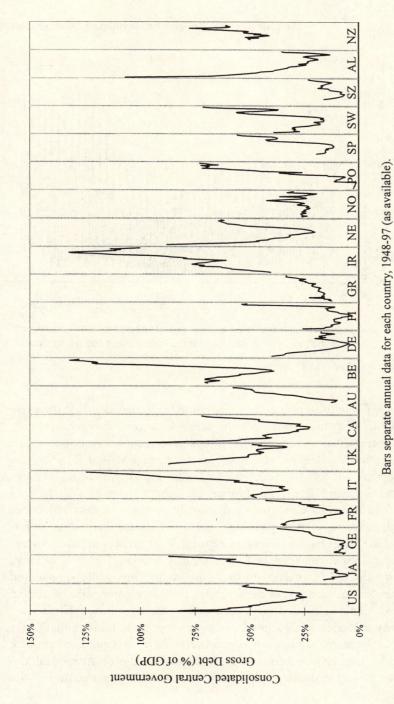

Figure 1.7 Public Debt by Country-Year

Bars separate annual data for each country, 1948-97 (as available).

23

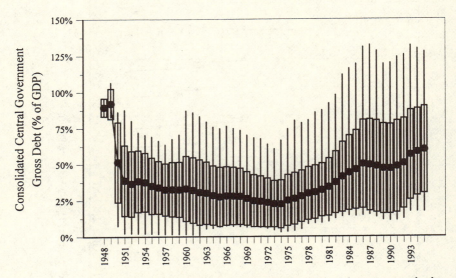

Dot marks 21-country mean; box extends plus to minus one standard deviation from mean; lines extend to maximum and minumum.

Figure 1.8 Public Debt by Year

generally fell in most places until stagflation hit in the seventies to reverse the trend. Debt often rose swiftly thereafter, with some retrenchment only now apparent. Variation is again as notable as commonality, however. For example, Italian, Belgian, and Irish debts topped 100% of GDP by the late eighties after slight reductions in the fifties, whereas Swiss, Danish, French, German, Greek, and Norwegian debt remained below 50% of GDP and Australia even managed roughly continuous debt reduction. Indeed, the common time path highlighted in Figure 1.8 accounts for just 19% of the total variation shown in Figure 1.7; differences in postwar averages across countries (Figure 1.9), contrarily, account for 55% of total, leaving fully 26% of total unique to country-year. Thus, while some shared debt tendencies emerged in the seventies, debt levels and paths of decline and growth also exhibited vast cross-country and over-time differences.

Chapter 3 explores these public-debt developments, reinforcing themes from Chapter 2's exploration of transfers. First, economic conditions, especially the adverse terms-of-trade shocks in the seventies and the ensuing slow growth and high unemployment, were again central to the

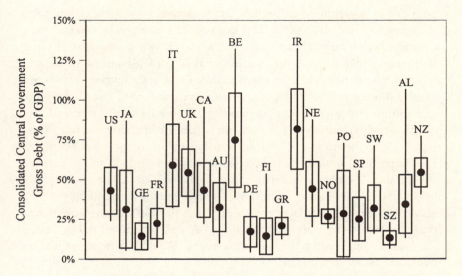

Dot marks postwar mean; box extends plus to minus one standard deviation from mean; lines extend to maximum and minumum.

Figure 1.9   Public Debt by Country

common time path.[16] Given governments' policy commitments, these shocks reduced revenues and increased expenditures, creating structural deficits that everywhere reversed downward trends. Then, as policy makers turned in the eighties toward monetary contraction to combat inflation, real interest rates skyrocketed, increasing interest payment burdens on their now accumulating debts, and inducing explosive debt in countries that entered this period with relatively large debt burdens, like Italy, Belgium, and Ireland. By themselves, these economic conditions, the variation across country-times in their incidence, and the temporal dynamics of debt can explain 43% of the total variation observed in Figure 1.7.[17]

Second, varying structures of political-economic institutions and interests, and certain key interactions among them, were again especially critical to cross-country and country-time-unique variation. Election-year

[16] For obvious reasons, demography drove debt less than it did transfers.

[17] I.e., $\bar{R}^2 \approx .43$ in a panel-weighted regression of deficits on lagged deficits and debts and the economic conditions mentioned (see Chapter 3).

politics and government partisanship, for example, played interesting roles (Chapter 3; Franzese 2000b). The extra deficits induced by election-year competition are large enough and debt adjusts slowly enough for election frequency, which depends on constitutional and other institutional factors, to impact long-run debt levels appreciably. Contrarily, partisan effects are usually shorter-term, smaller, and often counterintuitive, but can be large and intuitive if government-partisanship alternations are large and frequent, which again depends largely on institutional characteristics of the polity. Other broad macro-institutional aspects of the political economy, like central bank autonomy and conservatism, presidentialism, and perhaps the number of electoral districts and federalism,[18] also figure prominently in persistent cross-country differences. Varying tax system complexity may also have fostered differing degrees of "fiscal illusion" among voters (i.e., citizen difficulty in evaluating the full costs and benefits of public activities) and so produced important differences in public-debt accumulation over time by elected governments.

Most important and interesting, however, was how greater numbers of policy-making veto actors ("government fractionalization") – again, something largely determined by electoral, party, and governmental systems – retarded fiscal adjustments to the expenditure, revenue, and interest rate shocks described here. Absent adjustment, the adverse shocks would have created explosive debt paths in many countries. However, any proposed adjustment plan would typically favor some groups over others, so parties to budgetary legislation contested the allocation across their constituencies of these adjustment costs, even if they agreed on the necessity of fiscal redress. Where governments were more unified (e.g., single-party majorities in parliamentary systems), fewer veto actors operated on the policy-making process, so majorities could more easily shift the costs onto opponents' constituencies. Where governments instead contained multiple veto actors (as, e.g., in multiparty coalitions), these actors found plans that would distribute costs neutrally among themselves more difficult to devise. In such circumstances, governments delayed fiscal adjustments, magnifying the long-run impacts of *all* other factors, and especially the explosive impacts of the high real interest rates that followed stagflation. Notice in Figure 1.7, for example, that the United Kingdom, Canada, Italy, and Belgium had similar debts as the seventies began, yet debt exploded in Italy and Belgium, which had multiparty coalition governments, but

[18] See Chapter 3 for details, discussion, and qualifications.

not in the United Kingdom and less in Canada, which had single-party governments.

Thus, once again, similarly capitalist democracies faced similar economic challenges to their similar policy commitments, yet differences as large as the commonalities emerged in policy responses because policy makers' responses depend on interactions of differing structures of interests and institutions.

Chapter 3 then demonstrates that, at least in the short run, deficit spending by governments has had statistically and substantively significant impact on unemployment and inflation, generally reducing the former and increasing the latter, but has not had significant impact on growth. Thus, recent debates over fiscal "reforms" intended to reduce debt are, in fact, distributional more than efficiency issues, and so they more reflect than replace familiar partisan conflict. However, Chapter 3 also notes that large outstanding debts have increasingly constrained governments in their fiscal activities (see, e.g., Blais et al. 1993, 1996). Governments have felt this constraint, whether political or economic in origin, and increasingly turned toward monetary policy to implement their commitments to macroeconomic regulation and to try to sustain postwar coalitions behind them. As Chapter 4 demonstrates, however, monetary-policy efficacy depends critically on the relative strength of traded-sector over public-sector workers and employers within the wage-price bargaining system; yet, public employment, too, expanded dramatically over the postwar period.

1.3.2.3. Public Employment   Figure 1.10 plots public as a share of total employment. Unfortunately, data start only in 1960 at best,[19] yet the fairly common path since then is readably apparent. Public employment began this period rising everywhere, though at different paces, and finished the period shrinking virtually everywhere, though ceasing or reversal of growth began at different times, from different maxima.

Retrenchment began first in the United States in 1976, followed by New Zealand and Japan in 1980. In several others, it began later in the eighties – the United Kingdom, Canada, Belgium, Denmark, Greece, Ireland, the Netherlands, Sweden, Switzerland, Australia – while growth continued in Germany, France, Italy, Austria, Finland, Norway, and Spain until the mid-nineties and continues in Portugal as of 1997. Maximum

---

[19] Data refer to government civilian employment as a percent of total civilian employment and are from OECD, *Economic Outlook, Historical Statistics*, 6/97 disk, extended from print editions where possible.

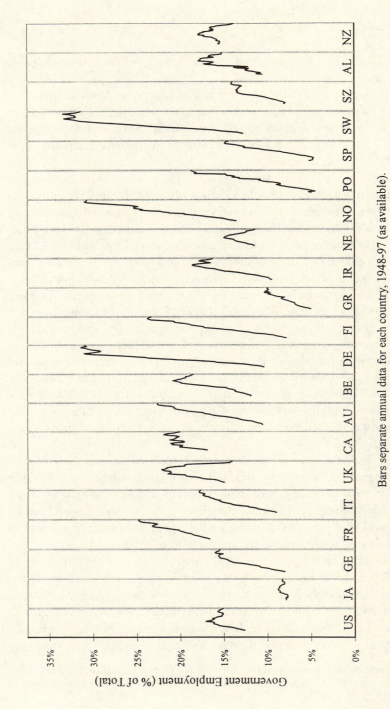

Figure 1.10 Public Employment by Country-Year

Bars separate annual data for each country, 1948-97 (as available).

28

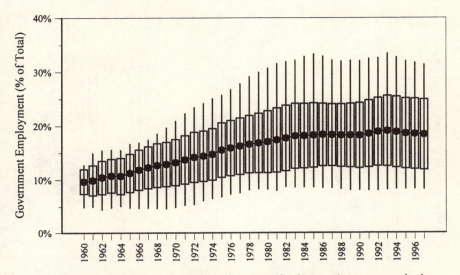

Dot marks 21-country mean; box extends plus to minus one standard
deviation from mean; lines extend to maximum and minumum.

Figure 1.11   Public Employment by Year

public-employment shares also vary widely, ranging from 8.8% in Japan
to 33.4% in Sweden.[20] Moreover, growth rates varied considerably, being
most dramatic in the social-corporatist countries: Denmark, Finland,
Norway, Sweden, and, less so, Austria. Three – Denmark, Norway,
Sweden – now top 30% of employment in the public sector. The share
remained relatively low and stable, contrarily, in the United States, Japan,
and New Zealand. Thus, while the average path is clear (Figure 1.11), from
9.7% to 18.4% in 1960–86 and flattening thereafter, growing divergence
is equally apparent; indeed, the common trend accounts for only 23% of
the total variation in Figure 1.10. Cross-country differences are far larger

[20] Retrenchment begins earliest in the United States (1976, from a maximum 17%), followed
by Japan and New Zealand (1980, 9% and 18%). Several others begin around 1984: the
United Kingdom (22%), Canada (22%), Denmark (31%), the Netherlands (15%),
Switzerland (14%), and Australia (18%). Sweden follows in 1986 (33%), then Belgium
(21%) and Ireland (19%) in 1987, while public employment seems to have leveled (at
10±%) in Greece since 1990. Growth continued in Germany until 1993 (16%), in Spain
until 1994 (15%), in Italy, Finland, and Norway until 1995 (18%, 24%, 31%, respectively),
and in Austria until 1996 (23%). France saw its highest level in 1996 (at 25%), and
Portugal is still rising (19% in 1997).

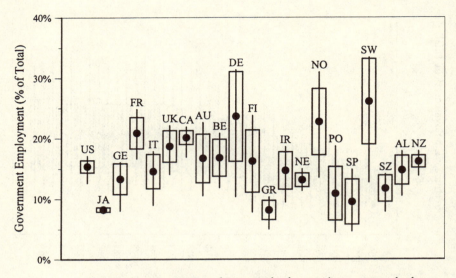

Dot marks postwar mean; box extends plus to minus one standard
deviation from mean; lines extend to maximum and minumum.

Figure 1.12   Public Employment by Country

(Figure 1.12), accounting for 63% of total variation, suggesting that key
sources of the observed differences must be factors that vary across countries but are relatively fixed over time.

As Chapter 4 elaborates, bargaining institutions that coordinate wage
levels (increases) across workers of varying productivity (growth) would
hinder private-sector provision of low-skill (growth) services. Governments in such countries therefore had either to accept low employment
growth or to absorb services growth into the public sector (see also Iversen
and Wren 1997, 1998). This may explain why public employment grew
most in the social-corporatist countries, which had left governments and
highly coordinated bargaining. Why, among these, Austria saw somewhat
less growth to lower levels is also explicable as its bargaining system has
allowed greater wage disparity than other coordinated systems. Such logic
suggests more-moderate growth most elsewhere in Europe, where some
combination of less coordinated, more wage-disparity-tolerant bargaining,
or more conservative governments operated. Japan and Switzerland,
meanwhile, had *employer-led* bargaining coordination, lesser wage equality,
and more conservative government and so retained small public-sector

employment. The rest – the United States, United Kingdom, Canada, Greece, Portugal, Spain, Australia, New Zealand – have more liberal-market or less wage-equality-inducing bargaining systems, so their private sectors could absorb the rising service-sector employment demand. In these countries, shifts of interests in the polity or of government partisanship more exclusively drove the evolution of public-sector employment.

Chapter 4 also and more directly addresses the consequences of public-employment growth for macroeconomic management, showing that monetary regulation of inflation and unemployment is more effective (i.e., achieves long-run lower inflation at lower unemployment) where credibly conservative monetary authorities face coordinated wage-price bargainers led by the traded sector. Where bargaining is less coordinated, or the public sector is more dominant, reliance on monetary policy for macroeconomic management raises less-favorable trade-offs. Thus, once again, recent shifts in political debate toward dispute over putatively more efficient monetary policy-making institutions ("reform") simply recast familiar left-right battles in somewhat newer and only marginally different terms.

To sum, the postwar commitments in developed democracies to public provision of insurance, goods, and macroeconomic management do seem to have produced some common tendency toward expanding government involvement in the economy. These universal pressures ultimately emanate from the differing distributions of political and economic influence in capitalist democracy, but the similar pressures induced varying degrees of government growth depending on the interactions of structures of interests and institutions in different country-times. However, merely noting that public transfers, debt, and employment rose starkly establishes neither that democratic management of the macroeconomy is in "crisis" nor much at all regarding the origins of these trends or their implications for the continued viability and utility of governments' policy commitments.

1.3.3. Macroeconomic Performance

1.3.3.1. Unemployment As Figure 1.13 reveals, unemployment increased through the oil-crises-plagued seventies in every country except oil-exporting Norway, rising from the lower levels most enjoyed through the fifties and sixties.[21] However, the rise was massive in some countries and

---

[21] Data refer to the internationally comparable definition of unemployment from the OECD, *Economic Outlook*, *Historical Statistics*, 6/97 disk, extended from print editions where possible.

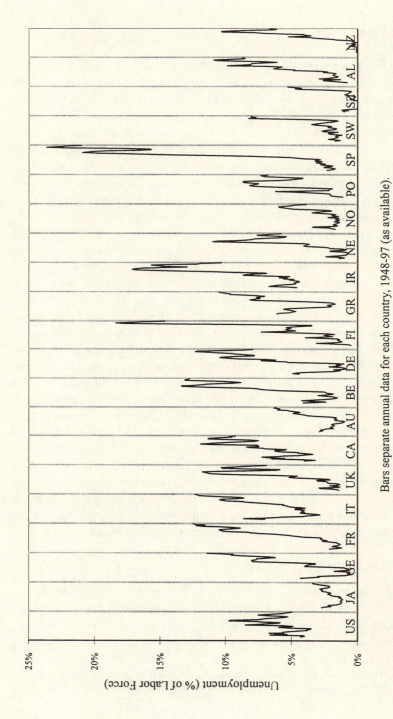

Figure 1.13 Unemployment by Country-Year

Bars separate annual data for each country, 1948-97 (as available).

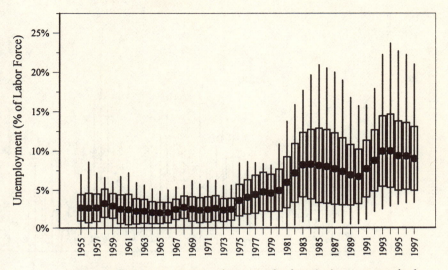

Dot marks 21-country mean; box extends plus to minus one standard
deviation from mean; lines extend to maximum and minumum.

Figure 1.14   Unemployment by Year

almost unnoticeable in (very) few others, opening large differences across
countries. Unemployment did not return to pre-oil-crises levels in most
places; in some it hardly budged; and in others it continued to rise, further
widening disparities. The nineties saw still further deviation as macroeconomic conditions improved in some places but worsened elsewhere.

As Figure 1.14 tracks, the OECD average floated between 3.3% and
2% in 1955–73. The 1973–4 oil crisis pushed it sharply to 4.8% by 1978,
where it leveled before rising sharply again after the 1979–80 oil crisis to
8.3% by 1984. It sank gently to 6.7% by 1990 before spiking to 10% in
1992–3, and returning only to 9% by 1997. This shared time path accounts
for 45% of the total variation, but the increasing divergence from the
1970s to 1990s is equally clear. Cross-country differences in postwar averages (28% of total variance) and ranges are quite apparent (Figure 1.15).
Unemployment differs remarkably across countries, more since than
before the oil crises, but it has always differed notably.

What, then, might explain this varying performance, and is it somehow
linked to the policy developments tracked in Figures 1.1–12? The con-

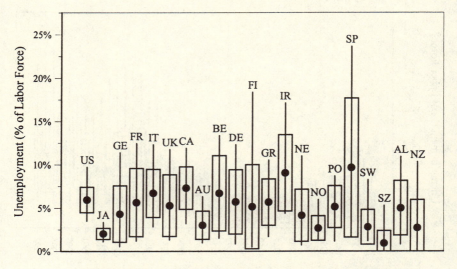

Dot marks postwar mean; box extends plus to minus one standard
deviation from mean; lines extend to maximum and minumum.

Figure 1.15   Unemployment by Country

clusions to Chapters 2–3 raise these questions, and Chapter 4 addresses
them more directly. Summarizing very briefly: first, shared exposure to
adverse international shocks clearly underlies the commonalities. Next,
Chapter 3 finds evidence that debt tends, if anything, to reduce unemployment,[22] suggesting that its evolution bears little relation to these trends
unless recent debt reductions share some blame for the failure of unemployment to decline much in the nineties. Contrarily, transfers growth
(Chapter 2), by increasing labor market rigidities, exacerbated especially
long-term unemployment problems, and so may relate to the tendency,
more pronounced in some countries than others, for unemployment to
ratchet upward after each shock. More critically, Chapter 4 shows that the
antiinflation policy shifts since 1980 were also detrimental, especially in
countries with uncoordinated or public-sector-led bargaining. Thus, as
Hibbs concluded over a decade ago for *The American Political Economy*

---

[22] As explained there, especially because no effect on growth is apparent, this likely reflects
differences in public- and private-sector borrowers' spending priorities rather than some
beneficial effect of public-borrowing per se.

(1987), policy maker reactions often exacerbate rather than alleviate the impacts of macroeconomic shocks. Additionally here, though, the degrees to which democratic policy makers made antiinflationary policy shifts and to which equivalent such shifts worsened unemployment depended on political-economic conditions that varied across country-times according to multiple interactions among their structures of interests (e.g., public- versus traded-sector-led bargaining) and institutions (e.g., bargaining coordination and monetary-authority credibility and conservatism).

1.3.3.2. Inflation As Figure 1.16 shows, inflation also varied radically across countries and over time. After extreme volatility in the early postwar years, more-moderate volatility around lower inflation rates reigned under the Bretton Woods fixed-exchange-rate regime, the OECD average fluctuating mildly between 2% and 5% in 1953–69. Inflation then began to rise, spurred by the U.S. monetization of its increasing expenditures in the wars on poverty and in Vietnam, which Bretton Woods spread to the other countries. The oil crises brought two spikes, to 13% in 1974 and 11% in 1980, dipping to 9.5% in 1978 between. From 1980 the average fell relatively continuously, back to its precrises low of 2% by 1997.

The shared time path highlighted in Figure 1.17, a fairly common rise until 1980 and fall since, accounts for 40% of the total variation, underscoring the size and commonality of the antiinflationary policy shifts. Contrarily, cross-country variation in postwar average inflation (Figure 1.18) covers only 14% of total, so inflation has largely country-time-unique variation: 46% of total. As Chapter 4 demonstrates and Franzese (1999a,b) elaborates, so much country-time-unique variation arises not only from the varying political-economic challenges monetary policy makers face and the fluidity of inflation (a nominal outcome), but also from multiple interactions among the widely varying international and domestic institutions and interests that shape monetary policy makers' differing responses.

Figuratively, many different sets of institutionally determined hands, each responding to different sets of interests, were effectively on the monetary-policy wheel across these country-times. Under a fixed-exchange-rate regime, to the degree the fix holds and capital is mobile, domestic policy makers retain monetary-policy, and thus inflation, control only in the Nth country to which the others peg. In the other N-1 countries, policy and inflation are determined by the peg. Thus, U.S. inflation, and so the political-economic considerations to which U.S. policy makers

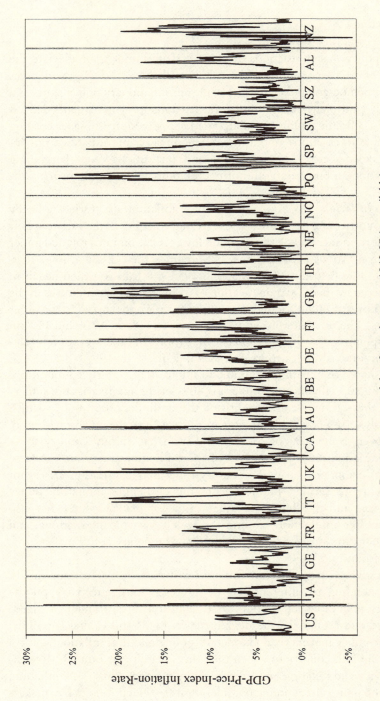

Figure 1.16   Inflation by Country-Year

Bars separate annual data for each country, 1948-97 (as available).

36

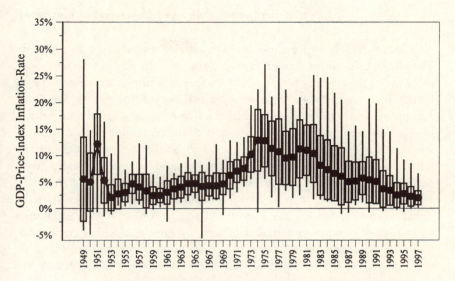

Dot marks 21-country mean; box extends plus to minus one standard
deviation from mean; lines extend to maximum and minumum.

Figure 1.17 Inflation by Year

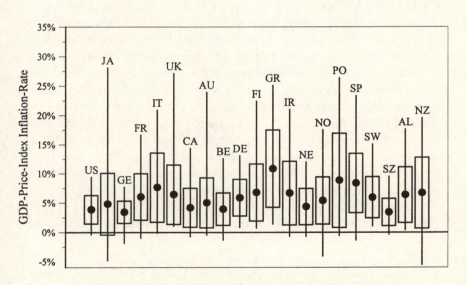

Dot marks postwar mean; box extends plus to minus one standard
deviation from mean; lines extend to maximum and minumum.

Figure 1.18 Inflation by Country

37

responded, largely drove most other countries' inflation under Bretton Woods. Furthermore, under that regime for the United States, and throughout the ensuing floating-rate era for all countries, domestic central banks controlled monetary growth *cum* inflation to the degree they had autonomy from political influence, and domestic political authorities (i.e., governments) affected inflation only to the remaining degree. Finally, whereas domestic governments respond to political-economic pressures felt domestically,[23] foreign governments respond to *their* domestic pressures, and autonomous and conservative central banks respond to neither, tending more to target fixed (and low) inflation. Thus, the considerable variation observed in Figures 1.16–18 reflects not only differing economic and political conditions but also differing degrees to which responsive domestic governments, as opposed to unresponsive central banks, and as opposed to foreign authorities, controlled monetary-policy reactions to those conditions.[24]

1.3.3.3. Growth Lastly, Figures 1.19–21 show real-per-capita-GDP growth rates, discussed more briefly here. Growth, though volatile like inflation, slowed visibly over the postwar era. OECD average growth (Figure 1.20) fell below 2.5% only three years in the fifties and not once in the sixties, but four years in the seventies, five in the eighties, and four of seven in 1990–6. As the (very) wide inter-standard-deviation (inter-extrema) ranges in Figure 1.21 attest, differences in postwar average growth across countries comprise little (9%) of total variation. The shared time path shown in Figure 1.22 accounts for more (29%), probably reflecting common exposure to oil crises and other international conditions, but that still leaves fully 62% of variation country-time unique. Like inflation, then, explanations for growth variation must largely involve county-time unique components. Chapter 2 suggests rising transfers may bear some blame for slowing growth by increasing labor market rigidities and so hindering growth-efficient resource allocation. Chapter 3, contrarily, finds little statistical case for claims that rising public debts reduced growth. Chapter 4, however, finds some simple evidence supporting claims that

---

[23] Such pressures may originate domestically or internationally.

[24] As Chapter 4 elaborates, these arguments and those regarding monetary authorities' interactions with wage-price bargainers in determining monetary-policy real-effectiveness, imply that pegged exchange-rate commitments will have very different economic and therefore political implications than will delegation of monetary-policy authority to central banks, even if they are equally credible and conservative.

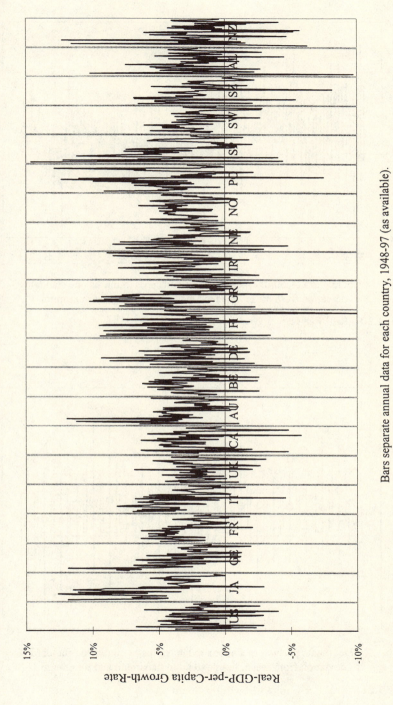

Figure 1.19 Real Per-Capita Growth by Country-Year

Bars separate annual data for each country, 1948-97 (as available).

39

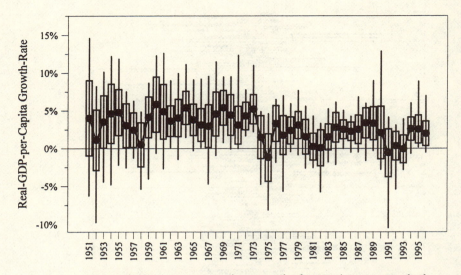

Dot marks 21-country mean; box extends plus to minus one standard
deviation from mean; lines extend to maximum and minumum.

Figure 1.20   Real Per-Capita Growth by Year

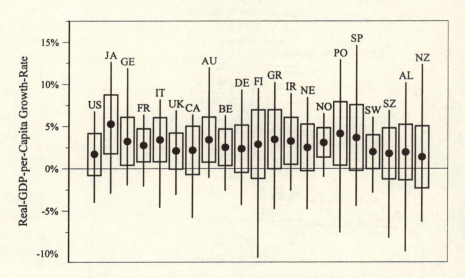

Dot marks postwar mean; box extends plus to minus one standard
deviation from mean; lines extend to maximum and minumum.

Figure 1.21   Real Per-Capita Growth by Country

40

public-employment growth reduced productivity growth and thus also real-GDP-per-capita growth. Otherwise, the arguments and evidence outlined earlier in relation to inflation and unemployment extend rather intuitively to growth.

Whatever *causal* connections may exist from the patterns of government growth documented in Figures 1.1–12 to those in economic performance shown in 1.13–21, their *coincidence* certainly drives the current outcry for public-sector "reform." This book explores and extends current political-economic theory on transfer-system, public-debt, and public-employment determination, seeking (1) to explain the patterns and variations exhibited in Figures 1.4–6 and 1.7–9 (Chapters 2 and 3) and, more summarily, those in Figures 1.10–12 (Chapter 4), and (2) to explore connections between these patterns and those of economic performance shown in Figures 1.13–21 (Chapters 2 and 3 more cursorily, Chapter 4 more deeply). This section demonstrated that the democratic commitments did tend to foster great extensions of government activity in the economy, yet, this common tendency notwithstanding, considerable differences remain. The section also presaged some of the specific arguments and evidence in Chapters 2–4 that explain these developments. The common exposure to similar economic conditions and the universal differences between the distributions of economic and political influence explain the commonalities, and interactions among differing structures of interests and institutions explain the differing policy and outcome responses thereto. The next section introduces a *cycle of political economy* framework, which diagrams this interactive view of comparative political economy and that guides the theoretical and empirical analyses of macroeconomic policy making and outcomes throughout the book.

1.4. Explaining Policy and Outcome Variation across Democracies over Time

1.4.1. Overview of the Approach

Not every developed democracy has equally large transfer systems, public debt, or difficulties in simultaneous management of inflation and unemployment; yet, country-times where at least one of these elements does not seem overextended are exceedingly rare. That is, at different times in different places, the universal pressures on democratic policy makers manifest different consequences for policies and outcomes. If the *same* fundamental conflicts underlie differing policies and outcomes in different times and places, explanations for the *varying* postwar experience of developed democracies cannot come from those common roots. Explanations must, instead, lie in *differences* across country-times (1) in the degrees and types of pressures upon policy makers to alleviate market-economy vicissitudes, and/or (2) in the incentives created by these common pressures on policy makers for how to respond to such pressures, and/or (3) in the economic or political effectiveness of policy makers' possible reactions to relieve that pressure. This book develops such explanations within an approach to comparative and international political economy that gives equal weight to *domestic* and *international*, *political* and *economic*, *institutional* and *structural* characteristics of the environments in which *strategic* public policy makers and private actors make choices, emphasizes the *interaction* of these institutions and structures to produce the set of incentives applying to the strategic actors that make and influence policy,[25] and stresses theoretically informed empirical analysis that incorporates such interactive propositions as *directly* as possible into statistical specifications.

1.4.2. *The Cycle of Political Economy*

This book studies macroeconomic policy making in developed democracies in the postwar era, asking why some country-times saw certain policies and other country-times saw others, and why similar policies sometimes produced markedly different outcomes across such similar country-times. The view of comparative, democratic policy making guiding the exploration of these questions – in the contexts of the postwar commitments to social-insurance, public-goods, and macroeconomic-management provision via transfers, debt, and monetary regulation of wage-price bargaining – may be condensed to a paragraph.

Macroeconomic *policy* is made by politicians who, in democracies, are *elected* by populations with different demographic, political, and economic *structures*. They are elected to make policy as *partisan* actors and do so in an *institutionalized* environment.[26] Those policies, coupled with more-exogenous factors like economic conditions abroad and endogenous ones

---

[25] In these senses, it answers Pontusson's (1995b) challenge that institutional political economists "put structure in its place and take interests seriously."

[26] Democratic policy makers do generally fulfill their electoral and partisan promises; see, e.g., Klingemann et al. 1994. Gallagher et al. 1995: ch. 13 summarizes some of the (generally favorable) evidence.

like the actions of nongovernmental actors, then produce political and economic outcomes about which the electorate cares. These outcomes may also alter the structure of interests in the electorate, which then chooses its policy-making representatives anew. At each stage, all the actors in this cycle know its circuit and realize that it cycles, so their incentives emanate both from other actors' decisions and other aspects before them in the current cycle, which determined their current situation; and from their expectations of other actors' choices and other aspects later in the current cycle and of the structure of future cycles and their situation in them. Figure 1.22 offers a schematic representation of this cyclical view of political economy.

To elaborate, the policy-determination arguments in this book begin by characterizing the interests of the electorate, focusing on demographic, institutional, and structural aspects of the polity and economy.[27] For example, the age and income distribution in the polity are center stage in Chapter 2; in Chapter 4, the sectoral structure of wage-price bargaining – the size and roles of public-, traded-, and sheltered-sector bargainers – are key; and the international exposure of the economy enters throughout. These structures of interest are then funneled through, and so generally interact with, for example, electoral and government-formation processes to determine the incentives facing policy makers.

When that interested population elects its representatives to government, it does so largely according to their partisan reputations in serving those interests.[28] In the process, the legal-institutional structure of the electoral system profoundly impacts not only the outcomes of the elections themselves (Lijphart 1994; Taagepera and Shugart 1989; Rae 1967) but also the policy implications of those elections and their outcomes (Tufte 1978; Dye 1979). Chapter 2, for example, shows how voter participation, which depends, inter alia, on electoral law regarding polling scheduling and registration (Powell 1982; Jackman and Miller 1995; Franklin 1996), modifies the impact of the income distribution on welfare policies. As another example, Chapters 2 and 3 both find that electioneering effects on fiscal policies are large enough and fiscal policies adjust

---

[27] That is, in the classic cleavage-structure terminology of comparative politics, the focus at this first stage is on *attitudinal or opinion cleavages* (Rae and Taylor 1970), on *economic-function cleavages* (Flanagan 1973), or on *disagreement over policy issues* (Eckstein 1966) within the polity. Lane and Ersson (1994: 52–6) give a particularly useful, succinct summary of these cleavage-structure schema.

[28] See Downs 1957; Keech and Lee 1995 offers recent supportive evidence.

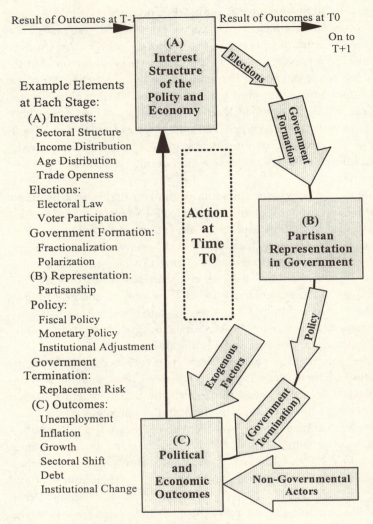

Figure 1.22 The Cycle of Political Economy

slowly enough for variation in election frequency to impact long-run transfers and debt shares of GDP appreciably. And election frequency depends on constitutional provisions regarding whether and under what conditions the government may call early elections and the maximum interelectoral period and on other institutional-structural features of the political economy that determine the types and durability of governments formed. Chapter 3 also shows that fractionalized governments magnify the long-run fiscal effects of electoral frequency (and all other political-economic factors) because multiparty governments delay policy adjustments.[29] Thus, the impacts of the election process on policies and outcomes, like those of interest structure, depend on (interact with) many other aspects of the political-economic cycle.

These elected, partisan representatives then form governments to make policy within the institutionalized setting of the legislature and executive.[30] In general, the policies governments enact follow from their incentives in democratic competition, specifically, their electoral promises and partisan preferences. Chapters 2–4, for example, find that governments tend to increase transfers, deficits, and monetary growth *around* elections, that is, in the years before and *after* elections. The preelectoral effect was long expected (Nordhaus 1975; Tufte 1978) but often proved hard to find empirically (Alesina 1988b, 1989; Alesina and Roubini 1992; Alesina, Cohen, and Roubini 1992; Alesina et al. 1997), partly because post-electoral effects were not sought.[31] Yet, because governments generally fulfill electoral promises (Alt 1985; Klingemann et al. 1994; Gallagher et al. 1995), and because campaigns tend to induce competitive escalation in promised largesse (Tufte 1978), policies will tend to provide excess economic stimulation after elections as well. Previous empirics also tended to ignore differences in policy-making processes across country-times. For example, in some countries, voters elect executives and legislatures separately, suggesting that policy will only partially respond to each

---

[29] Lin (1999) finds, similarly, that greater numbers of partisan veto actors in government retard transfer-payment responses to domestic economic and political influences, suggesting that these considerations also operate in that venue.

[30] While theoretical structures for analyzing such activity comparably across both parliamentary and nonparliamentary democracies are lacking (see Tsebelis 1995 for a recent ingress), work on parliamentary government formation and dissolution is vast and growing. (A thorough review might follow Riker 1962; Axelrod 1970; DeSwaan 1973; Dodd 1976; Browne and Dreijmanis 1982; Morgan 1976; Taylor and Laver 1973; textbook treatment: Gallagher et al. 1995: ch. 12; with, e.g., Diermeier and Stevenson 1994; King et al. 1990; Laver and Budge 1991; Laver and Hunt 1992; Laver and Schofield 1991; Laver and Shepsle 1994, 1996; Lupia and Strom 1995; Martin and Stevenson 1995; Stevenson 1994a,b, 1997; Strom 1984, 1985, 1988, 1990a,b; Strom et al. 1994; Warwick 1992a,b,c, 1994, 1996; Warwick and Easton 1992.)

[31] Thus, empirical work typically compared preelection periods with other periods, including the immediate postelection period, which evidence presented here demonstrates was at least as stimulative.

election if the election periods are staggered. Elsewhere, governments share control of some of these instruments with other agents less interested in such electioneering – for example, of monetary policy with central banks or, through fixed exchange rates, with foreign governments (Chapter 4; Clark et al. 1998; Franzese 1999a,b; Oatley 1999).[32] In short, these considerations and others from elsewhere in the cycle modify governments' incentives to provide economic stimuli around elections and/or their ability to act on those incentives, implying conditional (i.e., interactive) electoral cycles.

The policy and outcome effects of government partisanship also vary with other aspects of the political-economic cycle. For example, international and institutional constraints dampen partisan as well as electoral monetary-policy effects (Clark et al. 1998; Clark and Hallerberg 1999; Franzese 1999a,b; Oatley 1999). Moreover, partisans may have mixed incentives over deficits and debts. Right parties rely for electoral support partly on their reputation for fiscal conservatism; but, if voters suspect the left is more default-prone (n.b., inflation partially defaults on nominal debt outstanding), the right can broaden its electoral appeal by increasing the (nominal) debt that voters hold. Left parties, conversely, rely on reputations for responsive fiscal policy, but would narrow their electoral appeal by increasing outstanding debt if they are suspected default-risks.[33] Chapter 3 shows that which consideration dominates depends on partisan polarization across governments: that is, on the ideological distance in budgetary terms between alternative governments and their frequency of alternation. Governments with more security in office fear replacement less and so might use fiscal policy strategically for the electoral effect of debt accumulation. Governments in more polarized, volatile systems

---

[32] In others, subnational governments may have partial control over policies; and, in still others, multiple parties in coalition governments, each with potentially conflicting interests over the degree and type of electioneering stimulus to support, control policy. The book less directly examines these considerations.

[33] The literature has long linked left and right government-partisanship to responsive and minimalist fiscal policy (Hibbs 1977, 1986, 1987, 1992, 1994; Hibbs et al. 1996; Cameron 1978; Castles 1982; Alt and Crystal 1983; Alt 1985, 1987; Alesina 1988b, 1989; Alesina, Cohen, and Roubini 1992; Alesina, De Broeck et al. 1992; Alesina et al. 1993; Alesina et al. 1997). Literature on strategic debt policy is more recent and varied in its predictions (Persson and Svensson 1989; Aghion and Bolton 1990; Alesina and Tabellini 1987, 1989, 1990, 1992; Tabellini and Alesina 1990; Drazen and Grilli 1993; Spolaore 1993; Milesi-Ferretti and Spolaore 1993, 1994; Milesi-Ferretti 1995). See Chapter 3.

cannot afford to jeopardize their partisan reputations by such untoward policies; there, the left (right) tends toward fiscally responsive (conservative) policy.[34] Again, this polarization across governments and their alternation frequency depend on governmental and electoral institutions, and so partisan fiscal effects, like electoral ones, depend on other aspects of the political-economic cycle in that country-time.[35]

Fractionalization and polarization *within* governments also alter the impact of other conditions on macroeconomic policy. As Tsebelis (1995) argues, greater numbers of and ideological spaces between actors possessing policy-making vetoes complicate bargains over policy changes, reducing winsets (i.e., sets of politically feasible policy moves), and thereby privileging the status quo. In the public-debt context, scholars (Roubini and Sachs 1989a,b; Alesina and Drazen 1991; Drazen and Grilli 1993; Spolaore 1993; Alesina and Perotti 1994, 1995a,b) argued that such immobility delayed fiscal adjustments and so contributed to greater deficits in democracies with fractionalized and polarized governments than in those with more-unified governments. The evidence was mixed (Roubini and Sachs 1989a,b; De Haan and Sturm 1994; Edin and Ohlsson 1991; Borelli and Royed 1995; Hallerberg and Von Hagen 1999), but these empirical studies generally failed to consider the way the delayed stabilization that

---

[34] Lambertini 1999 also addresses the strategic literature empirically, but finds no evidence of strategic manipulation of debt to constrain the opposition. The findings here and in Franzese 2000b relate differently to the conditions of government alternation that foster traditional or counterintuitive fiscal policy.

[35] Many other political-economic conditions modify the impacts of government partisanship on fiscal policy. Some emphasize international considerations (Alt 1985, 1987; Garrett 1995, 1998a,b,c, 2000; Garrett and Lange 1991, 1995; Hall 1986, 1989; Gourevitch 1986; Iversen 2000a; Iversen and Cusack 1998), or interactions with bargaining organization (Alvarez et al. 1991; Beck et al. 1993; Garrett and Lange 1986; Hall 1986, 1989; Iversen 1998b, 1999a; Lange 1984; Lange and Garrett 1985, 1987; Lange et al. 1995; Scharpf 1984, 1987), or with other institutional and structural characteristics of the economy more generally (Alt and Alesina 1996; Berger 1981; Esping-Andersen 1985; Garrett and Lange 1989; Goldthorpe 1984; Gourevitch 1986; Hall 1986, 1989; Hall and Soskice 2000; Heclo 1974; Korpi 1980; Katzenstein 1985; Lehmbruch and Schmitter 1982; Lindblom 1977; Mosher and Franzese 1999; Offe 1984; Olson 1982; Pontusson 1995b; Pontusson and Swenson 1993, 1991; Scharpf 1991; Shonfield 1965; Swenson 1989, 1991). Others stress restraints inherited from previous fiscal excesses (Blais et al. 1993, 1996), the location of partisan veto actors in the legislature and executive (Alt and Lowry 1994), the ideology of the opposition in the legislature (Hicks and Swank 1992), and the government's majority or minority status and the influence of the legislative opposition more generally (Strom 1984, 1985, 1990a,b; Stevenson 1994b). Chapters 2–4 explore some of these interactions.

multiple veto actors induce would interact with other political-economic considerations to determine long-run debt effects. Fractionalization and polarization produce *inaction*, and the impact of inaction depends on what would have happened under the status quo. Thus, as Chapter 3 demonstrates, not only did democracies with more partisan veto actors delay stabilization longer and accumulate more debt following the oil shocks, as the original argument expected (see also Alesina and Perotti 1995b), but the number of veto actors also magnified the long-run impact of *all* other fiscal-policy determinants, such as those mentioned earlier (see also Franzese 1998a, 2000b).[36] Thus, once again Figure 1.22's *cycle of political economy* framework highlights that international and domestic political-economic conditions and structures of interests and institutions *interact* to determine policies and outcomes.

Finally, completing the political-economic cycle, the policy actions that these elected partisan governments take; those taken by nongovernmental actors such as central banks, unions, and firms; those taken by foreign actors; and more-exogenous factors like international economic conditions, all combine to produce the political and economic outcomes that form anew the interest structure of the polity and economy. Then, the cycle begins again, from the structure of interests in polity and economy, to election of partisan representatives, to the formation of partisan and unified or fractionalized-polarized governments, to their making of policies that depend on their electoral and other incentives and the reputations on which they rely for reelection. Policies are made, other actors move, exogenous conditions change, occasionally governments fall, and so new outcomes are determined, perhaps altering the previously existing structure of interests further.

A final complication: at every stage in the cycle, the actors might behave *strategically* because, at least at some simple level, they all know the structure of the game and that it cycles. Elected representatives, for example, know that their policies may alter private-actor choices and that they will face the electorate again. Thus, any actor may be motivated at any time by concerns emanating from either direction relative to that actor's current position in the cycle. Actors look forward to how their current choices may alter others' decisions as the cycle continues and may even, thereby

---

[36] Chapter 3 and Franzese 1998a, 2000b also offer important improvements on the measurement of fractionalization and polarization within (and across) governments, which likely also contribute to the stronger results here.

or autonomously, alter the future conditions in which they will act again. In the foregoing debt example, democratic governments may choose fiscal policies as much to change the structure of interests among the voters that they must face again as to fulfill electoral promises made to the current electorate. As another example, Garrett (1992, 1994), Garrett and Heath (1991), and Hall (1986) describe how the Thatcher government's attacks on collective bargaining rights and public housing served Tory electoral purposes by weakening Labour's union base and turning some public-housing Labour voters into Tory homeowners and the rest into nonvoting homeless. Similarly, Hibbs (1987) describes how the Reagan government's tax policies, which brought windfalls to the wealthiest and also massive debts, created a "more-debt-holding" public that soon became more anti-inflationary and anti-government-spending (i.e., more Republican).

In short, the policies and outcomes studied here emerge from the choices of reasoning, strategic human beings, generally aware of the cycle within which they are acting (if perhaps only vaguely) and capable of fore-seeing the likely impact of their possible actions on other actors and, with those reactions, on outcomes (if perhaps only with great, and usually uncomfortable, uncertainty). Therefore, public and private decision makers are likely to be at least partially motivated by the expected reac-tions of others to their actions and the outcomes of those interactions, and so scholars must look forward and backward around the cycle just as the political-economic actors that they are studying do. This highly interac-tive "cycle of political economy" framework guides the derivation of argu-ments and the search for evidence throughout the book.

1.5. The Political-Economic Implications

1.5.1. Economic Impacts

Public transfers (Chapter 2) are often posited to have two main effects. First, they alleviate the immediate economic hardships of those receiving them: the unemployed, aged, and disabled. Second, contrarily, they are often blamed for reducing economic efficiency by weakening the harsh incentives of the market. Thus, while critics claim the side effects of social insurance may actually worsen the broad problems to which it is addressed – poverty among the unemployed, aged, and disabled – no one seriously challenges that, at least in the short run, the receipt of transfers lessens current individual economic hardship (see, e.g., Hibbs 1987). In fact, empirical connections between government size and economic growth have proved difficult to establish,[37] as, initially, did connections between transfers and unemployment. Recent work stresses, however, that unemployment insurance should relate more directly to the duration of unemployment stints than to the unemployment rate per se, and the evidence very strongly favors that claim (e.g., Meyer 1990, 1995; Layard et al. 1991). Thus, transfers have lessened the current impact of economic difficulties on individuals but have also rendered unemployment and poverty "stickier" and less responsive to, for example, policy.

Additionally, as noted earlier and shown in Chapter 2, transfers growth tended to drive more general growth of government, and that tended to drive debt accumulation proportionately. The meteoric rise in transfers, therefore, also served to tighten governments' budget constraints, thereby reducing their discretion over other expenditure goals. Moreover, to the extent transfers are deficit-financed, the impacts of public debt are attributable that far to growth in transfers as well.

Regarding those public-debt effects, most macroeconomists had agreed until the late seventies that deficits increased real demand and, thereby, real output and income in the short run but that accumulated debt also *crowded out*[38] private investment in the long run, thereby hindering growth. The logic was simple. Public borrowing represents a demand for savings, so, absent some increase in private actors' willingness to save, higher debt would raise interest rates and so prohibit some investments that may have profited at lower rates. Thus, public deficits increase disposable income (i.e., raise government expenditure net of taxes), giving a short-run consumption-based boost to the economy. In the long run, though, public borrowing may *crowd out* private borrowing, but the size of that long-run effect depended on two factors: the interest elasticities of savings and investment, and what the government did with the borrowed funds. The (more) less responsive was savings (investment) to interest rates, the more *crowding out* occurred, and, of course, the more inefficient public

[37] Although Cameron's (1978) finding that the tax share of GDP related weakly negatively to the investment share may have been some support, later work (Barro 1990) has even suggested that, to the degree governments optimize, the observed relationship should be zero (because a derivative at an optimum is zero). Empirical support for a negative relationship is, in any event, weak at best.

[38] Actually, if the term and risk structure of public debt made it an appropriate portfolio complement to private assets, public debt could "crowd in" private investment, but most economists considered that a mere theoretical curiosity.

consumption and investment decisions relative to private ones, the more deleterious the effects of *crowding out*.

The rational-expectations revolution in macroeconomics, however, rebirthed the *Ricardian equivalence* theorem that whether the government borrows or taxes to finance a given amount of spending is irrelevant (Barro 1974, 1979). Basically, private actors know that borrowing today requires taxes tomorrow to repay the debt, so their willingness to save increases with government borrowing. Because their optimal intertemporal consumption choices require that they increase savings by the present value of future taxes, which is also the price efficient markets place on the current bonds, real interest rates remain unchanged. Thus, public debt per se is no drag on the real economy, although, of course, what the government does with the borrowed money remains critical.

Therefore, the real economic costs of public debt depend on the empirical relevance of the Ricardian equivalence theorem, the interest elasticities of savings and borrowing, and the efficiency of public relative to private spending. Chapter 3 offers some simple evidence suggesting that debt effects are negligible on real-per-capita-GDP growth but are appreciable on unemployment (–) and inflation (+). This, in turn, suggests that, from a political-economy viewpoint, the growth effects of public debt were never the primary issue for those concerned, on either side, over the development of massive public debts. Rather more central was how governments spent the borrowed funds compared with how the private sector would have spent them. Governments spent with some concern for macroeconomic management, aiming to reduce unemployment even if this tended to increase inflation, perhaps by raising public-sector employment.

Another effect of public debt, also important for present purposes and, surprisingly, relatively neglected in the literature (but see Blais et al. 1993, 1996), is that debt accumulation tends to constrain future governments from appropriate use of fiscal policy. Chapter 3 argues that this, in turn, spurred the shift in policy emphasis to monetary management of the macroeconomy, especially inflation control, and, subsequently, to institutional "reform."

Lastly, public employment (growth) is argued to reduce productivity (growth) and, as a public economic-activity, also partly to counteract adverse distributional and unemployment outcomes. Chapter 4 offers simple evidence that supports a strong negative productivity relationship, with obvious growth implications. Public employment also obviously reflects a different weighing of societal equity than does private. But beyond these effects, Chapter 4 argues and finds a strong wage-price-regulation impact. The relative insulation of public-sector workers from international and domestic competition profoundly weakens the ability of coordinated-bargaining institutions to deliver real-wage restraint (Franzese 1994, 1996b; Garrett and Way 1995b, 1999a,b) and, furthermore, renders bargaining less responsive to monetary-policy reactions, which could otherwise reinforce such restraint. Thus, beyond the direct adverse productivity and beneficial distribution effects, public-sector employment growth also tended to raise the real costs at which monetary and bargaining institutions could interact to regulate inflation and unemployment simultaneously.

To sum: transfers and spending growth alleviated the economic hardships to which they were addressed but also rendered unemployed spells more durable, thereby reducing fiscal-policy efficacy in fighting unemployment. They also drove public-debt growth that, while perhaps not harming growth, highlighted conflicts between unemployment and inflation reduction and increasingly constrained governments' fiscal maneuverability. As growing transfers, spending, and debt increasingly constrained their fiscal options, governments turned toward monetary "rigor" intending to recreate broad political coalitions behind fighting inflation (from those behind the postwar commitment to "efficient" macroeconomic management). However, the public-employment-growth aspect of this fiscal expansion also increased the real-growth and unemployment costs of the antiinflationary monetary-policy shift, again highlighting conflicts between inflation and unemployment reduction. Thus, modern political conflicts over various structural-institutional "reforms" intended to redress burgeoning transfers or debt or to enforce credibly antiinflationary monetary policies essentially retain all the left-right efficiency-equity trade-offs long-familiar to political economists.

1.5.2. Political Consequences

In addition to the specific political implications explored thus far, four general implications merit further review.

First, insofar as citizens hold governments responsible for economic performance, economic effects *are* political effects. That citizens do evaluate governments thus is a central tenet of political economy, and supportive empirical evidence across countries abounds (e.g., Lewis-Beck

1990; Powell and Whitten 1993). Thus, most broadly, if the trends in public-sector growth bear some blame for deteriorating economic performance, then some part of the public disaffection with governments and parties that is currently epidemic in developed democracies (see, e.g., Koole and Mair 1994) can likewise be blamed on these policy trends.[39]

Second, public-sector growth in each of these three aspects created new social cleavages or exacerbated existing ones. For example, as public debt grows, conflicts of interest between those holding relatively more public debt and those obtaining relatively larger benefits from debt-financed public spending likewise grows (Aghion and Bolton 1990). As emphasized in the conclusion to Chapter 3, this extends the usual conflict between human and physical capital holders and the less skilled and unemployed, exacerbating the tendency for the former's antiinflationary biases to conflict with the latter's relatively lower inflation concerns.

Third, in some countries, public-sector growth and its popular linkage to declining economic performance have profoundly impacted support for other political-economic institutions. For example, as decreasing fiscal maneuverability became apparent, support in more antiinflationary segments of the polity for increasing central bank autonomy grew, whereas in other segments – those most vulnerable to macroeconomic fluctuations, and so most desirous of retaining political-monetary discretion, especially with fiscal maneuverability declining – it decreased.[40] Similarly, as argued in Chapter 4, public-employment growth sapped the ability and willingness of coordinated bargainers to deliver real-wage restraint, inducing employers and some workers to abandon such bargaining institutions in some coordinated political economies.

Finally, if, as likely, voters' distaste for higher taxes increases with total tax burdens, then fiscal expansion became increasingly unviable for democratic governments as debt-financing burdens increased. Thus, they relied increasingly on monetary policy or sought to renounce Keynesian fiscal policy in toto in favor of various institutional-structural "reforms." In fact,

---

[39] More precisely, public disaffection would likely arise from the *perception* of a causal link even if such a link cannot be found objectively. Another question, then, is whether the perception was warranted.

[40] Missale and Blanchard 1992 builds from Calvo and Guidotti 1990 and Calvo et al. 1991 to suggest, relatedly, that high public debt raises debt holders' fear of inflationary default, raising interest premia, and so increasing pressure on governments to index or denominate in foreign currency. See also the second point in this subsection and Aghion and Bolton 1990.

the pattern since the sixties seems to follow these options in sequence. First, the U.S.-led inflation of the late sixties spurred the abandonment of Bretton Woods, freeing monetary policy to domestic purposes. Then, after the oil crises, focus shifted to antiinflationary monetary policy, as fiscal policy proved politically problematic or economically ineffective. Then, as real growth and unemployment continued to worsen through the eighties, focus fell finally on institutional "reforms" and other "supply-side" policies: major alterations in transfer systems (e.g., in the United States), in labor market regulation (e.g., in the United Kingdom), in monetary policy-making institutions (e.g., central bank autonomy or renewed fixed-exchange-rate schemes across Europe and elsewhere). As noted already and demonstrated throughout the book, though, none of these shifts succeeded in avoiding the replication of familiar political-economic struggles in capitalist economies: the conflict between the goals of fostering capitalist growth and alleviating its distributional outcomes, and the universal tension between distributions of political and economic influence.

1.6. Conclusion

This book explains the postwar evolution of macroeconomic policy in developed democracies. It argues that common exposure to political-economic policy challenges and universal tensions between distributions of political and economic influence and between goals of fostering capitalist development and alleviating its distributional consequences explain the expanding commitments of democratic governments to political provision of social insurance, public goods, and macroeconomic management. It argues that and shows how domestic and international political-economic conditions and structures of institutions and interests moderate public and private actors' responses to these similar stimuli. Moreover, it stresses theoretically and shows how empirically the policy and outcome effects of these institutions, interests, and conditions are generally complex because they *interact* to shape public and private actors' incentives.

Substantively, it shows the commonalities in transfers and debt growth and monetary policy to arise primarily from the reaction of similarly democratic governments to similar domestic and international political-economic (mostly economic) conditions. The key differences arise from multiple interactions among the broad configuration of (primarily domestic) institutions within which public and private actors respond to those conditions. Transfers grew most where proparticipatory electoral institutions induced greater government responsiveness *and* underlying economic disparity was greatest. Debt grew most where party systems and governmental institutions produced more veto actors in policy making *and* other political-economic conditions had created larger structural deficits from the seventies' stagflationary shocks. These trends reduced fiscal-policy efficacy and maneuverability, pushing governments toward monetary and other institutional "reforms" to restrain inflation, but again the impact depended on interactions of many other factors. Where domestic political-economic conditions most favored antiinflationary interests, monetary-institutional "reforms" had little further antiinflationary bite, being essentially unnecessary thereto, but the policy shift had real (e.g., unemployment) effects regardless of its nominal impact. The trade-off was most adverse where market structures and institutions induced uncoordinated or public-sector-led bargaining and least where bargaining was coordinated and trade-sector-led. Finally, the book shows how recent political struggles over "reforms" in these areas more replicate than replace classical left-right debates.

In these tasks, this book complements five prominent theoretical strands in recent contributions to comparative and international political economy. These strands (1) revisit electoral and partisan cycles in macroeconomic policies and outcomes; emphasize continuing partisan differences (2) in macroeconomic policy, despite increasing international exposure, or (3) in supply-side, microeconomic, structural policies, despite international and institutional constraints; (4) explore political contestation over the institutional structure of the economy; and (5) stress the complex effects of broad national networks of political-economic institutions.

1.6.1. Other Recent Contributions

Modern heirs to Tufte (1978) and Hibbs (1987) explore electoral and partisan cycles in macroeconomic policies and outcomes, stressing monetary and fiscal policies with rational policy makers and voters. Alesina et al. (1997), for example, argue that private actors' rational expectations limit real economic outcome cycles to brief, short-run responses to partisan electoral surprises, and virtually eliminate election-year policy and outcome effects.[41] This book has much broader aims, but it also explores electoral and partisan cycles in monetary, transfer, and debt policy. However, it stresses more the dynamic nature of macroeconomic policy making and wide institutional variation across country-times that condition policy makers' incentives. These emphases reveal much stronger, contingent electoral effects and more-strategic, contingent partisan effects. For example, because candidates make promises and usually fulfill them if they win, *post*electoral policy manipulation is at least as strong as preelectoral. Because policy makers have mixed incentives over deficits and debts and the latter adjusts slowly, institutional conditions that enhance incumbent security in office allow strategic policy makers to manipulate *debt* for partisan purposes, and conditions that foster frequent partisan alternation focus partisan strategies on *deficit* policies (see Chapter 3). In both these cases, and even more so in monetary policy, elected partisan governments share control of policy making and, a fortiori, outcomes with other institutionalized actors. For example, central bank autonomy or delegation to foreign authorities via exchange rate pegs mutes electoral and partisan (among other domestic factors') effects on monetary policy (as clarified precisely in Chapter 4). Moreover, the real-outcome effects of public policies depend also on private actors' strategic responses, and so vary with the structure of institutions and interests in the private sector. Monetary-policy efficacy, for example, depends on the organizational and sectoral structure of wage-price bargaining. Similarly, the effects of deficit spending depend, inter alia, on the differences between the uses to which public and private borrowing are put. Thus, in both policy and outcome terms, the strategic-interactive approach taken here complements the more exclusive focus on private-actor rationality in modern electoral and partisan cycle theory.

International political economists focus more on the implications of trade and monetary exposure and of international institutions for the conduct and effects of domestic macroeconomic policy. Some (e.g., Clark 2000; Oatley 1997) stress the constraints that trade exposure and exchange rate arrangements plus capital mobility place on domestic policy makers. Others, while recognizing these constraints, suggest that partisan governments can leverage domestic institutional differences to respond differently to common international pressures (e.g., Garrett 1998a; Milner 1997; Simmons 1994). This book shares these agendas (among others), but

[41] Franzese 2000c offers a more thorough review.

stresses that institutional differences *interact* to produce differing policy responses under common pressures, international *and domestic*. That is, first, it shows how the effects of international institutions and conditions differ complexly across country-times because they interact with domestic conditions, interest structures, and institutions to shape domestic policy makers' incentives. For example, domestic government fractionalization and central bank autonomy, respectively, retard fiscal and dampen monetary policy reactions to (i.e., interact with) global economic conditions. Second, the book also clarifies the roles and assesses the relative weight of international influences and domestic factors in producing cross-country similarities in policies and outcomes. For example, it shows that the similarities across developed democracies in the postwar evolution of transfers and debt stemmed primarily from policy maker reactions to *domestic* economic and demographic trends. Although some of these trends have foreign origins (in, e.g., the oil crises), the theoretical view taken here clarifies that analytic primacy accords to domestic conditions because the governments that make policy are elected domestically and so, naturally, respond to domestic conditions. Global conditions and international institutions are critical, but because of and through their impacts, in interactions with other domestic and international factors, on the domestic stimuli to which policy makers and other domestic actors respond.

Another view holds demand management as less central to partisan policy and economic outcomes, stressing instead partisan differences in microeconomic, structural, "supply-side" policies that persist despite international and institutional constraints. Boix (1998), for example, shows persistent wide partisan differences in public investment for human (education) and physical capital, in active labor market policies (training, employment subsidies, etc.), in taxes at high income, and in privatization. In this view, conservatives and social democrats both seek growth, but the left relies on public investment whereas the right reduces taxes and public economic activity to free (assumed efficient) private resource-allocation. Macroeconomic policy is more institutionally and internationally constrained.[42] Complementing that supply-side study, which underemphasized interactions and assumed interchangeability of the alternative partisan strategies and inaccessibility or inefficacy of macroeconomic policy, this book explains how *degrees* of policy control and efficacy, and the effects of those gradated policies, varied and evolved across

---

[42] Franzese 2000d offers a more thorough review.

country-times depending on multiple interactions of their differing structures of interests and institutions. Chapter 4, for example, measures quite
directly the varying degree to which institutions (central bank autonomy)
constrained partisan and other influences on monetary policy (see also
Franzese 1999a,b). Also, as shown sequentially through the book, public
transfers and debts grew most, sapping the efficacy of fiscal and monetary
policy the most, where domestic institutions fostered popular participation and fractionalized government. These developments spurred antiinflation monetary-policy shifts to that varying degree, and those varying
shifts had larger real costs where bargaining was least coordinated or most
public-sector dominated. And those varying costs, lastly, fed varying
degrees of shifts toward institutional-structural "reform." Yet, those
"reforms," too, have strong distributional impacts, which is where this
contribution rejoins the supply-side approach. Thus, this book complements the supply-side view, emphasizing institutional and interest interactions in showing how, to what degree, and with what distributional and
efficiency effects macroeconomic policy-options have become constrained,
leaving greater relative emphasis on structural policies.

Others explore political contestation over the institutional structure
of the economy. Iversen (1999a), for example, stresses contestation over
alternative institutional arrangements for managing, especially, monetary
policy and wage bargaining. This book again complements, elaborating
how the rising political and policy focus on that particular institutional
interaction arose from the cumulative outcomes of previous democratic
contestations over the policy commitments to social insurance, public
goods, and macroeconomic management. The shift in political emphasis
toward monetary policy, and then monetary- and bargaining-institutional
"reform," emerged endogenously from the growth in transfers and debt,
which reduced fiscal policy efficacy, and public-sector employment
growth, which sharpened trade-offs between the real (employment) and
nominal (inflation) effects of the monetary control of inflation. The
emphasis in the *political-economy cycle* framework on interactions of institutions with interest structures (here: bargaining coordination with its
sectoral composition) also helps resolve a conflict among several recent
arguments and findings on this particular institutional interaction.

Lastly, especially qualitative comparative political economy has long
stressed the complex effects of broad national networks of political-
economic institutions (Katzenstein 1985; Gourevitch 1986; Hall 1986). In
its most modern statement, Hall and Soskice (2000) stress institutional

complementarities (i.e., interactions) between the organizational structure of national education-and-training, finance, interfirm, and industrial-relations systems. While managing to encompass only a far more limited range of institutional interactions, this book formalizes and may clarify some of them, and adds interactions of some political institutions. It contributes in this regard some bridging of the theoretical and empirical gaps between qualitative and formal or quantitative comparative political economy. For example, the more formal theoretical elaboration than typical of previous work stressing institutional interactions helps specify certain interactions intuited there and uncovers some new ones, while the consideration of broader sets of potentially conditioning factors than that found in most others attempting some degree of formality illuminates institutional interactions more usually suppressed in such work. And, here, as also in relation to previous work in the four areas discussed earlier, the more precise transportation of interactive theoretical propositions into quantitative empirical specification enables the available data to speak more clearly and definitively to the hypotheses and, ultimately, to inform better our theories and understanding of economic policy making and outcomes in democracy.

1.6.2. Road Maps to the Rest of the Book

As noted above, this book undertakes five theoretical and empirical tasks to make its arguments. (1) It conducts three specific studies of transfers, debt, and monetary/wage-price policy making in developed democracies. Through these, (2) it develops a theoretical view of democratic political economy in which universal tensions between the allocations of political and economic influence manifest differently across country-times depending on multiple interactions among the international and domestic political-economic structures of institutions and interests characterizing those country-times. (3) It demonstrates methodological techniques for gaining powerful, substantively meaningful empirical leverage from the limited data available on the complexly interactive and dynamic propositions that emerge from that view. Through these, (4) it offers an aggregate empirical history of macroeconomic policy in developed democracies, and (5) it demonstrates, from that view and in those studies, how modern conflicts over institutional-structural "reforms" replicate rather than replace long-familiar left-right struggles. Several road maps to the rest of the book correspond to these tasks.

First, regarding the specific studies: Chapter 2 offers and evaluates several theories to explain the political-economic determination of transfer-system size and growth; Chapter 3 similarly studies public-debt determination; and Chapter 4 considers the interaction of monetary policy and the sectoral and institutional structure of wage-price-bargaining institutions in macroeconomic management. Those interested exclusively in those topics, can read the relevant chapters independently and Section 5.1 for a conclusion to them as a set.

Second, regarding the comparative, aggregate, empirical historiography, refer back to Figure 1.22. Chapters 2 and 3 focus on the top-right of the political-economic cycle, from the structure of interests in the polity through democratic policy making. Chapter 4 focuses instead on the bottom-left, that is, on how policy and the institutional and structural features of the polity and economy interact to produce political and economic outcomes and on how those outcomes alter the structure of interests in the polity. The cycle is closed in the "Discussion, Conclusions, and Implications" section that concludes each chapter, thus completing the empirical history in Chapters 2–4 read consecutively.

Finally, together, these studies develop a broad framework for analyzing macroeconomic policy making comparatively across capitalist democracies and show how this framework continues to illuminate democratic policy making as governments shift toward institutional-structural "reform" because the conflicts underlying the debates have not changed, whatever the protagonists might claim.

That last and broadest *road map* includes this introductory chapter, which provided: (a) introduction and motivation, giving a brief background on the postwar policy commitments; (b) a brief comparative empirical history of the evolving policy commitments and concurrent developments in macroeconomic performance; (c) an outline of the underlying view of political economy, which explains how the common disparity between distributions of political and economic influence in capitalist democracy manifests differently across country-times depending on multiple interactions of domestic and international political-economic institutions, structures, and conditions; (d) an overview of the theoretical and empirical framework applied to study the problematics illuminated by that view; and (e) a quick presaging of the implications of this postwar policy-evolution for the continued viability and utility of the policy commitments and for modern political conflict over "reforms" of the institutions within which democratic governments may continue to attempt to fulfill those commitments. The roles of Chapters 2–4 in consummating these promises were already detailed. Section 5.2 returns to the broadest of these questions and problematics for further reconsideration in light of the intervening arguments and findings.[43]

---

[43] The web appendix at <http://www-personal.umich.edu/~franzese> offers a convenient outline summary of the arguments developed and supported through the book.

2

**The Democratic Commitment to
Social Insurance**

2.1. Introduction: Motivation, the Explanandum,
and a Road Map

Almost every developed democracy has at least doubled since World War
II the share of its GDP allocated to tax-and-transfer (T&T) systems (see
Figure 1.4).[1] Notwithstanding this large and fairly common upward trend,
however, much variation remains. For example, eight countries amassed
T&T over 20% of GDP by 1995, while five had T&T closer to 10%; and,
whereas Dutch T&T more than sextupled before growth abated, German
T&T less than doubled in the same time. This chapter applies the *cycle of
political economy* approach to comparative democratic policy making introduced in Chapter 1 and diagramed in Figure 1.22 to guide theoretical and
empirical exploration of these commonalities and differences. The total
variance in Figure 1.4 can be segregated into three parts to explain: cross-
country postwar-average differences, a shared cross–time path, and variation unique to country-time (i.e., the remainder).[2]

Figure 1.5 plotted transfers (% of GDP) averages and variation by
country. The wide differences across countries' postwar averages shown

[1] Transfers are the sum of social-security benefits, social-assistance grants, and unfunded
welfare and pension payments by general government (items 30–32 in OECD, *National
Accounts*, vol. 2: *Detailed Tables*, 1996 disk). These three are the most clearly "transfers" and
relate most directly to the "welfare spending" and "social transfers" used elsewhere (e.g.,
Pampel and Williamson 1988; Hicks and Swank 1984, 1992; Hicks et al. 1989).
[2] Cross-section and time-period indicators are orthogonal by construction in time-series-
cross-section data. Thus, R^2 from regressions on the full set of country or time dummies
reveals the share of total variance covered by differences in country or year averages, respectively. The remaining variance is country-time unique. A graphic adding a plot of the
country-time-unique component to Figures 1.4–6 is available on the author's web page
<http://www-personal.umich.edu/~franzese>.

there covers 42.9% ($\pm$) of the total variation,[3] and differences in postwar variation of T&T experiences within countries are also large. For example, Dutch and Belgian T&T averaged well over twice Japanese T&T, and a plus-or-minus standard deviation range around the Dutch mean quadruples ($\pm$) corresponding Australian and German ranges. Similarly, Figure 1.6 plotted T&T by year, highlighting the shared time path and variation about it. The mostly upward time path of the cross-country average covers almost 48% of total variation,[4] yet it is hardly uniform or linear. Variation and skew across countries rose visibly over time, especially since 1975. This finding – that, with the Bretton Woods collapse and two oil crises, policy and outcome differences have widened across countries since the seventies – recurs throughout the book. How structures of interests and institutions induce varying policy maker responses to such changes are exactly the subject here and elsewhere. Such country-time-unique experiences (i.e., those covered by neither country-specific nor year-specific means) are the remaining 9.5% of total variation.[5] The United States, United Kingdom, Japan, Canada, and Australia managed mostly to reduce GDP shares of T&T relative to their means and the common trend; others, notably Sweden and the Netherlands, mostly increased it in the same relativity; in a few others, such as Belgium, shares rose and then fell in relative terms; and the rest, including France and Switzerland, kept mostly to the common trend and their national average, varying little around them. This country-time unique variation, though just 9.5% of total, is appreciable. Even net of country-specific means and the common time path, the country-time-unique component retains interextrema and standard deviation ranges as large as 15% and 5% of GDP ($\pm$).

Jointly, these graphs detail this chapter's explanandum and define its central empirical question: how well does current theory, with the amendments and additions to be offered here, explain the common and variant T&T experiences of developed democracies in the postwar era?

The chapter is structured to provide some answers to this question as follows. Section 2.2.1 presents a simple heuristic model of T&T

---

[3] I.e., $R_c^2 \approx .429$ from a regression of transfers on the full set of country indicators.

[4] I.e., $R_t^2 \approx .476$ from a regression of transfers on the full set of year indicators. Some countries enter the sample after 1950 – all but Australia (1960) enter by 1955 – and some leave before 1995 due to data availability; therefore, excluding one's focus in this graph to the period from 1955 to 1990 is advisable.

[5] I.e., $1 - R_c^2 - R_t^2 \approx (100 - 42.9 - 47.6)\% \approx 9.5\%$ of the total.

determination intended to reflect the core elements of the influential static, median-voter, neoclassical-macroeconomy models of Romer (1975) and Meltzer and Richard (1981). Section 2.2.2 then briefly considers a dynamic extension, similarly intended to reflect a simplified Alesina-Rodrik (1994) model. These sections aim, with minimum formality, to clarify the necessary assumptions of such models, to state the key predictions pertaining to T&T system-size determination emerging therefrom, and to provide a formal basis for further theoretical discussion. Section 2.3 then applies the *cycle of political economy* framework to extend the analysis in three relatively ignored directions. Section 2.3.1 considers the implications of forward-looking median voters or governments (the bottom of the cycle). Section 2.3.2 moves back in the cycle to consider elected partisan representatives that form governments that, although somewhat responsive to the median, may not exactly mirror its preferences but, rather, jointly straddle them. Finally, section 2.3.3 turns in the cycle to the structure of interests in the economy and polity and how those interests elect their partisan representatives, stressing that not everyone in the economy participates in the polity and that the interests of the politically active and inactive systematically differ in ways relevant to the empirical predictions emerging from median-voter models of T&T. Section 2.4 then details the data and methodology, and 2.5 conducts and discusses the empirical estimation. Section 2.6 concludes, first with implications and suggestions for further research specific to T&T, and then with broader discussion relating back to comparative democratic management of the postwar policy commitments discussed in Chapter 1.

2.2. Economic Inequality and Demand for Transfers in Pure Democracy

2.2.1. A Static Median-Voter Model of Tax-and-Transfer Systems

The static, median-voter, neoclassical-economy model of democratic choice over a strictly proportional T&T system presented here is intended as a simplified, reduced-form of Romer (1975) or Meltzer and Richard (1981). The model highlights the main factors determining the median voter's ideal T&T rate in a static world: the pretax income distribution, total wealth in the economy, and marginal rates at which taxes decrease output. These models underscore the central problematic of capitalist democracy, the differing distributions of electoral and economic power stressed in Chapter 1 (see also Meltzer and Richard 1978). The impetus for redistribution, they argue, derives from the median voter being poorer than the economy average. The median seeks larger transfers the greater that discrepancy. In focusing on partisanship (e.g., Castles 1982; Hicks and Swank 1984, 1992; Hicks et al. 1989) or demography (e.g., Pampel and Williamson 1988), however, previous empirical work has left this hypothesis largely untested. In emphasizing the derivation of formal theoretical models, and perhaps believing that income skew cannot be adequately measured, even the literature deriving the hypothesis has not generally tested it directly.[6] This chapter provides a direct empirical examination of that core hypothesis.

First, for simplicity and illustrative clarity, let $y_i \equiv y_i(\tau)$, the output (income) of individual i, decrease in tax rates,[7] and consider only strictly proportional T&T systems that tax all persons and income equally and return all revenue evenly. That is, all individuals will be taxed the same flat rate, τ, on all their income, y_i, and all revenues will be redistributed equally, $\tau \sum_{i=1}^{N} \dfrac{y_i}{N} \equiv \tau \bar{y}$ to each person ($N \equiv$ population size). This reduces the complicated (multidimensional) choice of the T&T system to a simple (one-dimensional) choice over a single parameter, τ, the T&T rate. Obviously, this grossly simplifies any actual T&T system, but the hypotheses derived under this simplifying assumption will remain substantively unchanged provided that transfers cannot be targeted to specific individuals and that feasible T&T systems have the properties that net transfer payments weakly decrease in income.[8] Finally, assume that utility for each person i increases in their disposable income (a hopefully noncontentious

---

[6] But see Rodríguez (1999) who tests the theory directly in U.S.-state data, finding no support. Hypothesis 7 suggests (empirically supported) theoretical additions that might explain this failure. Also, Alesina and Rodrik (1994) find a negative correlation between income disparity and growth. They assumed the distortionary impacts of redistribution to drive this result but do not directly test that link.

[7] One can derive such $y(\tau)$ from a fuller model where individuals choose how to allocate labor and leisure time given taxes. Taxes decrease output in such models by inducing substitution of leisure for labor. Output must decrease as tax rates rise (at least beyond some rate) for these models to have informative solutions; thankfully, theorists and practitioners, regardless of ideological predisposition, generally accept this contention (see, e.g., Esping-Andersen in Offe 1984).

[8] And the function is reasonably smooth. Actually, these conditions are stronger than the minimum needed (i.e., sufficient) but seem plausible enough. For other considerations, see also Alt 1983, Bergstrom and Goodman 1973, Berry and Lowery 1987, Kramer 1983, Larkey et al. 1981.

generality). This gives utility (log-utility for simplicity) of person i compactly and intuitively as:

$$u_i = \ln[\, y_i(\tau) + \tau \cdot \bar{y}(\tau) - \tau \cdot y_i(\tau)\,] \tag{1}$$

The optimal T&T rate for the median-income person, subscripted m, will be implemented in a median-voter polity deciding over a one-dimensional policy like this one, and is found by maximizing equation (1) with respect to τ, giving:[9]

$$\tau^* = \left(1 - \frac{\bar{y}'}{y'_m}\right)^{-1} + (y'_m - \bar{y}')^{-1}\cdot(\bar{y} - y_m) \equiv a + b \cdot (\bar{y} - y_m) \tag{2}$$

The last term on the right is the difference between average and median income, that is, the income distribution skew: $\bar{y} - y_m$, which is positive for typical, right-skewed income distributions (many poor and middle class, fewer, but some very, rich). Its coefficient, b, reflects differences between the responses of the median person's income and of average income to tax rates, y'_m and $\bar{y}'$. It is positive if the output of the relatively wealthy is more responsive to tax rates than those of the relatively poor – a property of all utility functions with decreasing marginal utility of income. The intercept, a, relates to these two terms also.

Thus, the median voter's optimal T&T rate lies between zero and one,[10] and depends on the economy's average and median incomes, $\bar{y}$ and

---

[9] These are the first-order conditions. The second-order conditions will hold for well-behaved (defined in note 10) $u(\cdot)$ and $y(\tau)$.

[10] Conditions under which $0 < \tau^* < 1$, however banal that might seem, follow less directly than one might like from many such models, yet any model concluding that democratically chosen T&T rates would be negative, zero, or one would lack empirical relevance. Fortunately, equation (2) identifies a set of sufficient conditions to assure interior solutions ($0 < \tau^* < 1$), which are quite plausible empirically. First, income distributions must be skewed right (positive), $\bar{y} - y_m > 0$, an absolute empirical regularity. Given that, the remaining sufficient conditions are:

$$\frac{\partial^2 y_i(\tau)}{\partial \tau \partial y_i} < 0 \tag{2a}$$

$$\lim_{\tau \to 1} y_i(\tau) = 0 \tag{2b}$$

$$|y'_m(0)| < \bar{y}(0) - y_m(0) \tag{2c}$$

Condition (2a) indicates higher-income people's output is more sensitive to taxes. This plus positive skew, assures nonnegative τ^*. Condition (2c) states that marginal τ-increases from zero do not so lower the median person's output that the added redistribution does not compensate. That assures nonzero τ^*. Condition (2b), stating that 100% tax rates

y_m, and the derivative of each with respect to the tax rate, τ. More simply, the core result of such models and the one primarily emphasized here and in the previous literature is that the median-income person typically[11] desires greater τ (i.e., larger T&T) as the societal income distribution, $\bar{y} - y_m$, becomes more skewed.

Several further results surround the way output decreases as taxes rise, that is, the magnitudes of $\bar{y}'$ and of $\dfrac{\partial^2 y}{\partial \tau \partial y} \equiv \dfrac{\partial \frac{\partial y}{\partial \tau}}{\partial y}$. For example, the more negative these terms, the smaller the median's desired T&T. Intuitively, the more that everyone substitutes leisure for labor as taxes rise, or that specifically the rich do relative to the poor, the more average income will decrease as taxes rise, implying that raising taxes ceases to give the median voter greater transfers at a lower τ. A *distribution-neutral* rise in national income likewise reduces the median voter's desired T&T. Intuitively, a distribution-neutral boon leaves the skew unchanged, but everyone is wealthier and so more willing to substitute leisure for labor. Thus, deadweight losses from taxes are larger, so the median desires less T&T. To summarize:

Hypothesis 1: The median voter's desired T&T increases in the (rightward) skew of the income distribution (ceteris paribus).[12]

Hypothesis 2: The median voter's desired T&T decreases with distribution-neutral increases in aggregate income.

Hypothesis 3: The more negatively output responds to taxes and the more that responsiveness increases (absolutely) with income, the less T&T the median voter desires.

Further implications could be teased from equation (2); however, Hypothesis 1 is the key, Hypotheses 2 and 3 illustrate that others, in principle,

---

reduce output to zero, assures $\tau^* < 1$. These are reasonable enough, so they are assumed throughout. Romer's (1975) model, for example, with Cobb-Douglas preferences over labor and leisure, assures conditions (2a) and (2b) and, for reasonable parameterization, (2c). N.b., these *sufficient* conditions are likely stronger than actually needed (i.e., than necessary-and-sufficient conditions).

[11] Only *typically* because income skew could (unlikely) increase while, given condition (2a), the denominator in equation (2) rises in absolute value even more.

[12] All hypotheses are ceteris paribus.

arise from this framework, but only Hypotheses 1 and 2 are actually tested here.[13]

2.2.2. *Dynamic Considerations: The Optimal Plan*

Adding a dynamic element, economic growth, would require investment and capital stock in a fully specified model (see Alesina and Rodrik 1994), but a reduced form capturing the relation between growth and the T&T rate can suffice for present purposes. First, summarize the impact of investment decisions, optimized given tax rates, τ, on growth rates, γ, by: $\gamma \equiv \gamma(\tau)$ *with* $\gamma' < 0$, $\gamma'' < 0$. That is, in addition to the level effects highlighted by the preceding static model, higher T&T rates diminish growth and do so at an increasing rate as τ increases. (Not only do higher tax rates lead some not to work as much, but they also lead some not to invest as much.) Next, model the intertemporal utility for each member of society as a simple extension of the static utility expressed in equation (1):[14]

$$U_i = \sum_{t=0}^{\infty} \left\{ \left[\frac{\{1 + \gamma(\tau)\}}{(1+\delta)} \right]^t \ln[y_i(\tau) + \tau\{\bar{y}(\tau) - y_i(\tau)\}] \right\} \tag{3}$$

The main differences from the static case are fully apparent in comparing equations (3) and (1), so an explicit solution for the median's optimal τ is unnecessary. The expression following the discount and growth rates, $ln[\cdot]$, is exactly the utility in the static model; therefore, the only additional concerns in the dynamic model are that the individual discounts the future (at rate δ) and that, beyond output-*level* effects from the static case, τ also retards output *growth*, γ. Thus, with positive discount and growth rates, the median voter prefers less T&T in the dynamic than in the static model. Alternatively, with greater empirical relevance, this difference manifests in the median voter desiring less T&T the more she weights the future in

---

[13] Testing Hypothesis 3 would require estimates by country and by individuals' income level of the marginal rate of substitution of leisure for labor with respect to increases in taxes, a task well beyond the current enterprise's scope.

[14] Thus, individuals maximize the present value of all current and future income. Summing over all time with a fixed discount rate assumes that people live forever, highly unrealistic, or that every member of each generation is equally linked to the next through, e.g., concern for their children, slightly more realistic. For present purposes, however, only the difference between the dynamic and static models matters, and that depends qualitatively neither on whether one models infinitely lived family units or finitely lived individuals nor on details of the latter.

evaluating policy (i.e., the longer her "time horizons"). Also, the more sensitive the growth rate to increases in taxes, that is, the more negative γ' and γ'', the more deleterious the tax effect on long-run wealth, and so the less T&T the median desires.

Hypothesis 4: The median voter desires less T&T the less she discounts the future.

Hypothesis 5: The median voter desires less T&T the more negatively sensitive the growth rate to tax rates.

Empirical evaluation of Hypothesis 5, analogously to Hypothesis 3, lies beyond the present scope; it serves here only to illustrate that further hypotheses could be derived. Hypothesis 4, contrarily, has extensions that will be evaluated here.

2.3. Democratic Management of Transfer Systems by Elected Governments

2.3.1. Policy Makers Looking Forward: The Time-Inconsistency Problem

The foregoing assumed all actors believe that the intertemporally optimal τ the current median voter chose will reign indefinitely. However, once the capital that increases next period's income is invested based on the existing τ, the median voter can then raise τ, garnering more transfers without reducing growth.[15] The implications of such time-inconsistency problems can be profound (Kydland and Prescott 1977). Suppose, for example, that this period's median voter is uncertain she will be next period's median. For illustrative clarity, suppose she were certain she will *not* be the median next period and cannot know who will succeed her. She cannot affect next period's τ under these conditions; it will be whatever the next median wants. Thus, her preferred T&T rate depends only on this period's outcome,[16] and so she chooses the static optimum from equation (2), which, as noted, will be higher than her intertemporal optimum. Alternatively, with more empirical relevance, this period's median voter increases τ as her uncertainty rises over the identity of next period's median

---

[15] Against this incentive are arrayed the usual contrary concerns like policy-making reputation, etc.

[16] Her choice of τ affects only this period's investment, which has vanishingly small impact on her utility relative to the level effects of this year's τ.

voter. Intuitively, greater uncertainty is analogous to a higher discount rate. Restating Hypothesis 4 accordingly:

Corollary 4a: The median voter desires more T&T the more uncertain she is that she will be the median in the future.

If, then, political entities with more durable control of the policy making agenda than the current median voter did not exist, democratic economies would risk serious redistributive overload indeed. The fears (or hopes) of Marx, Mill, and others that capitalism and democracy could not coexist (see Chapter 1) might well have been fully warranted. However, representative democracy mitigates the problem because political parties aggregate voters into fewer groups of competing interests with correspondingly larger spaces between the median incomes of each party than between each voter, implying that perturbations in the distribution of voters' incomes alter which party controls the agenda much less than they would which voter controls it in a pure median-voter setting.[17] Thus, because parties will control the policy agenda on behalf of their constituencies for longer periods than would median voters in pure democracy, and because parties, like firms (Kreps 1990), are long and indefinitely lived and reputationally tied to the future, parties are less susceptible to time inconsistency problems than median voters would be.

In short, partisan representation mitigates time inconsistencies, thereby reducing T&T, relative to a pure-democracy, median-voter ideal. The empirical implication is simple: the longer a party expects to control the policy agenda, the more it weights the future and so the smaller its desired T&T. The logic extends naturally to the horizon length of any potential agenda-controlling entity. For example, *governments* generally control policy in parliamentary democracies, so their expected tenure, as opposed to some citizen's, citizens', party's, or parties', establishes the relevant horizon affecting T&T-determination.

Corollary 4b: Policy makers desire less T&T the longer they expect to control the policy agenda.

2.3.2. *Characteristics of Governments: Partisan Redistributive Politics*

Party systems in representative democracy could be organized so that, when parties obtain agenda (government) control, the median voter in the

---

[17] This complements other mitigating aspects of party democracy (Offe 1984).

median party of government may not correspond to society's median-income voter. Far more commonly, parties jointly straddle the median and governments oscillate left to right of it. The implication for T&T determination is simple. Suppose for illustrative clarity that there are two parties that, because they have extra incentive to appeal to activists who are generally more extreme than the median (Aldrich 1983a,b, 1995; Aldrich and McGinnis 1989), jointly straddle rather than converge to polity's median. The median voter for the left or right party will, then, generally be left or right of (i.e., poorer or richer than) the polity's median. The optimal τ from equation (2), then, directly implies that the left party will desire more T&T than the median voter and, a fortiori, than the right party and vice versa:

> *Hypothesis 6*: Left governments desire more T&T than the median voter who, in turn, desires more than right governments.

Obviously, similar predictions emerge from class- or partisan-based views of political economy that rely less heavily on median-voter principles (e.g., Heclo 1974; Hibbs 1977; Castles 1982; Esping-Andersen 1990; Korpi 1980, 1983).[18] The point here is more the converse that, incorporating Aldrich's insights, the partisan identity of the government remains relevant *even controlling for the position (preferences) of the median voter*.

2.3.3. Interests Represented in the Polity: Participation and Redistribution

The discussion heretofore assumed that all members of society participate equally in the political process and, thus, that democratic governments respond to the *unweighted* distribution of societal interests, with perhaps a fixed partisan bias. However, not everyone votes, or otherwise participates equally, even in the most participatory democracies, and many scholars (e.g., Dye 1979; Pampel and Williamson 1988) argue that higher voter turnout should produce greater T&T.[19] The latter argument – a loosely

---

[18] Arguments that centrist governments, especially Christian Democrats, desire more T&T for their own reasons (Wilensky 1981; Castles 1982; Esping-Andersen 1990; Hicks and Swank 1992) are less amenable to translation into a single-dimensional median-voter framework.

[19] The degree of electoral competition, typically operationalized as the evenness of the vote distribution across legislative parties, is also emphasized. This variable has not proved robustly predictive, though, so it is omitted here.

specified link between more-participatory democracy and progressive policy (plus an assumption that redistribution is progressive) – neglects that the effects of participation must depend on who is joining the electoral pool as voter turnout increases. Thus, although empirical correlations between voter participation and T&T size seem fairly strong (Pampel and Williamson 1988; Hicks and Swank 1992), equally strong theoretical reasons to expect greater electoral participation to correlate with more pro-T&T elements comprising the politically relevant pool are more lacking. Many – for example, Meltzer and Richard (1981) and philosophers of all ideological views before them (Aristotle, Tocqueville, Mill, Marx, etc.) – simply assumed that franchise expansion would increase the political weight of the less-well-off. Historically, this is indubitably accurate, but whether the same holds for increases in voter turnout given universal suffrage and whether that implies that greater electoral participation increases governmental responsiveness to higher economic inequality remains more assumed than established.

Verba et al. (1978), Wolfinger and Rosenstone (1980), Conway (1985), Harrop and Miller (1987), and subsequent researchers all demonstrate the relatively wealthy to be more likely to vote than the relatively poor. Moreover, Nagel (1987: 117–19) shows that, in the United States at least, this has indeed implied generally wealthier voters than nonvoters; using the 1980 Census, he estimated the median-person's income as $18,267 and the median-voter's as $20,698. That voter participation varies radically across democracies and, less so, across time is also well known (Jackman and Miller 1995; Franklin 1996). Do these observations link more generally and comparatively to imply that, ceteris paribus, country-times with higher voter participation have wealthier median voters relative to median persons than those with lower voter participation so that the relationship between participation and T&T hypothesized by Dye (1979) and found by Pampel and Williamson (1988) and Hicks and Swank (1992) can be derived from the preceding model? Nagel's (1987) finding that higher voter turnout favors Democratic presidential candidates is highly suggestive, but should one expect the relationship more generally?

Consider the following heuristic model in which citizens decide whether to vote by a simple cost-benefit analysis in which the net benefits of voting (which may be largely subjective) vary by country, time, and individual. The positive correlation between income and voting propensity established by the empirical literature implies that the net benefits of voting generally increase with income. Furthermore, because this correlation is observed over many different country-times with widely variant average incomes, and because participation has not generally risen with aggregate income, *relative* rather than *absolute* income must be the determinant of voting propensity. This suggests an individual voting decision like:

(i) Vote if: $V(y_{ijt}, X_{ijt}) \geq 0$, otherwise abstain.

(ii) Define: $y_{ijt} \equiv i$'s income relative to country j's mean income at time t,

$X_{ijt} \equiv a$ vector of other aspects of i, j, t relevant to voting

(iii) Assume: the function $V(\cdot)$ is the same for all i, j, t

$E[\partial V/\partial y] > 0$

$E[\partial^2 V/\partial y \partial x] = 0 \ \forall \ x \in X$ (4A)

The key features here are that *relative* income, y_{ijt}, matters; that net voting benefits are determined similarly for all voters (here, $V(\cdot)$ is invariant); that net benefits, on average, increase in individual relative income (i.e., $E[\partial V/\partial y] > 0$); and that, on average, other factors affecting the propensity to vote fall similarly on relatively well- and worse-off (i.e., $E[\partial^2 V/\partial y \partial x] = 0$). These other factors, X_{ijt}, might reflect, say, institutional and cultural differences. For example, democracies differ in whether the individual or government is responsible for registration; the individual's cost of voting is clearly less where government bears responsibility.

Next, aggregate voter participation in country j at time t is just the sum of all persons, i, for whom the net benefit of voting is positive:

$$VP_{jt} = \sum_i [V(y_{ijt}, X_{ijt}) > 0]$$ (4B)

Equations (4A) and (4B) combine to imply that, on average, country-times with higher voter participation will have a poorer (in relative terms) "marginal voter" – the person for whom voting just has net benefits – than country-times with lower. Formally:

$$VP_{oo} > VP_{11} \Leftrightarrow E(y_{ioo}|b_{ioo} = 0) < E(y_{i11}|b_{i11} = 0)$$ (4C)

If this characterization of the decision to vote is reasonably accurate, then increases in voter participation will correlate positively across countries and over time with increases *from right (rich) to left (poor)* in the proportion of the income distribution voting. This, in turn, implies that, for any given median income in society, the effective median income represented by electoral input to the political process is decreasing in the voter participation rate. Thus, the raw income distribution skew and voter participation rates interact in determining T&T.

Hypothesis 7: The positive effect of the raw income skew on T&T size (Hypothesis 1) is increasing in the voter participation rate.

The logical converse is also new; the effect of voter participation on T&T is increasing in the underlying income disparity. Generally positive effects of voter turnout were hypothesized and found before (Dye 1979; Pampel and Williamson 1988; Hicks and Swank 1992); the greater formalism here clarifies, more subtly, that the impact of higher voter participation on government responsiveness varies with the structure of interests among those joining the pool of voters.

Corollary 7a: The effect of the voter participation rate on T&T increases in the skew of the underlying income distribution.

These arguments emphasize voting, but other modes of political participation – contributions, lobbying, contacting representatives, letters to editors, and the like – also provide influence. Indeed, considering the minuscule probability that one vote can alter an election outcome, other forms of participation are likely more influential than an individual vote. One might wonder, therefore, whether this undermines the empirical relevance of Hypothesis 7 and Corollary 7a, but two considerations suggest to the contrary that it strengthens them. First, as electoral participation declines, both the prevalence and the influence of alternative participation-modes logically tend to increase, at least relatively.[20] Second, socioeconomic status correlates even more strongly with other modes of participation than with voting (Verba et al. 1978; Conway 1985; Rosenstone and Hansen 1993; Verba et al. 1995). Therefore, as voter participation declines, not only does representation of the relatively less-well-off decline in the electorate, but the prominence and political influence of nonvoting participation tend to rise and, there, the relatively poor are even less well represented. As Rosenstone and Hansen argued and found, "class differences in mobilization typically aggravate rather than mitigate the effects of class differences in political resources" (1993: 241). In short, for

---

[20] The little evidence available suggests aggregate voting and other political-participation rates correlate negatively across countries (e.g., Verba et al. 1995).

present purposes, voter participation is a legitimate summary statistic for political participation more generally, and, indeed, it is intended as such in the foregoing theoretical analysis and subsequent empirical analysis.

2.4. The Data and Empirical Methods

2.4.1. The Dependent Variable

The appropriate dependent variable to evaluate these hypotheses is T&T size relative to GDP, but no public-accounts data correspond to this theoretical concept directly.[21] Of available data, social-security benefits, social-assistance grants, and pension and welfare benefits (items 30–2 of "Table 6: General Government" in OECD, *National Accounts*, vol. 2: *Detailed Tables*) are most unambiguously *transfer* in nature. The appropriate temporal unit of analysis is annual since governments budget yearly. The dependent variable, *TT*, therefore sums these items divided by GDP (same source) measured annually.[22] Figures 1.4–6 already displayed these data in various formats; descriptive statistics appear in the web appendix (<http://www-personal.umich.edu/~franzese>).

2.4.2. Controls and Variables Reflecting Other Hypotheses

To control for economic conditions is critical in examining any political-economic proposition, but also problematic. On one side, policies and, a fortiori, outcomes will often respond "automatically" to domestic and foreign conditions about which current policy makers could do little. Omitting *exogenous* controls like these would bias results in directions hard to determine a priori. On the other, economic controls will dampen the estimated effects of political variables relative to their true, full effect if the political impact occurs in any part by altering these *endogenous* conditions. Statistical techniques to distinguish endogenous from exogenous factors are unobtainable, so, rather than assuming conclusions by using the theory

---

[21] All data used in Section 2.4 plus supplementary analysis, statistics, tables, figures, and other materials are in an appendix at <http://www-personal.umich.edu/~franzese>.

[22] Usable observations are maximized by taking the raw data (1960–93) from OECD, *National Accounts*, vol. 2: *Detailed Tables*, 1996 disks and augmenting with print-edition (various issues) data, which fill some missing and add some pre-1960 data, ratio-splicing from 1993 back, thereby resolving conflicts to favor the later, disk publication.

to be tested to determine exogeneity,[23] this book errs toward downplaying political effects by controlling for economic conditions extensively.

Transfer payments will obviously respond to unemployment and the age structure of the population, these being much of their purpose, so such economic controls include the *unemployment* rate (*UE*: internationally comparable annual figures, OECD sources)[24] and the pension-*age* share of the population (*POP65*: population 65+ as a percent of total; UN, *Demographic Yearbook*). Transfers may also respond immediately and semi-automatically to *inflation* rates. T&T systems could be insufficiently indexed to keep real payments unchanged, so that inflation lowers *TT* (a ratio to GDP and therefore real) without any current policy maker response, or they could be "overindexed" or recipients could usually succeed in pressing policy makers to "overrespond" to inflation. Either way, controlling for inflation (*CPI*: consumer-price inflation, IMF sources)[25] seems wise.

Previous theoretical and empirical studies of government size stress at least six further variables, without typically stating whether the predicted effects should occur in transfers or elsewhere on the budget. Controlling for them seems prudent. First, nearly every empirical study begins with Wagner's Law that the public share of total spending increases with aggregate wealth because, in short, public goods are luxuries. If the law applies specifically to transfers, it (partly) contradicts Hypothesis 2 that T&T decreases in wealth (controlling for the income skew). The law's applicability to T&T depends on whether transfers are national luxury or necessity. If one assumes transfers are luxuries – poorer countries generally eschew them, so they probably are – the estimated T&T effect of wealth (*Y*: the natural log of real GDP per capita; *Penn World Tables*, v. 5.6) will reflect the net effect of these two, countervailing but not logically exclusive, forces.

---

[23] So-called tests for exogeneity only test overidentifying restrictions and must *assume* some other set of variables exogenous, which assumptions, if violated at all, render the "tests" meaningless. Similarly, in practice, instruments are only partly exogenous, and so they swap *some* endogeneity bias for *some* inefficiency. Which sin is worse depends on the degree of endogeneity relative to the explanatory power of the instruments for the instrumented variables (see Bartels 1991).

[24] "OECD sources" are *National Accounts*, vol. 2; *Detailed Tables*, 1996 disk; *Economic Outlook and Reference Supplement* no. 62, 1998 disk, and various print editions thereof; and *Labor Force Statistics*.

[25] "IMF sources" are *International Financial Statistics*, 6/96 CD-ROM, supplemented from print editions.

Second, Cameron (1978) argued and demonstrated that government size (measured as revenue share of GDP) tends to increase in *trade openness* (*OPEN*: exports plus imports share of GDP, IMF sources). Katzenstein (1985) and others (most recently, Rodrik 1998) argue that demand for government action in a social-insurer role specifically increases with exposure, which also suggests a positive *OPEN-TT* correlation. Garrett and coauthors[26] argue, alternatively, that openness would constrain *market-subverting* government action but, if anything, foster *market-augmenting* intervention. Whether T&T is subverting or augmenting will depend on the system's details. Either way, controlling for *OPEN* seems prudent.

Third, the social-democratic-corporatist scholarly tradition emphasizes the organizational strength of labor in the polity and economy (plus left-party strength in government). Whether *union density* or coordination (corporatism) is causally relevant is debated,[27] but indices of either have found strong support in previous empirical work, so the issue may be tangential to these control purposes. The simpler union density (*UDEN*: unions' share of labor force, Golden et al. 1995) is used here as it is more transparently understood and measured.

Fourth, others argue that federalization of fiscal policy making may reduce general government budgets.[28] Sharpe (1988), for example, notes that federalized policy making reduces fiscal authorities' ability to externalize the costs of locally desired spending to larger, aggregate decision-making units. Peterson (1990), for example, adds that federalized policy making, especially in T&T, may induce a "race to the bottom" as localities compete for investment by lowering taxes. To control for these possibilities, *fiscal centralization* (*CTAX*, OECD sources) is measured as the central government's share of general government revenues.

---

[26] See Garrett 1995, 1998a,b,c, 2000; Garrett and Lange 1991, 1995; and Garrett and Mitchell 1999. This argument often works via financial openness especially, but trade and financial openness correlate highly.

[27] One could infer from Lange 1984, Regini 1984, Crouch 1985, Lange and Garrett 1985, Katzenstein 1985, and others that T&T systems both support, in providing side payments, and are supported by corporatist bargaining institutions: large, effective political units that internalize many T&T benefits. Fragmented but strong unions, conversely, may spur unemployment, while remaining effectively sized politically: small enough to solve collective-action problems (Olson 1965, 1982) in lobbying for T&T but large enough together to make such pressure work.

[28] Weingast et al. (1981) argue, relatedly, that geographic districting of *national* legislatures fosters distributive overspending because coordination problems among localities make the sum of their separate wishes greater than the national aggregate would wish. See also Franzese and Nooruddin 1999 for an extension.

Penultimately, complicated fiscal systems may hinder voters' assessments of the full costs and benefits of government programs – that is, they may worsen *fiscal illusion*. Such illusion could induce under- or overestimations of net costs or benefits (Buchanan and Wagner 1977) or, as logically, the opposite (Downs 1960); which dominates depends on the relative opacity of spending and revenue. Either way, the greater the fiscal complexity, the greater the illusion, and so the more or less public spending. Again, one controls for either possibility by including indirect taxes (*ITAX*: complexity) and total and central-government taxes (*TTAX*, *CTAX*: simplicity) as shares of total general-government revenues (OECD sources).[29]

Finally, political economists have long suspected governments of seeking to manipulate transfers to rise before elections to garner electoral boons from fiscally illuded voters (Tufte 1978), though they might also manage to garner such boons from nonilluded voters (Rogoff and Sibert 1988; Rogoff 1990).[30] Thus, a variable equal to 1 in *preelection years* (*ELE*) is also included.[31]

2.4.3. Measuring the Factors Identified by These Hypotheses

Hypothesis 1 argued that T&T should increase in the difference between the mean and median income in the society. Hypothesis 7 extended the

---

[29] Indirect taxes are presumably more complicated than direct ones, but taxes are simpler than other means of revenue generation. More completely, one would also like measures of spending-side complexity, but this must await future research.

[30] Schultz (1995) notes that manipulating the economy has costs: e.g., lost reputation for sound policy or detrimental future economic repercussions. Thus, incumbents likely attempt it only when deemed most necessary, as when the upcoming election is expected to be close. Moreover, governments obviously cannot manipulate budgets in years prior to unforeseen elections. Thus, more ideal would be a variable that is nonzero only to the degree a coming election was foreseen and that increases in the expected closeness of such elections. Creating such a measure comparably across countries remains for future research.

[31] To be precise, in election year t, $ELE_t = M/12 + (d/D)/12$ with M the completed months preelection, d the day of the incomplete month, and D the total days in that month. $1 - ELE_{t-1}$ is allocated to the previous year. If preelection years overlap, ELE can exceed one, as perhaps it should, but this is rare enough that capping ELE at one changes no result appreciably. The United States, Finland, and the French Fifth Republic are problematic, being presidential systems. The general rule applied throughout is that presidents and cabinets in Finland and the French Fifth Republic are each one-half the government and in the United States that the president and each house are one-third. E.g., the year prior to a presidential election only would be scored one-half or one-third as appropriate.

prediction, arguing that this relationship should itself increase in the voter participation rate.[32]

Data for *voter participation* (*VP*: Mackie and Rose 1991 and *European Journal of Political Research*, various data annuals) are not annually observable like the dependent variable. Theory stresses the politically (electorally) active's share of the population; a reasonable annual estimate of such may be interpolated by fixing voter turnout from each election until the next and then smoothing the resulting series by a moving average covering this and the previous three years.[33]

Measuring *income disparity* is notoriously more difficult. To obtain the income distribution skew for which Hypotheses 1 and 7 call specifically requires median and mean income measures. The mean is just GDP per capita, but median income proved impossible to measure directly yet comparably across countries and time. Therefore, consider an alternative expedient based on manufacturing wages and GDP per capita (IMF sources), indexed equivalently. To the degree that manufacturing workers are the median actors or that their wage-income plight reasonably tracks the median's, the ratio of GDP-per-capita to manufacturing-wage indices gives a measure of the mean-to-median ratio that is cross-time-comparable within country, equal to one in index-year 1986, and increasing in income skew. Then, cross-country-comparable GINI index measures for 1986 or as close thereto as possible (Atkinson et al. 1995), normalized to one in a base country (United States), and multiplied by the within-country measure produces a cross-country- and cross-time-comparable index of the income skew: the *relative wage position of manufacturing workers* (*RW*). *RW* increases in income skew and compares all other country-times to the U.S. situation in 1986 where it equals 1.[34]

[32] As noted earlier, the unemployed and pensioners receive transfers. Because age and employment status also relate to voting propensities, participation should also interact with unemployment rates and the age distribution in T&T determination. Unfortunately, attempts made here to estimate all three interactive effects ran afoul of severe multicolinearity, and techniques such as in Chapters 3–4 cannot apply because employment, age, and income status relate to participation differently. These and similar hypotheses therefore remain open empirical matters.

[33] *VP* covers only lower-house national elections in cases where all elections do not coincide. The four-year blocks cover exactly one presidential-election year in the United States, thus smoothing the (possibly theoretically spurious) spikes in measured electorally relevant population that would otherwise occur every four years.

[34] The web appendix at <http://www-personal.umich.edu/~franzese> offers further details of *RW*'s construction and the arguments and assumptions underlying its use to measure

Hypothesis 3 related aggregate marginal rates of labor-leisure substitution and their pattern across individuals of different incomes to T&T. In principle, one could estimate these quantities for every country-year, given the necessary microeconomic data. In practice, such data are lacking, so the proposition must remain untested. Likewise, Hypothesis 5 related the tax sensitivity of the economy's growth rate negatively to T&T. Empirical evaluation would require estimates of that elasticity by country-time, which is beyond the present, and so remains for future, research.

Hypothesis 4 and its corollaries related the *median voter's uncertainty* and discount rate positively and *policy makers' expected duration* of agenda control negatively to T&T. Neither concept is terribly directly measurable, but some attempts are made. First, if variation within the income distribution over time correlates with variation of its skew across time – intuitively appealing and likely, but not mathematically necessary – then a moving standard deviation of the skew index will correlate with the median's uncertainty over whether she will remain such. Thus, *SDRW*, a five-year, centered, moving standard deviation of *RW* is included. Second, to the degrees that governments control policy, hazard rates of collapse are constant within governments, and governments' predictions of their own hazard rates are relatively accurate (i.e., have small mean-squared error), the inverse of the incumbent government's actual duration will well approximate policy makers' expected hazard rates (*HR*).[35]

Hypothesis 6 stated that, even controlling for the median voter's interests (the income skew), *government partisanship* affects T&T, the left implementing more T&T than the right. To index government partisanship, first code all parties in government since 1945 in these 21 developed

income skew. Other indices constructed from the *Luxembourg Income Study* (Atkinson et al. 1995) were also considered. A broad-coverage estimate of comparable GINI indices was constructed from its set of country-specific-study estimates, ranging from annual 1967–90 U.S. data to one observation for Greece and New Zealand, filling years between observations by fixed-growth extrapolation up to 1995 and back to 1950 by autoregression. The result is made internationally comparable by repeating the process for ratios of available data from comparative studies and multiplying that by the country-specific series. The resulting GINI index performed broadly similarly, though with slightly larger standard errors, to the *RW* measure, which better matches the present theory.

[35] Government-duration data are from Woldendorp et al. 1994, 1998 and Lane et al. 1991. U.S., French Fifth Republic, and Finnish presidential systems again complicate. The durations inversed are one-half each the president's and cabinet's in France and Finland, and one-third each the president's and each house's in the United States.

democracies, 0 at far left to 10 at far right.[36] Then, these codes plus each party's number of cabinet ministers in each government (Lane et al. 1991; Woldendorp et al. 1994, 1998) give a government's average left-right position or its partisan *center of gravity* (*CoG*).[37]

2.4.4. Specifying the Empirical Model

With hypotheses derived and operationalized, as Table 2.1 summarizes conveniently, this section turns to specifying an empirical model for evaluating the emergent positive political economy of T&T-size determination. Theory is ambiguous on many hypothesized signs and provides even less guidance on the functional form for the equation. The first issue, given the strong trends in the dependent and many independent variables, is appropriate time-serial control.

Tests reveal that *TT* may have a *unit root*,[38] so proceeding with simple lagged-dependent-variable models could be highly misleading; an error-correction model (ECM) is advised. Several likely candidates for co-integration exist; *UE*, *POP65*, and *RW* all may have unit roots, a necessary condition for co-integration. However, Beck (1992) suggests a simpler alternative to the common two-stage method of estimating ECM's that requires stark a priori decisions neither about which variables co-integrate with the dependent variable nor about the order of co-integration. He suggests simply regressing the change in the dependent variable on its lagged

---

[36] Each party's code is the rescaled (0–10) average of expert indices published in Laver and Hunt 1992 and other secondary sources, including those listed in Laver and Schofield 1991 and additionally in Blair 1984, Bruneau and MacLeod 1986, Castles and Mair 1984, DeLury 1987, Harmel et al. 1995, Inglehart and Klingemann 1987, Kerr 1987, Mavgordatos 1984, Sani and Sartori 1983. The web appendix at <http://www-personal.umich.edu/~franzese> gives complete details.

[37] The *CoG* term is originally Thomas Cusack's; the measure here is new. For years with more than one government, weigh each by the fraction it held. For the French Fifth Republic and Finland, $CoG = \frac{1}{2}(CoG_{president}) + \frac{1}{2}(CoG_{cabinet})$; for the United States, $CoG = (CoG_{president} + CoG_{senate} + CoG_{house})/3$. See the web appendix currently located at <http://www-personal.umich.edu/~franzese> for more details.

[38] N.b., unit roots in the factors underlying bounded variables, like $TT \in \{0 \ldots 100\}$, produce unit-root-like behavior in those variables. Augmented Dickey-Fuller (ADF) tests with various lagged differences and with and without trends and/or country fixed effects were considered. In levels, the tests always fell well shy of the .10 level even with fixed effects (which is most appropriate here). Rejection was overwhelming in any of the test formats in differences.

Table 2.1. *Variable Definitions and Hypothesized Signs of Transfers Effects*

Theory	Variable Abbreviation	Variable Short Name	Hypothesized Sign of Effect
Demographic control	POP65	Age distribution	+
Economic controls	UE	Unemployment	+
	CPI	Inflation	+/−
	ΔY	Growth	−
Economics/Wagner's Law	Y	Wealth	+/−
International exposure	OPEN	Trade openness	+/−
Labor-organizational power	UDEN	Union density	+
Fiscal-system centralization/ complexity and fiscal illusion	CTAX	Central-tax share	+/−
Fiscal-system complexity and fiscal illusion	ITAX	Indirect-tax share	+/−
	TTAX	Total-tax share	+/−
Electoral politics	ELE	Election-year indicator	+
Partisan politics	CoG	Government partisanship	−
Government time-horizons	HR	Government hazard rate	+
Median-voter time-horizons	SDRW	Income skew variability	+
Political participation, economic inequality, and their interaction	VP	Voter participation	+[a]
	RW	Income skew	+[a]
	VP·RW	Interaction term	+

[a] *Effects* of voter participation and income skew should be positive and also depend positively on their interaction. Only the expected *coefficient* on the interaction term is therefore unambiguous (see, e.g., Franzese et al. 1999).

level, its lagged differences as necessary, the lagged level of each potential co-integrating factor, and whatever other levels or differences theory or empirics may suggest. This simpler approach is equivalent to the two-stage approach asymptotically and produces statistically valid estimates, provided the coefficient on the lagged dependent-variable level is comfortably negative (i.e., has a large enough t-statistic to have satisfied an ADF test).[39]

Beck's suggested approach also has strong clarity advantages in coefficient interpretation. Those on differenced independent variables refer to

[39] The proviso is this author's suggestion, not Beck's; the author takes full responsibility for its accuracy.

82

momentum-like relations between *changes* in independent and dependent variables, loosely: *short-run* or *transitory* effects; those on levels refer to *equilibrium-like* (loosely: *long-run, permanent*) relations between *levels*. Both multiply and dissipate over time through the coefficients on the lagged dependent variable, reflecting rates of adjustment of levels to equilibrium relations, and on its lagged differences (if present), reflecting adjustment rates in momentum.[40] For example, if x increases once and remains at its new level, what is called here the *transitory* impulse to y also lasts only that one period and then dissipates as determined by the dynamics estimated in y and Δy. Contrarily, *permanent* effects indicate long-run relations between the levels of x and y. A one-time, permanent increase in x produces a permanent increase in y that propagates through y's (and, in the short run, Δy's) estimated dynamics.

In the present application, some variables should operate immediately and virtually automatically (*UE, POP65, CPI, ΔY*) but may also have long-run effects, perhaps through the changes they induce in the polity's structure of interests. For example, a rise in the over-65 population raises the proportion drawing pensions, which will have an immediate and somewhat automatic effect on *TT*, but it may also increase political pressures on policy makers to enlarge T&T, which has an indirect, long-term effect. Such variables enter the regression in current changes and lagged levels. Other variables are aspects of, or otherwise relate to, the current government (*ELE, CoG, HR*). These too should have an immediate effect that may also be persistent, so they also enter in current differences and lagged levels. The third category (*CTAX, ITAX, TTAX, UDEN, SDRW, VP, RW, VP · RW*) relates to the interests or perceptions of the polity and so needs time to work from there to representatives in government to impact policy, but these variables should have persistent impacts once they have done so. These enter in lagged levels only.[41]

[40] Moreover, even if this specification does not actually represent a co-integrating equation and yet the coefficient on the lagged level of the dependent variable remains very highly significantly negative, which would imply unit-root concerns were actually unfounded, the regression is still interpretable in this way.

[41] If direct, indirect, or centralized taxation primarily finances T&T, estimating contemporaneous effects of tax structure would greatly risk endogeneity. Lagging allows control for past T&T, much alleviating the danger. Economic variables, unemployment especially, also risk endogeneity. Their main purpose here, though, is to control for economic conditions when estimating other effects more central to present arguments, so less concern regards misestimating their impact than poorly instrumenting for them and so undermining their strength as controls.

All of these considerations combine to produce this estimation equation:

$$\Delta TT_t = \mathbf{C'B_0} + \beta_1 TT_{t-1} + \beta_2 \Delta UE_t + \beta_3 UE_{t-1} + \beta_4 \Delta POP65_t$$
$$+ \beta_5 POP65_{t-1} + \beta_6 \Delta CPI_t + \beta_7 CPI_{t-1} + \beta_8 \Delta(\Delta Y_t)$$
$$+ \beta_9 \Delta Y_{t-1} + \beta_{10} Y_{t-2} + \beta_{11} OPEN_{t-1} + \beta_{12} CTAX_{t-1}$$
$$+ \beta_{13} ITAX_{t-1} + \beta_{14} TTAX_{t-1} + \beta_{15} UDEN_{t-1}$$
$$+ \beta_{16} \Delta ELE_t + \beta_{17} ELE_{t-1} + \beta_{18} \Delta CoG_t + \beta_{19} CoG_{t-1}$$
$$+ \beta_{20} \Delta HR_t + \beta_{21} HR_{t-1} + \beta_{22} SDRW_{t-1} + \beta_{23} VP_{t-1}$$
$$+ \beta_{24} RW_{t-1} + \beta_{25} VP_{t-1} \cdot RW_{t-1} + \varepsilon_t \tag{5}$$

C represents the time series cross-section controls determined appropriate: one lagged difference of the dependent variable (ΔTT_{t-1}); the full set of country indicators; indicators for nondemocratic periods in Greece, Portugal, and Spain; and a variable equal to the average TT in the other countries in that sample-year.[42] Note also that the natural log of real GDP per capita, Y, enters in second difference, $\Delta(\Delta Y_t)$, lagged first-difference, ΔY_{t-1}, and twice-lagged level, Y_{t-2}. This is because the change in Y is also (a property of logs) the growth rate of real GDP per capita, which likely has immediate, and may have persistent, effects. Thus, per-capita growth, ΔY_t, is an economic condition that enters in current differences, $\Delta(\Delta Y_t)$, and lagged levels, ΔY_{t-1}. Hypothesis 2 and Wagner's Law, in turn, argue for the inclusion of the real GDP per capita in lagged levels, Y_{t-2}. The next section uses the postwar experiences of developed democracies[43] to esti-

[42] Methodological notes: (1) Cross-section indicators are disputed in TSCS analysis. If absent when they should be present, omitted-variable bias occurs; if present, they monopolize cross-sectional variance thoroughly unsatisfactorily theoretically. Wald tests rejecting their omission were too significant to ignore here: p < 1e⁻⁶. (2) Current and three lags of the nondemocracy indicator (p ≈ .035) are included to parallel the period covered by *VP*'s moving average. Measuring nondemocratic *VP*, *CoG*, *ELE*, and *HR* also involves very arbitrary assumptions, so including the dummy is prudent to ensure nondemocratic country-years do not overly influence estimates. (3) Controlling for the lagged changes and level of *TT*, Ljung-Box Q and Lagrange-multiplier tests fail by large margins to reject nulls of no remaining serial correlation in residuals. (4) Average *TT* in other countries in that sample-year is included to bring spatial correlation of the dependent variable into the model's systematic component. This should add some efficiency to Beck-Katz panel-*consistent* standard errors (PCSE), which were also employed.

[43] The usable sample includes the United States, Japan, Germany, France, Italy, the United Kingdom, Canada, Austria, Belgium, Denmark, Finland, Greece, Ireland, the Netherlands, Norway, Portugal, Spain, Sweden, Switzerland, and Australia from as early as 1956 through as late as 1991 (due to missing data, the sample is not quite rectangular).

mate equation (5) and applies the results to evaluate the emergent positive political economy of T&T.

2.5. Empirical Evaluation of the Positive Political Economy of Transfers

Table 2.2 summarizes the estimation of equation (5). Note first the negative coefficient on *the lagged level of TT* (–.06). Its large t-statistic, t ≈ 4.3, should satisfy even an ADF unit-root test, so inferences from these estimates should be free of unit-root concerns. The estimate implies that T&T policies adjust very slowly indeed; 94% (1 – .06 = .94) of a shock in one year persists into the next, then 94% of that into the following year, and so forth. Thus, the long-run impact of any permanent shock is about 16.67 (≈ .06^{-1}) times its immediate impact, and it takes about 11.2 (37) years for 50% (90%) of a shock's long-run impact to emerge.

2.5.1. The Impact of Economic and Demographic Developments

Unemployment is not surprisingly estimated to have a statistically strong (p ≈ 0), though short-term, positive T&T effect. A temporary 1% unemployment rate rise is estimated to produce a *transitory* 0.22% of GDP transfers-increase. Not much long-run relation between levels of unemployment and transfers appears, though; a permanent 1% unemployment rise induces an insignificant (p ≈ .25) .2% of GDP long-run transfers decline.[44] If anything, the higher costs of T&T from persistently high unemployment eventually persuade governments to reduce transfers slightly. However, even the transitory effects accumulated noticeably in the 1970s. As Figure 2.1 illustrates, OECD-average unemployment rose from 2% to over 8% from 1973 to 1982; by these estimates, governments accumulated almost 1% of GDP extra T&T in response.[45] The shallow

---

[44] In a difference model with one lagged dependent-variable like this, the long-run effects of permanent changes in x are $-\beta_x/\beta_{y-1}$, and estimated variances thereof are:

$$\left[-\beta_{y-1}^{-1}, \beta_x\beta_{y-1}^{-2}\right] \cdot \begin{bmatrix} V(\beta_x) & Cov(\beta_x, \beta_{y-1}) \\ Cov(\beta_x, \beta_{y-1}) & V(\beta_x) \end{bmatrix} \cdot \left[-\beta_{y-1}^{-1}, \beta_x\beta_{y-1}^{-2}\right]'.$$

[45] The estimated responses plotted in graphs like these are calculated by inserting the OECD-average series into spreadsheet formulas reflecting the estimated dependent-variable dynamics and independent-variable coefficients. Standard errors for such responses are computationally burdensome but could be simulated. To avoid clutter, however, they are omitted because the reader may safely rely on the relevant coefficients' standard errors to gauge them approximately.

Table 2.2. *Transfer-System-Size Determination: Estimation Results*

Variable	Coefficient	Panel-Corrected Standard Errors	t-Test p-Levels	Joint Hypothesis (Wald χ^2) Test p-Levels
Controls				
TT_{t-1}	−0.0601	0.0139	0.0000	—
ΔUE_t	+0.2238	0.0308	0.0000	} 0.0000
UE_{t-1}	−0.0131	0.0113	0.2446	
$\Delta POP65_t$	+0.1382	0.1393	0.3215	} 0.4426
$POP65_{t-1}$	+0.0265	0.0300	0.3762	
ΔCPI_t	−0.0365	0.0075	0.0000	} 0.0000
CPI_{t-1}	−0.0049	0.0066	0.4559	
$\Delta(\Delta Y_t)$	−8.0556	0.9409	0.0000	}
ΔY_{t-1}	−5.0930	1.3323	0.0001	} 0.0000
Y_{t-2}	+0.3621	0.2023	0.0739	}
$OPEN_{t-1}$	+0.1602	0.3565	0.6534	—
$CTAX_{t-1}$	−0.2131	0.5175	0.6806	—
$ITAX_{t-1}$	+0.8443	0.8535	0.3229	—
$TTAX_{t-1}$	+0.1051	1.0002	0.9164	—
$UDEN_{t-1}$	+0.0078	0.0035	0.0266	—
ΔELE_t	+0.1043	0.0535	0.0518	} 0.0274
ELE_{t-1}	+0.2259	0.0847	0.0078	
ΔCoG_t	−0.0391	0.0239	0.1030	} 0.1755
CoG_{t-1}	−0.0215	0.0155	0.1670	
ΔHR_t	−0.1010	0.1072	0.3465	} 0.5567
HR_{t-1}	−0.0105	0.1081	0.9223	
$SDRW_{t-1}$	+2.4838	1.4956	0.0972	—
VP_{t-1}	−0.3688	0.5498	0.5026	} 0.0203 }
$VP_{t-1} \cdot RW_{t-1}$	+1.1382	0.4720	0.0162	} 0.0496
RW_{t-1}	−0.3280	0.3396	0.3346	} 0.0451 }

Number of observations (degrees of freedom)	701 (650)
Adjusted R^2 (Standard error of the estimate)	0.477 (0.478)
Lagrange-Multiplier Residual Correlation Test, 1 Lag	0.4949

Notes: Dependent Variable = Change in Transfers as a Fraction of GDP (ΔTT_t). Ordinary least-squares estimation with panel-corrected standard-errors. Variables listed as controls are described more fully in the text. *t*-test *p*-levels are probabilities of false rejection from two-sided tests. Wald-test *p*-levels are the probabilities at which null hypotheses that the relevant coefficients are simultaneously zero are rejected. The single-lag Lagrange-multiplier test is the least favorable.

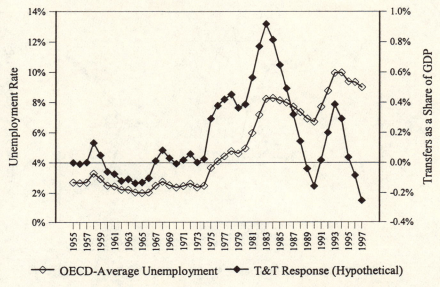

Figure 2.1 Estimated Transfers Response to OECD-Average Postwar Unemployment Path

recovery from 1982 to 1990 sufficed to erase that, but the 1991–3 recession added .4% back.

Inflation also has highly statistically significant transitory (p ≈ 0) but a negligible and insignificant long-run effect (p ≈ .456; jointly, p ≈ 0). The transitory effect, while statistically clear, is not large; a 1% CPI-inflation increase reduces *TT* only about 0.035% of GDP. Substantively, as shown in Figure 2.2, the OECD-average inflation, which spiked from 4% to 13% (±) from 1969 to 1973 and remained near 11% through 1982–3 before trending downward, would induce a nearly .5% of GDP transfers-reduction by 1974, lingering around there through 1983, before fading gradually thereafter. This likely indicates that transfers are generally slightly inadequately indexed, but, in the long-run, political pressures counteract that, leaving neither statistically nor substantively significant effect.

The impact of the *age distribution* on T&T, finally, is surprisingly weak statistically, though positive as expected. Neither change- nor level- (p ≈ .322, .376) relations attain standard significance levels (p ≈ .444 jointly). The low significance likely arises because the upward trend in the

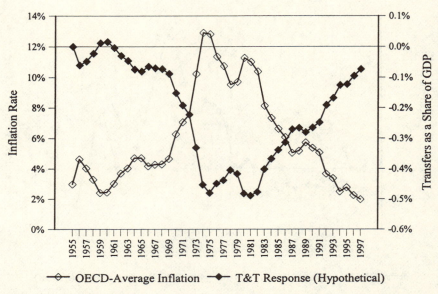

Figure 2.2 Estimated Transfers Response to OECD-Average Postwar Inflation Path

over-65 population share was largely shared across these countries, and so would have had common effect across them, and the regression already controls for average T&T movements in other countries each year.[46] The substantive magnitude of the long-run effect, if these estimates can be trusted, is nonnegligible though. As Figure 2.3 shows, the OECD-average 5.5% (±) rise in *POP65* from 1950 to 1995 might account for transfers increases of almost 2% of GDP, about one-seventh of the total common T&T trend seen in Figure 1.5.

The impacts of *aggregate growth and wealth* are more interesting. The change and level effects of growth, reflected in the coefficients on $\Delta(\Delta Y)$ and ΔY, are both very strong statistically (p ≈ 0, p ≈ .0001) and substantively. A 1% rise in the growth rate ($\Delta(\Delta Y) = +.01$) induces an immediate 0.08% of GDP transfers-decline; if the increase is permanent, the growth effect sums to a 0.85% of GDP long-run decrease. Counter to this,

---

[46] Official data also interpolate demographic variables between censuses, partly in ways that carefully specified autoregressive models will replicate (absorb).

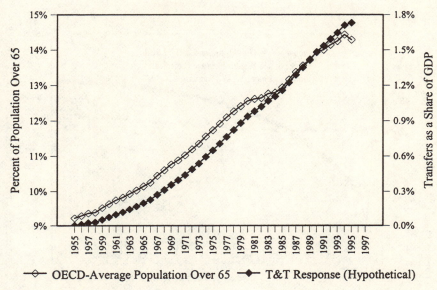

Figure 2.3 Estimated Transfers Response to OECD-Average Postwar Age-Distribution Path

though, the effect of accumulated aggregate wealth is positive and moderately significant (p ≈ .074). *Each* 1% permanent rise in wealth (a .01 rise in Y) produces a long-run 0.06% of GDP transfers-increase. The combination of slowed growth since the seventies yet high and accumulating wealth, therefore, likely induced large transfers increases across all developed democracies. However, these estimates are of the effects of changes in growth and wealth, keeping the other constant. Neither is logically possible, so the substantive size of the estimated effects is difficult to grasp without graphical aid.

Figure 2.4 helps, plotting estimated T&T responses to a onetime 1% real-wealth increase from a base of about US$3,000 1985 (left scale) and to a permanent 1% increase in growth rates (same base, right scale), including all the implied GDP dynamics in both cases. As seen, the semiautomatic transfer-reducing impact of growth dominates in the first 10 to 12 years. (This might also reflect Hypothesis 2, that median voters wish less T&T as wealth rises neutrally, but the estimated size and precision rather suggest automaticity.) Over that period, the onetime wealth rise

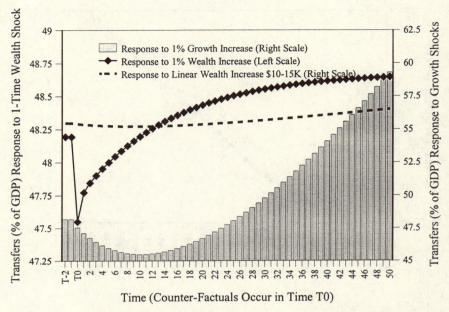

Figure 2.4 Estimated Transfers Responses to Hypothetical Growth and Wealth Shocks

yields a .65%, and the 1% permanently higher growth a 3%, reduction in transfers share of GDP. After that, Wagner's Law dramatically takes over, inducing a long-run +.5% of GDP transfer response to the onetime wealth increase and an explosive response to *any* permanent growth increase (as wealth also explodes). More substantively in Figure 2.5, OECD-average real GDP per capita increased from about 4,200 to 13,400 (constant 1985 U.S. dollars), but at generally slowing growth rates, over the postwar era. The estimated T&T response, likely reflecting both Wagner's Law and semiautomatic impacts of slower growth, was a fairly steady 6.25% increase in transfers share of GDP.

To sum, refer to Figure 1.5. OECD-average T&T rose fairly smoothly from about 7% to nearly 20% of GDP from 1955 to 1993, with some extra upward "bumps" in the late 1950s, mid 1970s, early 1980s, and, sharply, early 1990s. Economic and demographic conditions over this period can explain about three-fifths of these developments. The relatively smooth accumulation of wealth, slowing of growth, and aging of populations

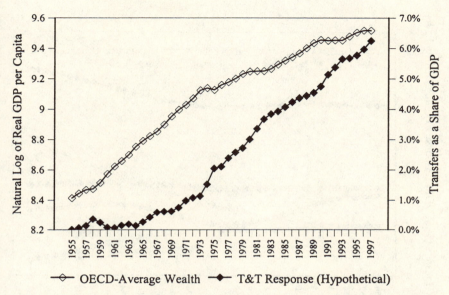

Figure 2.5 Estimated Transfers Response to OECD-Average Postwar Real-GDP-Per-Capita Path

account for 6.25% + 1.75% = 8% (±) of the 13±% OECD-average T&T growth. Likewise, some of the "bumps" seem attributable to the net of inflation (smaller downward) and unemployment (larger upward) effects. Other political-economic considerations explain much of the rest.

2.5.2. The Impact of Other Political-Economic Conditions

Neither *trade openness* nor any of the *tax-structure* variables relate statistically significantly to transfers by this analysis. However, these variables also exhibit mostly cross-national variation, especially trade openness (82%) and central-government share of revenues (80%), but also indirect (60%) and total tax shares (52%) of revenues. Thus, this regression, in which fixed effects absorb all cross-national variation, was biased against findings for such variables.[47] Still, the estimate for indirect tax share, substantively largest (a permanent 10% rise inducing a long-run +1.4%

---

[47] Trade exposure, tax centralization, and indirect tax-shares, but not total tax-shares, perform better in models without country fixed-effects.

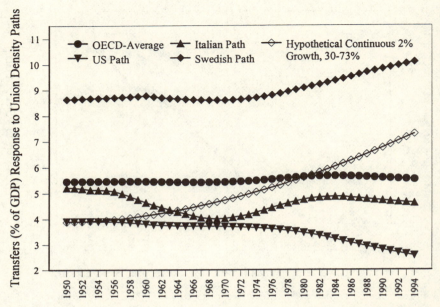

Figure 2.6 Estimated Transfers Responses to OECD-Average, U.S., Italian, Swedish, and Hypothetical Union-Density Paths

transfers) and statistically most significant ($t \approx 1$), suggests that fiscal-illusion may be present and appreciable. Contrarily, if trusted, these estimates suggest there is little to gain or fear from decentralizing T&T. Neither a competitive race to the bottom (Peterson 1990) nor an overspending-inducing collective-action problem among fiscal jurisdictions (Weingast et al. 1981) appears, at least in the cross-time variation. The effect of openness, finally, may be noticeable, its estimate suggesting a permanent 10% rise induces a long-run .27% of GDP transfers-increase, but *OPEN* has far too little cross-time variation to obtain an estimate precise enough ($t < .5$) to warrant further comment.

The transfers impact of *union density*, contrarily, is both substantively and statistically ($p \approx 027$) significant. A 5% rise in union density, which the OECD averaged from 1950 to 1979, would induce governments to increase T&T about .65% of GDP, about equal to what aging populations may have produced in that period. The hollow diamonds in Figure 2.6 show that steady 2% union-density growth from 30% to 70% from 1951

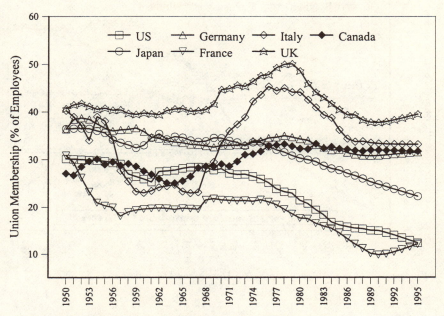

Figure 2.7 Union Density in Seven Developed Democracies

to 1973 (also roughly the Finnish experience) would produce about a 3.3% of GDP transfers-increase. However, as the circles show, the OECD-average path in *UDEN* was less monotonic and smoother, producing only a .21% of GDP increase from 1951 to 1985, which faded to +.13% by 1997 (beyond sample). Plus, country experiences with unionization varied radically as seen in Figures 2.7–9 and thus so did their T&T responses shown in 2.6. The fairly steady decline in U.S. union density induced a 1.5% of GDP drop in T&T, while Swedish union density hovered between 64% and 70% until 1970, when it rose steadily from 66% to 83% by 1990, producing 3.1% of GDP increase in T&T. Italy, meanwhile, saw sharper union-density fluctuations: from 40% in the early fifties, to 23% in 1966, back to 45% by 1978, then to around 33% by the nineties. These brought corresponding T&T responses of −1.2% by 1970, +1.9% from there by 1985, and −.2% from there to the early nineties. Labor organizational strength is clearly among the domestic structures of interests that are critical to the cross-national and country-time-unique variation in developed democracies' T&T experiences.

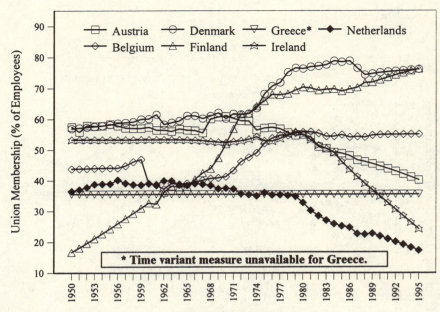

Figure 2.8   Union Density in Seven Developed Democracies

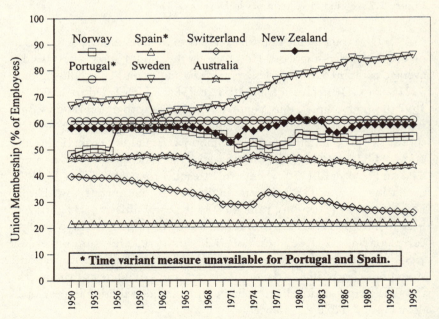

Figure 2.9   Union Density in Seven Developed Democracies

94

Turning from societal characteristics to those of government, *electoral manipulation* of transfers is strongly evident, contrary to some recent pessimism about such budget cycles in the literature (e.g., Alesina et al. 1997). The estimated coefficients on ΔELE_t and ELE_{t-1} reveal that transfers tend to rise the year before elections by about 0.10% of GDP ($p \approx .052$) and by about 0.12% ($p \approx .022$) further the year *after* elections (joint significance: $p \approx .027$).[48] An extra 0.22% of GDP is noticeable electoral manipulation itself, but, because governments adjust T&T policies very slowly and all democracies hold elections minimally every five years, the impact of one electoral manipulation has hardly faded when another, perhaps conducted by a different government, occurs. Figure 2.10 illustrates the interesting implications, three aspects of which merit particular attention.

First, the T&T cycle peaks the year *after* an election. In order of increasing substantive interest, this could reflect (1) merely lingering differences between calendar-year measured *ELE* and fiscal-year measured *TT*, or (2) slow budgeting procedures in government that delay retractions of election-year generosity, or (3) the facts that preelectoral and postelectoral policy makers may differ and that, in office, candidates tend to fulfill their promises. On this last, as Tufte (1978) noted, election campaigns tend to spark spiraling rounds of incumbent and challenger promises. If, ceteris paribus, the candidate with greater, more credibly promised, largesse wins, then pools of policy makers in preelection years (incumbents) tend to contain those seeking to buy votes by increasing current transfers, but pools of policy makers in postelection years will contain policy makers (some returned incumbents and some freshman) who, more frequently still, promised greater still transfers because some incumbents will have promised or started giving too small transfers and lost. Indeed, this would also explain the slightly larger and more significant coefficient on ELE_{t-1} than on ΔELE_t.

Second, the frequency of elections also has a sizable long-run impact on T&T system size. Democracies with elections every two (three, four) years average over 1% (0.5%, 0.19%) of GDP more transfers than those with elections every five years. This, as noted already, is because T&T adjusts slowly enough that one electoral manipulation lingers into the next. How much lingers thus depends on the time between elections, so

---

[48] Leads and lags up to five years on *ELE* were considered; these two and only these two years were significant, and they were so comfortably robustly.

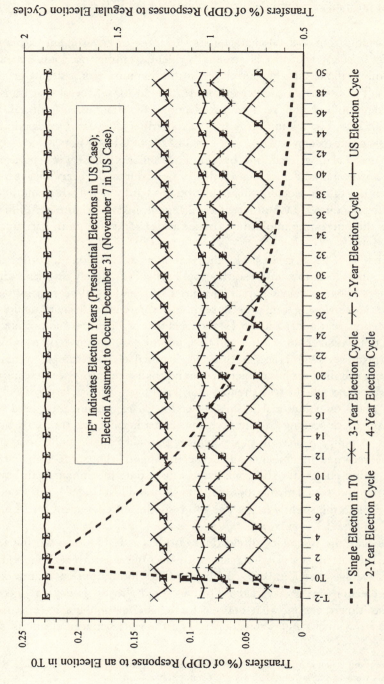

Transfers (% of GDP) Responses to Regular Election Cycles

Transfers (% of GDP) Response to an Election in T0

"E" Indicates Election Years (Presidential Elections in US Case);
Election Assumed to Occur December 31 (November 7 in US Case).

- - · Single Election in T0   —✳— 3-Year Election Cycle   —✳— 5-Year Election Cycle   —+— US Election Cycle
—— 2-Year Election Cycle   —— 4-Year Election Cycle

Figure 2.10   Estimated Transfers Responses to One Election and to Regular Elections of Various Frequencies

democracies with more-frequent elections accumulate larger long-run-equilibrium T&T. Third, for the same reason, the amplitude of electoral T&T cycles is increasing in the time between elections: .008%, .074%, .116%, and .141% of GDP for two-, three-, four-, and five-year cycles respectively.

The United States, with its presidents, representatives, and one-third of the senate elected every four, two, and two years, respectively, and with all elections occurring the first week of November, has an odd electoral-cycle that illustrates all three results. *ELE* codes the U.S. electoral-cycle (.0491, .2843, .1145, .6633), with the last being the presidential election year. The estimated T&T dynamics and the coefficients on ΔELE_t and ELE_{t-1} produce from this pattern a corresponding long-run T&T cycle of about (1.068, 1.042, 1.023, 1.044). Note that the U.S. cycle peaks the year *after* the presidential election. Also, compared with a simple four-year cycle $(0,0,0,1 \Rightarrow .9997, .9451, .8840, .9304)$, the U.S. cycle has smaller amplitude and larger long-run average: because off presidential election years have some elections and so produce some T&T response and because, relatedly, elections are more frequent.

Thus, democratic policy makers' attempts to manipulate transfers for electoral purposes not only explain some of the cross-country time fluctuation in T&T growth (via varying electoral timing), but their doing so at varying electoral frequencies also explains some of the cross-national variation in the pace of transfers growth and in long-run levels. Chapter 3 finds similar and similarly strong evidence for deficit-policy manipulation (see also Franzese 1998a, 2000b).

Likely, some combination of the following explains how so many previous studies missed this evidence for electoral cycles. First, Tufte's (1978) emphasis on *transfers* manipulation seems well founded but was too-often ignored (cf. Schultz 1995). Because policy makers wish economic benefits to arrive near election time and to be easily recognized and attributed to them, directly manipulable and observable outcomes, like transfer payments, will be their favored tools. Second, the dynamics of the policy variables in question and those of the electoral cycle itself have received insufficient attention. Transfers, like most policies, adjust neither automatically nor quickly, and democratic competition involves campaigns before and sometimes changes in policy makers after elections. Third, previous empirical studies often focused on frequent-election countries like the United States where budget-cycle magnitudes will be small. In any case, scholars have prematurely abandoned electoral-budget-cycle theory;

to paraphrase Mark Twain, rumors of its empirical demise have been greatly exaggerated.[49]

2.5.3. The Impact of Political-Economic Conditions Emphasized Here

First, Hypothesis 6 argued that *government partisanship* should retain T&T impact even controlling for median voters' interests. Although coefficient estimates are correctly signed, indicating the right (left) reduces (increases) T&T, the change and level effects attain only marginal statistical significance (p ≈ .103, p ≈ .167, and p ≈ .176 jointly). This seems at odds with stronger partisan findings in previous studies, but those results were likely overstated for statistical reasons now better understood.[50] Moreover, previous studies did not control for income skew or, usually, for the breadth of controls included here. The present estimates reflect government-partisanship effects *net of* (i.e., controlling for) the income distribution

---

[49] Economists returned to reconsider Nordhaus's (1975) *political business cycles* from a rational-expectations view, finding *equilibrium budget cycles* (Rogoff and Sibert 1988; Rogoff 1990). These results suggest that political scientists should likewise return to Tufte's (1978) *Political Control of the Economy*; more politics are afoot than mere election-year dummies will locate. E.g., Schultz (1995) argues and shows that policy makers will and do not manipulate T&T equally before every election; likely they manipulate only to the degree *close* elections are *foreseen* (see note 30). Estimates here and elsewhere effectively average such variations, under-(over-)estimating electoral manipulation in close contests (landslides). Such measurement errors would also have hindered finding signicant effects.

[50] Pampel and Williamson (1988) and Hicks and Swank (1992) find significant partisan effects; the latter also find a significant interaction between government and opposition partisanship. However, both employed Parks's GLS procedure for TSCS estimation, which Beck and Katz (1995, 1997) demonstrate is problematic in samples where time periods (T) do not greatly exceed cross sections (N). In the former study, N > T, so the estimation was actually mathematically undefined. It also reports a (defined) lagged-dependent-variable model; there the left-partisan effects were positive but insignificant. In the latter study, T = 23 > N = 18, so the estimation was defined, but Beck and Katz estimate that Parks's standard errors in such sample-sizes are likely three to four times overconfident. Thus, the present results are likely actually somewhat stronger. (That study also found the center more welfare-expansive than the left, which possibility was not considered here, confounding the comparison.) Finally, Hicks et al. (1989) estimate a (defined) IV-GLS model with Cochrane-Orcutt and fixed effects. They find negative coefficients on left government *in corporatist countries* with t ≈ 2, slightly stronger support than here, but only for those countries. They note (but do not report) negligible effects in other democracies, so averaging across all democracies as done here may have dampened the partisan estimate. The present results are thus much less surprising and even about the same as or stronger than others in light of these reinterpretations.

among voters and, more generally, controlling for the underlying structure of interests as represented in the all other independent variables.[51]

Aldrich's insights added to a Romer–Alesina-Rodrik type model suggested government partisanship should retain T&T effect even controlling for income skew and other underlying interest structures in the polity;
these estimates, in short, suggest such a remainder exists but is not overlarge. Each 1-unit rightward *CoG*-shift, ceteris paribus, reduces transfers
by 0.04% of GDP in the first year, by .18% after 12 years in office, and
ultimately by a long-run 0.36% if the shift were permanent.[52] Figure 2.11
graphs estimated T&T responses to such counterfactuals (right scale).
It also plots (left scale) estimated partisan T&T cycles for *typical* majoritarian and coalitional government systems, assuming governments 3 and
1 *CoG*-unit(s) apart exchange T&T-policy control every four and one
year(s) in majoritarian and coalitional democracies. As seen, partisan T&T
cycles are typically moderate (.2% of GDP in amplitude) in majoritarian
but tend to be tiny (.05% of GDP) in coalitional democracies. Thus, government partisanship effects, while perhaps noticeable and occasionally
appreciable, are not typically very large, controlling for the structure of
interests that elected those governments.

Consider next Corollaries 4a and 4b, which argued that *median-income
voters' uncertainty* that they will remain such and *incumbent governments'
uncertainty* that they will retain office should each relate positively to T&T.
Little evidence emerges that government instability increases T&T. If anything, it reduces transfers, at least short term, though the relevant coeffi-
cient estimates are quite insignificant ($p \approx .35$, $p \approx .92$, and $p \approx .56$ jointly).
The coefficient on *SDRW*, contrarily, is mildly significant ($p \approx .07$) and
suggests an appreciable T&T effect of median-voter uncertainty: a standard deviation increase in income-skew volatility (+0.023 *SDRW*), if permanent, would raise democratic pressures on governments to increase
transfers almost 1% of GDP long run. However, income volatility tended
more to fluctuate than trend in these countries, suggesting that it might
explain some country-time-unique variation in T&T but not much of its

[51] Conversely, when income-disparity effects are analyzed later, recall that they are effects
controlling for government partisanship. Similar interpretations, of course, apply to all
coefficient estimates in the model.
[52] Permanent partisan shifts are unlikely in democracies, but 90% of long-run T&T effects
occur within 37 years, which Swedish Socialists and Japanese Liberal Democrats (and
many others in coalition) exceeded.

100

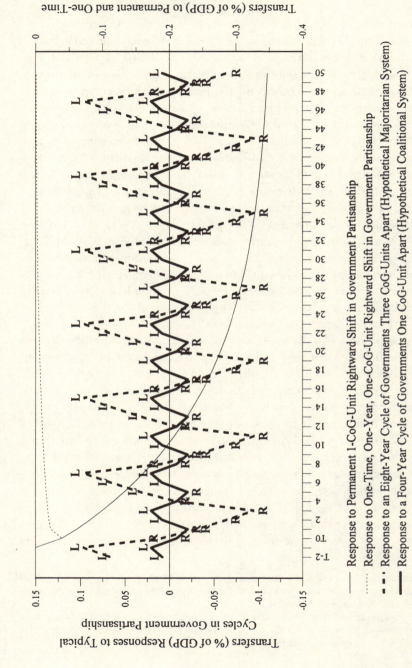

Figure 2.11 Estimated Transfers Responses to Government Partisanship

Transfers (% of GDP) to Permanent and One-Time
One-CoG-Unit Right-Shift in Government Partisanship

Cycles in Government Partisanship
Transfers (% of GDP) Responses to Typical

——— Response to Permanent 1-CoG-Unit Rightward Shift in Government Partisanship

·········· Response to One-Time, One-Year, One-CoG-Unit Rightward Shift in Government Partisanship

– · – Response to an Eight-Year Cycle of Governments Three CoG-Units Apart (Hypothetical Majoritarian System)

——— Response to a Four-Year Cycle of Governments One CoG-Unit Apart (Hypothetical Coalitional System)

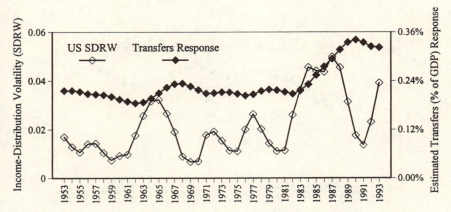

Figure 2.12 Estimated Transfers Response to Income-Distribution Volatility in the United States

Figure 2.13 Estimated Transfers Response to Income-Distribution Volatility in Germany

cross-country shared time path (*SDRW*'s shared path is only 5±% of its total variation).

Rather than estimated responses to OECD-average paths, Figures 2.12–14 thus plot the income-skew-volatility impacts in three countries with very different experiences. The United States, for example, saw a moderate, fluctuating response to mild skew-volatility oscillation until the steadily increasing effect of rising volatility under recent Republican

101

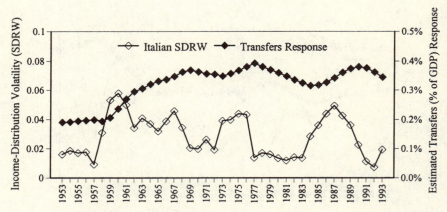

Figure 2.14 Estimated Transfers Response to Income-Distribution Volatility in Italy

presidents. Germany, instead, had steady pressure toward reduced transfers from a population experiencing falling income-skew volatility, until postunification turmoil reversed both. Italy, meanwhile, experienced a sharp response to sharply rising skew volatility in the early 1960s as a less wealthy democracy grew quickly through the ranks, and more erratic volatility thereafter.

In sum, governments do seem to provide more social insurance as citizens' uncertainty over the future distribution of income rises, though the effect is not overlarge (responses in Figures 2.12–14 span just .2–.4% of GDP); governmental uncertainty is insignificant, however. This could imply time inconsistencies plague T&T less than other policies, perhaps because policy makers find ex post levies easier to extract with relatively fluid, technocratic instruments like money supply, where voters need some economic sophistication to notice the seignorage, than in stickier, simpler instruments like T&T, where voters need no expertise to notice smaller transfers or larger tax bills. Transfers responses to *SDRW*, contrarily, reflect popular demands for insurance against income volatility (see also Iversen and Cusack 1998; Garrett and Mitchell 1999), and government time horizons are irrelevant to that.[53] In any event, conclude for now only

[53] Alternatively, time-inconsistency problems may be as strong in T&T as in other policies but more evident at individual than government levels because some other consideration induces governments to reduce transfers as their instability increases. For example, gov-

that income-skew volatility correlates with T&T size while government instability does not.

The interactive effects of *voter participation (VP) and income skew (RW)* are the final and core features of the amended model. The joint significance ($p \approx .05$) of *RW*, *VP*, and their interaction indicates that skew, participation, *and/or* their interaction affect transfers, broadly supporting Hypotheses 1 and 7. Other tests indicate that income skew "matters," by itself *and/or* interacting with *VP* ($b_{rw} = b_{vp \cdot rw} = 0 \Rightarrow p \approx .045$), and that voter participation matters, by itself *and/or* in interaction with *RW* ($b_{vp} = b_{vp \cdot rw} = 0 \Rightarrow p \approx .02$). The significant, positive interaction-term ($p \approx .01$) implies, lastly, that the T&T effects of *RW* and of *VP* each become less negative or more positive as the other increases. Graphics again help to interpret the substantive import of these statistically significant results because interaction terms like $VP \cdot RW$ imply that the *effects* reflected in these three coefficients and the standard errors of those effects depend on, and so can only be interpreted as a function of, the levels of other variables (see Franzese et al. 1999).

Figure 2.15 graphs estimated immediate T&T responses to a 0.1 rise in the income-skew index as a function of voter participation; that is, it plots $.1 \cdot (b_{rw} + b_{vp \cdot rw} VP)$ (and 80% confidence interval, which corresponds to a one-sided .10 t-test)[54] over the sample range of *VP*. Countries are labeled on that "effect line" at their postwar average participation.[55] As seen, governments tend to respond to more-skewed income by raising transfers at any *VP* rate (Hypothesis 1), but more so at higher participation (Hypothesis 7). For example, the U.S. and Swiss governments, which operate in the lowest-participation democracies, respond least to skew; indeed, their estimated responses are statistically indistinguishable from zero. In more-participatory democracies like Australia and Austria, contrarily, T&T responses to income skew are statistically and substantively

ernments may become stable precisely by responding to tenure uncertainty with larger transfers. Also possible is that, because both of these variables are crude proxies, measurement error could easily have been high enough to have produced weak or misleading coefficient-estimates.

[54] Significance tests have already established strong joint and interactive effects, so, because significance of each variable's effects will vary over the other's range, one need not hold the estimated effects at *each* level of the other variable to as high a standard as the usual 90% (.05) or 95% (.025) confidence interval (α level). A one-sided .10 test (80% c.i.) seems adequate to assess certainty across those ranges.

[55] These labels are informative because 68±% of total voter-participation variation is cross-national (excluding nondemocratic periods for which dummies control).

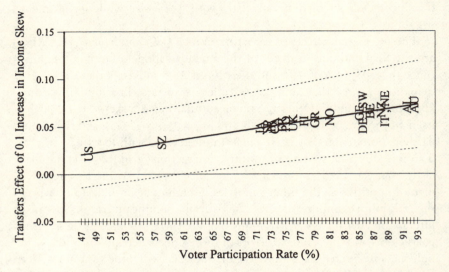

Figure 2.15 Estimated First-Year Impact of Income Skew on Transfers, as a Function of Voter Participation

significant: a 0.1 increase in *RW* induces an immediate +.075% and, if permanent, long-run +1.15% of GDP.

Figure 2.16, analogously, plots governments' estimated T&T responses to a 10% rise in *voter participation* as a function of the underlying income skew, with countries labeled on their postwar average *RW*.[56] As seen, voter participation generally increases transfers as argued and found before, but the relationship also becomes more positive and significant as population income-skew increases, as Corollary 7a suggested. Substantively, these effects can be appreciable: in the United States in 1986 (*RW* = 1, its base), a 10% voter-participation increase induces an immediate .077% and, if permanent, a long-run 1.28% of GDP transfer increase. Thus, the impact of expansion of the politically active population depends on who is joining that pool.

Figures 2.17–18 facilitate further substantive discussion of these results, plotting estimated T&T responses over time to sustained 10% increases

[56] Of total variation, 69±% is cross-national.

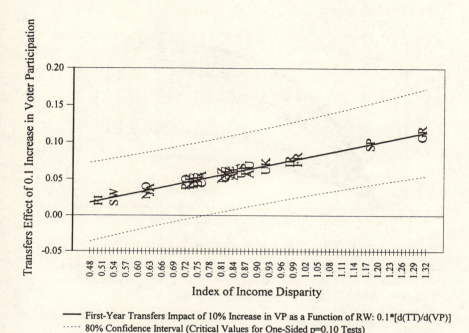

Figure 2.16 Estimated First-Year Impact of Voter Participation on Transfers, as a Function of Income Skew

in income skew (*RW*) and in voter participation (*VP*) at substantively informative levels of the other variable, namely at the postwar *RW* and *VP* averages of several countries arrayed from near sample-minimum to near maximum. The figures also list all countries' postwar average *VP* (democratic periods only) and *RW*, so T&T responses at any country's average *VP* or *RW* can be approximately visualized.

These graphs illustrate the strong empirical support for Hypothesis 7 that, adding previous insights about who votes to a simple neoclassical model of T&T, concluded higher income skew would foster popular demand for transfers and that this *popular* demand would be increasingly *politically* effective as the proportion of the population that votes increases. For example, Figure 2.17 shows that when nearly everyone votes, as in Austria or Australia, which fine(d) abstention, a sustained standard deviation increase in income skew (about +.22 *RW*) would press governments

105

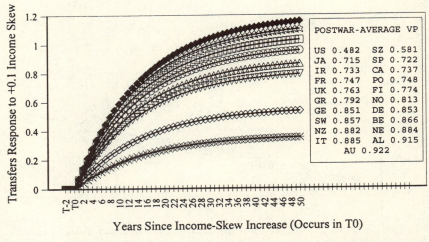

Figure 2.17   Estimated Cumulative Impact of Income Skew on Transfers, as a Function of Voter Participation

to increase T&T by 2.6% of GDP in the long run. When, contrarily, participation is near its democratic nadir, say at the U.S. average 48%, a sustained 10% income-skew rise draws only a statistically insignificant and small 0.37% long-run T&T response from governments. Conversely, Figure 2.18 shows that a sustained 10% increase in participation induces a 4.8% of GDP long-run T&T rise at the sample-maximum income skew (1.54 in 1965 Greece) and a negligible decrease at the sample minimum (.29 in 1956 Japan). These differences in government T&T responses are also statistically significant.[57] Lastly, as Figure 2.19 shows, the OECD-average *VP* and *RW* paths were slightly downward and erratically upward respectively, yielding net pressures on governments accounting for almost 1% of GDP of T&T's shared upward time path.

---

[57] I.e., the general proposition that *RW*'s effects differ with *VP* is significantly supported ($H_o : b_{vp-rw} \Rightarrow p \approx .016$). Whether any two country-times differ significantly will depend on the exact difference in their participation levels in the year tested.

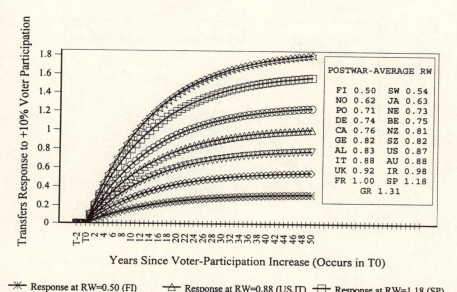

Figure 2.18 Estimated Cumulative Impact of Voter Participation on Transfers, as a Function of Income Skew

Thus, varying degrees of political participation moderated democratic governments' responses to the pressures they all felt toward redistribution from underlying distributional inequities, and, conversely, the impact of greater popular participation on governments' T&T policies depended on the degree of relative inequality reflected in the pool of voters from which the increased democratic pressures emanated. Indeed, this interactive combination of participation and inequality has T&T effects of sufficient magnitude to explain about half of the country-time-unique variation left unexplained by economic conditions alone. That is, whereas these capitalist democracies' common exposure to similar political-economic challenges explains much of their shared T&T time path, these similar tensions and challenges led some, those with more-participatory politics, to expand their transfer systems faster and farther, though at different times in different places.

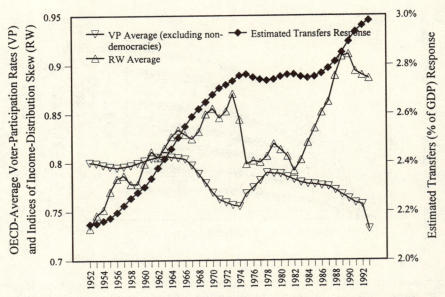

Figure 2.19 Estimated Transfers Response to OECD-Average Income-Skew and Voter-Participation Paths

2.6. Discussion, Conclusions, and Implications

2.6.1. Summary of the Empirical and Theoretical Results

Table 2.3, listing the short-run effects of transitory and long-run effects of permanent standard deviation increases in each variable, facilitates concluding discussion. As seen, the factors with appreciable impact are aggregate wealth, unemployment, inflation, income-distribution volatility, labor-organizational strength, government partisanship, electioneering, and the interaction of voter participation and income skew, plus, perhaps, age demographics and tax structure complexity. Together, these factors explain about half of the total variation in developed democracies' postwar experiences illustrated in Figure 1.4. Moreover, one can show the commonalities in those T&T-policy experiences arose primarily from these countries' shared exposure to similar structural-economic conditions, whereas cross-country and country-time-unique variations arose primarily from how differences in (domestic) structures of political-economic

sustained standard deviation adverse growth-shock (–2.9%), roughly average for this period, would induce +2.5% of GDP long-run T&T, about 17% of the average trend. Indeed, including both growth and wealth effects, the actual path of OECD-average real GDP per capita accounts for a 6±% rise (43% of the trend; see Figure 2.5). Other macroeconomic conditions, unemployment and inflation, had smaller persistent effects, but their fluctuations were central to shared short-term moves. A standard deviation unemployment rise (+3.6%) and inflation decline (–5.15%) induce +.8% and +.2% of GDP T&T-responses, combining to about 20% of T&T's standard deviation (see Figures 2.1–2). Over-65 population shares, lastly, rose from 8.75% to 14.25% from 1950 to 1993 on average, which could account for 1.7% more of GDP allocated to transfers if its coefficient estimate is trusted (only p ≈ .37). All told, over half the OECD-average T&T time path can be attributed to responses of existing policies to these common economic and demographic conditions. As Chapter 1 claimed, much of the shared experience across developed democracies reflects simply that the costs of their governments' postwar commitments to provide social-insurance increased as growth and inflation slowed, unemployment rose, and populations aged.

Other political-economic structures, institutions, and conditions primarily explain the differing responses of these similarly democratic governments to these common economic and demographic challenges. A standard deviation (16%) rise in union density, for example, increases the organizational efficacy with which labor support for transfers presses upon governments, inducing a substantively and statistically significant +2.1% of GDP in transfers. Voters' fiscal illusions and the changing budgetary complexity may also have modified popular pressures; while statistically insignificant, such effects equaled the estimated demographic effect in magnitude. However, average movements in union density (up, then down) and tax structure (toward transparency) were small, and the latter actually worked against the generally upward T&T path, respectively inducing policy responses of ±.25% and –1.4% of GDP. Similarly, elections, election frequency, partisanship, and income-distribution volatility played strong roles in explaining cross-country and country-time-unique variation, but showed little shared time-trend, and so were not central to the common upward T&T time path. Likewise, movements in the income skew and voter participation had strong impacts in democracies where both were high – adverse standard deviation movements in either would induce +3% of GDP in "transfer-responsiveness" in such cases – but were much less relevant in country-times where one or both remained low. On average, their postwar paths accounted for about +1% of GDP of the shared upward T&T trend (Figure 2.19).

Thus, shared exposure to similar macroeconomic-demographic conditions explains about half the OECD-average T&T trend ({6 + 1.7}/14.5 ≈ 53%) plus some common fluctuation around it: 46±% of transfers' total variance in all. Domestic political-economic institutions and interests add little to explaining the trend, +1% by income skew and voter participation, perhaps −1.4% by budgetary complexity, but may have strongly affected cross-country variation. In fact, despite being unable to render the set of atheoretical country-dummies statistically redundant, the theoretical variables could explain about half the cross-country variation in average T&T size (43±% of the total), and much of that by political-economic structures of interests and institutions as Table 2.4 and Figure 2.20 illustrate.[58]

As the last rows of Table 2.4 reveal, the economic conditions underlying cross-country variation in T&T size are *not* cyclical factors like growth, inflation, and unemployment but more durable socioeconomic structural conditions like, especially, the aggregate wealth of and, less so, age distribution in society. And these factors induce governments to increase T&T at least partly by their effects on the polity's structure of interests in addition to their more purely economic ramifications. That is, (a) wealthier and (b) older polities also demand more social transfers from their governments (a) as a normative luxury (Wagner's Law) and (b) because more citizens receive public pensions. Moreover, after wealth, the most important factors in explaining cross-country variation are the interaction of voter participation and income skew and then union density. Again, these factors foster government transfer-responsiveness via their effects on popular demand for redistribution (income skew, blue-collar shares of employment) and the efficacy with which those preferences are pressed upon government (political participation rates and labor organizational strength). The only other factor with appreciable cross-sectional impact is budgetary complexity (*ITAX*): varying fiscal illusion, while statistically insignificant, may not be substantively negligible, accounting for fourth-most cross-country variation. Thus, whereas shared exposure to global

---

[58] The table and figure assume that the coefficient estimates, which, due to the country indicators, relied solely upon time-serial variation, can be safely used to calculate differences in long-run T&T levels. This assumption may seem strong, but any model estimating fixed coefficients must make assumptions that imply it.

Table 2.4. *Long-Run Transfer Effects of Postwar Average Political-Economic Conditions*

	UE	POP	INF	d(Y)	Y	OPEN	CTAX	ITAX	UDEN	ELE	CoG	HR	SDRW	VPRW	SUM	FIX. EFF.	NET	T&T
US	-0.7	2.5	-0.2	-0.7	30.1	0.2	-1.0	3.0	1.6	0.5	-1.2	0.0	0.5	0.1	34.8	-29.4	5.4	8.0
JA	-0.2	2.1	0.0	-2.2	27.7	0.3	-1.0	3.3	2.1	0.8	-1.6	-0.1	0.7	0.4	32.3	-27.4	5.0	7.2
GE	-0.2	3.2	-0.2	-1.4	28.9	0.5	-0.7	3.3	2.3	0.5	-1.1	0.0	0.6	1.9	37.8	-30.4	7.4	14.2
FR	-0.2	3.1	-0.2	-1.2	28.8	0.4	-1.0	3.6	1.3	0.5	-1.1	0.0	0.5	2.2	36.7	-26.4	10.2	16.7
IT	-0.5	2.9	-0.3	-1.4	28.2	0.4	-1.2	3.2	2.3	0.5	-1.0	-0.1	0.6	2.4	35.9	-27.3	8.6	14.5
UK	-0.4	3.3	-0.3	-0.9	28.8	0.5	-1.4	3.9	2.9	0.5	-1.2	0.0	0.3	1.9	37.9	-32.2	5.6	9.4
CA	-0.6	2.2	-0.2	-0.9	29.5	0.6	-1.0	3.7	2.1	0.6	-1.0	0.0	0.5	1.0	36.5	-30.5	6.0	9.0
AU	-0.2	3.3	-0.1	-1.4	28.3	0.6	-1.0	3.7	3.7	0.6	-0.9	0.0	0.4	2.6	39.5	-29.9	9.6	16.4
BE	-0.4	3.2	-0.2	-1.1	28.6	1.4	-1.2	3.1	3.3	0.7	-1.1	-0.1	0.5	1.5	38.3	-26.1	12.2	18.5
DE	-0.5	3.1	-0.2	-1.2	29.0	0.7	-1.3	3.8	4.6	0.8	-1.0	-0.1	0.3	1.4	39.5	-31.3	8.2	11.9
FI	0.1	2.5	-0.3	-1.2	28.5	0.6	-1.1	3.4	3.6	0.4	-0.9	0.0	0.4	-0.1	35.9	-28.3	7.6	10.2
GR	-0.4	2.8	-0.4	-1.5	26.2	0.4	-1.1	4.2	2.4	0.5	-1.4	-0.1	1.4	2.6	35.8	-29.3	6.4	8.9
IR	-0.8	2.6	-0.3	-1.5	27.2	1.1	-1.6	4.8	3.3	0.6	-1.1	0.0	0.6	2.0	36.8	-30.6	6.3	9.9
NE	-0.3	2.6	-0.1	-1.2	28.8	1.3	-1.2	2.9	2.2	0.6	-1.0	0.0	0.4	1.5	36.3	-23.0	13.3	17.3
NO	-0.2	3.2	-0.3	-1.4	28.9	0.8	-1.3	3.6	3.7	0.5	-0.7	0.0	0.4	0.6	37.6	-28.8	8.8	11.5

SP	−0.2	2.6	−0.3	−1.4	27.3	0.3	−1.2	3.1	1.5	0.2	−1.4	−0.1	1.1	−1.0	30.4	−25.3	5.1	12.5
SW	0.0	3.5	−0.3	−0.9	29.3	0.6	−1.1	2.8	5.0	0.7	−0.7	0.0	0.3	0.3	39.5	−29.9	9.7	13.1
SZ	0.1	2.9	−0.1	−0.7	29.8	0.7	−0.6	2.3	2.2	0.5	−1.1	−0.1	0.5	0.5	37.0	−30.2	6.8	10.0
AL	−0.2	2.2	−0.2	−0.9	29.3	0.4	−1.5	3.7	3.1	0.8	−1.1	0.0	0.5	2.2	38.3	−34.1	4.2	7.6
NZ	0.0	2.2	−0.3	−0.7	29.0	0.6	−1.5	2.9	4.0	0.7	−1.1	−0.1	0.5	2.0	38.3	N/A	N/A	N/A
Avg.	−0.3	2.8	−0.2	−1.2	28.4	0.6	−1.1	3.5	2.9	0.6	−1.1	−0.1	0.6	1.2	36.4	−29.1	7.4	11.6
% of T&T avg.	−3	24	−2	−11	245	5	−10	30	25	5	−9	0	5	10	314	−250	63	100
Var.	$5e^{-6}$	$1.6e^{-5}$	$1e^{-6}$	$1.2e^{-5}$	$1.2e^{-5}$	$1e^{-5}$	$6e^{-6}$	$2.8e^{-5}$	$1e^{-4}$	$2e^{-6}$	$5e^{-6}$	$3.8e^{-8}$	$7e^{-6}$	$1.1e^{-4}$	$5.8e^{-4}$	$6.4e^{-4}$	$7.7e^{-4}$	$1.3e^{-3}$
% of T&T var.	0.4	1.2	0.1	1.0	9.2	0.7	0.5	2.2	7.8	0.2	0.4	0.0	0.6	8.8	45.0	49.3	59.3	100

Notes: Table lists the accumulated T&T effect (% of GDP) of 35 years at that country's postwar-average independent-variable levels and changes. The last and antepenultimate rows are the preceding rows as a percent of T&T's cross-national variance (var.) and average (avg.), respectively.

economic shocks explains much of the OECD-shared time path of T&T, *political conditions* tend more to drive the cross-country variation in average T&T size.

Figure 2.20 reinforces this conclusion, plotting country-average deviations of transfers from the OECD postwar average due to each independent variable, labeling the factors that importantly (more than ±0.5% of GDP) impact these persistent cross-country deviations. As seen, wealth (Y) and its distribution among voters (VP, RW, $VP \cdot RW$) explain much of most countries' deviations from the OECD-average. Labor strength and fiscal illusion (but recall: *ITAX* is mildly insignificant) also induced large national deviations in some, and demographics (*POP65* mildly insignificant) and growth ($d(Y)$) in a few. Other factors enter noticeably only in extreme cases: partisanship (*CoG* nearly significant) in Japan, where the Liberal-Democrats held government this whole period; trade exposure in Ireland, Belgium, and the Netherlands (*OPEN* mildly insignificant); and fiscal decentralization (*CTAX* quite insignificant) in the almost confederal Switzerland.

To sum empirically, three factors – wealth, its distribution among voters (VP, RW, $VP \cdot RW$), and labor organizational strength – with lesser input from growth, age demographics, and budgetary complexity, explain almost half (45%) the variation across developed democracies in postwar average T&T size. These same factors, especially wealth and growth, also explain about half the shared time path of T&T: a 14±% upward trend, with some "bumps," which, in turn, are fairly well explained by cyclical macroeconomic conditions like unemployment and inflation. Finally, other considerations, like income-skew volatility, election-year politics, and government partisanship, also exhibited statistically significant and, in some country-times, substantively large impacts. These, then, must add to the others in explaining the variation that is unique to particular country-times. A very rough calculation[59] indicates about 41% of total variation accounted here by the explained portions of the common trend and cross-country deviations, implying that the full model explains about ($R^2 - .41 \approx$) 10% more, which is about 85% of the country-time-unique variation that remains. Thus, the expanded political-economic model offered here performs especially well in explaining particular county-times' deviations

---

[59] Cross-country variation is 43% of total and 45% explained; the shared trend variation is 46% of total and 46% explained. That gives $.45 \cdot .43 + .46 \cdot .46 \approx 41\%$ of total variation explained so far, implying the full model must explain $R^2 - .41 \approx .51 - .41 \approx 10\%$ more variation, which is about 85% of the country-time-unique variation that remains.

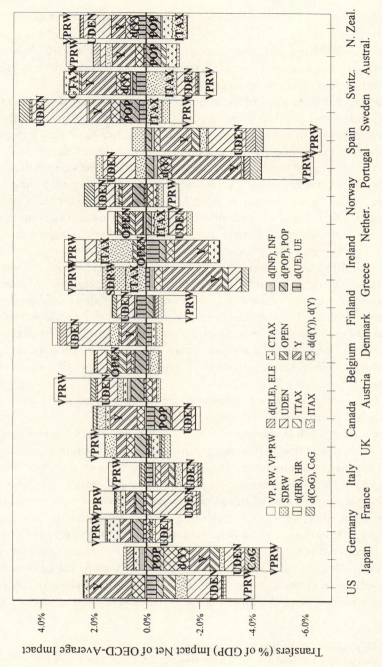

Figure 2.20 Transfers Impact by Country of Its Postwar Average Political-Economic Conditions Relative to OECD Postwar Average for Those Conditions

115

from the shared time path and varying country averages; that is, it best explains why governments' transfers policies respond to similar stimuli differently across democracies over time.

In terms of theory, many of the arguments drawn from previous studies and expanded here provide strong explanatory leverage. In particular, the evidence supports in a way the core prediction of the basic neoclassical model: democratic governments respond to median voters' demands for transfers as income skew increases.[60] However, what matters theoretically and, as now shown, empirically is income distribution *among the politically relevant segment of the population*. That segment's size and, critically, the proportion of the income distribution it represents vary across country-times, implying that the *effective* democratic pressure for transfers emanating from the underlying income distribution in the economy likewise varies with the domestic institutions that moderate political participation. That is, while societal income skew implies a poorer *population* median than average, effective democratic demand for redistribution emanates from the difference between the mean income among the *population* (taxpayers) and the median income among *voters*. The incomes represented in the electorate and, thus, the median voter's income will depend, in turn, on registration laws, ballot complexity, party-system competitiveness, and the like.

Most broadly, the view of political economy introduced in Chapter 1 and applied here uncovered theoretically and empirically important aspects of the political economy of T&T policy relatively ignored elsewhere. The concluding theme recurs through the book: popular participation highlights differences in the distribution of economic and political influence in capitalist democracy; these differences and shared exposure to economic challenges face all democratic governments with similar tradeoffs between their conflicting goals in economic policymaking; but the actual impacts on policies and outcomes of these common pressures vary across country-times depending on multiple interactions among differing structures of interest (e.g., more or less egalitarian income distributions) and institutional structures (e.g., pro- or antiparticipatory electoral institutions) within which government and private decision makers interact.

---

[60] Some less inspiring results for the basic model also emerged; most notably, its dynamic extension produced no readily testable predictions for T&T that passed statistical muster. That extension, however, also had other (growth) implications that Alesina and Rodrik (1994) tested successfully.

2.6.2. Implications

2.6.2.1. Economic Effects First, obviously, public transfers aim to ease the economic hardships of their recipients. Analyses of the best country-specific and comparative measures available of the incidence of poverty and government policies' impacts thereupon are unequivocal; unemployment or retirement with inadequate savings entails less disastrous individual consequences in country-times with more-generous transfers (Hibbs 1987; Coder et al. 1989; Layard et al. 1991; Danziger and Weinberg 1994; Marmor et al. 1994; Atkinson et al. 1995; Danziger and Gottschalk 1995; Primus 1996, 1998; Gottschalk and Smeeding 1997; Kamerman and Kahn 1997; Smeeding and Sullivan 1998; Smeeding et al. 1990). However, critics allege, generous transfer systems also weaken the harsh incentives of the marketplace and so, unintendedly but unavoidably, increase unemployment and hinder growth. Therefore, this section proceeds to sketch the outlines of some of the more-unfortunate consequences and side effects of transfers, taking as indisputable that, while disagreement over the degree of success may persist, they do alleviate the individual hardships of their recipients.

Figure 2.21 offers some simple vector-auto-regression (VAR)[61] evidence on the proposition that transfers growth eventually sapped capitalist

---

[61] VAR seeks to assess temporal and thus, by assumption, causal priority among sets of variables thought jointly endogenous but about which little else is assumed. VAR regresses each variable on a set of its own and the others' lags. Imposing restrictions on the variance-covariance matrix of the resulting residuals, which by construction no variable in the system could predict, then suffices to identify not the coefficients but the responses of each variable to the unexplained *shocks* in the others. These identifying conditions are called *ordering assumptions* because they attribute a temporal order to the shared error-covariance across the variables. *Ordering* essentially amounts to stating which variables move first when data could attribute some portion of the variance to several variables. Scholars obviously prefer VAR results that are robust to alternative orderings, and this book will note when such robustness is lacking. With these assumptions, the responses of all variables to an exogenous shock in one, called *impulse-response* functions, can be calculated. Several examples appear in Figure 2.21 and subsequently. Note, finally, that Monte Carlo studies (Freeman et al. 1996) have established that VAR is prone to Type II errors (i.e., failure to find significant effects when they in fact exist), especially but not exclusively in highly trended data. This results from the large number of very correlated right-hand-side variables (all the lags), some of which may be irrelevant (i.e., VAR is prone to overspecification). Thus, the large sizes of the confidence intervals in the reported impulse-responses are to be expected. Finally, note that the residual-covariance assumptions required to justify VAR in TSCS data are little more stringent than those which least squares requires, namely that the data emerge from a single, uniform stochastic process controlling for

117

efficiency, lowering output and/or raising unemployment.[62] The results indicate not only that exogenously higher unemployment raises transfers (third row, second column), reinforcing earlier findings, but also (second row, third column) that exogenously higher transfers tend to raise unemployment. Both effects are substantively appreciable: by five years on, a standard deviation transfers shock (+.5% of GDP) raises unemployment .2%, and a standard deviation unemployment shock (+.5±% of GDP) raises T&T .1±% of GDP (not much smaller than estimated earlier). Thus, as many others have found (e.g., Meyer 1990; Layard et al. 1991; Meyer [1995] reviews), transfers increase unemployment and unemployment increases transfers. (Importantly, this literature stresses that higher transfers particularly raise unemployment duration, implying "stickier," less policy-responsive unemployment.) Some, though weaker, evidence also emerges that transfers may have reduced growth (first row, third column), perhaps indicating that higher tax rates reduce (private) investment. Finally, transfers respond to wealth shocks first negatively but, in the long run, positively, as has already been found and illustrated more clearly.[63] In sum, the deleterious macroeconomic consequences argued to stem from transfers do seem to occur.

Chapter 1 also argued that transfers drove public-expenditure growth more generally and likely, thereby, tightened budget constraints on governments' other fiscal goals. Governments might raise taxes to meet social-insurance and other spending goals simultaneously, or they could borrow to avoid such tradeoffs for a time, but either approach might eventually limit fiscal maneuverability. Figure 2.22 presents a VAR relating transfers

---

right-hand-side variables. VAR assumes the same for each dependent variable, while allowing or assuming covariances among the dependent variables that are common over the sample.

[62] This VAR includes the nondemocracy indicator and full sets of country and year indicators. These partially and imperfectly substitute for whatever structurally independent variables may exist (e.g., those in Table 2.2). VARs with a constant or country fixed-effects only or with a reduced version of the theoretical model were also estimated. In the last, results broadly accorded with Table 2.2, though with much larger standard errors typical of VAR. Conclusions do not otherwise vary substantively across these alternatives. The country-year-indicators approach is reported because it is most certain to satisfy the common conditional stochastic process assumption (see note 61) required for VAR in TSCS. The ordering assumptions make little difference in any of these specifications.

[63] The size and significance of *TT*'s long-run effect on *Y* were somewhat smaller in some specifications and orderings; this is the only result in Figure 2.21 that was even slightly nonrobust. Still, the broad shape of the response was robust.

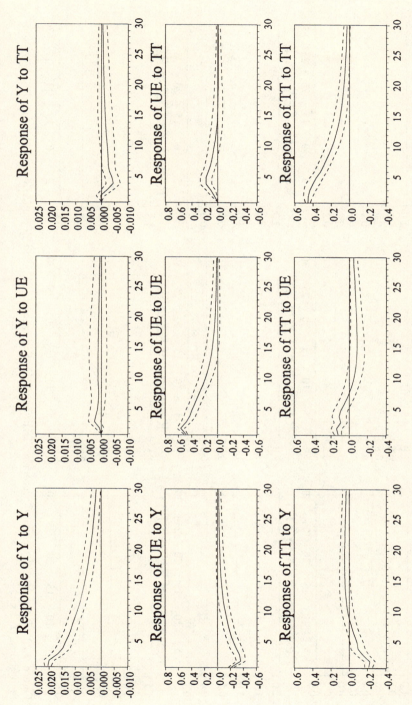

Figure 2.21 Responses of Transfers (TT), Unemployment (UE), and Wealth (Y) to One-Standard-Deviation Innovations (+/−2 s.e.)

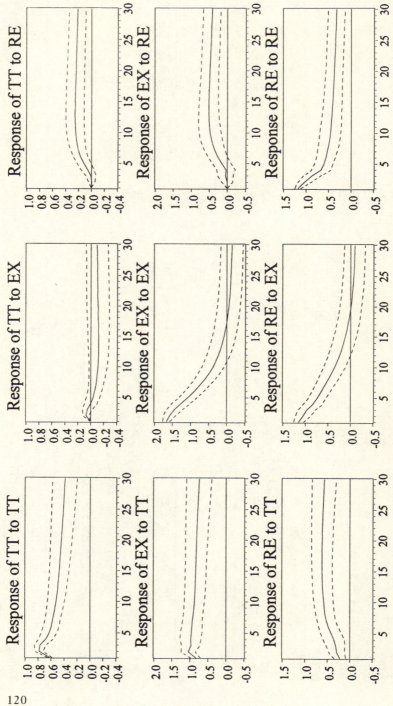

Figure 2.22 Responses of Central-Government Transfers (TT), Expenditure (EX), and Revenue (RE) to One-Standard-Deviation-Innovations (+/-2 s.e.)

120

and total expenditure and revenues to explore these possibilities. This is a purely descriptive exercise, aiming simply to gauge the degrees to which shocks in transfers typically fed into total expenditure and to which such spending increases were typically tax- or deficit-financed (and the inverse relationships). The assumed temporal ordering (see note 61) reflects a bottom-up view of government budgeting. That is, governments decide T&T policies and transfers occur first; they decide other spending next, amassing total expenditures; they decide taxation last, leaving primary deficits as residuals.[64]

Despite its simplicity, the exercise proved quite interestingly informative. Compare, for example, transfers response to its own exogenous shocks (first row, first column) and expenditures response to those transfer shocks (second row, first column), which show that virtually all of transfers increases reappear in total spending and that this persists over time. Governments do not typically reduce other spending to accommodate exogenous transfer increases. Contrarily, revenue responds by only 50% to 75% of the amount expenditure does to such transfers shocks (third row, first column), implying that, typically, transfers growth was 50% to 75% tax-financed and so must have been 25% to 50% deficit-financed.

Three other results are interesting. First, comparing spending responses to their own shocks (second row, second column) with revenue responses to those shocks (third row, second column) reveals that 25% to 50% deficit financing is the norm for all government spending. Second, comparing transfers responses to spending shocks (first row, second column) with their responses to revenue shocks (first row, third column) shows that governments generally do not reduce transfers to accommodate exogenous increases in other spending but they do at least partially spend exogenous revenue increases on transfers. Third, comparing spending responses to revenue shocks (second row, third column) with revenue responses to its own shocks (third row, third column) shows that, while exogenous revenue shocks are initially saved, policy makers eventually (7 ± years) adjust budgets to spend some and save some of the extra revenue that persists.

[64] The data are those from Figure 1.1. As a more descriptive exercise than the previous VAR, time indicators are omitted here, reflecting the lack of a theoretical model for them to proxy. The ordering assumption allows transfers to cause same-year and future changes in total spending and revenue, other spending to cause same-year increases only in revenue not in transfers but future changes in both, and revenue to cause only future changes in the other two.

Thus, as conservatives like to lament, notable asymmetries exist between democratic governments' responses to exogenous increases in program and other spending and in revenues. Looking along Figure 2.22's prime diagonal, transfers and tax-revenue shocks persist much longer than do expenditures, and, examining the other impulse responses, spending increases in one area are met more by deficit and tax increases, than by reductions in other spending. The differential distribution of political and economic influence thus tends to induce democratic policy makers to make trade-offs that keep transfers growing by increasing taxation and borrowing and not by reducing other spending. As expected, in making necessary trade-offs between their conflicting goals, democratic governments have tended to become "overcommitted" (with deleterious consequences for economic performance). Of course, however, the converses are also true: reductions in transfers and revenues will also persist longer, perhaps even when conditions would merit their increase.

2.6.2.2. Political Consequences First, Chapter 1 asked whether the growing popular discontent over T&T systems was not only understandable in that rising unemployment and slowing growth *accompanied* their meteoric rise but was also justified to assume implicitly that worsening macroeconomic performance *resulted* from growing government redistributive efforts. This analysis suggests that at least some of the worsening performance does indeed seem attributable to burgeoning T&T systems, probably via their alleviation of the harsh capitalist incentives that can foster employment and growth. The conflicts between democratic governments' commitments to social-insurance and public-good provision on the one hand and macroeconomic management on the other thus became increasingly problematic as transfer systems grew, which they did especially where political institutions favoring electoral participation produced governments highly responsive to the different distribution of economic and political resources in their societies.

The introduction also asked, more ambitiously, how these developments may have impacted the politics of economic policy making and the prospects, given these developments and their political impacts, for the continued viability and utility of the policy commitments. The arguments and evidence here suggest that the saliency of intergenerational and cross-class conflict will have risen as redistribution across cohorts and classes involved increasing shares of both GDP and government activity. Whereas the over-65 population and the economically disadvantaged have large incentives to sustain the size and growth of T&T, the younger population, and especially those well positioned to benefit from more flexible labor markets, have increasingly strong incentives to combat that trend and attempt to reverse it. As others have noted (Inglehart 1971, 1977, 1990; Kitschelt 1994), however, the increasing wealth of developed democracies may also have decreased the saliency of economic relative to other, *postmodern* or socio-ideological, concerns. In Maslovian fashion, with basic needs increasingly met, societal preferences begin to stress more-qualitative goals. Thus, while these economies grew wealthier and material saliency declined, their governments contrarily became more active in the allocation of that wealth, raising distributional saliency.

The old parties and new political movements that successfully navigated these complicated currents were those that built new broad coalitions that married either (left) concern to defend, or (right) discontent over, redistributional efforts with a (left) challenge to, or (right) defense of, traditional values and ideational systems. The new right sought institutional *reforms* (i.e., reductions in the size or duration of social insurance) that would induce people to "get off welfare and into jobs." This they linked to a defense of traditional moral values, including loose reference to "a work ethic" that generous transfers purportedly eroded, which played well with interests more concerned with various "social malaises" than with economic efficiency. The new left sought, instead, institutional *reforms*, that is, reorganization of social-insurance programs, which were intended to increase their efficiency in hardship alleviation and reduce their inefficient macroeconomic side effects. This they linked to "modern" concerns for "environmental, gender, and racial empowerment," which played well with interests as (or more) concerned about the social as (than) the economic inequalities characteristic of traditional modes of growth and government in industrialized democracies.

Notice, however, these strategies represent less a change in the substance of conflict over economic policy making than a shift in focus from the particular policies governments enact to the institutions and rules within which democratic conflict over future policy will continue. Indeed, the traditional right and left on the economic dimension of these microeconomic and institutional "reform" debates seems less changed than the traditional right and left on the social dimension. Moreover, such reemergent conflict seems likely to produce very different policies across countries depending on the nature of electoral competition. For example, transfers grew in response to rising income disparity only where and to the degree that most of the population actually involves itself in the electoral process. Thus, whereas governments have generally been faithful, perhaps too faithful, to their goal of alleviating inequality in more-participatory democracies, they have generally ignored that goal altogether in less-participatory democracies. The fears of some that democratic governments will, through inaction, allow a drastically bifurcated economic society to evolve could prove well founded in the less-participatory democracies. In more-participatory democracies, contrarily, the opposite fear, that democratic governments will do too much, may be more sound.

Indeed, if one presses harder on the arguments and findings here and elsewhere, four results combine to suggest possible equilibrium relations between transfers, unemployment, and participation levels. First, generous transfers tend to increase unemployment (Figure 2.21) and its duration (Meyer 1990, 1995; Layard et al. 1991). Second, the (especially long-term) unemployed are almost wholly unrepresented in the politically active population (e.g., Verba et al. 1978; Harrop and Miller 1987; Wolfinger and Rosenstone 1980). Third, only the politically active population affects the democratic determination of T&T (Figures 2.15–19). Fourth, permanent increases in unemployment do not permanently increase transfers (Figures 2.1, 2.21). Thus, an exogenous rise in unemployment produces a short-term transfers increase, but also a reduction in the electoral representation of the poorer end of the income distribution, which ensures that political support for T&T declines to bring transfers back down. Conversely, exogenous increases in T&T will tend to increase unemployment and its typical duration, raising the cost of that larger T&T and simultaneously diminishing political support for it by reducing representation of the at-risk population. Finally, an exogenous rise in participation increases effective democratic demand for T&T, but those transfers will tend to increase the duration and level unemployment, which will increase T&T costs and reduce participation. The equilibria in these recursive systems will likely vary across country-times depending on interactions of ranges of political-economic institutions that affect participation, such as electoral laws, and fiscal policy making, such as those affecting fractionalization and polarization across and within governments (see Chapter 3), and unemployment, such as monetary-policy and labor market institutions (see Chapter 4). Seemingly new democratic debates over "reforms" of these

124

institutions will likewise reflect familiar battles over desired government-policy, economic, and electoral outcomes.[65]

Common pressures on democratic governments to redistribute, arising from universal differences in the distributions of economic and political resources in capitalist democracy and from shared exposure to adverse economic shocks, produced a general tendency for transfers to rise dramatically across the OECD. Yet wide variation across countries in the pace of that growth also arose from interactions between the structures of interests and institutions (total wealth, its distribution, participation, labor organization strength, etc.) within which those governments enacted their T&T policies. To those varying degrees, in turn, rising transfer systems increased unemployment and elongated its individual incidence, reducing growth, employment, and the efficacy of macroeconomic policy in reducing unemployment, and also driving growth in spending more generally. Spending growth, in turn, was only partially tax-financed, producing common and varying pressures toward deficit-finance, partially driving the varying public-debt accumulation on which the next chapter focuses.

---

[65] Less pessimistically, other policy trends have increased the transparency of the trade-offs that governments choose in fulfilling their conflicting commitments and responding to the conflicting interests represented in their polities. While transfers and other fiscal activities of governments increased, taxation also became more direct, making it easier for voters to weigh the costs and benefits of the policy programs their governments administer. In the case of transfers, this generally led to reductions in the program. T&T reduction itself may be desirable or lamentable depending on one's predilections, but facilitating popular evaluation of public activities is a more universal democratic virtue.

3

Financing the Commitments: Public Debt

3.1. Introduction: Motivation, the Explanandum, and a Road Map

As Chapter 1 noted, high and/or swiftly rising public-debt-to-GDP ratios (henceforth: *debt*) have become major political issues recently in many developed democracies. As shown in Chapter 2, much of the impetus for this recent debt growth originates in the different allocation of political and economic influence in capitalist democracy, which fostered transfers growth, which drove total-spending growth, which, finally, governments typically partially debt-financed. Figures 1.7–9 plotted the historical record of the resulting public-debt accumulation (gross consolidated-central-government debt for 21 OECD countries from 1948 to 1997).[1]

Figure 1.7 revealed the relatively common experience of falling debt since World War II through 1972± and the dramatic reversal thereafter. Debt more than doubled in under 20 years in many countries, and in some it now tops 100% of GDP. The widespread and rising public concerns over these debt trends and levels and the number of theories emerging to

---

[1] The data, from IMF, *International Financial Statistics*, 6/96 CD-ROM, are gross debt of consolidated central governments (i.e., including social security). Where the CD-ROM gives no data but OECD sources or *International Financial Statistics* tape or print editions do, country-specific fitting regressions using all available other measures extend the data. R^2 from the fitting regressions usually well exceeded 90%. The same procedure maximizes available OECD data on gross and net general government debt (including subnational units). IMF data are used because they cover a far greater sample preextension, the theories mostly refer to central government, and OECD general-government debt data double-count for some countries. Still, the three debt series correlate highly as do their changes. IMF gross central and OECD net general debt correlate least at .74, with the other pairs between .84 and .89. The web appendix plots these data and offers a table of their correlations: <http://www-personal.umich.edu/~franzese>.

explain them are thus hardly surprising. Beyond these commonalities, however, lie large differences across countries and over time in the level and variation of debt.

Cross-national differences in postwar average debt (Figure 1.8) constitute 55% of the total postwar variation in developed democracies' debts. Belgian and Irish debt, for example, averaged over five times German and Swiss debt, whereas New Zealand and the United Kingdom debt averaged about twice that of Norway. Countries' debt ranges also varied greatly over the period; interextrema ranges in Australia, Italy, Japan, Belgium, and Canada, for example, dwarf those in Switzerland, Denmark, Germany, and France. Likewise, Figure 1.9 shows a clear shared time path, but rising intercountry variation and skew is as apparent, especially since the 1970s. As with transfers, the Bretton Woods collapse and two oil crises seemed to trigger widening differences across countries' debt policies. Indeed, the shared cross-time variation comprises only 19% of total variation. Thus, even netting country averages and the average time path, much country-time-unique variation, 26% of total, remains to be explained.[2] Striking among these unique experiences are the relative rise in Japan, Italy, Belgium, Ireland, and Portugal and the relative decline in the United Kingdom and Australia, especially since the 1970s.

The questions for theories purporting to explain public-debt accumulation, then, are, "Why have debt levels become inordinately large and/or grown rapidly in some countries and not others?" and "Why have they done so recently and not, in general, before?" (Alesina and Perotti 1994). This chapter applies the cyclic view of political economy diagramed in Figure 1.22 to guide empirical exploration of the burgeoning theoretical work claiming to explain the cross-country variation, shared time path, and variations around them shown in Figures 1.7–9. How well can current theory, with the additions and amendments offered here, explain the shared and variant debt experiences of developed democracies in the postwar era?

Excepting work on the tax-smoothing, economic-conditions model (e.g., Barro 1985, 1986), these theories have been little-examined empirically. Limited recent empirical attention focuses on theories of weak government and delayed fiscal stabilization (Roubini and Sachs 1989a,b; Edin and Ohlsson 1991; De Haan and Sturm 1994, 1997; Borrelli and Royed

---

[2] A figure adding a plot of the country-time-unique component to Figures 1.7–9 is in the web appendix: <http://www-personal.umich.edu/~franzese>.

1995; Alesina and Perotti 1995b; De Haan et al. 1999). Others stress the institutional rules of budgeting (Von Hagen 1992; Von Hagen and Harden 1994, 1996; Hallerberg and Von Hagen 1999; De Haan et al. 1997). Heller (1998) emphasizes instead bicameralism and partisan differences between legislative chambers. This chapter joins them in redressing imbalances between theoretical and empirical exploration, operationalizing and evaluating many contending explanations of when and where public debt amasses and/or grows rapidly, using the postwar history of debt in developed democracies as the data base. Having explored the determination of public debt, the chapter then discusses the political-economic implications of debt accumulation and its consequences for the evolving government policies to fulfill their democratic commitments.

The rest of this chapter unfolds thus to achieve these ends. Section 3.2 builds from Alesina and Perotti's (1994) excellent survey of the positive political economy of debt to identify the core arguments and to derive testable hypotheses from, and operationalize, them. Theory building follows the cycle in Figure 1.22 from the interest structure of voters who elect representatives to form governments to make policy, to the dissolution of those governments and their return to the electorate, whose interest-structure previous debt-policy may have altered. Section 3.3 offers empirical analyses, first of the tax-smoothing, economic-conditions default model, then of each political-economy model tested as an addition to the default (nested F-tests) and against each other (nonnested J-tests), and concludes with thorough substantive exploration of a regression model encompassing all the theories. Section 3.4 reevaluates the theories given this new evidence, addresses the empirical questions detailed here, suggests directions for future research, and, lastly, returns to the implications for the democratic management of the economy.

3.2. Democratic Management of Public Debt: Theories, Measures, Stylized Facts

3.2.1. Tax-Smoothing Theory and Economic Conditions

Basic tax-smoothing theory (Barro 1974, 1979; Lucas and Stokey 1983) notes that policy makers possessing rational foresight and utility-loss functions concave in taxes would estimate the present value of all expected public spending plus outstanding debt and set taxes to generate equal expected value of revenues.[3] With the concavity, varying the tax rate over time is costly, so, whatever level of spending desired, fixing the time path of tax rates, barring surprises, is optimal to finance it. Thus, optimizing governments will incur deficits when unanticipated or temporary shocks to revenues or spending occur. Moreover, when expected paths of the economy's real growth rate and the real interest rate on public debt differ,[4] governments can borrow or save beneficially. Governments borrow wisely, for example, when expected long-run growth rates exceed expected long-run real interest rates because those conditions imply the ability to repay is expected to grow faster via output-*cum*-tax-base growth than is the total debt burden via its real interest. Governments wisely reduce debt when the opposite relation holds.

Previous empirical work on the tax-smoothing hypothesis stressed atypical public-spending spurts associated with wars (Barro 1985, 1986). Since 1945, however, wars have not importantly impacted developed democracies' spending or revenue (possibly excepting Korea and Vietnam); large shifts in unemployment, growth, and interest rates, contrarily, have. Also, the theory was developed and tested primarily with closed-economy assumptions, but these apply dubiously to the United States and certainly not elsewhere. Luckily, the basic intuition that optimizing governments will debt-finance temporary and tax-finance permanent spending requirements extends easily to open economies. For example, weak economic performance due to adverse terms of trade, if expected to be temporary, will induce optimizing governments to issue debt. Thus, the empirical implications of tax smoothing relevant to this sample are that debt policy responds to movements relative to expected permanent levels in growth, unemployment, debt-service costs, differences between real growth and interest rates, and terms of trade.

Note, however, that any political-economic model of debt policy should control for these variables and that any theory that suggests *sticky* tax rates

---

[3] N.b., governments need not be benevolent social planners with definable social-welfare functions. Their concave losses in taxes, for example, could derive from office-seeking motives with voters who punish taxes increasingly. The tax-smoothing implications follow if they have such utility and optimize.

[4] Governments' time discount-rates should add to expected real interest rates in this comparison. That complication is generally ignored, implicitly assuming all governments discount time equally. The analysis here partially and indirectly incorporates varying government discount rates via their hazard rates of collapse.

is virtually indistinguishable from rational-expectations tax smoothing.[5] More unique to tax-smoothing theory is its distinction of temporary from permanent shocks, which models without such heroically foresighted policy makers would stress much less. Unfortunately, no commonly accepted method of empirically distinguishing expected permanent from unexpected or temporary shocks exists. Most empirical work implicitly assumes permanent levels are constant, thus rendering all changes unexpected and temporary. The models presented here follow that practice too, so, as elsewhere, the results cannot distinguish tax smoothing from any other model where these economic conditions matter. The theory was thus used simply to identify the economic variables for which any empirical exploration of public-debt policy should control, and the tax-smoothing, economic-conditions model is accordingly taken as the default in the analyses here, accepted by and controlled for in all the others.

In sum, tax-smoothing theory suggests several economic variables for the default model: the unemployment rate (spending shocks), real-GDP growth rate (revenue shocks), real-interest minus real-growth rates times the outstanding debt level (real debt-service-cost shocks), terms-of-trade shocks (open-economy shocks), and the difference between expected real interest and real growth rates (reflecting the expected relative trends in ability to pay and debt servicing).

Section 2.4.2 described the unemployment (UE) and real-GDP-growth (ΔY) data. Expected growth ($E(\Delta Y)$) is forecast by regressing ΔY on two lags, country dummies, and lagged per capita GDP.[6] Openness ($OPEN$) is export-plus-import share of GDP, and terms of trade (ToT) are export-import price ratios. Terms-of-trade effects being larger in more-open economies, models will include ToT, $OPEN$, and $ToT \cdot OPEN$. Expected GDP-index inflation rates ($E(\pi)$) are forecast from regressions with country dummies and two lags.

---

[5] Democratic governments may find raising taxes costly politically, regardless of expected present values of public spending; voters might, e.g., myopically punish them for higher taxes whatever the need. Surpluses would, however, be extremely rare in that case because voters always reward tax cuts, implying that governments will usually lower taxes with beneficial surprises but will debt-finance adverse movements more than tax-smoothing theory would predict because they are reluctant to raise taxes even when necessary in the long run because voters do not distinguish.

[6] Because lagged GDP per capita is used to estimate expected growth, coefficients on it in analyses here do not reflect the debt impacts of expected "catch-up" growth; those are reflected in $E(r - \Delta Y)$ as they theoretically should be.

Nominal interest-rate (i) data proved trickier to compile and are estimated from long-term government bond yields (*ltgby*); money-market, T-bill, discount, deposit, and lending rates; consumer- and wholesale-price inflation; and short- and medium-term government bond yields as follows. If available, *ltgby* are used. If not, available *ltgby* are regressed on the largest available subset of other interest rates to estimate *ltgby* for country-years in which data for that subset exist.[7] Differences between expected real-interest and growth rates are then simply $E(r - \Delta Y) \equiv i - E(\pi) - E(\Delta Y)$, and debt-service costs (interest payments) are just the product of *actual* real-interest minus growth ($i_t - \pi_t - \Delta Y_t$) and lagged debt (D_{t-1}): $(r_t - \Delta Y_t) \cdot D_{t-1}$. All data are from IMF and OECD sources (see 2.4.2).

Table 3.1 defines the study's variables, and Table 3.2 lists the theory to which each relates and signs their predicted debt correlation. Table 3.3 presents descriptive statistics for these variables and their correlations with debts and deficits. As indicated, the simple correlations of unemployment with deficits and debts are strongly positive as expected ($r \approx +.33$ and $r \approx +.45$). Deficit correlations with real-GDP growth ($r \approx -.35$), debt-servicing costs ($r \approx +.35$), and terms of trade ($r \approx -.23$), too, are all signed as expected and strong. If current trade openness is expected to produce future growth, as economic theory suggests, then the deficit ($r \approx +.12$) and debt ($r \approx +.46$) correlations with trade openness are also as predicted. However, positive correlation would also occur if openness simply reflected easier access to global capital markets.[8] Joint estimation of the debt impact of openness, terms of trade, and their product is especially critical before interpreting such a result too deeply. The oddly signed bivariate correlation of expected-real-interest-minus-expected-growth rates ($E(r - \Delta Y)$) with debts and deficits is likewise suspect because $E(r - \Delta Y)$ correlates highly positively with both unemployment and debt-service costs. Still, the correlations strongly support the applicability of the economic controls suggested by tax-smoothing theory and, coupled with the more-sophisticated multivariate analysis to follow, suffice to establish

---

[7] Three considerations allay concerns about this procedure. Theoretically, interest rates should overwhelmingly tend to move together; empirically, they do: R^2 from fitting regressions invariably exceeded 0.8; and the resulting series performs as expected. As concern here is more to control properly for economic conditions when testing other theories than in testing tax-smoothing theory itself, the third is a valid consideration. The resulting data comprise an internationally comparable interest-rate data base fully covering 21 countries and 50 years.

[8] Gratitude to Jeff Frieden for emphasizing this point.

Table 3.1. *Definitions of the Variables Employed in the Public-Debt Study*

Variable	Definition
D	Gross consolidated central-government debt as a percent of GDP[a]
UE	(Internationally comparable) unemployment rate[b]
ΔY	Real GDP growth rate[c]
y	Natural log of real GDP per capita[c]
$E(r - \Delta Y)$	Expected real interest rate minus expected real growth rate[a-c]
$OPEN$	Trade openness (exports plus imports as a fraction of GDP)[a]
ToT	Terms of trade (export price index/import price index)[a]
$(r - \Delta Y)D_{t-1}$	Debt-service cost (real interest less growth times outstanding debt)[a,b]
$TTAX$	Total taxes as a fraction of total current revenue[b]
$ITAX$	Indirect taxes as a fraction of total current revenue[b]
$CTAX$	Total current revenue of central as a fraction of general government[b]
OY	Ratio of population 65 and older to population 15 and younger[b,i]
RW	Relative real-wage position of manufacturing workers (income-skew index)[a-b]
$PRES$	Presidential-system indicator
FED	Number of federal regions
$ENED$	Effective number of electoral districts[j]
AE	Fraction of cabinet seats held by agrarian or ethnic parties[e-g]
ELE	Preelection-year indicator[d]
CoG	Partisan "center of gravity" of government[e-b]
$ENoP$	Effective no. of governing parties (fractionalization, influence conception)[e-g]
NoP	Raw no. of governing parties (fractionalization, veto-actor conception)[e-g]
$SDwiG$	Standard deviation within government (polarization, influence conception)[e-b]
$ADwiG$	Maximum deviation within government (polarization, veto-actor conception)[e-b]
RR	Replacement risk[e-b]
CBI	Central bank autonomy and conservatism index[k]

[a] IMF sources.
[b] OECD sources.
[c] *Penn World Tables*, v. 5.6.
[d] Mackie and Rose 1991.
[e] Woldendorp et al. 1994, 1998.
[f] *European Journal of Political Research Political Data Annuals*.
[g] Lane et al. 1991.
[b] Laver and Schofield 1991, Laver and Hunt 1992, and sources therein.
[i] UN, Age and Sex Demographics.
[j] Lijphart 1994.
[k] Cukierman 1992, Grilli et al. 1991, and Bade and Parkin 1982.

Table 3.2. *Theories, Variables, and Hypothesized Signs of Debt Effects*

Theory	Variable	Hypothesized Sign
Tax-smoothing/economic-control default model	UE	+
	ΔY	−
	$(r - \Delta Y) \cdot D_{t-1}$	+
	$E(r - \Delta Y) \cdot OPEN$	−/+
	$ToT/ToT \cdot OPEN$	−
Democracy and fiscal illusion	$TTAX$	−
	$ITAX$	+
	$CTAX$	−
Inter- and intragenerational transfer function of debt	y	−
	OY	+
	RW	+
	$OY \cdot RW$	+
Multiple constituencies[a]	FED[a]	+
	$PRES$[a]	−
	AE	+
	$ENED$	+
Electoral and partisan budget-cycles	ELE	+
	CoG	−
Fractionalized and polarized governments and delayed stabilization (influence or veto-actor conceptions)	$SDwiG$ or $ADwiG$	+ or 0
	$SDwiG \cdot D$ or $ADwiG \cdot D$	+
	$ENoP$ or NoP	+ or 0
	$ENoP \cdot D$ or $NoP \cdot D$	+
Central bank autonomy and conservatism as a debt-financing constraint	CBI	−
Strategic debt-use	CoG	?
Strategic debt-use	RR	
Alesina and Tabellini		+
Persson and Svensson		−
To alter electorate interests		?
Strategic debt-use	$RR \cdot CoG$	
Alesina and Tabellini		0
Persson and Svensson		+
To alter electorate interests		?

[a] *PRES* or *FED* may also be executive budgetary leadership or democracy and fiscal illusion, respectively.

Table 3.3. *Variables, Descriptive Statistics, and Correlations with Debt and Deficit*

Variable	Min	Max	Mean	Standard Deviation	Correlations with Debt	Deficit
Debt (D)	3.02	132	35.0	23.7	1.00	0.22
Deficit (ΔD)	−14.7	15.9	0.35	3.08	0.22	1.00
UE	0.00	20.9	4.53	3.64	0.44	0.33
ΔY	−8.72	13.5	3.47	2.78	−0.06	−0.32
$E(r - \Delta Y)$	−10.5	10.1	−0.97	3.07	0.14	0.17
$r - \Delta Y$	−16.1	10.7	−1.32	4.32	0.15	0.32
$(r - \Delta Y) \cdot D_{t-1}$	−825	644	−34.4	177	0.09	0.34
OPEN	0.07	1.40	0.47	0.24	0.43	0.21
ToT	0.70	1.82	1.01	0.15	0.01	−0.29
ToT · OPEN	0.09	1.33	0.47	0.25	0.43	0.14
ENoP	1.00	5.21	1.66	0.79	−0.13	0.01
$ENoP \cdot D_{t-1}$	4.44	295	55.1	44.5	0.80	0.14
SDwiG	0.00	2.51	0.60	0.61	−0.06	0.05
$SDwiG \cdot D_{t-1}$	0.00	194	19.7	29.8	0.54	0.15
NoP	1.00	5.92	2.09	1.21	−0.19	0.02
$NoP \cdot D_{t-1}$	4.44	480	66.7	62.1	0.68	0.14
ADwiG	0.00	5.41	1.34	1.47	−0.09	0.06
$ADwiG \cdot D_{t-1}$	0.00	400	43.2	66.8	0.53	0.16
y	7.75	9.8	9.12	0.37	−0.11	0.06
OY	0.18	1.05	0.52	0.19	0.01	0.15
RW	0.33	1.39	0.80	0.17	0.25	−0.03
OY · RW	0.06	0.97	0.42	0.17	0.10	0.10
ELE	0.00	1.41	0.31	0.34	0.02	0.00
CoG	2.78	9.40	5.54	1.54	0.06	0.06
RR	0.00	2.56	0.27	0.33	0.02	0.01
CoG · RR	0.00	14.8	1.42	1.84	0.02	0.02
PRES	0.00	1.00	0.17	0.37	−0.26	−0.07
CBI	0.15	0.93	0.48	0.20	−0.24	−0.06
FED	1.00	50.0	6.59	12.1	−0.12	−0.06
ENED	1.00	329	67.3	87.8	0.08	−0.16
AE	0.00	1.00	0.06	0.17	−0.33	−0.01
TTAX	0.81	0.98	0.91	0.03	−0.19	−0.19
ITAX	0.15	0.71	0.35	0.09	0.11	−0.18
CTAX	0.26	0.89	0.61	0.15	0.44	−0.10

the tax-smoothing, economic-controls model as an appropriate default. The "stylized facts" are empirically clear and substantively obvious: adverse growth, terms of trade, debt-service cost, and unemployment are all strongly associated with higher deficits.

3.2.2. Tax Structure Complexity and Voters' Fiscal Illusion

Moving from economic conditions to the demand the polity presses upon democratic policy makers, some argue that voters do not properly comprehend and internalize governments' intertemporal budget constraints but rather tend simply to reward spending and punish taxing. Specifically, voters do not fully incorporate the relation of current deficits to future taxes – they suffer *fiscal illusion* – and opportunistic officeholders can take advantage, seeking reelection by spending more than they tax (Buchanan and Wagner 1977; Berry and Lowery [1987] review and extend). This suggests further that voters' fiscal illusion should be greater the more complex government budgeting is, as opaque fiscal systems complicate cost-benefit analyses of public activities. Thus, democratic governments, especially those with more complicated fiscal systems, will accumulate larger debts pursuing electoral boons.

An indicator for nondemocracy (*DICT*) was created, but its interpretation proved problematic. History provides only three nondemocratic cases in the sample – Portugal and Spain through the late seventies, Greece from 1967 to 1974 – and only four changes in regime, with three shifting from autocracy to democracy and one the other way. Thus, comparative leverage was small to begin. Furthermore, other theories required measurement of governments' left-right partisanship and of their *replacement risk*. Even if one codes nondemocracies as farthest right, accurately coding their replacement risk and partisanship relative to democratic parties is dubious. Hope of adequately testing the democracy-versus-nondemocracy implication was therefore abandoned, and nondemocratic periods were excluded from the sample.[9] Thus, only budgetary complexity remains empirically testable in fiscal-illusion theory.

As detailed in Section 2.4.2, OECD sources give data on public revenue by source, allowing three measures applicable here: general-government indirect and total tax shares of current revenue (*ITAX*, *TAX*), and

---

[9] Four years before and after autocracies were also excluded so replacement risk measures would not depend on arbitrary coding for nondemocracy.

central-government share of general-government total revenue (*CTAX*).[10] The true costs of indirect taxes should be more difficult and of taxes should be easier to assess than of other revenue generation (e.g., seigniorage). Similarly, concentration of revenue generation in one central authority as opposed to many local or separate fiscal agencies should facilitate accurate cost-benefit analysis of public activity. Voters' fiscal illusion, therefore, should be more apparent in country-years with relatively high indirect tax and low total tax and central-government shares of revenue.[11]

These measures should produce reasonably direct evidence on fiscal illusion in democracy for two reasons. First, if voters have no fiscal illusions, and if all taxes have the same long-run growth effects, debt should be independent of the tax structure. Second, if the long-run growth effects of different taxes do vary, tax structure will correlate with debt even with fully rational voters without fiscal illusion. In that case, though, opaque tax structures should hinder efficiency more, so expected long-run growth rates would decline in indirect-tax and increase in total-tax and central-government-revenue shares of public revenue. If rational, illusion-free voters think growth responds thus to tax composition, they would demand *less* debt as indirect-tax shares rise and *more* debt as total-tax and central-government shares rise, directly opposite the fiscal-illusion predictions. One complication does arise though; the debt measured here is for central government. Because less centrally concentrated fiscal systems may tend to hold less of their total public debt at national levels, this could confound the *CTAX* results.

The simple correlations in Table 3.3 may hint at fiscal illusion. Indirect- and total-tax shares correlate with debt (r ≈ +.11, r ≈ −.19), and total-tax and central-government shares correlate with deficits (r ≈ −.19, r ≈ −.10). Central shares correlate highly positively (r ≈ +.44) with debt, though, which may reflect the suspected tendency for less-centralized systems to have less *central*-government debt. To control for federalism

---

[10] Direct and indirect taxes, and central- and general-government total current revenue were extended by splicing of data from print editions into the disk series.

[11] Future work should attempt to measure relative opacity of spending and taxing because, with fiscal illusion, government size depends on that relativity (see Downs 1960), and deficits are likely proportional to that size as Section 2.6.2 showed. To demonstrate theoretically, suppose democratic policy makers spend, G, tax, T, and borrow, $D \equiv G - T$, to maximize votes, $V = a ln G - b ln T - cD^2$. Then, $G^*/T^* = (a/b)$, implying $D^* = (1 - b/a)G^* = (a/b - 1)T^*$. Deficits are directly (inversely) proportional to size as voters reward spending more (less) than they punish taxing, $a > b$ ($a < b$).

directly will therefore be crucial. Moreover, these tax structure variables correlate highly among themselves, so bivariate analyses may be misleading. Conclude for now only that the stylized facts suggest some possible fiscal illusion among voters that worsens with budget complexity.

3.2.3. Inter- and Intragenerational Transfers Functions of Debt

Moving to the structure of interests among voters, Cukierman and Meltzer (1989) and Tabellini (1991) note the tax-smoothing theory assumes perfect capital markets allow poor parents to leave negative bequests. However, people cannot usually borrow based on their children's future earnings or, a fortiori, that of unborn descendants. Governments, contrarily, can borrow from future generations to spend more now. Therefore, they conclude that the relatively poor, old, and especially old poor, who most desire negative bequests and usually benefit most from public economic activity, should most favor public borrowing. Thus, democracies with poorer and older populations should experience higher and faster-rising debts. Furthermore, as noted in Chapter 2, unequal distributions of economic resources and more-equal distributions of political resources, that is many poor and middle class and few wealthy but one person–one vote, imply that more inegalitarian democracies, having poorer median voters, should also amass greater debt (controlling for aggregate wealth).

These arguments neglect, however, that governments can borrow to lower current taxes as well as to raise spending. To the degree they do the former, wealthier and especially older wealthier voters may favor public debt because both pay more taxes and the latter are also less likely to bear the future higher taxes or lower spending directly. Moreover, younger polities should borrow for efficiency reasons if youth portends future growth and especially if that expectation relies on current public investment in education (human capital).[12] Such considerations may confound the wealth- and age-distribution implications of the inter- and intragenerational-transfers role of debt. Debt will still likely correlate with these factors, but how is indeterminate.

In measurement, consider the likely views, by any of these arguments, of a senior with children and grandchildren, another with children only,

[12] Optimal public-finance theory generally suggests borrowing (taxing) to fund investments (consumption).

and a third without children. The first is most, the second intermediately, and the last least connected to the future where debt payment burdens will fall, so that likely also ranks their debt preferences. Similarly, the middle-aged link to both parents and children; the prevalence of the former over latter in the population should gauge middle-age debt preferences. Thus, ratios of over-64 to under-15 populations appropriately reflect the aspect of the age distribution relevant to intragenerational transfers; happily, the same ratio also reflects the incentive to borrow for current human-capital investment. Such old-young ratios (OY) are computed from OECD data.[13]

The natural log of real GDP per capita (y) measures aggregate wealth simply. Measuring income, and a fortiori wealth, distribution annually and cross-country and cross-time comparably is, contrarily, notoriously difficult. Section 2.4.2 detailed such a comparable indicator, the "relative real-wage position of manufacturing workers" (RW), which compares income skew in each country-year to a base, United States 1986, where $RW = 1$. Higher values indicate greater skew.

Measuring the joint distribution of age and income is more difficult still, but a crude attempt is made nonetheless by multiplying the old-young ratio by the income disparity index ($OY \cdot RW$). This at least distinguishes older populations in high-income-disparity country-years from those in lower ones and, vice versa, greater inequality in older polities from that in younger ones.

In the simple correlations from Table 3.3, aggregate wealth correlates negatively with debts ($r \approx -.11$) yet also mildly positively with deficits ($r \approx +.06$). The old-young ratio correlates little with debts ($r \approx +.01$) but positively with deficits ($r \approx +.15$). Income disparity also correlates positively with debts ($r \approx +.25$), but weakly negatively with deficits ($r \approx -.03$). The interaction of the old-young ratio and income disparity, lastly, correlates positively with both debts and deficits ($r \approx +.10$), though especially such interactions are perilous to analyze bivariately. Thus, the stylized facts do not strongly oppose the original inter- and intragenerational-transfers arguments, although they hardly offer unequivocal support.

[13] OECD, *Labor Force Statistics*, contains annual estimates of population and age breakdowns thereof from 1955 to present in most cases. The data are extended where necessary by linear extrapolation of quinquennial estimates of breakdowns from UN, *Age and Sex Demographics*, plus annual estimates of total population from IMF sources. Future work should use age ratios to estimate expected growth and so separate the expected efficiency and tax-burden incentives for debt to correlate with age distribution.

3.2.4. Multiple Constituencies and Distributive Politics

Moving to electoral institutions through which these potentially "fiscally illuded" and wealth- and age-differentiated voters choose their representatives, Weingast et al. (1981) argue that policy makers who represent subnational districts will tend to overestimate benefits of distributive spending and underestimate their costs because the benefits of such "pork-barrel" spending accrue largely within district, tax costs usually spread more equally across the polity, and voters reward or punish representatives accordingly. If budgetary-legislation majorities are assembled by logrolling compromises, then overspending on district projects increases in the number of constituencies represented by policy makers.[14]

To see the logic formally, assume for analytic clarity that benefits (B) of distributive projects concentrate entirely in district i and increase with project size or cost: $B_i = f(C)$. Diminishing returns imply $f' > 0$ and $f'' < 0$. Again for analytic clarity, assume costs are distributed perfectly evenly across n districts: $C_i = C/n$. Then, individual districts maximize net benefits, $Max_c f(C) - C/n$, by setting $f'(C) = 1/n$; thus, receiving districts prefer larger projects the greater number of districts. If legislatures decide by majority rule, with logrolling or side payments prohibited, all pork-barrel projects lose $n - 1$ to 1 because only receiving districts derive net benefits, $f(C) - C/n$, while the rest pay C/n. With side payments, however, district i must buy only $n/2$ votes to amass a minimum-winning coalition; it will pay and projects will pass if net benefits exceed required side payments: $f(C) - C/n > C/2$. Socially optimally, only projects where $f(C) > C$ should pass; minimum-winning coalitions instead pass projects capable of covering $\frac{1}{2}C$ in side payments plus C/n for the receiving district. Thus, districting in representative democracy implies slightly more distributive spending the greater n. Moreover, the small per-district costs of each project, C/n, might easily escape voters' notice in nonreceiving districts, especially if they are rationally ignorant (Downs 1957, 1960), while net benefits in receiving districts, $f(C) - C/n$, will surely attract those voters' attention. Thus, with imperfectly informed voters, legislators could

---

[14] Notice that the argument applies to *constituencies*, which may concentrate on dimensions other than geography, not *electoral districts* per se. Determining the relative weight of alternative *constituencies* on democratic policy making and measuring the effective number of such constituencies comparatively is beyond the present scope. Franzese and Nooruddin (1999) offer a first cut.

relatively easily form logrolling agreements to support each other's pork-barrel requests via, for example, tit-for-tat cooperative solutions to the iterated prisoner's dilemma they face (Axelrod 1984), especially because they are reasonably few actors, have fairly homogenous interests in this regard, and interact repeatedly and indefinitely. In the limit, such universalist logrolling passes distributive projects that maximize benefits district by district. Therefore, distributive spending strongly increases in the number of districts if voters are rationally ignorant.

As Alesina and Perotti (1994) note, overspending might not imply deficits. However, voters' fiscal illusion may lead elected policy makers to debt-finance a proportion of their spending (see note 11). Moreover, Velasco (1995) shows that multiple constituencies also induce dynamic common-pool problems that, even without voter fiscal illusion, lead elected policy makers to debt-finance some of their desired spending. Essentially, debt relocates some costs of current projects to the future, where districts again divide them. Common-pool problems thus enter twice when projects are debt-financed, suggesting that, indeed, deficits will be the preferred mode of financing distributive spending. Thus, with minimum-winning coalitions or logrolling, deficits, and not just spending, increase in the number of constituencies, especially if voters are fiscally illuded or rationally ignorant.

Calibrating numbers of constituencies comparably across democracies is challenging, even restricting attention to geographically defined constituencies (see note 14). Several imperfect measures here attempt to triangulate on the concept.

A first simple ingress is the number of regions in effectively federal states (*FED*).[15] However, problematically, federal regions will often contain all the costs as well as all the benefits of within-region spending; more than the one constituency implied by *FED* likely operates in unitary systems; federalism may also foster fiscal illusion as numbers of distinct fiscal authorities and of federal regions correlate highly; and federalism might lower *central-government* debt simply by substituting subnational debt. (*FED* will actually help to control for this last potentiality.)

---

[15] Considered effectively federal are the United States (48–50 regions in the sample), Germany (10; 16 postunification and out of sample), Canada (12), democratic Spain (17), Switzerland (23.9: cantons and half-cantons weighted as such), and Australia (8). The remaining unitary systems have 1 federal region. Numbers of regions, their natural logs, and a (0–1) indicator distinguishing federal and unitary systems were all considered. Including the number of regions and its square performed most consistently across empirical specifications.

Second, as an empirical regularity, agrarian- and ethnic-party electoral support (constituencies) tends to concentrate geographically, so common-pool problems should be more evident with them in government. Thus, such parties' shares of government (*AE*) also help gauge effective numbers of constituencies.[16]

Third, presidentialism may ease multiple-constituency problems because presidents have national constituencies whereas legislators represent more localized interests.[17] Therefore, an indicator set to 1 for the United States, Finland, and the French Fifth Republic, and 0 elsewhere (*PRES*) also helps. Again, though, presidentialism may have other effects. Political science has long known that legislative procedures and institutions strongly impact the policies that emerge from governments.[18] Regarding specifically budgets, Von Hagen and colleagues stress the strength of executives, that is, prime ministers or presidents, and of finance ministers in intragovernment budget negotiations. Deficits, they argue and evidence, are lower where executives set budgetary outlines first and hold cabinet and legislature negotiations to those outlines than where overall budgets emerge from less executively constrained, item-by-item, negotiations.[19] Thus, negative coefficients on *PRES* could as easily support presidential-leadership as multiple-constituencies effects on budgeting.

Fourth, and most directly, one can count effective numbers of electoral districts (*ENED*; data from Lijphart 1994).[20] Note however, that theory

[16] Lane et al. (1991) classify parties helpfully. Belgium's split liberal, socialist, communist, and Christian-Democrat parties are not considered ethnic for these purposes; only the strictly ethnic parties RW, FDF, and VU are. Germany's CSU is assumed ethnic/regional and, crudely, to hold 10% of the CDU's cabinet seats (CSU is not distinguished from CDU in all cabinet-composition data). Throughout, presidents and legislatures in Finland, the French Fifth Republic, and the United States are treated as equal parts of government (see Section 2.4.2 for details).

[17] Excepting legislators with one national district of course.

[18] See, e.g., Romer and Rosenthal 1978, Ferejohn and Krehbiel 1987, Ferejohn et al. 1987, Baron and Ferejohn 1989, Baron 1991, and Weingast and Marshall 1985 for the United States; and Wildavsky 1986 and Tsebelis 1995 for comparative views.

[19] Cf. Ferejohn and Krehbiel 1987. Von Hagen 1992, Hallerberg and Von Hagen 1997, and De Haan et al. 1997 also stress budgetary amendment and voting rules, transparency, and implementation flexibility. Unfortunately, their data on budgetary procedures cover only European Community countries, which would restrict the sample here too severely to include.

[20] Lijphart's numbers of electoral districts potentially vary within country only when electoral systems, as defined therein, change, and remain fixed at system average otherwise. *Effective* differ from raw district numbers due to multiple electoral tiers or rules. *ENED* weights by the proportion of government elected in each system. Also, presidential and bicameral differ from unicameral systems. Several weighting schemes were attempted,

regards numbers of *constituencies* not electoral districts (see note 14). A U.S. representative, for example, likely considers herself much more a representative of her electoral district than does a British Member of Parliament, who likely considers herself much more a representative of her party. Thus, the 650± electoral districts in the United Kingdom probably represent considerably fewer *constituencies* than do the 435± U.S. House districts.[21]

The combination of *FED*, *AE*, *ENED* (+), and *PRES* (–) will hopefully triangulate on the effective number of geographic *constituencies* stressed by this theory of debt determination. As shown in Table 3.3, presidentialism correlates negatively with debts ($r \approx -.26$) and deficits ($r \approx -.07$) as expected, but agrarian- and ethnic-party government representation actually correlates strongly negatively with debts ($r \approx -.33$), contrary to expectations. Effective numbers of electoral districts correlate positively with debt ($r \approx +.08$) as expected, but more strongly negatively ($r \approx -.16$) with deficits. Finally, numbers of federal regions correlate negatively with debts ($r \approx -.11$) and deficits ($r \approx -.06$), also contrary to expectations, though this could merely reflect the high empirical correlation of federalism and central bank independence ($r \approx +.57$)[22] or tendencies towards subnational rather than central-government debt in federal systems. Thus, the stylized facts are mixed to unfavorable regarding multiple-constituencies and debt.

Before proceeding, note that *FED* and *ENED* have highly outlying cases in their empirical distributions. There are many unitary systems and few federal ones, and the most subdivided United States has more than twice

---

ranging from lower house exclusive to equal weights, but none performed visibly better or worse across the empirical models than that reported. Finally, even distributive spending will not concentrate benefits within very small districts, so *ENED* adjusts for districts' geographic size. If average districts exceed 3,600 miles[2] (a 1-hour commute at 60 miles per hour), then apply no adjustment. If less, then adjust *ENED* halfway to the country's square milage divided by 3,600. Again, many alternative adjustment schemes were attempted, but none performed noticeably better or worse.

[21] Franzese and Nooruddin (1999) build from this consideration, suggesting weighting *ENED* inversely by party unity times *NoP* or *ENoP*, but lack of comparative measures of party unity constrains their empirics to the U.S. case. Janda's (1980) index of party cohesion, unfortunately, refers primarily to the 1960s, does not encompass this set of countries, and is time invariant. Adjusting *ENED* to consider the degree to which electoral rules allow candidate as opposed to party voting may also be appropriate if candidate voting makes electoral districts more relevant as constituencies. Preliminary attempts at such adjustments were not entirely satisfactory, leaving more possibilities for future research.

[22] The United States, Canada, Germany, and Switzerland are federal and have very or moderately highly conservative and autonomous central banks.

the regions as next most, Switzerland. Similarly, most countries have fewer than 100 effective electoral districts, but plurality systems in the United States, French Fifth Republic, United Kingdom, and Canada have 133 to 329. Given their extreme skews, the ensuing analyses allow nonlinear relations of these variables to debt by including *FED*, *ENED*, and their squares.[23]

3.2.5. Electoral and Partisan Budget Cycles

Consider next in the political-economy cycle, the electoral and partisan incentives of the governments selected by these voters through these institutions. At least since Nordhaus (1975) and Tufte (1978), political economists have suspected that democratic policy makers attempt to manipulate the economy for electoral purposes, employing more expansionary policies (here, higher deficits) immediately prior to elections. Incumbents may do so to win votes either because voters are fiscally illuded, rewarding spending and punishing taxes regardless of their economic-efficiency merit or long-run budgetary consequences (Nordhaus 1975; Tufte 1978), or because voters fully rationally expect policy-maker competence to persist over time and interpret increased spending or reduced taxes as a partial signal of the incumbent's actual ability to produce more for less (Rogoff and Sibert 1988; Rogoff 1990).

At least since Hibbs (1977), political economists have argued that right and left parties differ in their fiscal priorities. Because their core constituencies favor larger public economies, redistribution, and Keynesian expansion and activism, left-party-dominated governments are expected to run larger deficits than right. Rational-expectations additions to partisan theory (Alesina 1988b) moderate the predicted long-term economic effects of such partisan-differentiated macroeconomic policies, but do not challenge the policy implications.

Section 2.4.2 detailed construction of the indicator, *ELE*, which sums to one over the year preceding an election, and of governments' "partisan center of gravity" (*CoG*). For future reference: U.S. Democrats and Republicans and U.K. Labour and Conservatives are 2.8± and 4.9± *CoG* units apart (4.8 − 7.6±, 2.8 − 7.7±).

---

[23] Including a variable and its square more flexibly allows nonlinearity than using only the natural log of the variable as sometimes done. Including AE^2 was also considered but empirically rejected.

The bivariate correlations in Table 3.3 with deficits and debts of the preelection-year indicator ($r \approx .00$, $r \approx .02$) and of government partisanship ($r \approx .06$, $r \approx .06$) are weak (and the latter wrongly signed). This is unsurprising, though, because, in zero-order data without controls, the trends observed in Figure 1.7 would swamp the fluctuations predicted by electoral and partisan budget-*cycle* theory.

3.2.6. *Fractionalized and Polarized Governments and Delayed Stabilization*

Focusing on the fractionalization and polarization of the governments formed to make fiscal policies, Roubini and Sachs (1989a,b), Alesina and Drazen (1991), Drazen and Grilli (1993), and Spolaore (1993) develop "war of attrition" models of public-debt stabilization in which, given high outstanding-debt levels and/or persistent deficits, governing parties are likely to dispute who will bear the costs of fiscal adjustments even if they agree on their necessity. They argue that single-party governments can relatively easily shift such adjustment costs onto opponents' constituencies. Multiparty governments will also try to shift costs to outsiders, but adjustments that neutrally distribute costs among the governing parties' constituencies will be more difficult to devise. The more fragmented and polarized the coalition, the more difficult such neutral adjustment plans will be to devise. Finally, given some uncertainty among the governing parties over how long the others will tolerate steadily rising debt before capitulating to stabilization plans whose distributional consequences they dislike,[24] more polarized and fragmented governments will experience deadlock and delay implementation of stabilization plans longer than would more unified governments.

Previous evidence is quite mixed. Roubini and Sachs (1989a,b) find weak governments correlate with higher debts, but they simply categorize "weakness" 1–4, single- or multiparty and majority or minority. Using a separate indicator for each of these four categories, Edin and Ohlsson (1991) find support only for a positive relation between debt and minority government. De Haan and Sturm (1994, 1997) and Borrelli and Royed

---

[24] If parties had rational expectations and certainty over when each other would capitulate, the loser would cave immediately rather than allow debt to accumulate and (with certainty) have to capitulate later anyway.

(1995) find not even this, yet Alesina and Perotti (1995b) conclude (in a narrower, qualitative study) that coalitions implement stabilization plans less successfully than unified governments. More-careful operationalization of the theory may help by distinguishing fractionalization from polarization and between competing veto-actor and influence views of these theoretical concepts, and by appropriately modeling, in a wider sample, the *retardation of fiscal adjustments* rather than expecting an impact on the level of debt per se.

Arguments regarding weak governments and delayed stabilization stress the fractionalization and polarization of partisan interests within governments. Using the partisan codes compiled for *CoG*, one can calibrate polarization with standard deviations of government members' party-codes (*SDwiG*). Similarly, the effective number of governing parties (*ENoP*), which weighs each party by its share of government, can gauge fractionalization. Tsebelis (1995), however, argues for discarding such *weighted-influence* conceptions of policy making for a *veto-actor* conception, arguing that each member of a governing coalition is a potential veto-actor, their withdrawal threats being equally effective.[25] From this view, *ENoP* and *SDwiG* inappropriately weigh governing parties by the share of government they hold, embodying an *influence conception* of fractionalization-polarization. A *veto-actor conception* would instead measure maximum absolute differences between governing-party partisan scores (*ADwiG*) and raw numbers of governing parties (*NoP*) because, by that view, the polarization obstacle to fiscal adjustment is the whole span of member ideologies, any one holding a potential veto, and because each member adds equally to the fractionalization obstacle.[26]

---

[25] Logically, for each government member, at least one member essential to the coalition's hold on government must prefer a coalition with that member to one without it. If this were not so, no essential party sees that member as essential, and it would be excluded. Thus, every coalition member is critical, intrinsically or through another party, and so has equal potential veto power.

[26] Finnish and French presidents count as veto actors for *NoP* purposes, and as *N* ministers, with *N* = cabinet size, for *ENoP* and *SdwiG* purposes. U.S. presidents count as *N* and each senator as *N/100* representatives, with *N* = house size, for *ENoP* and *SDwiG* purposes. Each house and the president count as veto actors, so *NoP* = 1 when the president's party controls both houses and *NoP* = 2 when it controls one or neither house. When the president's party controls both houses, *ADwiG* is 0; otherwise, it is the distance between Democrats and Republicans (≈ 2.8). For country-years with multiple governments, their scores are averaged, each weighted by the fraction of year it held office.

Table 3.3 shows debts and deficits correlate weakly and often negatively with polarization and fractionalization in any of their competing conceptions. Given the Roubini-Sachs results and well-known coincidences of high debt and fractionalized, polarized government in Belgium and Italy, the weak correlations are surprising, though they resonate with the De Haan-Sturm and Borrelli-Royed nonfindings. Perhaps, though, the weak bivariate relations and the nonfindings of some previous studies stem from a common failure to consider the hypotheses properly. Fractionalization and polarization are expected to retard fiscal-policy adjustment rates, which will produce large deficits only or primarily where debt is already high. Accordingly, the multivariate analyses to follow also include $ENoP \cdot D_{t-1}$ and $SDwiG \cdot D_{t-1}$ or $NoP \cdot D_{t-1}$ and $ADwiG \cdot D_{t-1}$. Theories involving weak governments and delayed stabilization more directly predict positive coefficients on these interactions, which do correlate highly positively with debt and deficits, though that is virtually meaningless in bivariate analysis because lagged debt, D_{t-1}, will obviously correlate with debt regardless of whether stabilization is delayed.

3.2.7. *Autonomous, Conservative Central Banks as Borrowing Constraints*

Moving penultimately to the roles of nongovernmental actors, consider how central bank independence (i.e., autonomy plus conservatism) might alter the fiscal policies that seem best to these governments. Alesina and Perotti (1994) note that, historically, governments reduced massive debt burdens largely by inflation, which erodes the real value of outstanding nominal obligations. With independent central banks, however, this favored escape will be more difficult to implement. Assuming inflationary (partial) default is favored because it carries lower political or economic costs than alternatives, prudent governments would likely avoid accumulating debt where they face more-independent central banks. In fact, one could add, key components of central bank independence in several empirical indices are the conditions under which the bank legally can or must buy any public debt that the market will not absorb. Enforced or pressured buying usually produces a de facto inflation subsidy on public-debt interest, so central banks that are relatively free of such obligations and pressures raise debt-issuance costs quite directly. However, imprudent or recalcitrant governments that issue massive debt, despite facing highly independent central banks, lack the inflation escape. Central bank autonomy and conservatism could thus increase debt by constraining governments from cheap inflationary finance of it.[27]

Central bank independence (*CBI*) indices abound. Rescaling (0–1) and averaging two each from Cukierman (1992) and Grilli et al. (1991) and one from Bade and Parkin (1982) capitalizes on the most commonly used (presumably best) of these to broaden the country-years covered and, under most conditions,[28] to reduce measurement error. Preliminary empirics (Table 3.3) reveal a fairly strong negative relationship of *CBI* to debt (r ≈ −24) and a moderate negative relationship to deficits (r ≈ −.06), suggesting a dissuasion effect.[29]

3.2.8. Strategic Debt-Manipulation to Alter Future Governments' Policies

Finally, the cyclic view of political economy highlights policy makers' abilities to look forward and alter strategically the circumstances under which future policies will be made. Alesina and Tabellini (1990), for example, note that incumbents can accumulate debt to alter the fiscal situation inherited by future governments. In their model, incumbents accumulate more debt the greater the ideological distance (in desired spending composition) to its expected replacement and the more likely or sooner it expects to be replaced. Because incumbents dislike what their opponents will do with public funds, they aim to reduce future fiscal latitude by increasing future interest-payment burdens. The more likely or sooner incumbents expect to be replaced, and the less they like the expected policies of their expected replacements, the more they do so.[30] Persson and Svensson (1989) argue similarly, in a model where potential

[27] The multivariate analyses to follow control directly for debt-financing costs, so estimated coefficients correspond only to dissuasion effects. The estimated debt-service-cost impacts will contain any effects of the counterargument.
[28] If the individual indices' measurement errors are not too positively correlated, error variance is lower in the average than in picking one not knowing their relative quality. Even if one is known best, error variance in the average will still be lower if the others are not too much worse and error correlation is not too high.
[29] *CBI* changes little within countries in sample, so weaker deficit correlation means little. Cukierman's *LVAU* index and therefore the average potentially varies by "decade" (1950–9, 1960–71, 1972–9, and 1980–9), but little variation within countries occurs over this period anyway. If the indices extended beyond 1990, more within-country variation would emerge. Sadly, such extension still awaits.
[30] Tabellini and Alesina (1990) reach similar conclusions in a model with explicit voting; there the median voter has an interest in accumulating debt to constrain future spending-composition from drifting away from her preferences.

governments differ over spending level rather than composition. There, low (high) spending right (left) governments, when faced with prospects of replacement by their opponents, accumulate (reduce) debt, inducing the opposition to spend less (more). Again, the more likely or sooner the replacement and the more different the desired-spending levels, the more this counterintuitive incentive operates. Thus, these models emphasize strategic use of debt to add or remove constraints on the opposition's conduct of future fiscal policy.

Aghion and Bolton (1990), Milesi-Ferretti (1995), and Milesi-Ferretti and Spolaore (1993, 1994) stress instead that incumbents can affect their reelection probabilities by using debt to alter the partisan preferences of the population. Specifically, if the left is known or suspected to be more default-prone (direct or through inflationary partial default) than the right, then right governments can issue (especially nominal) debt, thereby raising the amount of voter-held debt and thus decreasing electoral support for the suspected default-prone left. The left, being a suspected default risk, could reduce (especially nominal) debt to alleviate default-risk concerns about it among the electorate. Again, the strategic uses of debt are emphasized, but, unfortunately, both types of models insufficiently explore the conditions that would bring such counterintuitive incentives for left and right to dominate the more familiar incentives emphasized in standard partisan theory.

Both arguments also stress government fractionalization and polarization, as did the war-of-attrition models, but *across* rather than *within* governments – that is, the expected ideological distance from incumbent to replacement governments. Directly measuring such *replacement risk* (*RR*) comparably across democracies with differing governmental systems would be very difficult, but available party left-right codes and government-composition data offer useful simplifications. Variations of government partisanship over time – say, standard deviations of *CoG* across nine years centered on the present – are as comparable as the *CoG* index itself and could measure the typical distance from itself an incumbent might reasonably expect potential replacements to be.[31] To complete the *RR* estimate requires measuring the incumbent's expected probability of losing office to that replacement. Ideally, such expectations formation would be modeled explicitly, but doing so comparably across 21 democ-

---

[31] Standard deviations across five, seven, and nine years, centered, present-forward and present-back were considered. None behaved very differently, but the nine-year centered measure gave most-consistent results across the analyses.

racies again eludes the discipline. A reasonable, simpler estimate is the inverse of the actual duration of the incumbent, which is the expected hazard rate (probability) of losing office in a year assuming that rates are constant within governments and that the incumbent knows or can estimate them well. Hazard rates times the standard deviations of CoG across governments then emerge as expedient, comparable estimates of the expected ideological deviation of next year's governments from the current incumbent.[32]

The theories also predict differing effects for this replacement risk (RR). Alesina and Tabellini (1990) argue that all governments accumulate more debt when facing higher replacement risk; RR suffices to explore that empirically, expecting a positive correlation. Persson and Svensson (1989) instead expect positive debt effects of replacement risk under right incumbents but negative effects under left. RR, CoG, and the interaction, $RR \cdot CoG$, are required to express that argument, with the expected pattern of coefficients such that increases in RR raise (lower) debt when the incumbent is sufficiently right (left), and, conversely, that rightward (leftward) shifts in CoG raise (lower) debt when RR is sufficiently high. This implies a positive coefficient on $RR \cdot CoG$ and likely negative ones on RR and CoG, but the latter signs and relative magnitudes are indeterminate with the relative strength of strategic-debt and (standard) partisan-deficit incentives unknown. When the incentives to deploy debt strategically to exploit or defend against partisan default reputations with the electorate should dominate standard partisan objectives is also unclear. However, presumably partisan governments employ debt strategically for this purpose either (a) when weakening opposition electoral support is especially desirable, which is when replacement risk is high; or when it is especially feasible, which is when incumbent office-security is high, that is, when replacement risk is low. Including CoG, RR, and $CoG \cdot RR$, therefore, should cover most possibilities and leave it an empirical issue.

The stylized facts favor none of the strategic-debt theories – $CoG \cdot RR$ and RR are uncorrelated with debts or deficits (r $\approx$ +.01 to +.02) – but,

---

[32] By itself, the standard deviation of CoG over time is insufficient. It does not, e.g., distinguish annually alternating governments of $CoG = 4$ and $CoG = 6$ from the same two alternating every 4.5 years. Replacement risk is higher in the former situation as incorporating the hazard rate will reflect. Hazard rates for Finland and the French Fifth Republic are one-half the president's and one-half the cabinet's. In the United States, they are one-third each the president's, the House's, and the Senate's, which happens to be constant at $1/[(1/3)4 + (1/3)2 + (1/3)6] = 1/4$. Again, RR averages governments in years with more than one government, weighing each by the part of the year it held office.

then, bivariate analysis is especially inept at exploring such conditional (interactive) hypotheses.

3.3. Empirical Evaluation of the Positive Political Economy of Public Debt

The usable sample is 618 country-years, encompassing the United States, Italy, France, Germany, Belgium, Denmark, Finland, Ireland, the Netherlands, Norway, Sweden, Australia, 1956–90; Japan, 1958–90; United Kingdom, Switzerland, 1963–90; New Zealand, 1969–90; Austria, 1973–90; Portugal, Spain, 1981–90; and Greece, 1961–2, 79–90.[33]

3.3.1. Multivariate Specifications and Methodology

As with transfers, the high temporal persistence of public debt suggests a *pseudo-error-correction* format (see Section 2.4.4) for the empirical models. The dependent variable is change in debt (ΔD_t), and independent variables include two lagged changes in debt (ΔD_{t-1}, ΔD_{t-2}) and one lag of debt level (D_{t-1}), which model momentum- and equilibrium-like persistence in changes and levels respectively, and averages of other countries' deficits that sample year ($\Delta D_{-i,t}$), which models the spatial correlation of debt.[34]

---

[33] Data availability and the need to exclude nondemocratic periods restrict the usable sample. All data used in this book are available from the author's web page, currently located at <http://www-personal.umich.edu/~franzese>.

[34] Methodological notes: Specifying a uniform base-model format requires some auxiliary analyses. (1) Augmented Dickey-Fuller tests fail to reject unit roots in D, UE, OY, $OY \cdot RW$, $OPEN$, and $ToT \cdot OPEN$, yet residuals of debt regressed on any permutation of the rest also potentially retain unit roots. Beck (1992) suggests an error-correction-model (ECM) form especially useful in such cases (Section 2.4.4 describes such *pseudo* ECM). Here, ΔD is regressed on (a) its lagged level and two lagged differences, and, the following being robustly consistent across specifications only in these forms, (b) OY and the economic conditions in levels and changes, (c) RW and $OY \cdot RW$ in changes, and (d) all other variables in levels. (2) The lagged-debt coefficient has t ≈ −3.7 in Table 3.7's encompassing model, which would likely pass ADF, so inferences should safely satisfy any lingering unit-root concerns. The model also passes Lagrange Multiplier (up to six lags) and Ljeung-Box (any lag-length) for autocorrelated residuals. Thus, inclusion of ΔD_{t-1}, ΔD_{t-2}, and D_{t-1} should satisfy all autocorrelation concerns. (3) Although a linear trend or one kinked at 1973 is significant in most models, including it alters other coefficient estimates little substantively, so, as their inclusion may obscure *theoretical* explanations for debt time-paths, they are excluded. (4) Regressing residuals from the full model on country indicators explores the validity of omitting fixed effects. F-tests of these regressions were never remotely significant. In contrast to one-stage tests of equal intercepts across countries, this two-stage approach gives pride of place to substantive variables. This is wholly as should be, but the more skeptical may note that the one-stage test did, in some specifications (but

Begin by gathering terms in theoretical groups to facilitate exploring whether each political-economic model adds explanatory power to the economic-conditions default (nested F-tests) and whether each adds explanatory power to each of the others plus the default (nonnested J-tests).

The first group contains the economic controls that tax-smoothing theory suggests (UE, ΔY, $E(r - \Delta Y)$, $(r - \Delta Y) \cdot D_{t-1}$, $ToT \cdot OPEN$, ToT, $OPEN$), in levels and in changes to allow both long-run-equilibrium and short-run-deviation relations, plus the temporal- and spatial-correlation controls. This constitutes the default, no other theory disputing that economic conditions and spatial and temporal correlation affect budgetary policies. The second group pertains to weak governments and delayed stabilization: $ENoP$, $ENoP \cdot D_{t-1}$, $SDwiG$, and $SDwiG \cdot D_{t-1}$ for an influence and NoP, $NoP \cdot D_{t-1}$, $ADwiG$, and $ADwiG \cdot D_{t-1}$ for a veto-actor conception. Group three derives from the arguments involving inter- or intragenerational transfers role of debt y_{t-1}, ΔOY, ΔRW, $\Delta OY \cdot RW$, and OY_{t-1}.[35] The fourth merges partisan-and-electoral-budget-cycle (ELE, ELE_{t-1}, CoG)[36] with strategic-debt-manipulation theories (CoG, RR, $RR \cdot CoG$) because these are partially nested theoretically also.

notably *not* in the full model), favor country fixed effects. Two notable differences in the fixed effects results from those reported: the macro-institutional variables were usually signed as reported but not or more-marginally significant (to be expected as they vary little over time), and the replacement-risk-augmented partisan-fiscal-cycles found here were *more* significant and unchanged in shape (see Franzese 2000b). (5) Analogous tests weakly supported time-period fixed effects, but, instead of 34 atheoretical year indicators, the average deficit in the *other* countries each sample-year ($\Delta D_{-i,t}$) was included. With $\Delta D_{-i,t}$, year-indicators were robustly rejected, and the substitution hardly altered substantive results (except: real GDP per capita is marginally significantly negative with time indicators). (6) OLS residuals in each model were squared and regressed on country indicators. F-tests of these auxiliary regressions, which test panel heteroskedasticity against homoskedastic nulls, were invariably high (p < .0001). The Durbin-Watson statistics there test first-order autoregressive conditional heteroskedasticity (ARCH) against panel-heteroskedastic nulls. DW > 1.84 in all models, so the panel-heteroskedasticity used suffices. All models also employ panel-corrected standard errors (PCSEs): Beck and Katz 1995, 1997. Thus, the reported results emerge from the following process: run OLS, saving residuals; regress squared residuals on country indicators, saving fitted values; inverse the square root of those fitted values as panel weights for WLS; run WLS and compute PCSE's using the weighted residuals. GAUSS code to implement such a procedure in nonrectangular samples like this is available at <http://www-personal.umich.edu/~franzese> (see also Franzese 1996a).

[35] The data show only change relations between debt and income disparity, in interaction with age distribution or separately, but a level relation between debt and age distributions, which did not depend on income disparity.

[36] As with transfers in Chapter 2, exploring the pseudo-error-correction format for these variables uncovered both pre- and *post*electoral fiscal expansions.

The remaining variables group less distinctly by theory. One coherent scheme would distinguish tax complexity and fiscal illusion ($TTAX_{t-1}$, $ITAX_{t-1}$, $CTAX_{t-1}$, FED, FED^2), macro-institutions (CBI, $PRES$, $ENED$, $ENED^2$, FED, FED^2), and multiple constituencies ($PRES$, FED, FED^2, $ENED$, $ENED^2$, AE). The categories highlight some of the specification difficulties in these theories. For example, a strong empirical correlation of federalism with CBI confounds interpretation of the former's coefficients in the first and last group and ambiguity remains in whether presidentialism pertains more directly to multiple-constituency or budgetary-institutions arguments. Such complications, and that the three groups are nearly coterminous anyway, argue for a final, residual set merging all ten factors: a nested model involving tax structure, macro-institutions, and multiple constituencies.

Multivariate analyses will show how J- and F-tests of the theoretical groups provide leverage to evaluate their explanatory power. Data show at least minimal support for each political-economy model, suggesting an empirical model encompassing all the theories, as in equation (1), merits estimation. The coefficients' hypothesized signs are superscripted where unambiguous. The key theoretical ambiguities regard strategic-debt and federalism variables as noted earlier. Other ambiguities regard nonlinear or interactive effects.[37]

$$
\begin{aligned}
\Delta D_t = {} & \beta_0 + \beta_1^+ \Delta D_{t-1} + \beta_2^+ \Delta D_{t-2} + \beta_3^- D_{t-1} + \beta_4^+ \Delta D_{\sim i,t} \\
& + \beta_5^+ \Delta\!\left((r - \Delta Y) \cdot D_{t-1}\right) + \beta_6^+ (r - \Delta Y)_{t-1} \cdot D_{t-2} + \beta_7^+ \Delta UE_t + \beta_8^+ UE_{t-1} \\
& + \beta_9^- \Delta(\Delta Y)_t + \beta_{10}^- \Delta Y_{t-1} + \beta_{11}^- \Delta(E(r - \Delta Y)_t) + \beta_{12}^- E(r - \Delta Y)_{t-1} \\
& + \beta_{13}^? \Delta OPEN_t + \beta_{14}^? OPEN_{t-1} + \beta_{15}^? \Delta ToT_t + \beta_{16}^? ToT_{t-1} \\
& + \beta_{17}^+ \Delta(ToT \cdot OPEN)_t + \beta_{18}^+ (ToT \cdot OPEN)_{t-1} + \beta_{19}^? NoP_t \\
& + \beta_{20}^+ NoP_t \cdot D_{t-1} + \beta_{21}^? ADwiG_t + \beta_{20}^+ ADwiG_t \cdot D_{t-1} + \beta_{23}^+ ELE_t \\
& + \beta_{24}^+ ELE_{t-1} + \beta_{25}^? CoG_t + \beta_{26}^? RR_t + \beta_{27}^? (CoG \cdot RR)_{i,t} + \beta_{28}^- y_{t-2} \\
& + \beta_{29}^+ \Delta OY_t + \beta_{30}^+ \Delta RW_t + \beta_{31}^+ (\Delta RW \cdot \Delta OY)_t + \beta_{32}^+ OY_{t-1} \\
& + \beta_{33}^- TTAX_{t-1} + \beta_{34}^+ ITAX_{t-1} + \beta_{35}^- CTAX_{t-1} + \beta_{36}^? FED_t \\
& + \beta_{37}^? FED_t^2 + \beta_{38}^? ENED_t + \beta_{39}^? ENED_t^2 + \beta_{40}^+ AE_t + \beta_{41}^- PRES_t \\
& + \beta_{42}^- CBI_t + \varepsilon_t
\end{aligned}
\tag{1}
$$

---

[37] For example, the multiple-constituency model expects effective numbers of electoral districts to induce debt, but different sign patterns on $ENED$ and $ENED^2$ could produce that. Similarly, the economic-conditions and weak-governments models are unambiguous

Table 3.4. *The Tax-Smoothing/Economic-Conditions Default Model*

Independent Variables	Coefficients	Standard Errors	p-Levels
C	+.2056	.9647	.8313
ΔD_{t-1}	+.4511	.0545	.0000
ΔD_{t-2}	+.6567	.0460	.0109
D_{t-1}	−.0047	.0048	.3289
$\Delta D_{-i,t}$	+.2057	.0562	.0003
(1) $\Delta((r - \Delta Y)_t \cdot D_{t-1})$	+.0056	.0008	.0000
(2) $(r - \Delta Y)_{t-1} \cdot D_{t-2}$	+.0047	.0009	.0000
(3) ΔUE_t	+.6104	.1000	.0000
(4) UE_{t-1}	+.0310	.0244	.2046
(5) $\Delta(\Delta Y)_t$	−.0396	.0351	.2592
(6) ΔY_{t-1}	−.0045	.0399	.9109
(7) $\Delta(E(r - \Delta Y))_t$	−.0358	.0449	.4249
(8) $E(r - \Delta Y)_{t-1}$	−.1400	.0344	.0001
(9) $\Delta OPEN_t$	+13.36	5.950	.0251
(10) $OPEN_{t-1}$	+2.343	2.919	.4225
(12) ΔToT_t	+4.156	2.267	.0673
(13) ToT_{t-1}	−.3543	.8785	.6868
(14) $\Delta(ToT_t \cdot OPEN_t)$	−15.29	6.107	.0125
(15) $ToT_{t-1} \cdot OPEN_{t-1}$	−2.064	2.781	.4583
N (° Free)	618 (599)	s.e.e.	2.328
Adjusted R^2	.430	Durbin-Watson	1.995
Omit (1) to (15):	$p(\chi^2) \approx .0000$	Omit (5) and (6):	$p(\chi^2) \approx .3558$
Omit (1) and (2):	$p(\chi^2) \approx .0000$	Omit (7) and (8):	$p(\chi^2) \approx .0001$
Omit (3) and (4):	$p(\chi^2) \approx .0000$	Omit (9) to (15):	$p(\chi^2) \approx .0429$

Notes: Dependent variable is change in debt (ΔD). Panel-weighted least squares (PWLS) regression with panel-corrected standard-errors (PCSE); p-level is probability of false rejection from a two-sided t-test; s.e.e. is the standard error of the estimate (it and adjusted R^2 are from the unweighted data); Durbin-Watson is from the weighted data. $p(\chi^2)$ are the results of a Wald joint significance test of the terms identified to their left.

3.3.2. Examining the Political-Economy Models against the Economic-Conditions Default

Table 3.4 reports the default model of the economic conditions suggested by tax-smoothing theory plus time and spatial correlation. Substantive

regarding the debt effects of openness and terms-of-trade shocks and of fractionalization and polarization, but that determines only the sign of the respective interaction-term coefficient (see Franzese et al. 1999).

153

Table 3.5. *Tests of Political-Economy Models Added to Economic-Conditions Default*

Theory		Variables Added to Default Model	p-level
(1a)	Weak governments, influence conception	$ENoP_t$, $ENoP \cdot D_{t-1}$, $SDwiG_t$, $SDwiG \cdot D_{t-1}$	.0462
(1b)	Weak governments, veto-actor conception	NoP_t, $NoP \cdot D_{t-1}$, $ADwiG_t$, $ADwiG \cdot D_{t-1}$	.0038
(2)	Inter- and intragenerational transfers	y_{t-1}, ΔOY_t, ΔRW_t, $\Delta(OY \cdot RW)_t$, OY_{t-1}	.0071
(3&4)	Electoral and partisan budget-cycles + strategic	ELE_t, ELE_{t-1}, CoG_t, RR_t, $(RR \cdot CoG)_t$	.0018
(5)	Distributive politics and multiple constituencies	$PRES_t$, FED_t, FED_t^2, $ENED_t$, $ENED_t^2$, AE_t	.0008
(6)	Tax structure and fiscal illusion	FED_t, FED_t^2, $TTAX_{t-1}$, $ITAX_{t-1}$, $CTAX_{t-1}$	.0469
(7)	Macro-institutions	CBI_t, $PRES_t$, FED_t, FED_t^2, $ENED_t$, $ENED_t^2$	.0007
(8)	Nested multiple-constituency, fiscal illusion, and macro-institutions model	CBI_t, $PRES_t$, FED_t, FED_t^2, $ENED_t$, $ENED_t^2$, AE_t, $TTAX_{t-1}$, $ITAX_{t-1}$, $CTAX_{t-1}$	.0001

Notes: As in Table 3.4; *p*-level is from a Wald χ^2 test that the coefficients on all the added variables are jointly zero.

discussion of estimated effects is deferred until reporting the encompass-ing regression for which the ensuing tests argue. The default model per-forms remarkably well. All but one of its variables (growth) are jointly significant in changes and levels and many are individually significant in both changes and levels. Every coefficient is signed as expected, and economic conditions, plus time and space correlation, explain an adjusted 43% of the variance in developed democracies' postwar debt experiences (59.5% of the weighted data). No other model performs near as well with the time and space controls alone, justifying further the economic-conditions model as the default in subsequent analyses.

Table 3.5 examines whether each political-economy theory reviewed here adds statistically significant explanatory power to the economic-conditions default. The Wald test reported is from a regression adding that theory's variables to the economic conditions; it thus tests the default model as a restriction on each of the others. In every case, the evidence rejects that restriction (p $\leq$ .05), favoring adding the political-economy variables. (Notice also that omitting the veto-actor conception is more strongly rejected than omitting the influence conception of the delayed-stabilization model.) The question remains, though, Which to add? Are any of these models redundant, adding explanatory power that some other political-economic considerations wholly encompass?

3.3.3. Examining the Political-Economy Models against Each Other

The political-economic models are *nonnested*; none can be expressed as a restriction on any other simply by setting some coefficients to zero. Davidson and MacKinnon (1981) *J-tests* facilitate direct comparisons of such nonnested linear models of the sort $Y = f(X)$ and $Y = g(Z)$ thus. First, estimate the model suggested by $Y = f(X)$ and save its predictions, $\hat{Y}$; then, estimate the $Y = g(Z)$ model, but add $\hat{Y}$ to that regression. If the coefficient on $\hat{Y}$ is significant, then $Y = f(X)$ rejects $Y = g(Z)$. Reversing the order treats $Y = f(X)$ as the default and determines whether $Y = g(Z)$ can reject it. J-tests thus explore whether a null model *encompasses* an alternative, a significant coefficient on $\hat{Y}$ indicating that the alternative contains empirical information not completely covered by the null. One unfortunate property of J-tests, though, is that rejection of $f(X)$ does not always (or even frequently) imply nonrejection of $g(Z)$ and viceversa. Failure to reject either is also possible. The only conclusive result is when $f(X)$ rejects $g(Z)$ but $g(Z)$ fails to reject $f(X)$ or vice versa; such results imply conclusively that one model encompasses the other. One permissible and reasonable conclusion when $f(X)$ rejects $g(Z)$ and $g(X)$ rejects $f(Z)$, as happens in many cases, is that neither model encompasses the other and therefore that each adds unique information to the other. When each fails to reject the other, conversely, that likely implies that neither adds much unique information.

Table 3.6 presents J-tests of each political-economy model (plus the default) against every other (plus the default). The p-levels give the significance at which to reject the null that the column model encompasses the row model. Read the table thus: "Does the null (column) model encompass the alternative (row) model?" Significant p-levels answer negatively; insignificant results leave open the possibility that the null encompasses the alternative. Most of the table can be summarized very succinctly: nearly every political-economy model rejects each of the others, often overwhelmingly. That is, the data insist that each of the theories adds explanatory power to any of the others with three important exceptions.

Table 3.6. *Pairwise Comparisons of the Political-Economy Theories*

Alternative		Null (1)	(2)	(3)	(4)	(5)	(6)	(7)	(8)
Weak governments (influence)	(1)	XXX	.8056	.0039	.0008	.0017	.1421	.2076	.0470
Weak governments (veto-actor)	(2)	.0136	XXX	.0003	.0000	.0001	.0845	.1092	.0292
Inter- and intra- generational transfers	(3)	.0002	.0003	XXX	.0000	.0000	.0000	.0001	.0000
Political budget-cycles and strategic debt manipulation	(4)	.0000	.0000	.0000	XXX	.0000	.0012	.0017	.0006
Fiscal illusion and budgetary complexity	(5)	.0011	.0010	.0000	.0012	XXX	.0038	.0103	(1.0)
Macro-institutional model	(6)	.0004	.0016	.0000	.0001	.0000	XXX	.5348	(1.0)
Multiple-constituency model	(7)	.0004	.0013	.0000	.0001	.0000	.6441	XXX	(1.0)
Nested institutions, constituencies, and tax structure	(8)	.0000	.0000	.0000	.0000	.0001	.0010	.0008	XXX

Notes: As in Table 3.4. Entries are the probability of a false rejection of the null model in favor of the alternative using a two-sided test. The artificially nested (8) encompasses (5), (6), and (7) by construction.

First, and most theoretically interesting, the data do *not* reject that the veto-actor conception of the weak-government model encompasses the influence conception, yet they easily reject the converse that the influence encompasses the veto-actor conception. Moreover, if one reads across the first two rows, the veto-actor conception more strongly rejects being encompassed by any of the others, whereas, if one reads down the first two columns, it is less strongly rejected as covering the others. Thus, Tsebelis's (1995) veto-actor conception of fractionalization and polarization clearly dominates the influence conception. The other exceptions are that macro-institutional and multiple-constituency models each cannot reject the other encompassing it, but this is unsurprising because each has only one unique variable relative to the other. The failures to reject in the upper-right quadrant are too marginal to merit emphasis. In short, Table 3.6

strongly suggests artificially nesting all the models, that is, compiling all variables into one large equation, using the veto-actor conception that has now emerged clearly to dominate the influence conception.[38]

3.3.4. Estimating and Evaluating the Encompassing Model

Table 3.7 presents the encompassing model results. Figures 1.7–9 can give scale to the substantive magnitudes of estimated effects to be discussed. Table 3.8 in the next section will also help, giving immediate-deficit and long-run-debt effects of permanent, standard deviation increases in the independent variables.

Note first that debt adjusts very slowly and at rates that depend critically on real-interest-net-of-growth rates ($r - \Delta Y$), and the fractionalization (NoP) and, less so, polarization ($ADwiG$) of governments. At sample means (-1.3, 2.1, 1.3), the estimates indicate that the long-run debt effect of any permanent shock[39] is about 75 times its immediate deficit impact. However, where and when real-interest rates rise relative to growth rates and fractionalized, polarized governments retard policy adjustment, this multiplier increases, magnifying the long-run debt impacts of *all* other political-economic conditions. Until otherwise noted, though, all discussion and figures below assume $r - \Delta Y$, NoP, and $ADwiG$ at sample means and that debt is initially stable and all else is constant.

3.3.4.1. Tax Smoothing and Economic Conditions
The coefficient on every economic condition is signed as expected, and most are highly significant, even controlling for all 43 other variables in this large regression. Unemployment changes (ΔUE), for example, relate tightly positively to deficits ($p \ll .01$), and unemployment levels (UE) relate positively to long-run debt ($p \approx .03$). Substantively, a one-standard-deviation unemployment rise, $+3.6\%$, increases deficits immediately (i.e., the first year) by 2% of GDP. Most of the debt-effect would fade within five years if UE returns to its original level, but, if permanent, the estimated effects cumulate to 15% of GDP greater long-run debt. *Real-GDP growth* changes and levels also reduced deficits and debt as expected, though not as significantly

---

[38] Other variables' results are little different using the influence conception.

[39] *Permanent shocks* are increases or decreases in the independent variables that persist rather than reverting to their preshock level. *Transitory shocks*, contrarily, are one-time, one-year increases that revert to previous levels.

Table 3.7. *Encompassing Model of the Political Economy of Public Debt*

Theory	Independent Variable	Coefficients	Standard Errors	p-Levels
(1) Tax-smoothing/economic-conditions	D_{t-1}	−.0321	.0086	.0002
	ΔUE_t	+.5335	.1005	.0000
	UE_{t-1}	+.0570	.0261	.0294
	$\Delta(\Delta Y)_t$	−.0592	.0394	.1330
	ΔY_{t-1}	−.0730	.0487	.1346
	$\Delta(E(r - \Delta Y))_t$	−.0314	.0458	.4931
	$E(r - \Delta Y)_{t-1}$	−.1082	.0467	.0207
	$\Delta((r - \Delta Y)_t \cdot D_{t-1})$	+.0046	.0007	.0000
	$(r - \Delta Y)_{t-1} \cdot D_{t-2}$	+.0039	.0009	.0000
	$\Delta OPEN_t$	+22.49	5.597	.0001
	$OPEN_{t-1}$	+10.83	3.316	.0012
	ΔToT_t	+6.749	1.888	.0004
	ToT_{t-1}	+1.387	.9579	.1480
	$\Delta(ToT \cdot OPEN)_t$	−23.12	5.598	.0000
	$ToT_{t-1} \cdot OPEN_{t-1}$	−9.599	3.125	.0022
(2) Weak governments and delayed stabilization	$ADwiG_t$	+.1122	.1275	.3794
	$ADwiG_t \cdot D_{t-1}$	−.0025	.0039	.5151
	NoP_t	−.3043	.1698	.0736
	$NoP_t \cdot D_{t-1}$	+.0129	.0045	.0046
(3) Inter- and intra-generational-transfers role of debt	Y_{t-1}	+.5506	.3628	.1296
	ΔOY_t	−46.48	10.94	.0000
	ΔRW_t	−27.01	5.931	.0000
	$\Delta(RW \cdot OY)_t$	+47.63	11.52	.0000
	OY_{t-1}	−1.905	.6468	.0034
(4) Electoral and partisan budget-cycles + strategic debt-manipulation	ELE_t	+.4425	.1707	.0098
	ELE_{t-1}	+.5080	.1750	.0038
	CoG_t	+.1273	.0606	.0360
	RR_t	+.9741	.7151	.1737
	$RR_t \cdot CoG_t$	−.1990	.1201	.0982
(5) Macro-institutions	CBI_t	−1.277	.6793	.0607
(6) Macro-institutions and multiple constituencies	$PRES$	−1.333	.4472	.0030
	$ENED_t$	+.0064	.0070	.3608
	$ENED_t^2$	−2.2e^{-5}	2.0e^{-5}	.2696
(7) Multiple constituencies	AE_t	+.8158	.5089	.1094
(8) Macro-institutions, multiple constituencies budgetary complexity, and fiscal illusion	FED_t	−.1013	.0347	.0037
	FED_t^2	+.0022	.0006	.0003

Table 3.7 (*continued*)

Theory	Independent Variable	Coefficients	Standard Errors	p-Levels
(9) Budgetary complexity	$TTAX_{t-1}$	−3.913	3.072	.2032
and fiscal illusion	$ITAX_{t-1}$	+3.987	1.824	.0292
	$CTAX_{t-1}$	−4.859	1.033	.0000
N (° Free)	618 (575)	s.e.e.		2.252
Adjusted R^2	.466	Durbin-Watson		2.001
Omit (2):	$p(\chi^2) \approx .0047$	Omit (7):		$p(\chi^2) \approx .0046$
Omit (3):	$p(\chi^2) \approx .0000$	Omit (8):		$p(\chi^2) \approx .0008$
Omit (4):	$p(\chi^2) \approx .0038$	Omit (9):		$p(\chi^2) \approx .0000$

Notes: As in Table 3.5.

so ($p \approx .13$). Recall, though, that growth reduces debt-service costs, and this effect is highly substantively and statistically significant. Excluding its debt-service-costs effects, a standard deviation growth-rate decline (−2.8%) produces a small (.16% of GDP) immediate deficit increase, but cumulates, if permanent, to a long-run debt impact of +15%, as strong as a similar adverse unemployment shock if less statistically certain ($p \approx .28$).

Thus, the strong rise in unemployment, given these countries' democratic commitments to social insurance and the tendency to deficit-finance a proportion of public expenditures, and the slower real-GDP growth, even excluding its debt-servicing effects, each made substantively important contribution to the dramatic post-seventies reversal of the OECD-average debt path. Figure 3.1 illustrates, plotting estimated debt-responses to permanent and transitory (one-year) adverse shocks. OECD-average growth and unemployment from 1973 to 1990 each worsened by just under a standard deviation compared with the prior period's average. Reading the debt impacts of such sustained lower growth and higher unemployment after 18 years from Figure 3.1 reveals that over half (13±% of GDP) the OECD-average rise in debt from 1973 to 1990 (24±% of GDP, see Figure 1.9) can be attributed to the direct impacts of higher unemployment and slower growth prevailing since 1972.

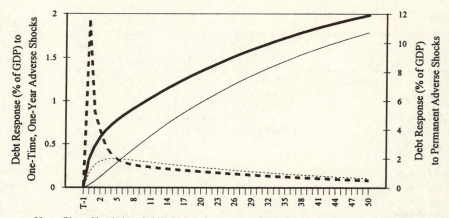

Figure 3.1 Estimated Debt Responses to Adverse Unemployment and Growth Shocks

No such secularly adverse *terms-of-trade* (*ToT*) trend covers this period; rather, the 1973 OECD average of 1.12 falls to .93 in 1981 before recovering to 1.00 by 1988. Thus, the statistically and substantively significant debt effects of *ToT* shocks per se – that is, excluding their impacts on macroeconomic outcomes like growth and unemployment controlled here – are primarily relevant to debt fluctuations, and that especially in more-open economies. A standard deviation adverse *ToT* shock (−.15) produces immediate deficit responses of +.6% of GDP in economies of average openness but +1.5% or more in very open economies. To illustrate, Figure 3.2 plots the estimated debt responses to hypothetical transitory, standard deviation adverse shocks at three trade-openness levels: the sample mean (.47), mean minus, and mean plus one standard deviation (.22, .71). As seen, *ToT* shocks per se have negligible impact at low openness, but appreciable effect at average openness, and adds fairly large deficit-impetus in very open economies.

If a standard deviation adverse *ToT* shock were permanent, it induces +8% of GDP long-run debt at low, +34% at average, and +60% at high

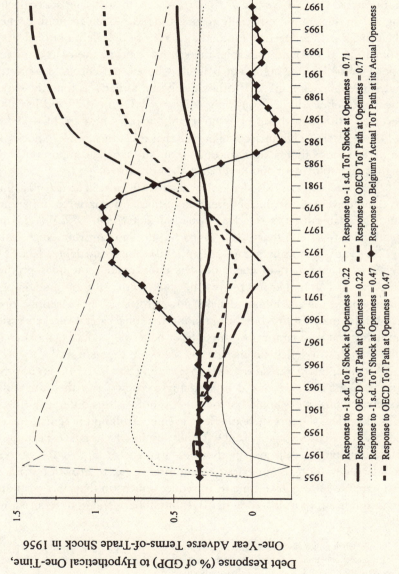

Figure 3.2 Estimated Debt Responses to Terms-of-Trade Shocks at Various Trade Openness

Debt Response (% of GDP) to Actual Paths of OECD-Average,
or Country-Specific Terms-of-Trade Shocks 1956-97

Debt Response (% of GDP) to Hypothetical One-Time,
One-Year Adverse Terms-of-Trade Shock in 1956

— Response to -1 s.d. ToT Shock at Openness = 0.22   · · Response to -1 s.d. ToT Shock at Openness = 0.71
— Response to OECD ToT Path at Openness = 0.22   – – Response to OECD ToT Path at Openness = 0.71
· · · · Response to -1 s.d. ToT Shock at Openness = 0.47   ◆ Response to Belgium's Actual ToT Path at its Actual Openness
– – Response to OECD ToT Path at Openness = 0.47

161

openness, again excluding effects via other outcomes, but *ToT* shocks tend to be temporary (e.g., the two oil shocks). Figure 3.2 therefore gauges longer-term impacts by tracking debt responses at these openness levels to the actual OECD-average *ToT* path. As seen, the debt impact of declining *ToT* in this era was especially apparent in more-open economies where the shocks' path induced an estimated +8.5% of GDP debt rise on average from 1974 to 1985. In principle, the effects could be even larger in very open economies, like high-debt Belgium whose experience is also plotted, but, although Belgium's *ToT* difficulties began as early as the mid-sixties, their peak-effect on debt was only +4.6% of GDP in 1979 and has since reversed. Although this peak is noticeable, it pales next to the +80% of GDP total debt Belgium accumulated in that time. In sum, *ToT* shocks per se were at most, that is, in more-open economies, half as important as the higher unemployment and lower growth they caused.

Trade openness per se also had some impact. Calculated at *ToT* = 1, about its sample average and, in the intention of these price indexes, at its long-run sustainable level, a standard deviation increase in *OPEN* (+.25) has negligible (−.07%) short-term impact but substantively appreciable (+22%) and statistically significant (p < .01) long-run debt effect. The neoclassical explanation would be that more-open economies produce (expectations of) higher future growth, which, with tax smoothing, implies an incentive toward higher deficits now. However, more simply, open economies may just find borrowing in international capital-markets easier, implying that democratic governments, or benevolent social democrats for that matter, will deficit-finance greater shares of expenditure.[40]

When *expected real-interest-net-of-growth*, $(E(r - \Delta Y))$, is positive, governments are expecting debt servicing to grow faster than the ability to repay. Thus, they should borrow less or more as this difference rises or falls. The data support such an effect, even controlling for actual, current debt-service costs $((r - \Delta Y)_t \cdot D_{t-1})$ and despite the crude expectations-formation model reflected in the measurement of $E(r - \Delta Y)$. A one-standard-deviation rise in expected real interest net of growth (+3.1%) is estimated to induce governments to reduce deficits in the short term only an insignificant (p ≈ .49) −.1% of GDP, but, if permanent, to reduce long-

---

[40] Future work could distinguish these possibilities by including openness in the equation estimating expected growth. The openness result is less strong omitting Belgium as a potential outlier but remains easily significant.

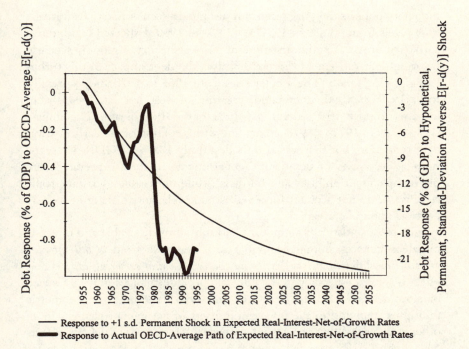

Figure 3.3 Estimated Debt Response to Expected-Real-Interest-Net-of-Growth Rates {E[r − d(y)]}

run debt by 24.4% of GDP (p ≈ .02). Figure 3.3 plots the estimated smooth accumulation of debt in response to a hypothetical, permanent, standard deviation rise and also the estimated debt response to actual OECD-average $E(r - \Delta Y)$ 1955 to 1995.

The OECD-average postwar path of expected real interest net of growth was erratic, though. It fluctuated around −2.7% to −3.5% from 1955 to 1964, implying faster expected real growth than interest, favoring debt issue. As real interest rose in the late sixties, an upward trend −3.6% to −1% from 1965 to 1970 began, muting this prodebt incentive. Rosier expectations dropped $E(r - \Delta Y)$ to −2.7% by 1971–2, but the Bretton Woods collapse and the first oil shock brought nominal interest expectations that regained on inflation and growth, raising $E(r - \Delta Y)$ to −1.9%. Then, with renewed expected growth, $E(r - \Delta Y)$ fell below −3% in 1975–7. The second oil shock, stagflation, and the ensuing conservative shift in monetary policies then triggered and sustained a secular rise to historically high levels from –3.6% in 1977 to +2.9% in 1990. Expected real interest surpassed growth for the first time in postwar history, a gloomy scenario favoring debt retirement. Figure 3.3 plots the debt impact of this turbulent $E(r - \Delta Y)$ path. The secular rises from 1965 to 1970 and, especially, from 1977 to 1990, dominated, creating modest but fairly consistent impetus toward debt reduction (–1±% of GDP at peak). The impact reversed from 1971 to 1978, coinciding with cessation of the early postwar debt reduction, but that was also modest, only +0.4% of GDP. Thus, the rational responses of democratic governments to their expected future interest-payment abilities and burdens, while noticeable and statistically significant, do not account for a very sizable substantive share of OECD postwar public-debt experiences.

The most statistically significant and substantively sizable and interesting debt impacts among economic variables arise from *actual interest/ growth-rate differentials ($r - \Delta Y$) and the implied debt-servicing costs.* Their effect is critical especially in the long run because changes in $r - \Delta Y$ speed or slow debt's adjustment rate and thus help determine the geometric multiplier applying to the long-run impacts of permanent changes in *all* other variables. When real growth exceeds interest, current deficits' effects on debt-to-GDP ratios fade over time (as the denominator grows faster than numerator), but, when real interest exceeds growth, the opposite occurs, so the effects of *any* current prodeficit impetus expand over time. This implies also that the debt effects of $r - \Delta Y$ shocks depend on the outstanding-debt levels at which they occur. At *low debt* (sample mean minus a standard deviation: 11% of GDP), a standard deviation rise in $r - \Delta Y$ (+4.32%) centered on its mean (–3.5% to +.85%) raises current deficits just .23% of GDP but would foster +36% long-run debt if the shift were permanent. At *average debt* (35%), the same $r - \Delta Y$ shift would yield 0.7% greater current deficit and +111% long-run debt (to 146% of GDP!) if permanent. At *high debt* (mean + standard deviation: 59%), such adverse $r - \Delta Y$ shocks would be devastating, inducing noticeable +1.2% deficit and, if permanent, a whopping long-run +136% in debt (to almost 200% of GDP!).

As Figure 3.4 illustrates, the actual historical sequence of average $r - \Delta Y$, rising real interest net of growth in the 1980s as governments shifted to antiinflationary monetary policy following the 1970s terms-of-trade, growth, and unemployment shocks, was almost as nasty a combination. Democracies whose political economies had induced relatively low debt to

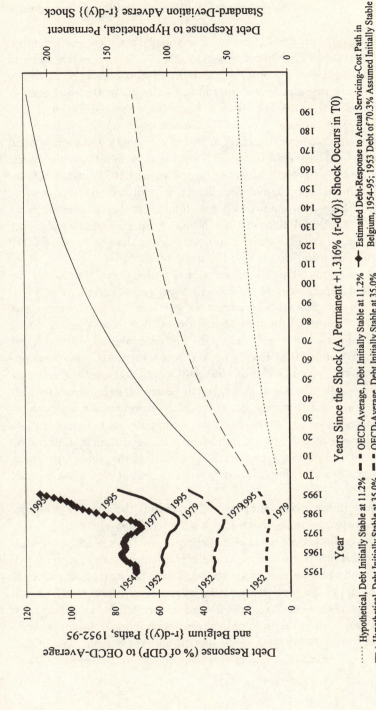

Figure 3.4   Estimated Debt Responses to Debt-Servicing Costs $\{r - d(y)\}$

165

start the period weathered these debt-servicing-cost increases tolerably, but the cumulative debt effects of the adverse shocks and policy shifts in places whose political economies had induced above-average debts are striking in both magnitude and duration. As seen, debt that was initially stable in 1952 at the OECD postwar average (35%), would rise to 47% of GDP by 1995 in response to the OECD-average $r - \Delta Y$ path alone and ceteris paribus. A country starting at stable 59% debt and facing equal conditions would have debt rise to 78% over that period. Importantly, the real-interest-net-of-growth adversity begins around 1978, just as stagflation was hitting its depths, so these effects are hardly merely hypothetical, especially in high-debt countries like Belgium. As shown, starting from Belgium's 70% of GDP debt in 1953, if one assumes it initially stable, the actual Belgian $r - \Delta Y$ path alone would have driven debt to 114% of GDP by 1995, not far from its actual 132% peak in fact.

In sum, economic conditions account for much, but not all, of the postwar debt experiences of developed democracies. Briefly, the 1970s adverse terms-of-trade shocks triggered worsening unemployment and growth, which reversed the immediate postwar debt reduction that most countries had managed largely due to the high growth and low real interest in the 1950s and 1960s. Then, as governments turned to monetary conservatism to combat the inflation aspect of stagflation, real interest rose and high unemployment and slow growth persisted, causing stagflation's debt effects not just to persist but to multiply exponentially as net debt-servicing costs rocketed. These effects were especially pronounced in those democracies whose political economies had induced higher outstanding debt to enter the period. Countervailing effects of the 1980s improving terms of trade and rising expected real interest net of growth were swamped.

However impressively simple but powerful the pure economic-conditions explanation is, Sections 3.3.2–3 conclusively established a statistically significant political side to the story also. Indeed, the time-and-spatial-correlation controls alone could explain an adjusted (unweighted) .33 of the total variance, and, while economic conditions raise that by 29% to .43, the full political-economic model increases it by 39% to .47 of total variance. Thus, very crudely, time and space correlation can tell at most one-third of the story; the full political-economic model tells almost one-half of the story with at most three-fourths and at least one-half of that from economic conditions and at least one-fourth and at most one-half from the political-economic factors.[41] Moreover, recall that this book errs toward understating political effects by assuming economic conditions fully exogenous to politics. Especially critical here: the huge effects of rising real interest net of growth is largely due to governments' antiinflationary policy shifts following the stagflationary seventies.

3.3.4.2. Tax Structure Complexity and Voters' Fiscal Illusion

Proceeding empirically now through the political-economy cycle, begin with fiscal complexity, which democratic policy makers can leverage to obfuscate citizen evaluation of public budgets, fostering voter fiscal illusion that facilitates deficit finance of government activity. The data suggest some fiscal illusion. If voters had rational expectations and no illusions, then either debt and tax structure would be independent or, if one assumes simpler fiscs more efficient, tax complexity would reduce debt by inducing expectations of lower future growth. Contrarily, coefficients on fiscal simplicity (total-tax and central-government shares of total revenue: *TTAX* and *CTAX*) are negative ($p \approx .20$, $p \approx .00$) while that on complexity (indirect-tax share of total revenue: *ITAX*) is positive ($p \approx .03$), suggesting fiscal illusion. Jointly, these effects are statistically ($p \approx .00$) and, for some tax structure shifts, substantively significant. A standard deviation rise in the direct-tax share of revenues (*TTAX* + 2.9% with *ITAX* fixed) reduces next year's debt little, $-.11\%$, and, if permanent, long-run debt only by 8.3% of GDP (both insignificant), but a standard deviation shift in revenue shares from direct to indirect taxes (*ITAX* +9.1% with *TTAX* fixed) significantly raises short-run debt by .36% and, if permanent, long-run debt by 26.6% of GDP. Most dramatically, a standard deviation rise in central-government share of revenue (*CTAX* + 15%) decreases deficits by .73% and, if permanent, long-run debt by 53.6% of GDP.

In principle, then, fiscal-system opacity can importantly influence voter demand for (tolerance of) public debt. However, *TTAX*, *ITAX*, and *CTAX*, being related proportions, tend to move together, so, to evaluate their substantive impact more fully, consider Figure 3.5, which plots estimated cumulative debt-responses to the actual OECD-average paths of these tax structure variables from 1951 to 1990. As seen, tax-structure-varying fiscal

[41] The *worst (best) case* division of explained-variance attributes all shared covariance of economic and political variables with debt to economic (political) variables. Both cases attributed all debt-covariance shared with the time-space correlation factors to simple time-space correlation.

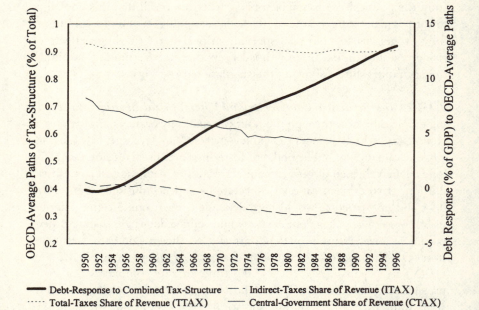

Figure 3.5 Estimated Debt Response to Tax Structure

illusion did, on average, contribute importantly and continually to debt accumulation since 1950. It accounts for a 13% of GDP secular rise as the debt-favoring combination of declining reliance on taxes and, more importantly, of declining central-government shares of total public revenue swamped the debt-hindering effects of declining reliance on indirect taxes.

3.3.4.3. Inter- and Intragenerational Transfers Next in the cycle, consider the structure of interests that voters press upon governments, specifically the wealth and the age & income distributions of the polity. The historical record fails to support inter- or intragenerational-transfers explanations of debt that predict wealthier, more equal, and younger democracies accumulate less debt. The coefficient on aggregate wealth is incorrectly signed and nearly significant ($p \approx .13$). Coefficients on income and age distribution and their product are highly significant ($p \approx .0001$), but neither the change effects nor the level effects of age distribution ($p \approx .003$) correspond with those predictions. Figures 3.6–9 show the estimated effects best (graphically).

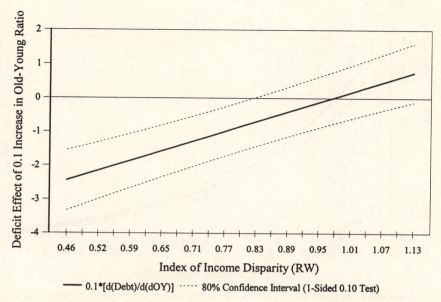

Figure 3.6 Estimated First-Year Impact of the Old-Young Ratio on Debt, as a Function of Income Disparity

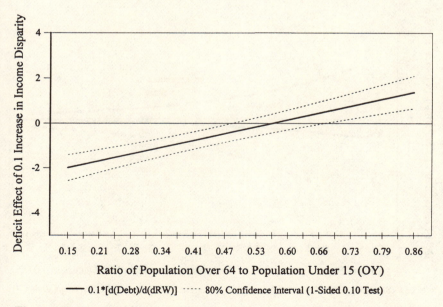

Figure 3.7 Estimated First-Year Impact of Income Disparity on Debt, as a Function of the Old-Young Ratio

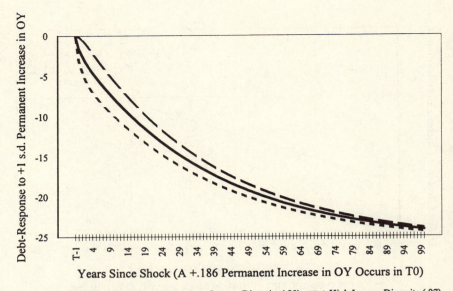

Figure 3.8 Estimated Cumulative Impact of the Old-Young Ratio on Debt, as a Function of Income Disparity

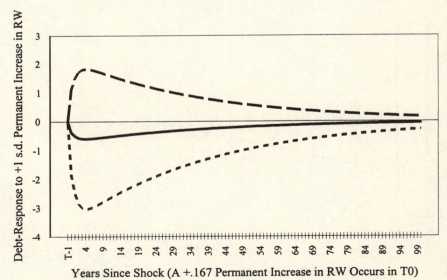

Figure 3.9 Estimated Cumulative Impact of Income Disparity on Debt, as a Function of the Old-Young Ratio

Figure 3.7 plots estimated current-deficit responses to a +0.1 change in the income disparity index, $\Delta RW = .1$, over a meaningful range (mean ±2 s.d.) of the old-young ratio. As seen, the prediction that governments in less-equal economies run higher deficits holds only in older polities; in average-to-young polities, more than half the sample, governments *decrease* deficits in response to increases in income disparity. Worse for the original theory, Figure 3.6 shows that, over most of the sample range of income disparity, estimated deficit impacts of aging societies are negative. Both of these conditional effect-lines do slope in the predicted direction though, so, in the oldest and most unequal polities at least, increases in income disparity and population age do tend to induce higher deficits.

Longer-run hypotheticals provide an even clearer and still less supportive picture. Figure 3.8 plots estimated debt-responses to a permanent, standard deviation (+.19) increase in the old-young ratio at high, average, and low income-disparity levels. The level effects of age distribution, which the data found not to depend on income distribution, dominate these long-run responses and are sizable (−26% of GDP), negative, and significant. Figure 3.9 plots estimated debt responses to a permanent standard deviation (+.17) increase in income disparity at high, average, and low old-young ratios. Despite their transitory nature, the effects of income distribution are also appreciable: +2% of GDP at high and −3% at low OY, peaking 3 to 4 years after the permanent shock, then fading slowly.

What do these results imply for inter or intragenerational-transfers theories of debt? First, the inability to measure the joint age-income distribution is unlikely to underlie the anomalies as omitting the interaction term leaves only the *negative* level relation between OY and debts significant. Instead, the problems with the age- and income-distributional hypotheses may be twofold and distinct to each.

Regarding the income distribution, the original argument neglects that the wealthy typically have political resources beyond their numbers. While income skew may imply a majority that favors debt, Chapter 2 demonstrates that wealth concentration among the politically active generally partially offsets this and, in particular, offsets it more in less-participatory democracies. Moreover, that small groups find it easier to mobilize for political effect (Olson 1965) also suggests that the relation between the numbers of poor and wealthy and their relative political weight could be nonlinear and even nonmonotonic. In extremely inegalitarian economies, and especially in smaller polities, the (very) wealthy may (will) be a small group in Olsonian terms *and* have highly effective means of extraelectoral political participation. Future work might explore some of these conjectures by combining empirical and theoretical insights from this and the previous chapter.

Similar logic may apply to age-distribution results, but, because the 65+ do not compose a particularly small group and need not have wealth advantages in political efficacy, other considerations likely dominate. The original theories may simply wrongly attribute prodebt preferences to older generations in this sample. Sociologically, as Depression survivors, this older generation likely developed a strong distaste for indebtedness, their own and, by analogy, public. Alternatively, reasoning from the denominator in OY, citizens and policy makers in countries with relatively large youth populations should be able to expect greater future growth. Even assuming no productivity growth, larger current youth populations imply more future workers and thus more future output with which to repay debt. Furthermore, educational and other public investments may be needed to realize that future potential fully, and debt finance of such investments may actually be optimal. To explore these ideas, future empirical and theoretical work may benefit by introducing an expected-growth effect of currently youthful populations. The sociological hypothesis might be explored by allowing past bankruptcy frequency and severity to modify the debt response to the 65+ population-share.

3.3.4.4. *Multiple Constituencies and Distributive Politics*   Moving now to the political institutions that mold voter interest-structures into electoral pressures on democratic policymakers, consider the constituency structure arguments. Although the variables derived therefrom are jointly significant (p ≈ .005), the results do not support their expected debt effects so strongly as that suggests. The strongest finding (p ≈ .003) is for presidential systems, with an estimated 1.3% of GDP lower deficit per year than pure parliamentary systems, amassing to −90% if permanent (as is all but true). But, this sizable estimate relies on the presidential systems of just the United States, French Fifth Republic, and Finland. The estimate could also, as noted earlier, more reflect presidents' leadership roles in the budgetary process than their single electoral district. Thus, the presidentialism result is best viewed as tentative.

Excepting the extreme U.K. case where the estimated impact is negligible, greater effective numbers of electoral districts do appear positively related to deficits as the multiple-constituency argument predicts, but not

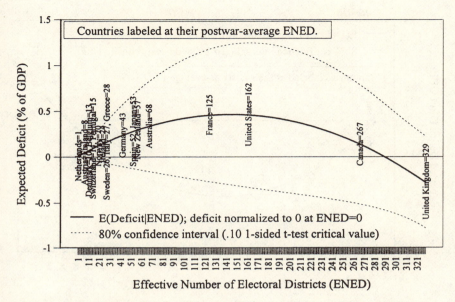

Figure 3.10 Expected Deficit Given the Effective Number of Electoral Districts

significantly so (p ≈ .33 for *ENED* and *ENED²* jointly). The effect could be large – increasing *ENED* from its median (27: about Italy's 1958–90 level) to a standard deviation above mean (115: about France's Fifth Republic level) is estimated to raise deficits by .3% and long-run debt by 21% of GDP if permanent – but the statistical confidence is low. Figure 3.10 illustrates, plotting estimated deficits as a function of the number of electoral districts (i.e., of *ENED* and *ENED²*) from sample minimum, 1 in the Netherlands, to maximum, 329 in the United Kingdom along with an 80% confidence interval, which corresponds to a one-sided .10 *t*-test. The graph clearly demonstrates that, at most, *ENED* produces some small impetus toward greater deficits in the lower half of the sample range, but nowhere are these effects statistically significant.[42]

Worse, as Figure 3.11 shows, the number of federal districts is negatively significantly related to deficits (p ≈ .0004, *FED* and *FED²*), opposite

---

[42] As with interactive effects, the standard errors of nonlinear effects depend on the variable value. Because the significance of the terms involved has already been gauged, holding this conditional effect over its whole sample range to usual two-sided confidence levels is excessive. The one-sided .10 significance *cum* 80% confidence interval used here is an arbitrary compromise.

173

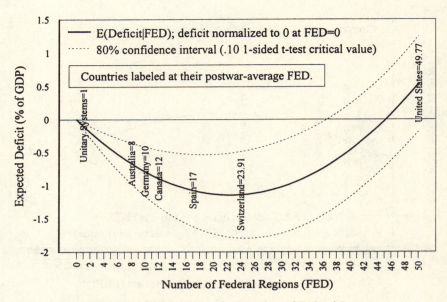

Figure 3.11 Expected Deficit Given the Number of Federal Regions

expectations, excepting the extreme U.S. case where the impact is negligible.[43] These effects are also substantively sizable: raising the number of federal regions from 1 (median) to 12 (Canada, roughly median + standard deviation) reduces *central-government* deficits by .79% and long-run debt by 58% of GDP. The likeliest explanation for this is that effectively federal systems simply transfer fiscal onus to subnational governments where perhaps greater debts occur – indeed, that the estimated effects of both tax *centralization*, *CTAX* (Figure 3.5), and regional *federalization* were negative strengthens the interpretation of the former as influencing voters' fiscal illusion and the latter as inducing fiscal transference to subnational governments.

The most trustworthily direct result for multiple-constituency effects on debt, then, regards agrarian- and ethnic-party government representation (*AE*), which relates weakly positively to deficits (p ≈ .11). If reliable, the estimate implies a standard deviation increase in *AE* (+17%) induces +1.4% of GDP in deficits.

---

[43] The results do not depend on Switzerland alone as reestimation including a Swiss indicator-variable verifies.

In sum, evidence regarding the debt impacts of multiple-constituencies is mixed at best. These macro-institutions are clearly central to explaining persistent cross-national differences in postwar-average debt levels. Presidentialism and federalism correlate strongly with lower central-government debt (although the latter's relation to *total* public debt may differ), and geographically concentrated party support almost as strongly with higher, but the mechanisms of these relationships remain uncertain. Recall that the multiple-constituencies argument was also least well operationalized. One key obstacle to both theoretical and empirical progress is the underexplored link from the theoretical concept of *constituencies*, in which distributive spending and, by extension, debt increase, and empirical observations of *districts*, *regions*, and *parties*, which relate to the former only problematically.[44]

3.3.4.5. *Weak Governments and Delayed Stabilization* Continuing

through the political-economy cycle to the characteristics of the governments formed by elected representatives to make policy, data strongly support the weak-governments theories. The highly significant ($p \approx .005$) positive coefficient on $NoP \cdot D_{t-1}$ indicates that fractionalized governments do retard fiscal-policy adjustment as argued. However, if the number of governing parties are controlled, their partisan polarization bears no significant relation to deficits or debt-adjustment rates ($p \approx .38, .52$ for $ADwiG$, $ADwiG \cdot D_{t-1}$; $p \approx .67$ jointly).[45] NoP and $NoP \cdot D_{t-1}$, contrarily, are significant jointly ($p \approx .012$), as are the two interaction terms ($p < .005$), which correspond to a slow adjustment by *either* fractionalization or polarization hypothesis, as is the sum of the interactive coefficients ($p < .005$), which corresponds to the impact of, for example, adding one party one-CoG-unit away from a single-party government to form a coalition. Thus, the evidence establishes unequivocally that fractionalized governments slow debt-adjustment rates, though, that controlled, government partisan-polarization seems less relevant.

Figure 3.12 shows the estimated current deficit-effect of adding one party to government as a function of outstanding debt levels, plotted over

---

[44] One step for future research must be to bridge this currently wide gap; see Franzese and Nooruddin 1999 for a beginning.

[45] The opposite signs on fractionalization and polarization effects may suggest that they are imperfect, correlated measures of a single underlying factor. Achen (1983) discusses sign reversal in such cases, showing that the more reliable measure attains correctly signed significance and the other reverses signs.

175

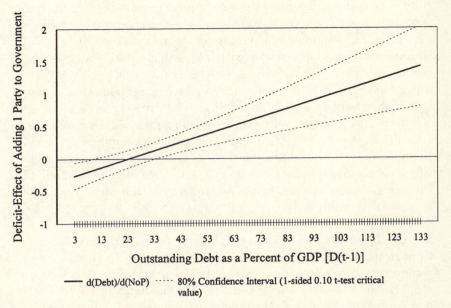

Figure 3.12 Estimated First-Year Deficit-Impact of Government Fractionalization, as a Function of Outstanding Debt Level

the sample debt range, 3% to 133% of GDP.[46] Adding a partisan veto-actor to government reduces deficits when outstanding debt is very low (below 25% of GDP) but raises them at higher debt, quite appreciably so at very high debt. This accords with the revised weak-governments argument suggested earlier; namely: veto actors induce *inaction*. Inaction prevents fiscal adjustments that would reduce deficits when big debts already exist as argued before, but it likely also prevents introduction of new deficit-financed programs when debt is currently low. As seen, standard deviation rises in fractionalization centered on the mean (i.e., +1.2 parties, from 1.5 to 2.7) raise deficits .2% of GDP at average debt, but the same *NoP* increase induces a .2% of GDP deficit *reduction* at low debt and a .55% of GDP increase at high. At very high debt, the deficit effects are

---

[46] These are fractionalization effects holding polarization constant, so the counterfactual specifically is to add a party to government that lies *ideologically within the current governments' partisan (CoG) range.*

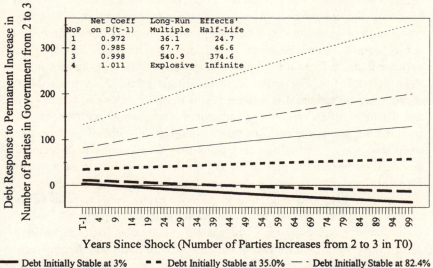

Figure showing plot with table:

NoP	Net Coeff on D(t-1)	Long-Run Multiple	Effects' Half-Life
1	0.972	36.1	24.7
2	0.985	67.7	46.6
3	0.998	540.9	374.6
4	1.011	Explosive	Infinite

Y-axis: Debt Response to Permanent Increase in Number of Parties in Government from 2 to 3

X-axis: Years Since Shock (Number of Parties Increases from 2 to 3 in T0)

— Debt Initially Stable at 3%   ▪ ▪ Debt Initially Stable at 35.0%   — ˙ Debt Initially Stable at 82.4%
— Debt Initially Stable at 11.2%   —— Debt Initially Stable at 58.7%   ····· Debt Initially Stable at 133%

Figure 3.13   Estimated Cumulative Debt-Impact of Government Fractionalization, as a Function of Outstanding Debt Level

quite large; in Belgium, Ireland, and Italy during the late 1980s through the 1990s where debt topped 100% of GDP, for example, adding a party to government is estimated to yield over 1% of GDP larger deficits *per year*.

Indeed, if fractionalization persists, its long-run effects can be as dramatic, and as interesting, as those of debt-servicing $(r - \Delta Y)$ costs. Figure 3.13 plots debt responses to a hypothetical permanent increase from two to three governing parties at six initially stable outstanding debt-levels: 3% (sample minimum), 11% (low), 35% (average), 59% (high), 82% (very high), and 133% (maximum). As seen, if fractionalization were to increase by one permanently in a country where debt was already high, the long-run debt-effects are nearly explosive. In 100 years, if nothing were done to redress the situation, average debt will have become high, high would have reached the prior sample maximum, and very high debt would have reached 200% of GDP and would still be growing at almost 1% per year.

As the table in Figure 3.13 clarifies, these effects, like those of servicing costs, promulgate through fractionalization's hindrance of fiscal adjustment. The long-run debt-effects of *all* other political-economic factors are thus many times larger in democracies with more-fractionalized governments because greater numbers of partisan veto actors retard debt-adjustment rates and so increase the long-run geometric-multiplier on the impacts of permanent changes in *any* public-debt determinant. For example, while single-party U.K. governments more easily shifted fiscal-adjustment costs to oppositions and so navigated the 1970s stagflation and the subsequent stagnation without massive public-debt accumulation, multiparty Belgian and Italian governments were less able to find adjustment plans that distributed costs acceptably among their members and so allowed their debts to skyrocket, each waiting for others to cave. Indeed, *permanent* fractionalization of 4+ governing parties (veto actors) is estimated to produce explosive debt-paths in this sample ($r - \Delta Y$ and $ADwiG$ at sample means and ceteris paribus). In short, government fractionalization, specifically the number of partisan veto-actors, is a critical determinant of debt adjustment paths and thereby interacts with multiple other political-economic factors to play a central and large role in any explanation of the postwar debt experiences of developed democracies.

If one controls for the number of partisan veto actors, their polarization seems less important. However, interaction terms, even such insignificant ones, are hard to interpret fully without graphs, so Figure 3.14 plots estimated deficit-responses to a unit increase in government polarization as a function of the outstanding debt-level, with a confidence interval.[47] Note that the interval widens drastically beyond moderate levels of debt, much more so than the analogous *NoP* interval had relative to its size. This is not because high debt-polarization observations are few, so it could be because the *effect* of polarization at high debt is itself quite variant. One possibility is that "grand coalition" governments, which are highly polarized by nature, may often form when debt is high for the express purpose of reducing it. If they typically fail but occasionally dramatically succeed in that aim, Figure 3.14 would follow; the conjecture may merit future analysis.

3.3.4.6. *Electoral and Partisan Budget Cycles* Turning now to the electoral and partisan incentives of these governments to manipulate fiscal

---

[47] Controlling for the number of parties implies that the hypothetical considered here is a shift in the ideology of a party already in government, or a replacement of one with another, extending the ideological range of the coalition.

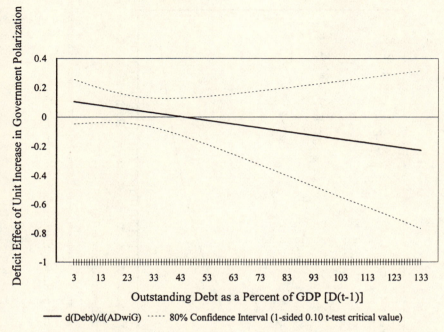

Figure 3.14 Estimated First-Year Deficit-Impact of Government Polarization, as a Function of Outstanding Debt Level

policy, both the year before *and after* an election are found to have significantly higher deficits (p ≈ .01, .004, and .003 jointly). Chapter 2 found similar transfer cycles; Section 2.5 (see also Franzese 2000b) explains such effects and elaborates on the briefer discussion here. Because debt adjusts so slowly and exhibits such strong momentum, the combined +1% of GDP debt-impetus of one election actually grows to +1.6% five years postelection before subsiding. Even this onetime effect is noticeable, but all these democracies have elections minimally every five years, so the debt effect of one election year at best just begins fading when another occurs. Figure 3.15 plots estimated debt response-paths to electoral politics in three-, four-, and five-year-cycle countries, whose elections begin in year T0, and the estimated response to a onetime election.

As seen, democracies averaging one election every three years accumulate 5.8±% higher long-run debt than those averaging one every four years, which, in turn, accumulate 3.5±% higher debt than those averaging one

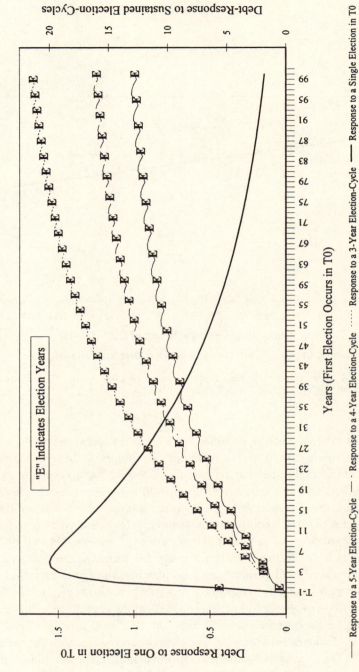

Figure 3.15 Estimated Debt-Responses to One Election and to Regular Elections of Various Frequencies

180

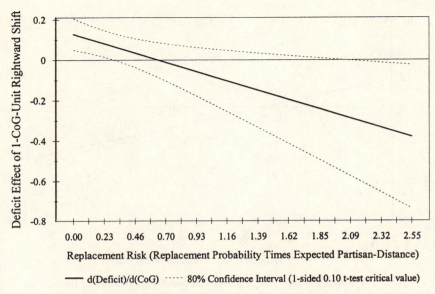

Figure 3.16 Estimated First-Year Deficit-Impact of Government Partisanship, as a Function of Replacement Risk

every five years. Electoral-cycle oscillation is also most visible in five-year-cycle countries and more muted in higher-frequency cycles. The two-year electoral debt-impetuses and the temporal dynamics produce this effect, which may have masked existing electoral policy-cycles in some previous empirical work. Again, reports of the empirical demise of electoral-cycle theories may have been greatly exaggerated.

The significant coefficients on *CoG* and *CoG · RR* (p ≈ .04, .10, jointly: .09) reveal that government partisanship also affects deficits, in ways that may depend on incumbents' perceived replacement risk. As seen in Figure 3.16, at fairly high replacement risk, a 1 − *CoG*-unit rightward shift has partisan theory's expected deficit-reducing effect, which can be noticeable, .4% of GDP at sample maximum of *RR* (2.6), though significance is only marginal in this range. However, a right government produces significantly (p < .1 one-sided), though moderately, *higher* deficits when replacement risk falls below 0.3± (e.g., a 25% risk of replacement by government 1.2 *CoG* units to its left), which covers almost 70% of the sample. Thus, partisan effects are usually relatively small and *opposite* standard

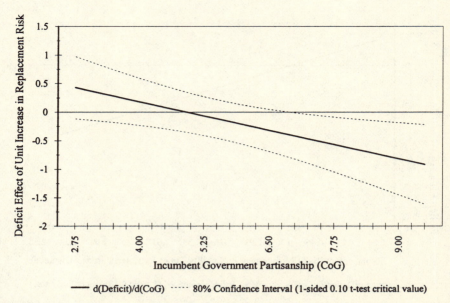

Figure 3.17 Estimated First-Year Deficit-Impact of Replacement Risk, as a Function of Government Partisanship

partisan-theory expectations. The replacement-risk-contingent nature of these partisan debt-cycles is more clearly seen in discussing replacement risk effects.

3.3.4.7. Strategic Partisan Fiscal Policy Strategic-debt-manipulation theories as originally argued find little support in these results.[48] Replacement risk, RR, and its partisanship interaction, $RR \cdot CoG$, are not quite significant (p ≈ .17, .10, jointly: .23), but CoG and $RR \cdot CoG$ do attain marginal significance (p ≈ .09). Thus, replacement risk may alter the partisan goals of strategic governments in manipulating deficit and debt, yet the estimated effects do not suggest attempts to constrain ideologically distant opponents with debt.

Figure 3.17 shows that higher replacement risk induces the left to raise and the right to reduce deficits, as in standard partisan theory but opposite the Persson-Svensson (1989) model. Alesina-Tabellini (1990) instead

---

[48] Lambertini (1999), using different measures and samples, finds likewise.

182

expect *RR* to induce both left and right to raise deficits, yet such positive effects obtain only left of $CoG \approx 5$, about 38% of the sample, and do not attain significance in sample *CoG*-range. Conversely, replacement risk induces *lower* deficits over 62% of the sample and marginally significantly (p < .1 one-sided) at $CoG \gtrsim 6.8$ (18% of sample).[49] Thus, rather than replacement risk enticing democratic governments to manipulate debt to constrain their expected opposition, the evidence suggests that *only* fairly high replacement risk induces left and right to pursue *standard* partisan deficit objectives, and that, with less replacement risk, the *right* amasses and *left* reduces debt.[50] Substantively, such replacement-risk effects on partisan debt-cycles can be noticeable, especially toward the far right. A standard deviation replacement-risk increase (+.33) would push the Japanese LDP (right-most democratic government, *CoG*: 8.9) to reduce deficits .8% of GDP. The same *RR* increase would push U.K. Labour (left-most, *CoG*: 2.8) to raise deficits .4% of GDP. At sample-mean *CoG* (5.54), typical of Democratic-president-led U.S. governments, for example, effects of replacement risk are small and insignificantly negative (−.13%). Thus, partisan-cycle-modifying effects of *RR* clearly dominate whatever debt-as-constraint effects it might have.

Figure 3.18 illustrates these replacement-risk-augmented partisan fiscal cycles clearly, plotting estimated deficits or surpluses as government partisanship oscillates regularly from $CoG = 4$ to $CoG = 7$ (mean ± 1-standard deviation) at frequencies of 1–5 years (sample range of the hazard rate is 0.4–5). Only when governments change frequently, each holding office for one or two years, do partisan deficits follow standard partisan theory; when governments retain office longer, the right runs deficits and the left surpluses, opposite partisan theory. Also opposite the Persson-Svensson model however, the *greater* the replacement risk the *more* the left and right

---

[49] These models were developed to explain presumed exceptional cases of right governments raising and/or left partisans reducing debt. By nature, data covering 600+ country-years swamp exceptional circumstances, *but* these results are almost significantly opposite of expected, suggesting minimally that these theories are insufficient to explain these (not so exceptional as it happens) circumstances.

[50] Joining nicely to Schultz's (1995) finding that incumbents engage in electoral manipulation especially when expecting close elections, this suggests that right and left governments must face stiff partisan competition to use deficits as their core constituencies desire. Sitting comfortably or facing less opposition threat, they are less solicitous or, perhaps, more cavalier about economic efficiency. Powell (1982: ch. 5) argues similarly that partisan differences in policy would only be apparent where regular left-right alternations in government occur.

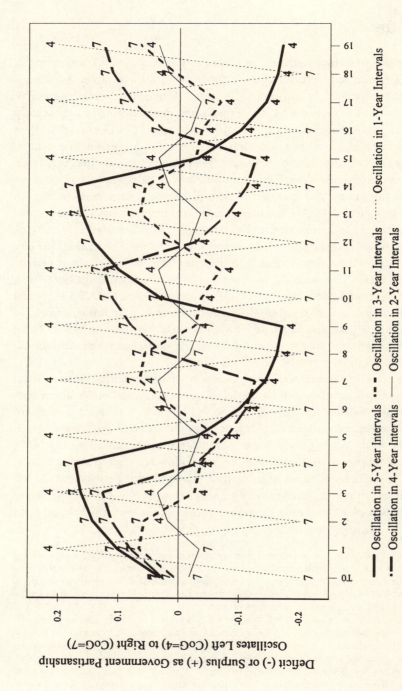

Figure 3.18 Estimated Deficit-Cycles as Partisan Governments Oscillate at Various Frequencies

184

act according to standard partisan theory. Thus, the results suggest both venerable partisan-budget-cycle and newer strategic-debt theories may need revision; perhaps the theories might usefully merge thus.

Theories that predict strategic use of debt to constrain oppositions seem to underestimate the persistence of debt and to ignore the logical connection between replacement risk and the frequency of partisan oscillation. Given extremely slow debt adjustment, right incumbents who expect frequent oscillation in government with the left may be unwilling to raise debt to constrain their opposition because they expect to hold office again soon when most of that debt will still constrain them. Only with less frequent government oscillation will expected time between stints in office suffice to begin considering strategic debt-manipulation. Moreover, only relatively secure right governments could risk their core constituency's ire by amassing debt in trying to augment the electorate's inflation aversion, thereby altering voters' partisan preferences toward them in the future. If, conversely, the left expected to hold office durably, it may wish to retain fiscal maneuverability precisely because its core constituency favors more fiscal responsiveness. Furthermore, a currently secure left can bolster its support by keeping voter-held debt, and thus voter's inflation-default concerns, low, but an insecure left must respond more quickly even to a relatively small downturn because it cannot risk its core-constituency support and because it expects that the right will react insufficiently (by left standards) to the downturn, which will likely persist into the right's quite imminent term. Thus, when both are secure, the left may be less likely than the right to tolerate structural deficits because the left needs fiscal maneuverability to respond to potential future economic difficulties whereas a secure right can spend some current core-constituency votes to buy with debt a larger future core.

This theory of *replacement-risk-augmented partisan budget cycles* accords with the findings here and with some stylized facts from developed democracies' postwar debt experiences. Sweden's long-secure left, for example, kept debt relatively low while it held power, yet Italy's long-secure center-right tolerated unrestrained structural deficits. Meanwhile, left and right were more associated with deficits and surpluses in places like the United Kingdom, where they oscillated with greater regularity. Although evidence regarding this reconsideration and broadening of partisan theory should not be drawn from the sample used to derive the argument, these findings recommend further theoretical and empirical analysis of the conjecture.

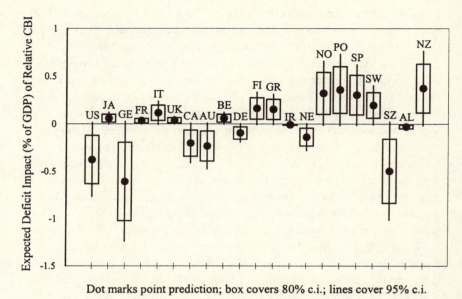

Dot marks point prediction; box covers 80% c.i.; lines cover 95% c.i.

Figure 3.19 Expected Deficit-Impact by Country of Its Postwar Average CBI Relative to OECD Postwar Average

3.3.4.8. Central Bank Autonomy and Conservatism Lastly, central bank independence (*CBI*), that is, autonomy and conservatism, does seem to dissuade governments from accumulating debt (p ≈ .06), likely by reducing access to inflationary default. As the political-economy cycle suggests, governments' policies depend on *CBI*, as on other macropolitical institutions like presidentialism and federalism, because they modify the policy options available or the relations between policies and outcomes. As a set, these political-economic institutions add significant explanatory power to the full model (p ≪ .01); all but *CBI* were discussed already. To complete the empirical tour: a standard deviation increase in CBI (+0.2), about the gaps from the Dutch to U.S. to German banks, yields .26% of GDP lower deficits and 19% lower long-run debt. *CBI* exhibits little cross-time variation, so its impact is best seen by comparing the estimated deficit-impacts of central-banking institutions across countries. As seen in Figure 3.19, *CBI* has been a strong obstacle to debt accumulation in some democracies. (Recall that, assuming average adjustment rates and countries' *CBI*

186

constant, the long-run debt effects are 75± times the immediate deficit-impacts shown.)

3.4. Discussion, Conclusions, and Implications

3.4.1. Discussion and Conclusions

Table 3.8 lists estimated current-deficit and long-run-debt impacts of permanent standard deviation increases in each independent variable, helping to gauge its importance in explaining debt variation across developed democracies since the war. Two prominent facts merit reemphasis. First, although economic conditions were clearly central to the shared experiences of declining debt ratios through the 1970s and rising ratios thereafter, institutional and other political factors were often as important. Second, high rates of real interest net of growth $(r - \Delta Y)$ and highly fractionalized governments (NoP) in particular had disastrous long-run consequences where other political-economic factors induced toward debt. Table 3.8 also reinforces several conclusions from this discussion.

1. Government fractionalization and (less so) polarization, the political factors receiving most prior empirical attention, are often no more important than other the political-institutional factors considered. Veto actors are indeed critical when and where other political-economic conditions push toward higher debt, by delaying its stabilization, but it has more-moderate influence near average debt and even hinders deficits at low debt. Its importance, like that of $r - \Delta Y$, dominates at high debt in magnifying the impacts of all debt determinants, including itself, dramatically. Elsewhere, macro-institutions like central bank independence or presidentialism played key roles in explaining cross-country variance.

2. While the evidence clearly rejects the specific predictions of previous inter- or intragenerational-transfers theories of debt determination, it equally clearly demonstrates some substantive role for age demographics to short- and long-run debt dynamics and of income distribution to short-run dynamics.

3. Despite much recent pessimism, a statistically and substantively clear pre- *and post*-electoral deficit-cycle emerges; plus, election *frequency* has sizable long-run impact (e.g., going from five- to two-year cycles $\Rightarrow$ +21.35% of GDP).

Table 3.8. *Change (Deficit) and Level (Debt) Effects of Variables*

Independent Variable (Standard Deviation)	Current Deficit-Effect of +1sd Shock	Long-Run Debt-Effect +1sd Shock
UE (3.64%)	+0.94*	+15.26*
ΔY (2.78%)	−0.16	−14.91
E(r − ΔY) (3.07%)	−0.10	−24.44*
r − ΔY (4.32%) at mean (*D*) − sd	+0.23*	+35.56*
r − ΔY (4.32%) at mean (*D*)	+0.70*	+110.75*
r − ΔY (4.32%) at mean (*D*) + sd	+1.18*	+185.94*
ToT (.151) at mean (*OPEN*) − sd	+0.24*	−8.39*
ToT (.151) at mean (*OPEN*)	−0.61*	−34.37*
ToT (.151) at mean (*OPEN*) + sd	−1.47*	−60.34*
OPEN (.245) at *ToT* = 1	−0.07*	+22.05*
ADwiG (1.47) at mean (*D*) − sd	+0.12	+7.93
ADwiG (1.47) at mean (*D*)	+0.03	+2.19
ADwiG (1.47) at mean (*D*) + sd	−0.05	−3.55
NoP (1.21) at mean (*D*) − sd	−0.19	−32.95
NoP (1.21) at mean (*D*)	+0.18*	+30.59*
NoP (1.21) at mean (*D*) + sd	+0.55*	+94.12*
y (.372)	+0.20	+15.03
OY (.186) at mean (*RW*) − sd	−3.05*	−25.98*
OY (.186) at mean (*RW*)	−1.57*	−25.98*
OY (.186) at mean (*RW*) + sd	−0.10	−25.98*
RW (.167) at mean (*OY*) − sd	−1.84*	[a]
RW (.167) at mean (*OY*)	−0.37	[a]
RW (.167) at mean (*OY*) + sd	+1.11*	[a]
ELE (1)	+0.95*	+21.35*
CoG (1.54) at mean (*RR*) − sd	+0.20*	+14.39*
CoG (1.54) at mean (*RR*)	+0.11	+8.33
CoG (1.54) at mean (*RR*) + sd	+0.01	+0.82
RR (.334) at mean (*CoG*) − sd	+0.06	+4.36
RR (.334) at mean (*CoG*)	−0.04	−3.15
RR (.334) at mean (*CoG*) + sd	−0.15	−10.66
PRES (.372)	−0.50*	−36.38*
CBI (.202)	−0.26*	−18.90*
FED (from 1 to 12)	−0.79*	−58.30*
ENED (from 27 to 115)	+0.29	+21.08
AE (.171)	+0.14	+10.24
TTAX (2.90%)	−0.11	−8.33
ITAX (9.07%)	+0.36*	+26.55*
CTAX (15.0%)	−0.73*	−53.61*

Notes: Long-run debt-effects are of permanent one-standard-deviation increases in the variables except: *FED* and *ENED* effects are of standard deviation increases from their medians, and *ELE* effects are of increasing its mean from .2 to .5 (from quinquennial to biannual). Current deficit-effects are the first-year impacts of one-standard-deviation increases in the variables except: *ELE* sums the two-year impact of one election. All long-run effects calculated at sample-means of *r − ΔY*, *NoP*, and *ADwiG*, except their own long-run effects, which are for standard deviation increases centered on their means. * = p ≤ .10.
[a] Long-run effects of income-disparity are zero by construction.

4. Partisan budget-cycles, contrarily, play rather lesser roles in explaining the postwar debt experiences of developed democracies, especially near sample means, and usually run opposite of conventional wisdom. Governments' strategic use of *debt* seems to focus on altering the inflationary preferences of voters to gain future partisan electoral advantages, which induces counterintuitive left or right deficits when incumbents are moderately secure in office. Political systems with frequent, regular, and clear shifts in government partisanship, however, can have appreciable partisan *deficit*-cycles that accord with conventional wisdom.

5. Macro-institutional changes – that is, in presidentialism or parliamentarism (*PRES*, –), in central bank autonomy and conservatism (*CBI*, –), in federalism (*FED*, –), and perhaps in electoral districting (*ENED*, +) have small-to-moderate current deficit-impacts but, because they are usually long-lived if not permanent, they can have very large long-run debt-effects. Thus, they have little role in cross-time variation but are often central to cross-country variation.

6. Finally, fiscal-illusion effects, as captured by debt responses to tax-structural complexity, are both statistically and substantively significantly present. Thus, increasing the ease with which voters can evaluate tax burdens that fund public goods and services would seem one simple (technically, perhaps not politically) but effective reform for reducing debt.

In sum, the evidence demands eclecticism in explaining the postwar debt experiences of developed democracies. Data support most arguments proposed in the literature, and almost all the suggested variables can have substantively strong debt impacts under the right (wrong) conditions. Thankfully, the analysis also demonstrated the utility of the cycle of political economy framework for organizing such an eclectic approach.

The pattern of answers to Alesina and Perotti's (1994) two questions – "Why more in some countries than others?" and "Why now and not before" – are now clear. The data respond to the second, mainly, that economic conditions worsened as the 1970s stagnation lingered through the 1980s, driving democratic governments, given their commitments to social insurance, public goods, and macroeconomic management, into debt. Then, as these governments shifted to monetary contraction to control inflation, real interest rocketed relative to the continuing slow growth, magnifying debt growth by increasing interest due on the newly accumulating debt. This had especially dramatic impacts in democracies whose broader political-economic conditions had hindered the reduction of wartime debt in the prosperous 1950s and 1960s, and debt growth was magnified again, especially in such places, by fractionalized governments delaying plans for stabilization. For example, Belgium, Italy, and the United Kingdom entered the 1970s with similar debts, but the U.K.'s single-party governments found shifting fiscal-adjustment costs onto their opposition's constituencies easier, whereas Italy's and Belgium's fractionalized governments were unable to find adjustment plans that would distribute costs acceptably among coalition partners. Thus, the United Kingdom mostly contained debt, but it skyrocketed in Belgium and Italy: see Figures 1.7, 3.4, 3.13.

Another key to answering "Why in some countries and not others?" lies in persistent macro-institutional differences (presidentialism, federalism, central bank independence, etc.) and in fiscal complexity, both of which had small but persistent deficit effects that accumulated to wide debt-level disparities across developed democracies over the postwar era. Election-year politics and electoral frequency played a subsidiary role but a larger one in explaining both short-term fluctuations and long-run differences across democracies than the literature has generally appreciated. Demographics, income, and their distributions also seemed to play some role, but one requiring theoretical revisit. Government partisanship, polarization, and replacement risk also played lesser roles, again with the evidence suggesting theoretical revisions. With all this, the full political-economic model still explains only about half ($R^2 \approx 53\%$, unweighted) of the total variation from 1956 to 1990 of developed democracies' debt experiences, so another half of Alesina and Perotti's two questions remains an unanswered challenge to political economists.

3.4.2. Implications

3.4.2.1. Economic Effects As discussed in Chapter 1, modern economic theory disputes the economic effects of public debt. Neoclassical arguments renew the Ricardian equivalence theorem, implying that public debt will not effect real outcomes (e.g., growth and employment). Neo-Keynesian theories, meanwhile, still imply important, short-run stimulative effects and perhaps more-negative long-run effects. Figure 3.20 offers some simple VAR evidence (see Chapter 2, note 61) on the issue. The reported VAR includes four lags of each endogenous variable – inflation

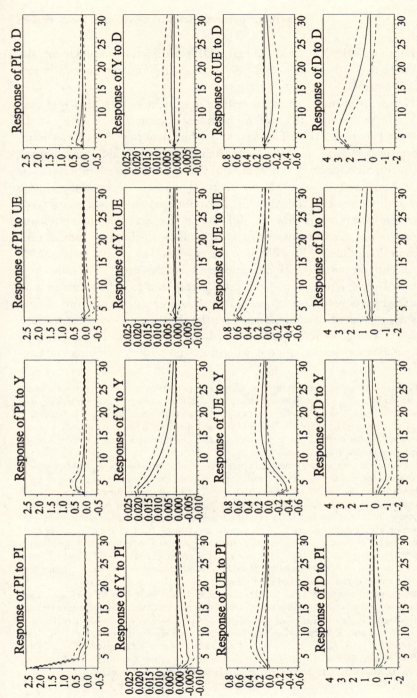

Figure 3.20 Responses of Inflation (PI), Wealth (Y), Unemployment (UE), and Debt (D) to One-Standard-Deviation Innovations (+/− 2 s.e.)

191

(GDP index), the natural log of real GDP per capita, unemployment, and the debt-to-GDP ratio[51] – and also included the full set of country and year indicators.[52]

First, real output (top right) responses to debt suggest that real neutrality of public debt (Ricardian equivalence) cannot be rejected in the intermediate term, 10 to 15 years, but public debt may even foster long-run growth slightly, perhaps by financing necessary public investments. However, even ignoring the latter (and the unemployment response), one should not jump to conclude for neutrality because, as simulations have shown (Freeman et al. 1996), VARs are quite prone to Type II errors (i.e., failure to reject when they should). When, for example, the systematic impact of one variable on another is 10% of the stochastic (residual) variance in that other, VARs will fail to reject when they should 20% to 60% of the time in samples with characteristics like this one.[53] Thus, the two-standard-error range around the growth response to debt in the first 15 years, which contains –0.4% to +0.7%, should give great caution. Simply, this *test* of Ricardian equivalence gave the theorem *the benefit of the null*, which is a huge benefit when standard errors are large. Moreover, even more Keynesian results emerge, with short-run positive and long-run neg-

---

[51] That is also the ordering chosen (see Chapter 2, note 61), reasoning that nominal variables (inflation) are most fluid and so set first, GDP generally reacts more quickly than unemployment, and debt comes last, being a policy variable that, as argued in Chapter 2, is a residual of prior determinations of taxes and spending. That ordering will generally produce smaller effects for debt on other variables than if debt were put earlier; thus, the ordering also expresses scientific caution.

[52] As before, country and year indicators here act as crude controls for systematic exogenous variation and to help ensure that, with these controls, the residuals come close to being drawn from *i.i.d.* random samples so that TSCS VAR can be meaningful (see Chapter 2, note 61). Results are insensitive or somewhat sensitive to excluding year or country indicators. Omitting country fixed effects, the results seem standard or neo-Keynesian (concurring with, e.g., Blanchard 1989, Blanchard and Watson 1986, Galí 1992; cf. Fair 1988, or Sims 1992). That is, short-run wealth responses are notably positive (2.3% increases in debt producing 0.25% to 0.5% growth within five years), but decay rapidly, and, by 10–15 years, become as notably negative. Standard errors were massive in that VAR, but both ends of this pattern approached significance.

[53] Refer especially to tables 1 and 2 of Freeman et al. 1996, which show Monte Carlo Wald-test sizes and powers in various samples with different stochastic assumptions (unit root, co-integration, near integration, stationarity). Sample size is nominally 720 here, but each country has only 35± observations, so the sample could also be viewed as a pool of 21 35-observation VARs. The tables imply that the actual power of a 5% test could be as low as 20%, viewing this sample as 700, or as low as 60%, viewing the sample as 35, advising great caution indeed in interpreting failure to reject as lack of causation.

ative growth effects of debt, if the country and time indicators are omitted (see note 52).

While VARs are prone to Type II errors, they are contrarily reasonably immune to Type I errors (i.e., false rejections).[54] Thus, one can have greater confidence in the significant, negative, short-run responses of unemployment to debt (bottom left: $p \leq .05$ over the first 12± years). Likewise, the significant, positive, short-run response of inflation to debt is trustworthily significant ($p \leq .05$ over the first 8± years). Substantively, each 2±% (exogenous) increase in public debt triggers a 0.4±% spurt in inflation over the next 4± years, which fades by 10–15 years on, and a more durable decrease in unemployment of 0.1±%.

3.4.2.2. *Political Consequences*
Thus, the economic debate about public-debt effects on output (efficiency) may have missed the political-economic (distribution) point. As Hibbs (1977, 1987) argued and demonstrated most thoroughly, people differ by partisanship and class in the relative emphases placed on inflation and unemployment. No one likes either, but the less-well-off have greater distaste for unemployment relative to inflation than the better-off. Figure 3.20 shows that debt has immediate and fairly clear opposite impacts on inflation and unemployment, but not much, less immediate, and less clear impact on output. Yet, while recent theoretical concerns emphasized the efficiency effects of public debt, the rather clearer distributional effects were neglected. Voters and policy makers, no doubt, never lost focus.

The battle over public debt is partially a battle over investment resources. When governments borrow, they remove private-sector investment resources and allocate them politically. Figure 3.20 shows that this affects efficiency less than distribution; public investment favors employment more heavily than the private investment it displaces. As Boix (1998) argues, left and right policies in modern political economies center on these conflicting partisan views of the appropriate investment control and

---

[54] If some variables have or very nearly have unit roots, and if the VAR fails co-integration, Freeman et al. (1996) find VARs can overreject by a factor of 3± in samples of 35 (see previous note). However, the estimated adjustment rates in this VAR (below .9) leave little to fear from this. Freeman et al. (1996) show VARs even with only 35 observations have at worst 1.5 to 2 times actual test-size as nominal. If this sample is viewed as fully 700, actual and nominal sizes are equal unless variables contain unit roots, in which case the 2-to-1 ratio could still occur. However, vector-error-correction models produce substantively similar results here, further testifying to the lack of unit-root concerns in this case.

allocation. The left pursues growth by public investment in human capital, with an eye to equity; the right aims to reduce public economic activity to free private resources to pursue profits and thereby secure growth and efficiency by Adam Smith's free hand, with tangential, if any, equity concern.

Moreover, as Figure 2.22 showed, governments usually debt-finance part of their economic activity, and, as Aghion and Bolton (1990), for example, argued, public debt also creates new or exacerbates existing political cleavages beyond those over the uses to which the borrowing is put. As governments borrowed to meet their commitments to insurance, public goods, and macroeconomic management, they increased public-debt holdings in the polity. That increased fear of default and, for nominal-debt holders, inflation. Thus, as these democratic governments borrowed, they increasingly shifted their electorates' interests toward fiscal and monetary conservatism. Indeed, the evidence here suggests that more-secure right governments, having stronger antiinflation and antidefault reputations than their adversaries, may even have leveraged this strategically, amassing debt to increase antiinflation sentiment in the electorate.

In short, the mounting evidence supports Chapter 1's suggestion that rising public indebtedness reinforced antiinflation versus antiunemployment cleavages in developed democracies. Not only do deficits induce the long-recognized short-run trade-offs between inflation and unemployment, but accumulating debt widens the disparity of interests between the well-off, whose relative dislike of inflation *and* debt holdings are greater, and the less-well-off, whose relative dislike of inflation *and* debt holdings are lower. Thus, battles over fiscal "reform," however couched in language of aggregate efficiency, reflect and sharpen rather than replace partisan and class cleavages long-familiar to political economists.

Finally, rising debts also increasingly constrained the ability of democratic governments to employ fiscal policy to meet their macroeconomic-management commitments. First, Missale and Blanchard (1992), building from Calvo and Guidotti (1990) and Calvo et al. (1991), argue and show that as debt rises, with it rise nominal debt-holders' fears of inflationary default and so the interest premia governments must pay on nominal, domestic-currency debt. These rising premia push policy makers toward reducing or issuing indexed or foreign-currency debt to allay those fears.[55] If, however, the latter suffice to evade premia, and if, as Figure 3.20 found,

---

[55] More precisely, they show a positive correlation between debt shares of GDP and shares of debt that are indexed or foreign-currency denominated.

debt does not harm output, then debt is no constraint on fiscal policy. As long as debt holders remain confident democratic governments will not default outright, no fiscal belt-tightening is ever required.[56] However, indexing and the like only partly evade premia (Missale and Blanchard 1992), so large deficits raise debt *and* the interest rate on it. This vicious circle, whose implications Figure 3.4 illustrated, increasingly limited the democratic governments' fiscal maneuverability for macroeconomic management (Blais et al. 1993, 1996). Meanwhile, as Chapter 2 showed, rising unemployment-insurance generosity was also rendering aggregate fiscal policy increasingly ineffective in that management.

In sum, debt produced a kind of *policy crowding out*; as public economic activity grew over the postwar era to fulfill the democratic commitments, fiscal-policy maneuverability and efficacy both shrunk. As fiscal-policy options closed, governments naturally turned toward monetary policy in attempting to fulfill their macroeconomic-management commitments and toward other putative substitutes for fiscal policy, such as "supply-side" policies (see Boix 1998), which have also come to include a fiercely anti-inflationary stance. This promonetary, antiinflationary policy shift exacerbated public-debt crises in many democracies as already shown. The analysis now turns appropriately to democratic governments' use of monetary policy for macroeconomic management. As shall be shown, other public-sector, institutional, and international developments had simultaneously sapped the effectiveness of and governments' access to that route as well.

---

[56] If this were so without limit, the so-called *no-Ponzi-game* limit-condition, which emerges as part of the solution to the Hamiltonian on which the Ricardian equivalence theorem is based, would not hold.

4

Monetary Management of the Macroeconomy

4.1. *Introduction: Motivation, the Explanandum, and a Road Map*

Through the 1970s into the 1980s, economic conditions deteriorated and public debt and transfers grew dramatically, though variably across countries, increasingly reducing democratic governments' fiscal-policy options and efficacy in fulfilling their commitments to macroeconomic management. With fiscal utility narrowing, and with the Bretton Woods collapse having removed fixed-exchange-rate constraints, governments turned toward monetary policy to combat at least the inflation part of stagflation. Concurrently, the rational-expectations revolution in economic theory (Lucas 1976, 1981) suggested that they could do so at little real cost, provided monetary authorities had sufficient conservative credibility (Barro and Gordon 1983a,b). Policy makers, however far they credited these theories (Hall 1989), seized upon them to justify shifting policy-emphases toward heavy reliance on antiinflation monetary policy, trying to rebuild broad postwar coalitions behind public macroeconomic management for putative efficiency, which stagflation and seeming Keynesian policy failure had weakened. Right parties turned first, easily restructuring their support coalitions behind this new conservative orthodoxy (Hibbs 1987). The left soon followed, caught between high transfers sapping fiscal efficacy (Chapter 2), high debts constraining fiscal maneuverability (Chapter 3), and high capital mobility and flexible exchange rates diminishing Keynesian policy efficacy (Alesina et al. 1994; Garrett 1995, 1998a,b,c, 2000; Garrett and Lange 1991, 1995; Clark 2000; Clark et al. 1998; Clark and Hallerberg 1999; Oatley 1999). They too restructured economic-policy platforms and coalitions, endorsing some macroeconomic, minimally

196

monetary, conservative orthodoxy, and adding an emphasis on public investment, especially in human capital (Boix 1998).

This chapter also shifts focus, to the bottom half of the political-economy cycle (Figure 1.22). That is, it begins with policy and explores how the institutional-structural composition of the polity and economy affect those policies' outcomes. Specifically, it asks theoretically and empirically how the institutional structure of labor and goods markets condition the effectiveness – that is, the real (unemployment) cost – with which credible monetary conservatism lowers inflation. From there, the chapter turns to the end (*cum* start) of the cycle, asking how the conservative monetary-policy shifts and their unemployment and inflation results have altered the interests and institutions that feed back into the electoral stage where Chapters 2 and 3 began.

Scholars interested in institutional-structural aspects of political-economic regulation of unemployment and inflation heretofore confronted two disparate and partially contradictory literatures. One approach derives from modern neoclassical theories of monetary policy and stresses central banks' antiinflation conservatism and autonomy from political authority. Its core claim is that *credibly* autonomous, conservative central banks offer nominal (e.g., inflation) benefits at little real (e.g., employment) cost on average. The other derives from studies of interest intermediation in democracy and stresses union- and, now, firm-bargaining institutions. Its core claim is that coordinated bargaining internalizes certain wage-price externalities, inducing bargaining restraint and thus producing real and, perhaps, nominal benefits. Each literature stresses *one* political-economic institution: the degree of central bank conservatism and autonomy from government or of coordination of wage-price bargaining across the economy. The exclusive foci aided theoretical development, and these are now among the most influential theories in political economy, academically and practically. However, monetary policy making and wage-price bargaining are intimately related activities, so institutional interactions of the sort this book emphasizes are especially likely to condition their conduct and effects.

Building on these well-developed theories and some recent contributions beginning to merge their insights,[1] this chapter demonstrates that

---

[1] Scharpf 1984, 1987, 1991 presage. Franzese 2000a reviews later advances (Agell and Ysander 1993; Bleaney 1996; Calmfors 1998; Cubitt 1989, 1992, 1995; Cukierman and Lippi 1999; De Haan 1999; Forteza 1998; Franzese 1994, 1996b, 1999a,b, 2000; Franzese and Hall 2000; Garrett and Way 1995a; Grüner and Hefeker 1999; Gylfason and

and shows how wage-price-bargaining and monetary-policy-making institutions interact with each other and with sectoral structure in macroeconomic regulation. Specifically, *CBI*, *CWB*, and strong traded relative to public sectors are *substitutes* in producing low inflation and *complements* in producing low unemployment. As stressed throughout this book more broadly, the incentives facing political-economic actors are determined by the *interaction* of the *set* of institutions and other political-economic conditions present in that country-time. Monetary regulation of unemployment and inflation, therefore, rests not on any one institution, *CBI* or *CWB*, but on the wider configuration of relevant institutions operating within the political economy.

The chapter develops these arguments, first, by synthesis, arguing that the insights of *CBI* and *CWB* theories are valuable but derive from contradictory foundations and suggesting a resolution, and, then, by extension, analyzing *CBI-CWB* interactions incorporating the sectoral structure within which they operate. Section 4.2 reviews each literature, offering a heuristic model that reproduces its core theoretical contentions and empirical predictions. Surveying each argument and associated evidence reveals their contradictory theoretical foundations and claims and some lingering empirical issues. Section 4.3 addresses these issues and contradictions, merging *CBI* and *CWB* insights and stressing a sectoral-structure extension, again using a simple heuristic model to guide argumentation. The synthesis and extension restore theoretical coherence and clarify the operation of important institutional-structural interactions in determining the unemployment and inflation effects of monetary policy. Section 4.4 then uses the post–Bretton Woods inflation and unemployment experiences of developed democracies to evaluate the hypotheses, finding strong support. Section 4.5 summarizes and considers implications of the arguments and findings for monetary policy making by a conservative and autonomous European Central Bank (4.5.1) and for the recent collapse of *CWB* in some countries (4.5.2). Section 4.5.3 concludes, returning discus-

Lindbeck 1994; Hall 1994; Hall and Franzese 1998; Iversen 1993a,b, 1994, 1996a,b, 1998a,c, 1999a,b, 2000a, forthcoming; Iversen and Eichengreen 1999; Iversen and Soskice 1999; Jensen 1997; Jonsson 1995; Ozkan et al. 1998; Rama 1994; Sibert 1999; Sibert and Sutherland 1998; Skott 1997; Soskice and Iversen 1998, 2000; Velasco and Guzzo 1999; Yashiv 1989; Zervoyianni 1997). See note 36 for a brief discussion, placing the present analysis in context.

sion to the implications of the arguments and findings for the postwar commitments and continuing democratic conflict over them.

4.2. Monetary-Policy-Making and Wage-Price-Bargaining Institutions

4.2.1. Central Bank Autonomy and Conservatism

Political scientists and economists agree that central bank independence (*CBI*) lowers inflation. Both also define *CBI* as the degree of autonomy of the conservative central bank from the political authority in monetary policy making. From political science, central banks are bureaucratic institutions, led by financial experts who are usually hawkish on inflation, whether socialized to that view or drawn from a population with those interests. Contrarily, governments, especially in democracies, are more responsive to societal pressures favoring inflation. Only the most conservative of governments would be as antiinflationary as its bank, so delegation of monetary-policy authority to central banks reduces inflation. From (neoclassical) economics, monetary policy involves *time-inconsistency problems* that produce pro-inflationary bias if responsive monetary authorities control policy. Credible delegation of monetary-policy authority to autonomous and conservative central banks can serve as a commitment device circumventing the time inconsistencies and therefore the inflationary biases.[2]

4.2.1.1. The Neoclassical Argument and Evidence
Economists in the 1980s and 1990s argued strongly that *CBI* lowers inflation without real costs on average. First, Kydland and Prescott (1977) showed that macroeconomic policy making suffers from *time inconsistencies*; policies, once announced, induce private-sector responses, which, once undertaken, alter the policies desired. Recall from Chapter 2, for example, that once policy makers set taxes and private investors fix capital based on them, policy makers can freely raise capital taxes because already fixed investment cannot be reduced. This suggests that governments cannot credibly

---

[2] From economics, see note 4. From political science, see Hirsch and Goldthorpe 1978; Beck 1984; Woolley 1984; Lindberg and Maier 1985; Mayer 1990; and Goodman 1992. Cf. Posen 1995, 1998, who argues essentially that *CBI* is epiphenomenal, produced by the same conservative forces that reduce inflation.

promise low taxes to investors, so only higher taxes are both optimal for governments, given what private actors expect, and rational for private actors to expect, given optimizing policy makers. Barro and Gordon (1983a,b) extended the logic to monetary policy, noting that if low money growth is announced, and private actors set wages expecting it, policy makers can optimally stimulate the economy with more money growth.[3] Only higher rates are both rational for wage setters to expect and monetary authorities to provide, given each other's expected (re)actions. A conservative central bank enjoying sufficient autonomy from elected governments, contrarily, can announce and provide lower inflation credibly, thereby inducing lower wage-settlements, and so achieving lower inflation without real economic costs (e.g., unemployment) on average.

One can summarize the neoclassical argument for present purposes thus.[4] Nominal contracting (Lucas and Rapping 1969), or *menu* pricing (Mankiw 1985), or *near rationality* or calculation costs in optimization (Akerloff and Yellen 1985) create incentives for monetary authorities to produce *surprise* inflation, thereby lowering real wages and prices and thus spurring employment and real demand.[5] Private actors, however, know these incentives and incorporate their inflationary consequences into wage and price setting. In rational-expectations equilibrium, policy makers cannot systematically surprise private actors, so real wages and prices and thus employment and output are unaffected on average while inflation is

[3] The inflationary motive could arise from an expectations-augmented Phillips Curve or from seignorage on outstanding nominal public liabilities (money or debt), which would be nondistortionary if unexpected.

[4] Kydland and Prescott 1977; Barro and Gordon 1983a,b. Important theoretical advances occur in Rogoff 1985 and Lohmann 1992, showing respectively that, *in this framework*, the median voter actually prefers a more conservative policy maker than herself, and credible conservatism trades output variability for low inflation and so the optimal degree of conservatism is intermediate. Cukierman 1992 gives textbook treatment and advances theory, focusing on uncertainty and information asymmetries, and empirics, providing excellent indices of legal independence. Bade and Parkin 1982 offered the first empirical support; Alesina and Summers 1993 graphically summarized the stylized facts. Eijffinger and De Haan 1996 and Cukierman 1996 give excellent brief theoretical and empirical reviews. See also Rogoff 1989; Alesina and Tabellini 1987; Alesina 1988b; Grilli et al. 1991; Cukierman et al. 1992, and Persson and Tabellini 1994.

[5] Ball and Romer (1990) show nominal rigidities, such as stressed in Lucas's supply model or Mankiw's menu costs, do not suffice to produce real policy effects on the scale suggested in the *CBI* literature. (*CBI* is not their example.) However, they continue, small real rigidities plus small nominal rigidities do provide the necessary effects. Akerloff and Yellen's *near rationality* is both. Any degree of bargaining power in labor or goods markets also generally implies both.

high. If, contrarily, monetary authorities could *credibly* promise to refrain from inflationary surprises, private actors could set lower wages and prices without fear, so once again real wages and prices and thus output and unemployment are unaffected on average, but inflation can be lower than without credibility. Finally, conservative central banks, if insulated from political authorities, can provide such credibility, so *CBI* reduces inflation without adverse real effects on average.

In more detail, the argument begins with the quantity theory of money:[6]

$$m + v = \pi + y \tag{1}$$

Money-supply growth, m, plus percent change in monetary-exchange velocity, v, equals inflation, π, plus real-output growth, y. Abstractly, one can define m, v, π, and y so that the quantity *theory* is an accounting *identity*. The *theory* amounts to assuming velocity and output fixed or exogenous, so money growth *is* inflation by definition, and then, usually, simplifying that policy makers directly control money growth *cum* inflation. Yet, policy makers do not directly control the money supply, much less inflation; inflation is the rate of change of *prices* set in the market, not of *money* "printed" by central banks. Money affects prices intimately, but it does not directly determine them. The assumption is just useful simplification in the neoclassical context, but, while money growth and inflation obviously cannot long diverge, the synthesis and extension stress that policy makers affect inflation only by altering the wages and prices that private actors set (bargain).

Next, monetary-authority preferences – that is, their utility functions, $V^m(\cdot)$ – are specified. Policy makers dislike employment, N, and inflation, π, deviations from some targets, N^* and π^*. A quadratic form and a zero-inflation target simplify:[7]

$$V^m = -\left[\frac{A}{2}(N^* - N)^2 + \frac{1}{2}\pi^2 \right] \tag{2}$$

A, the weight on employment relative to inflation, gauges the *conservatism* of the policy maker: lower $A \equiv$ more conservative. Now, with nominal contracting and market power in labor or goods markets, unexpected money

---

[6] The presentation builds from Cukierman 1992: 27–45.

[7] Replacing employment with other real quantities, like unemployment or output, is trivial. N.b. that equation (2) actually indicates policy makers dislike employment that is *too high*. To avoid this political absurdity, simply assume unobtainably optimistic targets; Cukierman (1992: 28), e.g., assumes $N^* > N$.

growth spurs employment beyond its natural rate, N_n. With expected inflation π^e:

$$N = N_n + \alpha(\pi - \pi^e) \tag{3}$$

Thus, an expectations-augmented Phillips curve describes the economy. Finally, abstracting from uncertainty, growth, real shocks, and changes in velocity, the rational-expectations equilibrium money-growth *cum* inflation rate is found by substituting equation (3) into (2), maximizing over π, and lastly setting $\pi^e = \pi$:

$$m \equiv \pi = \pi_d^* = A\alpha(N^* - N_n) \tag{4}$$

This *discretionary-equilibrium inflation*, π_d^*, is the only rate both rational for private actors to expect, given that they know policy maker incentives, equation (2), and the economy, equation (3), and for monetary authorities to produce, given their preferences, private actors' rational expectations, and the economy. Because π_d^* involves only A, α, N^*, N_n, which private actors know with certainty, expected and actual inflation are equal, $\pi^e = \pi_d^*$, so employment does not deviate from its natural rate, $N = N_n$, in rational-expectations equilibrium. If, contrarily, authorities could credibly commit to lower inflation (e.g., their target), expected would again equal actual inflation (at zero), and equilibrium employment would still be the natural rate, N_n. Call this *commitment-equilibrium inflation*: $\pi_c^* = 0$. Credibly conservative commitments thus reduce inflation without real costs on average.[8] More fully, institutionalizing some effective insulation of a conservative central bank from political authority allows central banks relatively to ignore political demands to respond to shortfalls in employment with monetary expansion,[9] thereby evading the time inconsistency.

That *CBI* lowers inflation at no real cost on average has been extensively, if simplistically, illustrated empirically.[10] The typical procedure

[8] With information asymmetry or uncertainty, *CBI* reduces inflation without affecting *average* real outcomes, but it raises their *variance* because credible conservatism sacrifices monetary stabilization policy, which is effective in this framework when monetary authorities enjoy private information. Still, the core conclusion remains that *CBI* lowers inflation practically costlessly, especially because evidence that *CBI* correlates with more-variant real outcomes has not surfaced. (Alesina and Gatti 1995 suggest that the omission of partisan fluctuations in fiscal policy may account for that null finding.)

[9] To do this, the political costs to current governments of removing central bankers must be raised: longer terms for central bank boards, constitutionally curtailing political review of central bank policy, etc. See the work cited in notes 2 and 4.

[10] Alesina and Summers (1993) provide a graphical summary, and Eijffinger and De Haan (1996) a review.

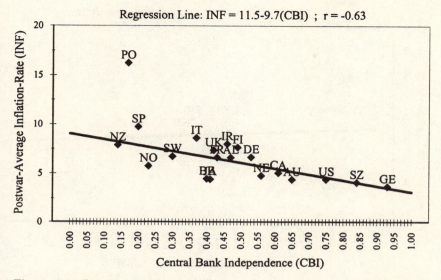

Figure 4.1 Bivariate Regression of Postwar Average Inflation on Central Bank Independence

regresses postwar averages of inflation and of real outcomes on some *CBI* index in cross sections of 15 to 21 OECD countries. Temporal disaggregation or controls for other explanators are rare.[11] As Figures 4.1–2 show, such cross sections find impressively strong negative correlations between inflation and *CBI* and no significant bivariate correlation between *CBI* and virtually any real outcome. Prominent empirical examples have also lent persuasive support. Germany, the United States, and Switzerland have the most notedly independent central banks, and they share the experience of relatively low inflation while their unemployment experiences differ considerably.

Such eloquent argument, simple but striking evidence, and prominent anecdotes have apparently convinced wide academic and policy-making

---

[11] Exceptions exist. Cukierman (1992) draws evidence from decade-frequency data, including developing countries, and an annual VAR with bank-governor turnover and inflation as dependent variables, finding *CBI* to correlate with low inflation and related nominal phenomena but offering no evidence regarding real effects. Cukierman et al. (1992) find beneficial relationships of *CBI* to some real variables in developing countries. Al-Marhubi and Willett (1995) and Havrilesky and Granato (1992) estimate the nominal effects of *CBI* controlling for corporatist structures. See also Eijffinger and De Haan's review (1996); cf. the emerging literature on *CBI* and *CWB* interactions, cited in note 1.

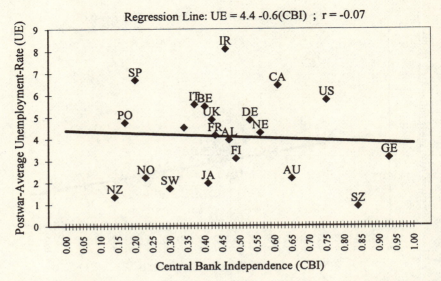

Figure 4.2 Bivariate Regression of Postwar Average Unemployment on Central Bank Independence

audiences. Raising *CBI* rose on policy agendas across the world, and many countries moved in that direction: Italy and New Zealand notably among developed democracies, and then much of Europe as it began preparations for monetary union under a credibly conservative European central bank, whose structure was clearly outlined with these arguments and evidence in mind and with the Bundesbank as template. The wide academic agreement and persuasive evidence helped solidify "responsible" monetary policy as a cornerstone of the macroeconomic conservatism underlying the reformulated left and right policy paradigms as each sought to reconstitute broad political coalitions behind their economic roles (see also Boix 1998).

4.2.1.2. CBI: Lingering Issues and Anomalies The discretionary-equilibrium inflation in equation (4) indicates more than merely that *CBI* reduces inflation. Also, anything that increases the (i) weight, A, that discretionary authorities (governments) put on employment, or (ii) their targeted employment or inflation, N^* or π^*, or (iii) surprise-money efficacy in spurring employment (the Phillips Curve slope, α), or that decreases

(iv) natural rates of employment, N_n, increases discretionary inflation. The degree of *CBI* then lowers the inflation that actually occurs from that discretionary toward the commitment level (i.e., the central bank target; here: zero). Thus, *CBI* lowers inflation *more* the higher discretionary inflation would have been. Points (i) and (ii), for example, suggest that *CBI* reduces inflation more when left than when right parties govern because the left weighs employment more than the right (or targets higher inflation or employment) and so would produce higher discretionary inflation. Points (iii) and (iv) begin to suggest one avenue for synthesizing the *CBI* and *CWB* insights because wage-price-bargaining institutions, both theories agree, alter monetary-policy efficacy, α, and natural rates of employment, N_n.[12] Therefore, defining *CBI* as the degree of central bank autonomy from the discretionary (i.e., political) authority, $0 \equiv$ none to $1 \equiv$ complete, the theory more precisely predicts:

$$\pi = CBI \cdot \pi_d^* + (1 - CBI) \cdot \pi_c^* \tag{5}$$

with π_d^* as in (4) and π_c^* usually assumed a small positive constant (here: zero).

Thus, even the neoclassical argument, properly conceived, concludes that the antiinflationary effect of *CBI* depends on *everything* that would determine discretionary inflation – that is, everything to which governments' and central banks' monetary policies would respond differently. The neoclassical theory of *CBI*, the theory of *CWB*, and the synthesis and extension to be offered here all agree on this point. The implications are pursued further here (and Franzese 1999a,b elaborate more fully), but the *CBI* theoretical literature has ignored them and the oversight translated into previous empirical misspecifications of *CBI*'s inflation effects.[13]

The behavior and public statements of central banks are also somewhat anomalous from a neoclassical view. For example, the U.S. Federal Reserve often contends that it must raise interest to defuse incipient inflationary

---

[12] Equation (4) also gives the antiinflationary benefit, by this theory, of instituting *CBI*, suggesting that governments in country-times with high A, α, and N^*, and low N_n should be more likely to increase *CBI*, ceteris paribus. However, as will be discussed, the evidence suggests moves toward *CBI* have occurred when the antiinflationary benefits of such moves had declined dramatically. See also Franzese 1999b.

[13] Partial exceptions abound; see note 1. Franzese (1999b) first incorporated the theoretically suggested functional form of equation (5) directly into empirical specification and fully into theoretical implications.

pressures, and it often does. However, such *incipient pressures* do not strictly exist in this model because inflation is money growth, which the bank fully controls; nor does relaxing the quantity theory's simplifying assumptions help. Discretionary inflation, π_d^*, depends theoretically on A, α, N^* and N_n as in equation (4), but these do not vary cyclically in a manner consistent with Fed behavior. By *incipient pressures*, the Fed means a strong real economy. Yet, if A and N^* (current government's employment weight and target), α (real efficacy of monetary policy), and N_n (natural rate) vary at all cyclically, it is to lower A, α, and $N^* - N_n$ in booms. That is, when economies push capacity: governments likely fret more over inflation than employment (A or N^* lower); monetary real efficacy, α, likely shrinks due to diminishing returns; and natural rates, N_n, are acyclical by definition. Strictly by this theory, then, *incipient inflationary pressures* should concern central banks *less* in booms than busts, and their contrary statements and behavior are therefore anomalous.[14]

The Bundesbank behaves similarly anomalously, and, moreover, it often directs pronouncements to governments or union-firm bargainers specifically: also inexplicable here. The Bundesbank often threatens (fairly overtly) to respond to wage-price settlements or public budgets it views as inflationary by raising interest.[15] It thus identifies the sources of the *incipient pressures* as governments and wage-price bargainers. Yet, public budgets cannot cause inflation in this model, so the bank has no reason to address the government except as price setter for public goods and employer for public-sector workers. Similarly, wage-price bargainers in the theory simply add expected money growth to desired real-wage growth. Again, no need to threaten a *response*; the bank should simply announce its *fixed* intended money growth.

In sum, the behavior and statements of both Bundesbank and Fed discord somewhat with *CBI* theory. That the Bundesbank speaks differently to different agents than does the Fed is also inexplicable. Moreover, the theory has not been appropriately tested even in its own terms, on the nominal side especially because the empirical model should reflect equation (5), but also on both real and nominal sides because controls were

---

[14] Moreover, financial-stability motives for countercyclical policy (Cukierman 1992: ch. 7) cannot explain the justification the Fed offers for its behavior even if they were considered to explain the actual countercyclicality.

[15] The Fed rarely mentions wage-price bargainers. Examples of quite different Bundesbank announcements are easily found: e.g., Kennedy 1991: 27–53 or *Financial Times*, June 24, 1993, 14.

too-often inadequate. The proposed synthesis and extension starts to resolve these theoretical anomalies – explaining why the Bundesbank speaks differently to different agents is especially key – and to fill these empirical gaps.

4.2.2. Coordination of Wage-and-Price Bargaining

4.2.2.1. Early Theory and Evidence
Another literature, developed concurrently, argued that encompassing (Olson 1965) wage-price bargaining can achieve real and perhaps nominal wage- and price-setting restraint and thereby has beneficial employment and perhaps inflation effects.[16] Simplified and summarized, the argument proceeds thus. One person's wage earnings or output price is another's wage cost or input price; thus, when bargaining occurs in very fragmented units, the externality of one bargain's wages (prices) lowering another's real value is ignored. Therefore, fragmented wage and price settlements are higher than need be because they must include increments to offset expected increases elsewhere in the economy.[17] If, contrarily, bargaining occurs in encompassing or coordinated units, these externalities are internalized, and such increments are neither necessary nor desirable. Thus, *CWB* induces wage-price restraint, thereby lowering unemployment and inflation.

A heuristic model from these first principles will prove useful. Following early theoretical development, start by identifying the value functions of j worker bargaining-units (*unions*), $V_j^u(\cdot)$. The argument's core is that these j unions derive utility from their real consumption value of wages,

---

[16] Headey 1970 presages. Berger 1981, Schmitter 1981, and Lehmbruch and Schmitter 1982 explored related issues in interest intermediation. Lange 1984 and Cameron 1984 laid the foundational work for the economic effects of *CWB*. Regini 1984 and Crouch 1985 explored its political underpinnings, and Scharpf 1984, 1987, 1991, Lange and Garrett 1985, Garrett and Lange 1986, 1989, and Alvarez et al. 1991 with Beck et al. 1993 extend the thread, explicitly analyzing partisan-government interactions with *CWB*. Bruno and Sachs 1987, Calmfors and Driffill 1988, Calmfors 1990, 1993a, Carlin and Soskice 1990, and Layard et al. 1991 provided formal macroeconomic theory for and extension of these arguments. Swenson 1989 and Soskice 1990 introduced key employer-side (price-setting) considerations. Cameron 1984, Lange and Garrett 1985, Bruno and Sachs 1987, and Alogoskoufis and Manning 1988 are the seminal empirical works.

[17] Bargains are thus seen as a multiplayer prisoner's dilemma with most preferred outcome that all but i, then all, none, and lastly only i exercise restraint. This ordering assumes actors have considerable market power since being the only unit to raise wages (prices) is most preferred, which is only likely if employment (demand) is quite wage (price) inelastic, which exactly defines market power.

ω_j^c, and employment prospects, ε_j, which latter improve in, inter alia, aggregate output-growth, y:[18]

$$V_j^u = V^u\left(\omega_j^c, \varepsilon_j(y,\cdot)\right) \quad with \quad V_\omega^u \equiv \frac{\partial V^u}{\partial \omega^c} > 0;$$

$$V_\varepsilon^u \equiv \frac{\partial V^u}{\partial \varepsilon} > 0; \quad \varepsilon' \equiv \frac{\partial \varepsilon}{\partial y} > 0 \tag{6}$$

Define terms in log changes (growth rates) for comparability with the *CBI* literature. Then, growth of real consumption-wages for union j, ω_j^c, is the difference between its nominal-wage growth, w_j, and consumer-prices inflation, π: $\omega_j^c \equiv w_j - \pi$. The value to j of gaining higher nominal-wage-growth for itself, w_j, is then found by substituting that into equation (6) and differentiating with respect to w_j:

$$\frac{dV_j^u}{dw_j} = V_\omega^u\left(1 - \frac{d\pi}{dw_j}\right) + V_\varepsilon^u\left(\frac{d\varepsilon}{dy} \cdot \frac{dy}{dw_j}\right) \tag{7}$$

Equation (7) reflects the *CWB* argument core. Unions perceive more or less real value for any given nominal wage-gain, and so exercise more or less wage restraint, the larger or smaller this derivative.[19] The first right-side term reveals that the real-wage gains j expects from given nominal-wage increases are lower the more aggregate-price inflation, π, moves in line with j's wage inflation, w_j. At one limit, when j's bargain is all-encompassing, this relationship is one-for-one ($d\pi/dw_j = 1$), and there are no perceived real-wage gains. j knows that its own nominal gains are matched across the economy. At the other limit, when j's bargain is too small for j's wages to affect national aggregates appreciably, no single union perceives aggregate inflation to respond to its own settlement ($d\pi/dw_j \approx 0$). In short, individual unions perceive nominal wage-gains to produce real wage-gains in inverse proportion to the share of all wages that their own individual settlements represent.

[18] Unions' wage-restraint incentives come from this sensitivity of their members' employment prospects to aggregate economic performance, which, in turn, responds to settlements in proportion to their encompassingness. The assumed monotonicity of these relationships has been much criticized recently, as will be discussed.

[19] More precisely, they exercise more or less wage restraint the lower or higher the dw_j (wage inflation) at which equation (7) is zero.

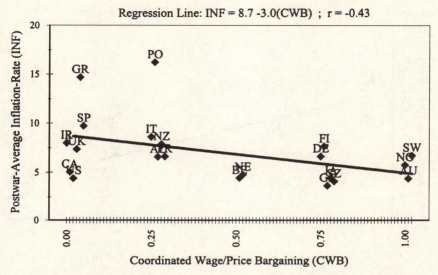

Figure 4.3 Bivariate Regression of Postwar Average Inflation on Coordinated Wage-Price Bargaining

The second right-side term in equation (7) reflects the negative aggregate-output effects of wage gains, dy/dw.[20] Output, y, and thereby j's employment prospects decline with *aggregate* (or average) wage-gains across the economy. Once again, though, *aggregate* output responds more negatively to j's settlement ($|dy/dw_j|$ is larger), and j's employment prospects respond more to *aggregate* output ($|d\varepsilon_j/dy|$ is larger) the more encompassing j's bargain. Thus, on both the real-wage-gain and employment-prospect-cost sides, unions are more disposed to deliver wage restraint the larger the share of the economy's wages their settlement determines.

As with *CBI*, the amassed evidence strongly supported *CWB* arguments (see note 16). Quantitative evidence again typically involved regressing postwar averages of some real (e.g., unemployment) and nominal (e.g., inflation) outcome on various indices of *CWB*.[21] Figures 4.3–4 illustrate. Prominent empirical cases again added convincingly; the Scandinavian

[20] The economics of this relationship was originally unspecified, but Bruno and Sachs 1987, Carlin and Soskice 1990, Layard et al. 1991, e.g., specify more-complete models that retain this general relationship.

[21] Exceptions were less rare (see, e.g., Alvarez et al. 1991; Layard et al. 1991).

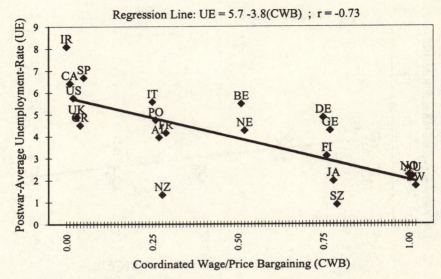

Figure 4.4 Bivariate Regression of Postwar Average Unemployment on Coordinated Wage-Price Bargaining

countries and Austria were well known to have high *CWB* and also admirable unemployment and fair inflation performance. And again, the intuitive argument, striking evidence, and prominent anecdotes put raising *CWB* on many economic policy agendas. Some countries (e.g., the United Kingdom, Italy) scrambled briefly, and mostly unsuccessfully, to institute such bargaining in their economies (Regini 1984).

4.2.2.2. Recent Theoretical Amendments

Two recent advances in *CWB* theory are critical. Swenson (1989, 1991), Soskice (1990), and Layard et al. (1991) drew attention to the, previously virtually ignored, employer role in wage-price bargaining: the *employer-side amendment*; Calmfors and Driffill (1988), Layard et al. (1991), and Calmfors (1993a) drew attention to the market-power assumptions implicit in the preferences assumed by the early *CWB* literature: the *market-competition amendment*.

Reformulate the simple *CWB* model slightly to consider these. Unions do not unilaterally *set* wages; wage-*and-price* settlements are *bargained* between *j* unions and their counterpart employer-groups (*firms*). Thus, analysis of the marginal utility unions perceive from nominal-wage gains, equation (7), does not suffice; those must be weighed relative to the marginal disutility firms suffer from ceding wage gains and to unions' and firms' relative bargaining strengths. Start again with j unions that value real-consumption wages, ω_j^c, and employment prospects, ε_j, which latter are now more sensibly modeled as rising in the output, y_j, of firms j. Firms value profits that, ceteris paribus, decline in *product* real-wages (input costs), ω_j^p,[22] and rise in real demand for their product, y_j. The value functions implied could be written:

$$V_j^u = V^u\left(\omega_j^c, \varepsilon_j\left(y_j, \cdot\right)\right) \quad with \quad V_\omega^u \equiv \frac{\partial V^u}{\partial \omega^c} > 0; V_\varepsilon^u \equiv \frac{\partial V^u}{\partial \varepsilon} > 0; \frac{\partial \varepsilon_j}{\partial y_j} > 0$$

(8)

$$V_j^e = V^e\left(\omega_j^p, y_j, \cdot\right) \quad with \quad V_\omega^e \equiv \frac{\partial V^e}{\partial \omega^p} < 0; V_y^e \equiv \frac{\partial V^e}{\partial y_j} > 0; \frac{\partial y_j}{\partial y} > 0 \quad (9)$$

Equations (8) and (9) clarify that, when firms and unions bargain wages knowing that prices will be marked-up accordingly, they are truly bargaining over how to trade wages against employment, (8), *and* prices against demand, (9). Thus, the employer-side amendment concludes first that the institutional and structural organization of unions and firms are *jointly* influential in *wage-price*-bargaining regulation.

Next, assuming union-firm dyads Nash-bargain over nominal-wage gains, some tedious algebra yields the obvious conclusion that wage-price settlements reflect unions' propensity to offer restraint and firms' rigor in demanding it in proportion to the relative strengths of their current bargaining positions.[23] Thus, derivatives of equations (8) and (9) will suffice,

---

[22] This assumes exogenous productivity growth; given that, assuming zero growth and dropping it from these models is no further loss of generality. Endogenizing productivity growth remains for future research.

[23] Nash bargaining, though a cooperative-game solution-concept, is convenient *and* especially appropriate here because its equilibria are identical to noncooperative games of offers and counteroffers like wage-price bargaining (Rubinstein 1982). Nash-bargaining solutions are found by maximizing bargaining-power-weighted products of bargainer utilities with respect to bargained variables (here, nominal-wage-growth, w_j): $\underset{w_j}{Max}\left[V^u\left(\omega_j^c, \varepsilon_j\left(y_j\right)\right)\right]^a \left[V^e\left(\omega_j^p, y_j\right)\right]^b$. The solution sets a weighted sum of unions' (firms') marginal (dis)utility from nominal-wage gain to zero. The weights reflect the exogenous bargaining powers and the initial utility levels of the unions and the firms: $\frac{a}{V_j^u} \cdot \frac{dV_j^u}{dw_j} + \frac{b}{V_j^e} \cdot \frac{dV_j^e}{dw_j} = 0$. Franzese (1994; 1996b: ch. 4) details derivation of this solution.

211

as those of (7) did, to characterize the implications of coordination for wage restraint; unions (firms) that derive more value (suffer less) from wage gains will settle on less restraint.

Now continue with the amendments by defining the new terms in equations (8) and (9). First, *product* real-wage growth, ω_j^p, is nominal-wage growth minus j's *product*-price growth, π_j, *not consumption*-price growth, π, as in *consumption* real-wages: $\omega_j^p \equiv w_j - \pi_j$. Second, real demand for j's products increases in aggregate income and, as importantly, decreases in j's price growth relative to its competitors' price growth, $\pi_{i(j)}$:

$$y_j = y_j(y, \rho); \quad \rho \equiv \pi_j - \pi_{i(j)}; \quad y_y \equiv \frac{\partial y_j}{\partial y} > 0; \quad y_\rho \equiv \frac{\partial y_j}{\partial \rho} \quad (10)$$

Substituting these definitions into equations (8) and (9) while differentiating with respect to w_j reveals the marginal (dis)utility unions (firms) perceive from nominal gains:

$$\frac{dV_j^u}{dw_j} = V_\omega^u \left(1 - \frac{d\pi}{dw_j}\right) + V_\varepsilon^u \cdot \frac{\partial \varepsilon_j}{\partial y_j} \cdot \frac{\partial y_j}{\partial y} \cdot \frac{dy}{dw_j}$$
$$+ V_\varepsilon^u \cdot \frac{\partial \varepsilon_j}{\partial y_j} \cdot \frac{\partial y_j}{\partial \rho_j} \cdot \left(\frac{d\pi_j}{dw_j} - \frac{\partial \pi_{i(j)}}{d\pi_j} \cdot \frac{d\pi_j}{dw_j}\right) \quad (11)$$

$$\frac{dV_j^e}{dw_j} = V_\omega^e \left(1 - \frac{d\pi}{dw_j}\right) + V_y^e \cdot \frac{\partial y_j}{\partial y} \cdot \frac{dy}{dw_j} + V_y^e \cdot \frac{\partial y_j}{\partial \rho_j} \cdot \left(\frac{d\pi_j}{dw_j} - \frac{\partial \pi_{i(j)}}{d\pi_j} \cdot \frac{d\pi_j}{dw_j}\right)$$
$$(12)$$

The differences in equations (11) and (12) illuminate both amendments. First, note that unions *value consumption* real-wages whereas firms *dislike product* real-wages, so the first right-side term is positive for unions and negative for firms. Thus, simply and obviously, firms are more disposed to demand than workers to offer wage restraint. However, more-coordinated bargains reduce the real-wage effects of any given nominal-wage increase, implying that unions become more disposed to offer but firms *less* to demand restraint as coordination increases. Next, unions' employment concerns virtually mirror firms' output concerns. Interestingly, they differ only by $\partial \varepsilon / \partial y_j$, which describes employment responses to output growth. Thus, wage-price bargaining is partly a struggle over how much labor to input for given output-demand at given prices. Indeed, this facet has become more central to collective bargaining in developed economies as outsourcing and related practices evolved. Third, the term $d\pi_j/dw_j$, describing responses of j's price growth to j's wage growth, reflects markup adjustments (e.g., fixed markups imply constant $d\pi_j/dw_j$). Another part of bargaining, then, is dispute over how far the product-price growth that markets will bear will bleed into wages: that is, over the distribution of productivity growth and extranormal profits between workers and employers. The competitive situation of group j firms crucially impacts the slack available in this struggle. As price competition among j's firms rises, their insistence on wage restraint obviously increases, but, because union j's employment prospects also respond negatively to ρ_j, they mostly share this sensitivity.

Regarding the employer-side amendment, all three points illustrate that both sides of the wage-price bargain are critical; the institutional structure of labor and goods markets *interact* to shape bargainers' incentives. Thus, *wage* bargains are more correctly conceived as *wage-price* bargains; union members' position in the labor market and their institutional structure are no more central to wage-price restraint than firms' goods-market positions and their institutional structure.

Regarding the market-competition amendment, compare equation (7) with (11) and (12). The first two terms of each are equivalent, so all the (dis)incentives for labor to exercise wage restraint from (7) remain in (11), and employers share or exceed them in (12). The third terms reflect market-competition considerations; namely, group j's workers' employment prospects and firms' profits respond positively to j's demand, which responds negatively to its products' relative price ($\partial y_j/\partial \rho_j < 0$). So, the more nominal-wage growth for j induces price increases for its products that competitors less than match (i.e., the greater $\partial \rho_j/\partial w_j$), the more unions (firms) have incentives to exercise (demand) restraint. Thus, as Calmfors and Driffill (1988) argued, incentives for unions and firms to exercise restraint also depend on their expectations regarding responsiveness of competitor's prices to their own.

This suggests that both very competitive and very coordinated structures can induce restraint. At one extreme: with perfect competition in goods and labor markets, competitors' prices do not respond at all to j's settlement, so firms cannot pass the costs of wage gains to consumers, and workers' wages cannot exceed marginal values of labor because employment prospects and profits are radically reduced by any nominal gains exceeding productivity growth (i.e., any lack of restraint). If unions (firms) in perfectly competitive labor (goods) markets exercise such insufficient restraint, they simply become unemployed (lose all their market) with

213

certainty. This incentive's force swamps the externality concerns stressed by early *CWB* work under perfect competition. At the other extreme: with perfect coordination across the entire *domestic* economy, all concerns about prices relative to *domestic* competitors vanish because all *domestic* wages rise with one's own. Thus, incentives for restraint stem *only* from national economic competitiveness considerations, as argued in early *CWB* work. Between extremes, some mix of incentives applies. For example, Calmfors and Driffill (1988) argue that industry-level bargaining allows unions and firms some shelter from competitive-pricing considerations as all their (domestic) competitors are within industry and so have the same wage-price settlement. At the industry level, however, national-level concerns are still mostly ignored because no industry is very large relative to the whole. Thus, they conclude that such intermediate coordination is inferior to both zero and full coordination, giving their famous hump-shaped hypothesis: low and high coordination produce better wage-price restraint than intermediate coordination.

In sum, modern *CWB* theory stresses the economy-wide coordination induced by the institutions and structure of both unions and firms (labor and goods markets). Modern theory also hypothesizes a hump-shaped relation of *CWB* to wage-price restraint. Zero and full coordination produce more restraint than intermediate. However, several theoretical and empirical issues and controversies remain.

4.2.2.3. Lingering Issues and Controversies First, disagreement persists over degrees of coordination actually existing in certain country-times. For example, Soskice (1990) and Calmfors and Driffill (1988) dispute the degree of *CWB* in Japan and Switzerland, the former including employer-side considerations on which account the two countries exhibit higher coordination. Second, a related but wider debate persists over how well union-membership structure might proxy for effective coordination (cf. Garrett and Way 1995a,b; Iversen 1994, 1996a,b; Hall 1994; Franzese 1994, 1996b: ch. 4; Franzese and Hall 2000). Clearly, resolving such disputes remains crucial to theoretical and empirical progress.

Second, the exact shape of the Calmfors-Driffill *hump* and where the set of empirically observed political economics lie on it relative to theoretical zero and full *CWB* also remain unresolved. Theoretically, *CWB* and restraint likely relate curvilinearly, but whether the *hump* declines quickly from zero coordination and rises gradually, vice versa, or anything in between, is ambiguous. Worse, however these measurement issues are resolved, where precisely the resulting *empirical CWB* index places the set country-times relative to *theoretical* perfect competition and full coordination on that ill-defined *hump* also remains unknown. Empirical work, therefore, must use disputed measures, whose placement as a set relative to theoretical extremes cannot be determined, to trace a curve of indeterminate shape, whose only determinate points are those theoretical extremes: a daunting task, especially given the relative lack of cross-time variation in *CWB*, which leaves virtually only cross-sectional leverage.

Some things are known, though. First, because every economy has some collective bargaining while perfectly competitive labor and goods markets would preclude it, theoretical zero *CWB* has never existed. Inversely, theoretical full *CWB* is also nonexistent because, even where one economy-wide bargain exists, some wages and prices are finalized outside it. For example, any international trade excludes full *CWB* because some relevant wages and prices are foreign and therefore set in other bargains. This limits the empirically relevant range, but that merely implies that the evidence will reveal only part of a *hump* whose shape remains unknown. The relationship could easily look linear within the empirical range for example.

Final resolution seems unlikely, but current theory suggests that empirics minimally should incorporate into measures of *CWB* coordination among unions *and firms* across the economy rather than rely solely on union-membership structure[24] and should allow *CWB*-outcome relations to reflect both competition-reducing and internalization-increasing effects of labor and goods market structures. Subsequent analysis uses a subjective index of economy-wide *CWB* that sides with Soskice (1990) and Swenson (1989, 1991) in incorporating employer coordination and that separates competition-reducing from internalization-increasing aspects of market organization, thereby splitting the *hump* into two opposite linear relations.[25]

Important theoretical omissions also remain. Just as key assumptions in *CBI* theory of direct control of inflation by policy makers and of

---

[24] See Golden 1993, Thelen 1994, and Golden and Wallerstein 1995, for further considerations.

[25] Others include measures of coordination and their squares instead. The approach here follows Layard et al. 1991 to distinguish competition-reducing from internalization-increasing aspects, using union density to capture the former and *CWB* the latter. If directly concerned with the *hump*, one should avoid reduced forms and estimate bargaining institution–wage restraint relations directly. That is not tried here or usually elsewhere (but see Alogoskoufis and Manning 1988; Layard et al. 1991).

exogenous natural rates and monetary efficacy hindered analysis of wage-price bargainers' interactions with monetary authorities, *CWB* theory tends to ignore monetary policy or assume it passive, and so is as ill-positioned to consider such interactions. Autonomous, conservative central banks would certainly react to inflationary bargains, so bargainers would likely consider that reaction in settling. Thus, wage-price bargaining and monetary policy making interact, and so must be analyzed jointly. Moreover, *CWB* theory usually assumes homogeneous workers (firms) that have similar interests. Yet, traded-sector actors have very different interests, both in general and vis-à-vis monetary policy, than do private-nontraded- (*sheltered-*) or public-sector actors. Accordingly, analysis now turns to a synthesis and extension that addresses these critical institutional-structural interactions.

4.3. A Proposed Synthesis and Extension: Institutional-Structural Interactions

CBI theory predicts centrally that *CBI* reduces inflation without real costs on average. That has been extensively examined empirically with strong seeming results. However, theory actually predicts more, describing *how much CBI* reduces inflation under different political-economic institutional-structural conditions (see equations (4), (5)), and this has gone unexplored theoretically or empirically. Moreover, central banks' actions and statements seem somewhat to contradict the standard model. Conversely, *CWB* theory predicts centrally that *CWB* induces real and nominal wage restraint, and thus reduces unemployment and inflation. This too received extensive and apparently favorable empirical evaluation. Two recent theoretical amendments introduce employer-side and competitive-exposure considerations in bargaining, but these also complicate empirical exploration. The theory also evolved without considering either possible monetary-policy reactions to wage-price settlements or sectorally differentiated interests among bargainers.

Indisputably valuable insights have emerged from both lines of research, and they appropriately draw attention to monetary-policy-making and wage-price-bargaining institutions as key to the political-economic regulation of inflation and unemployment. However, to consider the effects of democratic governments' shift toward monetary conservatism to fulfill their postwar commitments, analysis must begin to combine their insights, and doing so clarifies the incompatibility of their underlying assumptions. On one hand, *CBI* theory assumes that money growth is price inflation by identity and that both natural rates of employment and monetary efficacy are exogenous, thus not allowing the monetary stance to alter the impact of bargaining institutions on them. If wages and prices are bargained, however, inflation emerges from those settlements, and, if bargaining institutions confer *strategic capacity* (Iversen's apt phrase), bargainers' strategic reactions will condition both monetary efficacy and natural rates. On the other hand, *CWB* theory assumes (usually implicitly) that monetary policy accommodates wage-price settlements.[26] However, because monetary policy aims to restrain inflation, especially if a conservative central bank controls it, it will obviously respond to inflationary settlements, and strategic actors will consider that response in their bargaining. Thus, any synthesis must begin by redressing these contradictions.

4.3.1. A Neoclassical Synthesis

A possible *neoclassical synthesis* was begun earlier.[27] Cukierman (1992) notes that, in standard models, incentives toward surprise inflation only exist and so discretionary monetary-policy creates inflationary biases only if real wages are excessive, possibly due to union monopoly-power.[28] The advance is to endogenize natural rates of employment, N_n, to depend on real-wage excessiveness, ω, and ω to depend on *union power*, *UP*. Specifically, monopolistic unions gain real wages that exceed market clearing, which lowers natural rates and so induces monetary authorities to stimulate. In this framework, unions still set nominal wages simply by adding expected money growth, which remains inflation by identity, to the real wages they seek, but union power increases discretionary inflation because, by equation (4), π_d^* increases in $N^* - N_n$, and now N_n decreases in ω, which

---

[26] Scharpf's (1984, 1987, 1991) work is exceptional (both senses) and in some ways fore-shadowed the emerging synthesis (see note 1, and Franzese 2000a for a review) from which this current offering builds.

[27] Franzese (1999a,b) elaborates the theoretical and empirical implications of this synthesis.

[28] More precisely: "employment [must decrease in] the real wage rate," implying that "own effects [must] dominate cross-effects in labor demands or . . . the supply of labor . . . [to] the competitive segment . . . [must be] relatively irresponsive to the real wage rate, or . . . both conditions [must] hold" (Cukierman 1992: 41). If at least some unemployment is involuntary, then labor supply is effectively in excess, so it is not effectively wage elastic in that vicinity, and the conditions hold.

finally increases in *UP*. Adding that *CWB*, as opposed to *union power*, induces restraint not excess,[29] and natural rates, N_n, become increasing in *CWB* and decreasing in *UP*:

$$N_n = N_n(\omega(UP, CWB), \cdot) \quad with \quad \frac{\partial N_n}{\partial \omega} < 0, \frac{\partial \omega}{\partial UP} > 0, \frac{\partial \omega}{\partial CWB} < 0 \qquad (13)$$

This neoclassical combination of *CBI* and *CWB* logic predicts that: (a) unemployment decreases (increases) in *CWB* (*UP*); (b) inflation decreases in *CBI*, but less (more) so the higher is *CWB* (*UP*); (c) inflation decreases (increases) in *CWB* (*UP*), but less so the higher is *CBI*; and (d) unemployment is unaffected on average by *CBI*. Interactive hypotheses (b) and (c) derive from the combinatorial logic in equation (5): by (4), discretionary inflation increases as natural rates, N_n, fall; by equation (5), *CBI* lowers inflation less the higher is N_n; and, now, by equation (13), N_n increases (decreases) in *CWB* (*UP*). In words, high *UP* or low *CWB* bargainers show less restraint, lowering natural rates of employment, which increases political incentives to create surprise inflation. Thus, because governments holding monetary reins under these conditions would produce higher inflation, the antiinflation gains from delegating to conservative central banks are large (vice versa for low *UP* or high *CWB*). The logical converse also follows: *CWB* or *UP* raises or lowers natural rates, which lowers or raises discretionary inflation, implying that *CWB* or *UP* lowers or raises inflation but less so the higher is *CBI* – that is, the more a conservative central bank rather than a responsive democratic government controls monetary policy. This *neoclassical synthesis* retains real-nominal divides by assuming that bargainers set wages simply by adding expected money growth to real targets, implying that credibly conservative monetary policy, *CBI*, affects only nominal variables.

4.3.2. Strategic Monetary Authorities and Wage-Price Bargainers

As noted earlier, wage-price bargaining and monetary policy making cannot be so compartmentalized. Because bargaining implies market power, bargainers and policy makers can interact strategically. Bargains determine nominal wages *and* prices, leaving the monetary authority dis-

---

[29] Henceforth, "*CWB* produces wage-price restraint" means "*CWB* produces wage-price restraint possibly according to some curvilinear function as yet poorly estimated," and analogously for similar statements.

cretion over how monetary policy reacts to wage-price settlements rather than direct inflation-control. Cukierman et al. (1992), for example, implicitly recognize this, modeling inflation as determined jointly by money and nominal-wage growth[30] and showing empirically that more independent central banks accommodate nominal wage-growth less. Such nonaccommodation amounts to constriction of the *real* money supply and so produces *real* output and employment effects, but strategic bargainers must know this and can react to it. Knowing that inflationary settlements would produce greater real contraction when facing autonomous and conservative central banks than when facing responsive democratic governments, they would reasonably adjust their settlements accordingly. Thus, the neoclassical synthesis does not suffice; *CBI* will produce real effects on average by altering strategic bargainers' behavior.

Such strategic interactions can be analyzed again with the heuristic model of wage-price bargaining, now allowing monetary authorities to respond to wage-price settlements. As before, union-firm Nash-bargaining settlements are weighted averages of their marginal values from nominal increases, so it again suffices to examine these derivatives (simplify by assuming fixed markups):

$$\frac{dV_j^u}{dw_j} = V_\omega^u \left(1 - \frac{d\pi}{dw_j} - \frac{d\pi}{dm} \cdot \frac{dm}{dw_j}\right) + V_\varepsilon^u \cdot \frac{d\varepsilon}{dy_j} \cdot \frac{dy_j}{dw} \left(\frac{dy}{dw_j} + \frac{dy}{dm} \cdot \frac{dm}{dw_j}\right)$$
$$+ V_\varepsilon^u \cdot \frac{d\varepsilon}{dy_j} \cdot \frac{dy_j}{d\rho} \left(1 - \frac{d\pi_{i(j)}}{dw_j} - \frac{d\pi_{i(j)}}{dm} \cdot \frac{dm}{dw_j}\right) \qquad (14)$$

$$\frac{dV_j^u}{dw_j} = V_y^e \cdot \frac{dy_j}{dy} \cdot \left(\frac{dy}{dw_j} + \frac{dy}{dm} \cdot \frac{dm}{dw_j}\right) + V_\varepsilon^e \cdot \frac{dy_j}{d\rho} \cdot \left(1 - \frac{d\pi_{i(j)}}{dw_j} - \frac{d\pi_{i(j)}}{dm} \cdot \frac{dm}{dw_j}\right) \qquad (15)$$

The new considerations are the terms involving dm/dw_j, which is how the jth bargaining unit expects monetary authorities to alter money supply in response to j's settlement: the *monetary threat*. As noted earlier, monetary authorities often announce their intentions not to accommodate excessive wage settlements. If they can make that threat large and credible enough for bargainers to perceive the costs of expected

---

[30] The model is posited as a heuristic simplification rather than derived from bargaining. Later work (Cukierman and Lippi 1999) derives further results explicitly from strategic, inflation-averse bargainers. See also note 1.

monetary-reactions to excessive settlements to outweigh benefits, then the bargainers will refrain from inflationary settlements and the monetary threat need not be enacted. The neoclassical synthesis ends there: credible enough monetary authorities wielding big enough threats achieve low inflation at no average cost. However, with only one money supply, policy makers cannot promise different responses to each settlement; they can only respond to aggregates. Thus, monetary threats, dm/dw_j, as bargainer j perceives them, involve three substantive parts: the severity of the threatened response to aggregates, dm_t/dw, that threat's credibility, c, and the degree to which j expects its settlement to affect aggregates, dw/dw_j:

$$\frac{dm}{dw_j} \equiv \frac{dm_t}{dw} \cdot c \cdot \frac{dw}{dw_j} \tag{16}$$

CBI increases threat credibility, c, but it also raises the trade-off between employment and inflation that monetary authorities will accept since *CBI* means autonomous *and conservative*. Credibly autonomous banks can trade employment for inflation at better rates than can less-credible discretionary (i.e., political) authorities, but conservative banks will also accept higher unemployment for any inflation level if trade-offs must be made.[31] The questions, therefore, are whether trade-offs must be made on average and, if so, at what rates. The answers hinge critically on the institutional and sectoral structure of wage-price bargaining.

Note first that dw/dw_j increases in *CWB*. Thus, when coordination is full, all wages and prices are settled in a central or lead bargain, $dw/dw_j \approx 1$, so that one bargaining unit directly perceives all the monetary threat. Contrarily, with nearly nil coordination, unions and firms do not perceive other wages to rise with theirs, $dw/dw_j \approx 0$, so atomistic bargainers directly perceive almost none of the threat. Examining equations (14) and (15), monetary threats discourage unions from demanding and encourage firms in resisting excessive nominal increases by raising the real costs of such excessiveness. Nonaccommodation reduces real output and demand, which hurts both unions and firms.[32] However, when *CWB* is very low, the

---

[31] Formally, increasing *CBI* not only shifts expectations-augmented Phillips curves inward (credibility), but also increases the slopes at which monetary-policy authorities' indifference curves tangent to Phillips curves (conservatism).

[32] They might also increase the real-wage gains of unions and losses of firms from nominal increases, thereby increasing union propensity to offer but also firm convictions to demand restraint. Others emphasize the former effect (see note 1 and Franzese 2000a for a review), but generally do so in a context that ignores the employer side.

threat times its credibility, $(dm_t/dw) \cdot c$, would have to be extremely high for these aggregate real threats to restrain bargainers without being enacted.

In fact, for small bargaining-units, a little introspection reveals that the threat would have to be *incredibly* large to render threat enactment unnecessary. Suppose, for example, that professors have some market power and bargain with their university, which also has some market power. The professors' market power allows them to demand excessive raises, and the university's allows it to cede them if it must (passing costs to scholarship- and loan-subsidized parents). The settlement will be inflationary. Conservative monetary authorities might threaten to respond to *aggregate* inflationary signs with monetary contraction, but these bargainers are so small relative to aggregates that, from their perspective, however credible the threat, either money will contract or it will not and nothing they do will alter that. Any aggregate threat would have to be catastrophically large for such small units to appreciate sufficiently to restrain their settlements, but any such threat would also be thoroughly *incredible*.[33] No democratic government would so directly and observably impose catastrophe on its economy, nor would it allow a bank to impose catastrophe and remain autonomous. The situation is analogous for all bargaining dyads in strong market positions, so settlements become increasingly inflationary in aggregate as market power rises across the economy. For monetary authorities to restrain inflation, they must enact threats to create recessions to spur unemployment and dampen output enough to cut market power and shift bargaining power toward employers and consumers sufficiently to make ensuing wage and price increases less inflationary. Equilibrium is reached when bargainers seek no more nominal increases than the bank will tolerate.

To smooth nominal and real fluctuations, policy makers will likely try to keep the monetary reins tight enough, and so growth low enough, for market power never to rise sufficiently to allow such recalcitrant bargainers to emerge in the first place. This bargaining perspective thus explains central bankers' concerns over *incipient inflationary pressures*. The pressures emerge from excessive wage-price settlements, which market power allows, and market power in both labor and goods markets increases in booms and decreases in recessions. Monetary authorities can defuse these pressures only by preventing the real economy from becoming *too strong*. Perfect credibility, $c = 1$, and no uncertainty, would imply monetary threats need never be enacted and the neoclassical conclusions would hold. Absent

---

[33] More formally, it would be *trembling-hand* incredible.

perfect credibility, the threats must be enacted at least periodically (although, rather than induce volatility, conservative monetary authorities will likely keep the reins too tight continually). Periodic threat enactment to quash or continual monetary tightness to prevent incipient inflationary pressures implies familiar Keynes/Phillips-type trade-offs between inflation and unemployment. The terms of those trade-offs – that is, how strong the real economy may become before spurring inflationary pressure – depend on the institutional structure of the political economy, especially on that of wage-price bargaining, as equations (14) and (15) clarify.

Simply and generally: anything that lowers the enacted threat required to restrain the aggregate of bargainers improves the trade-off. Monetary-authority *credibility*, higher c in equation (16), is thus unambiguously beneficial because it raises the efficacy of any given threat's size and frequency in restraining all bargainers and so allows lower inflation at higher real strength. Contrarily, *conservativism* – that is, greater willingness to enact larger threats – is ambiguous.[34] Larger threats may be more effective in inducing restraint but may also need to be enacted depending not only on credibility but also on the institutions and structure of bargaining.

For example, equation (16) also reveals that greater *CWB* reduces required threats by increasing dw/dw_j. Coordinated bargainers perceive monetary threats as being more directed at them than do fragmented bargainers, so threats can be smaller and/or less frequently enacted when *CWB* is high than they must be when *CWB* is low. This explains the difference between Bundesbank and Fed behavior. The former addresses wage-price bargainers because German labor- and product-market actors have the institutionally and structurally determined incentives and *strategic capacity* to respond. The Fed simply has no such actors with whom to speak.

Further implications follow from the different impacts of monetary policy across economic sectors. Monetary tightening does two things; it raises interest rates and causes exchange appreciation. Higher interest reduces consumption and investment and so hurts firms and unions in all sectors dependent on domestic demand, that is, private sectors; formally in equation (14) and (15), $dy_j/dy \cdot dy/dm > 0 \ \forall j$ in the private sector. Public-sector workers' employment prospects, however, are unharmed or even benefit by private-demand reduction because public employment is acycli-

---

[34] The degree to which monetary *conservatism* and *credibility* are theoretically and practically separable is an important neglected line of research.

cal or countercyclical: $dy_j/dy \lessgtr 0 \; \forall$ public-sector j. Thus, private-sector bargainers fear monetary contraction more than public-sector bargainers.

The exchange appreciation triggered by enacted threats enters bargainers' calculations three ways. First, appreciation hinders demand for all goods produced domestically and so, again, harms all private-sector but leaves public-sector actors relatively unharmed to benefited: $dy_j/dy \cdot dy/dm > 0 \; \forall$ private-sector j and $\leq 0 \; \forall$ public-sector j. Second, appreciation also implies higher export relative to import prices and thus is especially painful to all units j who compete internationally: $d\pi_{i(j)}/dm < 0 \; \forall$ trade-sector j. Finally, appreciation lowers import prices and so reduces the consumption-price index. This actually benefits consumers and so works against forcing restraint from unions; it is irrelevant to employers as such, though of course as consumers they benefit by it too. This last effect is likely dominated by the first two, but notice that it implies, once again, that employer-led may be more conducive than labor-led coordination to wage-price restraint.[35]

In sum, monetary threat enactment is most costly to private- and especially traded-sector and least costly to (noncompeting) public-sector bargainers. Thus, traded-sector bargainers should be most, sheltered-sector intermediately, and public-sector least responsive to monetary threats. Also, coordinated wage-price bargainers should be more responsive to monetary threats, and all other actors should be more responsive to more-credible monetary authorities. Thus, monetary conservatism reduces inflation most efficiently (i.e., at least real cost) in political economies with credible monetary authorities and traded-sector-led *CWB* and least efficiently in political economies with less-credible monetary authorities and low or public-sector-led *CWB*. So, when stagflation and the rising fiscal-policy constraints described in Chapters 2 and 3 pushed democratic governments toward monetary conservatism in reconstructing their macroeconomic-policy paradigms, they paid real economic costs, even where they endeavored to increase the credibility of that antiinflationary shift, and they paid more in less-organized or public-sector-led economies, and less in more-organized and traded-sector-led economies.

Consider, finally, the interactions of *CWB* with sectoral structure. Public-sector bargainers have little incentive to exercise restraint

---

[35] Others focus on this effect as the center of the wage bargaining–monetary policy interaction, and thus arrive at somewhat different conclusions, but they generally also ignore employer-side considerations (see note 1).

autonomously or to respond to monetary threats; contrarily, traded-sector bargainers are especially disposed toward restraint and to respond to monetary threats. Thus, *CWB* operates differently depending on the sectoral composition of those coordinated (Franzese 1994, 1996b: ch. 4; Garrett and Way 1995b, 1999a,b). *CWB* is most beneficial, both per se and in interaction with monetary authorities, when traded sectors dominate bargaining and public sectors follow. In fact, provided traded sectors continue to dominate, *CWB* is more beneficial the larger the public sectors brought under the traded-sector bargain. Traded-sector bargainers deliver restraint relatively easily and require little monetary threat to enforce that restraint, so the rest of the economy need suffer less to control aggregate nominal increases when *CWB* coordinates traded-sector bargains across the economy. On the other hand, should public sectors dominate, *CWB* is less beneficial on both accounts and may even be costly because it then coordinates the public-sector *lack* of incentives toward restraint across the economy. Public-sector bargainers do not easily deliver restraint but rather require large monetary threats to force it upon them, so the whole economy must suffer more to control aggregate nominal increases when *CWB* coordinates public-sector bargains across the economy. Indeed, provided public sectors continue to lead, *CWB* is more costly (less beneficial) the larger the traded sector because the latter most directly and painfully bears the costs of public-sector lack of restraint and conservative monetary responses thereto.

So, the empirical implications of the proposed synthesis and extension are:

a1. Monetary conservatism, even if credible, has interactive real effects: it is less costly (more beneficial) when wage-price bargaining is coordinated and traded-sector-led and more costly when bargaining is uncoordinated or public-sector-led.

a2. Monetary conservatism, credible or not, has interactive nominal effects: it reduces inflation, though less when bargaining is coordinated and traded-sector-led and more when bargaining is uncoordinated or public-sector-led.

b1. Coordinated wage-price-bargaining has interactive real effects: if traded-sector-led, it is more beneficial the higher *CBI*; if public-sector-led, it is less beneficial (more costly) as *CBI* increases.

b2. Coordinated wage-price-bargaining has interactive nominal effects: it reduces inflation more when traded-sector-led and less (perhaps increasing it) when public-sector-led. The magnitude of these effects is dampened as *CBI* increases.

c. Sectoral structure has interactive real and nominal effects: Traded-sector dominance reduces inflation and unemployment by improving the efficacy of *CWB* in delivering wage-price restraint and so has more beneficial real effects the higher *CWB* and *CBI* and larger (smaller) beneficial inflation effects the higher *CWB* (*CBI*). The public sector operates oppositely and the sheltered sector intermediately.

Thus, this synthesis-and-extension uncover a highly interactive political economy; the effect of any single, institution, structural feature, or policy on real and nominal outcomes depends on the broader configuration of institutions and structures present (see also Hall and Soskice 2000). More specifically, *CBI* can complement coordinated wage-price-bargaining with dominant traded sectors and dominated public sectors in producing beneficial real outcomes; each factor tends to augment each other's efficiency in, for example, reducing unemployment. Conversely, monetary conservatism and *CWB* with dominant traded sectors and dominated public sectors are substitutes in producing beneficial nominal outcomes; either tends to reduce inflation.[36] Thus, when democratic

---

[36] The difference between this and the neoclassical synthesis offered earlier is primarily (a1) that *CBI* has real effects on average. The neoclassical synthesis (which Bleaney 1996, Forteza 1998, Jonsson 1995, de Haan 1999, e.g., also partially derive) maintains real-nominal divides, allowing no real effects of *CBI* on average, interactive or not. Even in that framework though, Calmfors (1998), Ozkan et al. (1998), Sibert and Sutherland (1998), and Sibert (1999) note that, if governments dislike inflation and control policies that can increase the natural rate, *CBI*, by reducing the inflation effects of "bad" policies, reduces government incentives to enact efficiency-improving "reforms." One could extend and summarize the logic: any nominal effects have real consequences if other strategic actors dislike inflation or behave differently depending on the monetary stance. Several others discovered more-direct real effects of a credibly conservative monetary authority interacting with a single, monopoly, inflation-averse union (Cubitt 1989, 1992, 1995; Yashiv 1989; Agell and Ysander 1993; Gylfason and Lindbeck 1994; Rama 1994; Jensen 1997; Skott 1997; Zervoyianni 1997; Grüner and Hefeker 1999). The offering here extends and modifies Franzese 1994, 1996b: ch. 4, by disaggregating the monetary threat in equation (16), addressing the difference between sectoral size and sectoral dominance in bargaining, more directly considering the nominal side (thereby also adding to 1999c,e), and studying the *CWB* interactions with sectoral structure. It extends and modifies Hall 1994, Hall and Franzese 1998, and Franzese and Hall 2000 in these ways and by considering sectoral structure. It differs from Iversen's approach (1993a,b, 1994, 1996a,b, 1998a,c, 1999a, forthcoming), which argues that *CBI* has unemployment benefits when *centralization* (not coordination) is intermediate, unemployment costs when centralization

governments turned toward monetary conservatism after the Bretton Woods collapse, the differing institutions and structure of their political economies rendered that policy shift differently effective in reducing inflation at low real (e.g., unemployment) costs. The next section tests this prediction, using the actual inflation and unemployment experiences of developed democracies in the flexible-exchange-rate era.

4.4. Empirical Evaluation of the Positive Political Economy of Monetary Policy Making and Wage-Price Bargaining

4.4.1. Previous Evidence of Institutional Interactions

Hall (1994), charting postwar average inflation and unemployment by *CBI* and *CWB*, first noted an interactive pattern. Hall and Franzese (1998) summarize that pattern tabularly, showing that postwar average (a) inflation declined in both *CBI* and *CWB*, (b) unemployment declined in *CWB* and rose in *CBI*, and that (c) the unemployment rise per unit *CBI* fell in *CWB* and decline per unit *CWB* rose in *CBI* (real complementarity), and (d) inflation declines per unit *CBI* and *CWB* each fell as the other rose (nominal substitutability). Their multivariate regression analyses, using postwar-average, *decade*-frequency,[37] and annual data in 18 OECD democracies support these conclusions, though point (d) only weakly.

Franzese (1994, 1996b: ch. 4) uses *decade*-frequency data in 21 OECD countries to examine the interactive real effects of *CBI*, *CWB*, and sectoral structure. Beyond the *CBI-CWB* interactions, which give results substantively congruent with and statistically minimally as significant as those in Hall and Franzese (1998), the model includes traded- and public-sector shares of total employment and their interactions with *CBI*. Results very strongly support hypotheses that public employment share and *CBI* inter-

is high, and little effect when bargaining is decentralized (see also Iversen 1999b on the nominal side). The differences, which are smaller than they first appear, arise because his wage bargainers also like wage equality and the hump-shaped hypothesis is incorporated differently. Cukierman and Lippi 1999 and Velasco and Guzzo 1999 also differ in that bargainers dislike inflation for consumption, not employment reasons, and price inflation is money growth, and unions *set* instead of bargain wages. Despite the theoretical differences, their theories (and evidence) broadly agree with the present analysis. See Franzese 2000a for a fuller review, and note 1 for the reference list.
[37] *Decade* refers to Cukierman's (1992) periodization of *CBI* (1950–9, 1960–72, 1973–9, 1980–9), which is the most frequent periodization of *CBI* measures available.

act harmfully in regulating unemployment. Where *CBI* was high, higher public employment share increased unemployment; where *CBI* was low, it reduced unemployment. Traded-sector employment share also seemed to improve unemployment outcomes, more so the higher *CBI*, although that result was somewhat less strong statistically.

Garrett and Way (1995a) criticize these studies for their subjective *CWB* indices. Using collective-bargaining concentration plus coverage, *union strength*, a procedure argued against here following Swenson (1989, 1991), Soskice (1990), they nonetheless find similar institutional interactions. Using five-year-average postwar data in 13 OECD countries, they find *CBI* and *CWB* interact beneficially in regulating inflation (weakest result), unemployment, and growth (strongest).

Garrett and Way (1995b, 1999a,b) more directly evidence the negative effect of public-sector employment on *CWB*'s ability to deliver wage-price restraint than Franzese (1994, 1996b: ch. 4). They estimate curvilinear relations between union strength and unemployment, allowing *public-sector strength*, public-sector shares of total union membership, to alter that curve. Using five-year-average unemployment data from 13 OECD countries, they find a Calmfors-Driffill (1988) hump-shaped relation between union strength and unemployment where *public-sector strength* was low, but also that union strength became increasingly monotonically detrimental to employment as *public-sector strength* rose.

Iversen (1994, 1996b, 1998a,c) also finds that monetary conservatism has real effects that depend on bargaining institutions and vice versa, but the nature of those effects differs from previous findings. He argues that conservatism reduces unemployment at intermediate wage-bargaining *concentration* (not coordination), increases unemployment at high concentration, and has little effect at low concentration (see note 36). His findings in quinquennial data from 15 OECD countries, 1973–93, support these predictions. The sample and the measure of bargaining *concentration* differ from the rest, notably over Japan and Switzerland, the empirical controversy that also divides Soskice (1990) and Calmfors and Driffill (1988). The measure of credible monetary conservatism also differs, using actual exchange-rate movements in conjunction with a *CBI* index. While sample and measurement might explain the differing result, these differences are still disturbing in that Iversen's findings suggest monetary conservatism has unemployment *benefits* over much of the sample and unemployment *costs* in the most-concentrated-bargaining countries: seemingly almost opposite others' results regarding the interaction of *CBI* and *CWB*.

Cukierman and Lippi (1999) find differently from both the earlier and Iversen's results. They regressed five-year averages of unemployment and inflation, centered on 1980, 1990, and 1994, in 19 OECD countries on three indicators of high, medium, and low *CWB*, a *CBI* index, and their interactions, finding that higher *CBI* increased unemployment at low *CWB*, reduced it at mid-*CWB*, and also, though more moderately, reduced it at high *CWB*. This accords with earlier results in finding that monetary conservatism had real costs at low *CWB* and that these costs generally decreased as *CWB* rose, at least from low to middle ranges. It accords with Iversen's results in that *CWB* had unemployment benefits at mid-*CWB*, but disagrees in finding costs at low *CWB* and in finding benefits at high *CWB* that differed little from those at mid-*CWB*.

The present synthesis and extension perhaps resolves these apparent controversies, but here note the points of agreement across all of these empirical efforts. First, all agree that the institutions of wage-price bargaining and monetary policy making interact in the determination of both nominal *and real* outcomes, so neoclassical divisions between the real and nominal economy are unfounded when bargainers and monetary policy makers are both strategic. Second, all agreed that monetary conservatism has more palatable (less unpalatable) real effects when monetary authorities face intermediately coordinated than when they face very uncoordinated bargainers. More disagreement regards high coordination. Third, to the degree nominal effects have been explored, all broadly agree on the effects of all institutional and structural factors considered here. Even the neoclassical synthesis offered earlier shares the agreement on the nominal side.

4.4.2. New Evidence on the Proposed Synthesis and Extension

Several testable hypotheses derive from this heuristic model of monetary policy making and wage-price bargaining in open economies. Empirical evaluation of these hypotheses follows five steps: determining the relevant sample and dependent variables, measuring the variables identified by the theory (and controls), specifying the empirical models suggested by the theory, estimating the model, and inferring from the results about the theory.

These arguments presuppose relatively liberal-market economies, where wages and prices are bargained, quasi-public bureaucratic institutions like central banks can have some effective autonomy from governments, and nationally distinct monetary policy is possible. These considerations suggest restricting the sample to capitalist democracies that are large enough to conduct minimally distinct policy and have strongly developed rule of law: the United States, Japan, Germany, Italy, United Kingdom, Canada, Austria, Belgium, Denmark, Finland, Greece, Ireland, Norway, Portugal, Spain, Sweden, Switzerland, Australia, and New Zealand.[38] Further, the Bretton Woods era of fixed exchange rates limited national monetary autonomy (Clark et al. 1998; Clark and Hallerberg 1999; Franzese 1999a; Oatley 1999). It is excluded for this reason and, subsidiarily, to increase comparability with Iversen's results, leaving annual data in 21 democracies, from 1974 to 1990.

The theory emphasizes three independent variables – *CBI*, *CWB*, and sectoral structure – and the two dependent variables of inflation and unemployment. Consumer-price-index growth rates measure inflation (IMF and OECD sources). Unemployment figures are internationally comparable (OECD sources). *CBI* is measured by a 0–1 index averaging the five most frequently used, and so likely the best, indices in the literature (Cukierman 1992; Grilli et al. 1991; Bade and Parkin 1982). This averaging procedure increases sample coverage and, under reasonable assumptions, reduces measurement error (see Chapter 3, note 28). *CWB* is Hall and Franzese's (1998) subjective index of wage-price-bargaining coordination, valued {0,.25,.5,.75,1}, which is built from Soskice's (1990) index of economy-wide coordination (EWC) and Layard et al.'s (1991) indices of business and labor organization (BO, LO) and secondary sources. It is extended here, using Layard et al. (1991), to Greece, Portugal, and Spain (0, .25, 0). Finally, the *desired* public-, sheltered-, and traded-sector data are shares of employment covered by wage-price bargaining in sectors whose products respectively do not compete in the market, do not compete with foreign products, and compete with foreign and domestic products. As the theory predicts oppositely for the traded and public sectors with the sheltered sector intermediate, public-sector divided by traded-sector employment efficiently summarizes the required information. The *available* data, however, are government employment and employment by

---

[38] Indicator variables for Greece, Portugal, and Spain, and one for authoritarian periods therein, are included in both equations, acknowledging those country-years' ambiguous membership in the sample.

single-digit ISIC sectors as shares of total (OECD sources).[39] Therefore, government, G, and manufacturing, M, sectors will proxy for public and traded sectors, yielding a summary sectoral measure: $S \equiv G/M$.

The unemployment (U) and inflation (π) equations specified here also include several controls, the results for which are suppressed as nonessential to the analysis: (1) time-serial controls,[40] (2) indicators for Greece, Spain, Portugal, and for their authoritarian periods, (3) trade-openness (O), (4) terms of trade (T), (5) their product ($O \cdot T$), (6) natural-log real-GDP per capita (Y), (7) government partisanship (CoG), (8) pre- and post-election-year indicators (ELE), and (9) union density (UD). The inflation model also adds (10) financial sector share of employment (F, OECD sources) to consider Posen's (1995, 1998) arguments and (11a) average inflation in the other sample countries each year (inflation abroad: π_a). The unemployment model likewise adds (11b) average unemployment abroad (U_a). Previous chapters detailed these controls. Note especially that union density (union share of total employment) is controlled, as discussed earlier, to distinguish the competition-reducing effects of labor market organization (UD) from the internalization-increasing effects of coordinated bargaining (CWB). This separates the Calmfors-Driffill (1988) hump into two oppositely signed linear relations. In the subsequent text, X_1 refers to controls (1) and (2) and X_2 to controls (3)–(11).[41]

To specify the empirical models, note first from equation (5) that observed inflation is a weighted average of what would have occurred if the responsive, democratic government fully controlled monetary policy, π_d^*, and what would have occurred if, instead, a fully autonomous, conservative central bank controlled it, π_c^*, with (1-CBI) and CBI giving the respective weights. Subsequent discussion highlighted that CWB, sectoral structure, and their interaction should be among discretionary inflation's (π_d^*) determinants. These are also among unemployment's determinants, though in a complementary rather than substitute (weighted-average) relationship. Lastly, in both cases, the impact of sectoral structure, S, should differ depending whether the public (numerator) or traded (denominator) sector dominates. Thus, the impact of $S \equiv G/M$ should be nonlinear in a

---

[39] The sectors are agriculture, extraction, construction, manufacturing, transport-shipping-communications, utilities, exchange, finance, other services, other.

[40] Three dependent variable lags sufficed in each to leave residuals uncorrelated serially. Their coefficients sum to well under one, leaving no unit-root concerns.

[41] The web appendix <http://www-personal.umich.edu/~franzese> tabulates the sample descriptive statistics and shows the full regression results.

manner most easily enabled by including S and S^2 in the empirical models. The specifications matching theory are therefore:[42]

$$E(\pi) = \alpha'_\pi X_1 + (1 + \beta_{I2}I) \cdot \gamma'_\pi X_2 + \beta_{I1}I$$
$$+ (1 + \beta_{I2}I) \cdot [\beta_c C + \beta_{s1}S + \beta_{s2}S^2 + \beta_{cs1}C \cdot S + \beta_{cs2}C \cdot S^2] \quad (17)$$

$$E(U) = \alpha'_u X_1 + \gamma'_u X_2 + \theta_i I + \theta_c C + \theta_{s1}S + \theta_{s2}S^2 + \theta_{ic}I \cdot C + \theta_{is1}I \cdot S$$
$$+ \theta_{is2}I \cdot S^2 + \theta_{cs1}C \cdot S + \theta_{cs2}C \cdot S^2 + \theta_{ics1}I \cdot C \cdot S + \theta_{ics2}I \cdot C \cdot S^2 \quad (18)$$

with C the CWB (0–1), I the CBI (0–1), and $S \equiv G/M$ the sectoral-structure index.

The expression inside square brackets in equation (17) reflects the effect of CWB and sectoral structure on political authorities' inflation policies (via their effect on natural rates of employment). The term $1 + \beta_{i2}I$, which multiplies that and the other factors (X_2) to which π^*_d responds, reflects the weighted-average manner in which CBI reduces realized inflation from that discretionary level toward banks' targets as autonomy increases. If the weighted-average formulation is correct, the models of π^*_d and π^*_c are well specified, and CBI is well measured, one expects $\beta_{i2} \approx -1$. Note more generally that the effects of CBI, CWB, and S on inflation are all interactive. For example, the impact of CBI on inflation is:

$$E\left(\frac{d\pi}{dI}\right) = \beta_{I1} + \beta_{I2} \cdot \gamma'_\pi X_2$$
$$+ \beta_{I2} \cdot [\beta_c C + \beta_{s1}S + \beta_{s2}S^2 + \beta_{cs1}C \cdot S + \beta_{cs2}C \cdot S^2] \quad (19)$$

which should typically be negative, although its magnitude depends on coordination and sectoral structure among bargainers, and, indeed, on every other factor to which conservative banks and responsive govern-

---

[42] Methodological notes: weighted (W) two-stage (2S) least-squares (LS) used. WLS is necessary because higher unemployment and inflation both exhibit greater (stochastic) variance. Weights are $(1 + Y)^{-.5}$ with Y the dependent variable. 2SLS mitigates endogeneity concerns, instrumenting with one-year lags of all variables. White's robust standard errors applied because scale is not likely the only source of heteroskedasticity. The weighted-average form of the inflation equation estimated by nonlinear (N) W2SLS. Beck-Katz PCSEs have not yet been implemented for NLS, so, for consistency across π and U models, White's robust standard errors are reported in both equations. The reported substantive findings are robust across applications of any subset combination of these techniques (right down to OLS), and are not oversensitive to any one country's inclusion or exclusion from the sample (see Beck and Katz 1993).

ments would respond differently (see Franzese 1999a,b). Similarly, the expected inflation effect of *CWB*:

$$E\left(\frac{d\pi}{dC}\right) = \beta_{I2} \cdot I \cdot [\beta_c + \beta_{cs1}S + \beta_{cs2}S^2] \tag{20}$$

depends on *CBI* and *S*. It should generally be negative also, but *CWB* may even increase inflation given sufficient public-sector dominance (high *S*). *CBI* should dampen the magnitude of this effect (a substitute relationship) regardless of sign. Finally, the expected inflation-effect of sectoral structure, specifically of an increase in government-relative-to-manufacturing employment ($S \equiv G/M$), is:

$$E\left(\frac{d\pi}{dS}\right) = \beta_{I2} \cdot I \cdot [\beta_{s1} + \beta_{s2}S + \beta_{cs1}C + 2\beta_{cs2}C \cdot S] \tag{21}$$

It analogously depends on *CBI* and *CWB* but also on the level of *S* itself because sectoral structure has nonlinear effects. Increases in public-sector size (*S*) should increase the inflation benefits of *CWB* when traded sectors dominate (*S* small), but will become increasingly detrimental as the public sector comes to dominate (*S* large), especially when such public-sector-led bargains are coordinated across the economy (*CWB* large). Again, *CBI* will dampen those inflation effects.

Similarly, equation (18) reflects the contention that monetary conservatism, bargaining coordination, and traded-sector dominance complement in reducing unemployment. Expected unemployment effects of *CBI*, e.g., are given by:

$$E\left(\frac{dU}{dI}\right) = \theta_i + \theta_{ic}C + \theta_{is1}S + \theta_{is2}S^2 + \theta_{ics1}C \cdot S + \theta_{ics2}C \cdot S^2 \tag{22}$$

which depends on *CWB* and sectoral structure. The effect may be positive or negative because *CBI* has both conservatism and credibility effects, but it should generally improve as *CWB* rises when the traded sector dominates (low *S*) and worsen as *CWB* rises when the public sector dominates (high *S*). Symmetrically, the expected unemployment effect of *CWB* is:

$$E\left(\frac{dU}{dC}\right) = \theta_c + \theta_{ic}I + \theta_{cs1}S + \theta_{cs2}S^2 + \theta_{ics1}I \cdot S + \theta_{ics2}I \cdot S^2 \tag{23}$$

which should generally be negative but depends on *CBI* and *S*, and may become positive with sufficient public-sector dominance (*S* large) and conservatism (*CBI* large). Finally, the expected unemployment-effect of sectoral structure depends on *CBI* and *CWB* and on relative dominance of public or traded sectors (*S*):

$$E\left(\frac{dU}{dS}\right) = \theta_{s1} + \theta_{s2}S + \theta_{is1}I + 2\theta_{is2}I \cdot S + \theta_{cs1}C$$
$$+ 2\theta_{cs2}C \cdot S + \theta_{ics1}I \cdot C + 2\theta_{ics2}I \cdot C \cdot S \qquad (24)$$

Larger public sectors should raise unemployment when *CBI*, *CWB*, and public-sector dominance (*S*) are large because, under those conditions, sectoral structure does not favor restraint, public-sector bargainers have captured coordination, and conservative central banks react with costly real consequences. Conversely, when public sectors are not large enough to dominate, increases in *S* will increase the value of coordination and independence, and so equation (24) could be negative at low *S*.[43]

Table 4.1 reports the inflation results. The core conclusion is quite clear: monetary, bargaining, and sectoral institutional structures interact to determine inflation. The negative and highly statistically significant b_{i2}, for example, reveals that credibly conservative monetary authorities dampen the inflation effects of (i.e., interact with) bargaining coordination, sectoral structure, their interaction, and, indeed, everything else (X_2) to which central banks and governments respond differently (also b_{i2} is not too far from the −1 predicted).[44] Similarly, the b_{cs} and b_{cs2} estimates strongly (p < .01) suggest that bargaining coordination and its sectoral structure interact to influence politically responsive governments' inflation policy. These coefficients alone do not reveal the substantive impact of the highly significant estimates very clearly because each factor's impact depends on other institutional and structural variables as shown in equations (19)–(21). Substantive discussion is deferred until after reporting the unemployment results, so the nominal and real effects of governments' shifts toward anti-inflationary monetary policy may be considered together.

---

[43] "Fuller syntheses" tend to produce complicated predictions as this discussion no doubt illustrated. Relatedly, their highly interactive models usually produce highly correlated regressors, complicating estimation – one reason quantitative scholars often avoid them. Here, theory allowed sufficiently precise specifications for multicollinearity not to preclude interesting, and robust, results.

[44] N.b. that one would expect $\beta_{i2} = -1$ exactly *iff* the model included all the true variables, entered in all the true forms, and that all variables, especially *CBI*, were measured perfectly.

Table 4.1. *The Estimated Inflation Equation*

$$\pi = \ldots b_c C + b_s S + b_{s2} S^2 + b_{cs} C \cdot S + b_{cs2} C \cdot S^2 + b_{i1} I + b_{i2} I \cdot [b_c C + b_s S + b_{s2} S^2 + b_{cs} C \cdot S + b_{cs2} C \cdot S^2]$$

Coefficient (Cofactor)	Estimate	Standard Error	t-Statistic	p-Level
Controls				
b_{cwb} ($C \equiv CWB$)	−28.150	5.818	−4.838	0.000
b_s ($S \equiv G/M$)	−34.834	9.968	−3.495	0.001
b_{s2} (S^2)	+16.000	5.301	3.018	0.003
b_{cs} ($C \cdot S$)	+43.699	11.734	3.724	0.000
b_{cs2} ($C \cdot S^2$)	−19.267	5.955	−3.235	0.001
b_{i1} ($I \equiv CBI$)	−8.954	11.748	−0.762	0.447
b_{i2} ($I \cdot [\bullet]$)	−0.691	0.157	−4.413	0.000
Number of observations	347	R^2		0.523
Degrees of freedom	323	Adjusted R^2		0.489
Durbin-Watson	1.976	Standard error of regression		1.960

Table 4.2's core result is also clear: monetary, bargaining, and sectoral institutional structures interact to determine unemployment. More exactly, a Wald test of terms (e)–(k), establishes the joint significance (p ≈ .02) of the full set of interactions. A test of terms involving *CBI* (b, e–g, j–k) as firmly (p ≈ .003) shows that even credible monetary conservatism has real effects, confirming the insufficiency of neoclassical syntheses. Tests of terms involving *CWB* and sectoral structure as strongly (p < .01) support those interactive claims. Coefficients alone again cannot clearly reveal the substance of these significant results because *CBI*, *CWB*, and sectoral structure have interactive unemployment effects as seen in equations (22)–(24).

To evaluate the substance of these results, one must consider the estimated impact of each variable over relevant sample ranges of the others: $CWB \in \{0 \ldots 1\}$, $CBI \in \{0.15 \ldots 0.95\}$, and $G/M \in \{0.25 \ldots 1.25\}$. Consider the estimated inflation effect of a 0.1 increase in *CBI* (about the gaps in the ascending sequence Sweden-Italy-Ireland-Netherlands-Austria-United States-Switzerland-Germany). As Table 4.3 shows, the effect depends on the degree of *CWB* and its sectoral structure in the polit-

Table 4.2. *The Estimated Unemployment Equation*

Variable	Coefficient	Standard Error	t-Statistic	p-Level
Controls				
(a) $C \equiv CWB$	+11.826	3.847	3.074	0.002
(b) $I \equiv CBI$	+20.314	6.885	2.951	0.003
(c) $S \equiv G/M$	+14.921	7.132	2.092	0.037
(d) S^2	−4.924	4.372	−1.126	0.261
(e) $I \cdot C$	−29.423	9.204	−3.197	0.002
(f) $I \cdot S$	−35.596	15.317	−2.324	0.021
(g) $I \cdot S^2$	+14.163	8.753	1.618	0.107
(h) $C \cdot S$	−22.523	8.465	−2.661	0.008
(i) $C \cdot S^2$	+8.385	4.740	1.769	0.078
(j) $I \cdot C \cdot S$	+54.697	20.051	2.728	0.007
(k) $I \cdot C \cdot S^2$	−22.201	10.651	−2.084	0.038
Number of observations	347	R^2		0.907
Degrees of freedom	320	Adjusted R^2		0.899
Durbin-Watson	2.082	Standard error of regression		0.637

ical economy where that increase occurs (all other variables set to sample means).[45]

Credible monetary conservatism generally lowers inflation; every entry but the extreme top right (and no country-year has such characteristics) is negative. Theory also implied that monetary conservatism should reduce inflation less when bargaining institutional and sectoral structure is also antiinflationary. That is, monetary conservatism, coordinated bargaining, and traded-dominating-public sectors are *substitutes* in producing low inflation, so monetary policy need do less when other institutional structures already keep wage-price growth low.[46] Thus, reading right to left in Table 4.3, *CBI*'s estimated antiinflation effect grows larger as *CWB*

[45] Statistical significance, whose general high level can be inferred from Tables 5.1–2, is omitted in the subsequent tables to reduce clutter (available on request). All substantive findings discussed in this chapter are strongly statistically supported.

[46] Recall that the antiinflation effect of delegation to a conservative central bank is also lower the more antiinflationary the pressures on government in general. The highly significant b_{i1} confirms this expectation also (see Franzese 1999a,b).

Table 4.3. *Inflation Effect of Credible Monetary Conservatism as Function of Bargaining Coordination and Sectoral Structure*

S ≡ G/M	CWB 0.00	CWB 0.25	CWB 0.50	CWB 0.75	CWB 1.00
Estimated impact of 0.1 increase in CBI					
0.25	−1.20	−0.88	−0.57	−0.25	+0.07
0.50	−0.81	−0.62	−0.42	−0.23	−0.04
0.75	−0.55	−0.44	−0.34	−0.23	−0.12
1.00	−0.43	−0.37	−0.30	−0.24	−0.18
1.25	−0.45	−0.39	−0.33	−0.27	−0.20

decreases. Similarly, as public-relative-to-traded-sector size (S) increases beyond some point where it starts to reflect public dominance, the anti-inflation effect of *CBI* should rise. Conversely, rising S below that point will reduce *CBI*'s antiinflationary effect because, with traded sectors dominant (low S), they have more antiinflation bite the larger the public sector they lead, again leaving less for conservative monetary policy to do. Table 4.3 reveals just such a pattern. In fact, how large public sectors must grow before they start to dominate declines as *CWB* increases, suggesting that public-sector unions have more say in coordinated than uncoordinated bargaining, which is also sensible. Specifically, the antiinflation bite of monetary conservatism (*CBI*) starts to rise, suggesting public-sector actors begin to dominate bargaining, at one-third± traded-sector size for *CWB* = 1, at two-thirds± for *CWB* = .75, at equal± for *CWB* = .5 or .25, and at 1.25+ for *CWB* = 0.[47]

Table 4.4 shows the estimated inflation effect of 0.25 increases in *CWB*. Theory suggests that coordinated bargaining generally reduces inflation; indeed, every entry is negative. It also argues that coordinated bargainers and monetary conservatives each reduce inflation less as the other rises because each needs do less itself with the other present: a substitute property; reading left to right, Table 4.4 supports this also. Finally, the theory holds that, as public-sector bargainers grow relative to traded, coordina-

[47] These sectoral results also support similar arguments in Franzese 1994, 1996b: ch. 4, 2001 and Garrett and Way 1995b, 1999a,b. The last result in fact suggests that public-sector bargainers are extremely weak, or perhaps public-sector bargaining is virtually non-existent, in very uncoordinated economies.

Table 4.4. *Inflation Effect of Bargaining Coordination as Function of Its Sectoral Structure and of Credible Monetary Conservatism*

$S \equiv G/M$	CBI 0.15	CBI 0.35	CBI 0.55	CBI 0.75	CBI 0.95
Estimated impact of 0.25 increase in CWB					
0.25	−4.13	−3.49	−2.86	−2.22	−1.58
0.50	−2.49	−2.11	−1.72	−1.34	−0.95
0.75	−1.39	−1.18	−0.96	−0.75	−0.53
1.00	−0.83	−0.70	−0.58	−0.45	−0.32
1.25	−0.81	−0.69	−0.56	−0.44	−0.31

tion becomes less able to deliver antiinflationary wage-price restraint. Table 4.4, reading top to bottom, supports this, too; the estimated antiinflation impact of *CWB* becomes smaller as *S* increases.

The remaining derivatives, giving the inflation effects of rises in public-relative-to-traded-sector employment shares, *S*, depend on *CBI*, *CWB*, and *S* itself and so require three dimensions to present. Thus, Table 4.5 lists separately the estimated inflation effects of increases from *S* = .25 to .5, *S* = .5 to .75, and so on, at various levels of bargaining coordination and monetary conservatism. As seen, when the traded sector dominates the public sector in bargaining (low *S*, the top 2–3 sections), increases in public-sector employment share generally reduce inflation. This is because public-sector share increases at low *S* levels raise the antiinflationary benefit of traded-sector dominance. However, at higher levels of *S* (the bottom 1–2 sections), which suggest public-sector dominance, further increases in public-sector employment generally raise inflation. Moreover, increases in public-sector shares raise inflation sooner under more coordinated bargaining: in the changes *S* = .25 to .5 at *CWB* = 1, in *S* = .75 to 1 at *CWB* = .75, and in *S* = 1 to 1.25 at lower *CWB*. These results obtain because *CWB* can coordinate public-sector-led as easily as traded-sector-led settlements across the economy, and the (latter) former tend to be (anti)inflationary. Finally, once again, delegation of monetary policy making to a credible conservative central bank dampens the inflation effects of these other institutional-structural factors; reading down columns within sections, the size of the sectoral-structure inflation effects diminishes as *CBI* increases.

Table 4.5. *Inflation Effect of Public-to-Traded Employment-Share as Function of Bargaining Coordination and Credible Monetary Conservatism*

CBI	CWB 0.00	CWB 0.25	CWB 0.5	CWB 0.75	CWB 1.00
Estimated inflation impact of change in S ≡ G/M from .25 to .5					
0.15	−5.12	−3.48	−1.84	−0.20	1.44
0.35	−4.33	−2.94	−1.56	−0.17	1.22
0.55	−3.54	−2.41	−1.27	−0.14	0.99
0.75	−2.75	−1.87	−0.99	−0.11	0.77
0.95	−1.96	−1.33	−0.70	−0.08	0.55
Estimated inflation impact of change in S ≡ G/M from .5 to .75					
0.15	−3.32	−2.23	−1.13	−0.03	1.07
0.35	−2.81	−1.88	−0.95	−0.02	0.91
0.55	−2.30	−1.54	−0.78	−0.02	0.74
0.75	−1.79	−1.20	−0.61	−0.01	0.58
0.95	−1.27	−0.85	−0.43	−0.01	0.41
Estimated inflation impact of change in S ≡ G/M from .75 to 1.00					
0.15	−1.53	−0.97	−0.41	0.15	0.71
0.35	−1.30	−0.82	−0.35	0.12	0.60
0.55	−1.06	−0.67	−0.29	0.10	0.49
0.75	−0.82	−0.52	−0.22	0.08	0.38
0.95	−0.59	−0.37	−0.16	0.06	0.27
Estimated inflation impact of change in S ≡ G/M from 1.00 to 1.25					
0.15	0.26	0.28	0.30	0.32	0.34
0.35	0.22	0.24	0.25	0.27	0.29
0.55	0.18	0.19	0.21	0.22	0.23
0.75	0.14	0.15	0.16	0.17	0.18
0.95	0.10	0.11	0.12	0.12	0.13

In sum, the inflation experiences of developed democracies under flexible exchange rates support all the nominal-side predictions of the proposed synthesis and extension. Thus, as governments turned toward monetary conservatism to restrain the inflation from the stagflationary seventies, monetary policy itself had to do most of the antiinflationary work where bargaining was uncoordinated or public-sector bargainers had captured coordinated bargaining and had to do less of the work itself where bargaining remained traded-sector-led and -coordinated. The theory also argued that governments' policy shifts toward monetary conservatism would have deleterious real effects under the former conditions

Table 4.6. *Unemployment Effect of Credible Monetary Conservatism as Function of Bargaining Coordination and Sectoral Structure*

S ≡ G/M	CWB 0.00	CWB 0.25	CWB 0.50	CWB 0.75	CWB 1.00
Estimated impact of 0.1 increase in CBI					
0.25	+1.23	+0.80	+0.37	−0.06	−0.48
0.50	+0.61	+0.42	+0.22	+0.03	−0.16
0.75	+0.16	+0.14	+0.11	+0.09	+0.07
1.00	−0.11	−0.04	+0.04	+0.12	+0.20
1.25	−0.21	−0.10	+0.01	+0.11	+0.22

(e.g., raising or leaving high unemployment). Where bargaining coordination and structure instead alleviated inflationary pressures on policy makers, monetary policy could also control inflation without requiring such adverse real effects, so unemployment could have fallen simultaneously. To support this, the data must show the unemployment effects of credible monetary conservatism (*CBI*) to be more detrimental (less beneficial) where coordination was low or captured by public-sector bargainers and more beneficial (less detrimental) where coordination remained strong and traded sector dominated. Table 4.6 gives the relevant estimated effects.

Reading Table 4.6 left to right shows, as predicted, the unemployment effects of credible monetary conservatism (*CBI*) become less detrimental or more beneficial as bargaining coordination (*CWB*) increases and public-to-traded-sector employment shares remain low ($S \lesssim .85$), implying traded-sector dominance, and the effect reverses as public-sector come to dominate traded-sector workers in bargaining ($S \gtrsim .85$). However, somewhat unexpectedly, where coordination is medium-to-low (*CWB* ≤ .5), credible monetary conservatism seems to have less detrimental (more beneficial) unemployment effects as public shares increase relative to traded. Again, this likely suggests that the bargaining strengths and rights of public-relative to traded-sector workers differ from high to low *CWB* countries (Franzese 1994, 1996b: ch. 4; Garrett and Way 1995a, 1999a,b). Where coordination is low – for example, in the liberal-market economies of Anglo-America – public-sector workers have relatively little bargaining power or are even legally denied bargaining rights. Thus, their increase relative to the traded sector tends simply to reduce the share of the

Table 4.7. *Unemployment Effect of Bargaining Coordination as Function of Its Sectoral Structure and of Credible Monetary Conservatism*

S ≡ G/M	CBI 0.15	CBI 0.35	CBI 0.55	CBI 0.75	CBI 0.95
Estimated impact of 0.25 increase in CWB					
0.25	+1.04	+0.18	−0.68	−1.53	−2.39
0.50	+0.38	0.00	−0.38	−0.76	−1.15
0.75	−0.12	−0.17	−0.21	−0.25	−0.30
1.00	−0.46	−0.31	−0.16	0.00	+0.15
1.25	−0.65	−0.43	−0.22	+0.01	+0.21

economy that bargains more than to condition aggregate bargaining efficiency. Political authorities could directly restrain their wage gains and perhaps do so especially in such liberal-market economies. That certainly demands further exploration but, for present purposes, the strong central conclusion is that *CBI* and traded-sector-dominant, public-sector-dominated *CWB* are *complements* in producing low unemployment. Reverse the sectoral structure, and *CBI* and *CWB* become complements in producing *high* unemployment.

Table 4.7 lists the estimated impact of .25 increases in *CWB*. The theory argues first that coordinated bargaining generally reduces unemployment; indeed, most entries are negative. Next, provided traded sectors dominate, *CWB* should reduce unemployment more under higher *CBI* because autonomous, conservative monetary authorities help enforce coordinated traded-sector bargainers' restrained wage-price settlements, and, vice versa, such bargainers respond best to credibly conservative monetary-threats. Table 4.7's top three rows, read across, confirm. However, where public sectors come to dominate bargaining, the theory predicts the reverse. Conservative monetary authorities will not accommodate coordination on an inflationary public-sector-led bargain, and so the unemployment effect of *CWB* should become detrimental, as *CBI* and S ≡ G/M both increase. That is, given a detrimental sectoral structure, coordination *raises* unemployment *if* the monetary authority is sufficiently autonomous and conservative to resist the inflationary results. Table 4.7's bottom two rows affirm this; the unemployment effects of public-sector dominated (S ≳ .8) *CWB* become more detrimental as *CBI* increases.

Table 4.8. *Unemployment Effect of Public-to-Traded Employment-Share as Function of Bargaining Coordination and Credible Monetary Conservatism*

CBI	CWB 0.00	CWB 0.25	CWB 0.5	CWB 0.75	CWB 1.00
Estimated unemployment impact of change in $S \equiv G/M$ from .25 to .5					
0.15	1.87	1.21	0.55	−0.10	−0.76
0.35	0.62	0.44	0.26	0.07	−0.11
0.55	−0.63	−0.33	−0.04	0.25	0.55
0.75	−1.88	−1.11	−0.34	0.43	1.20
0.95	−3.12	−1.88	−0.64	0.61	1.85
Estimated unemployment impact of change in S $\equiv$ G/M from .5 to .75					
0.15	1.52	1.02	0.52	0.02	−0.48
0.35	0.63	0.46	0.30	0.14	−0.03
0.55	−0.27	−0.10	0.08	0.25	0.43
0.75	−1.16	−0.65	−0.14	0.37	0.88
0.95	−2.06	−1.21	−0.36	0.48	1.33
Estimated unemployment impact of change in S $\equiv$ G/M from .75 to 1.00					
0.15	1.17	0.83	0.49	0.14	−0.20
0.35	0.63	0.49	0.34	0.20	0.05
0.55	0.09	0.14	0.20	0.25	0.31
0.75	−0.45	−0.20	0.05	0.31	0.56
0.95	−0.99	−0.54	−0.09	0.36	0.81
Estimated unemployment impact of change in S $\equiv$ G/M from 1.00 to 1.25					
0.15	0.82	0.64	0.45	0.27	0.08
0.35	0.63	0.51	0.38	0.26	0.14
0.55	0.45	0.38	0.32	0.25	0.19
0.75	0.26	0.25	0.25	0.24	0.24
0.95	0.07	0.13	0.18	0.23	0.29

Table 4.8, lastly, lists the estimated unemployment effects of sectoral structure, which depend on *CBI*, *CWB*, and *S* itself. To sum first: as argued, rising public-to-traded employment shares do tend to increase unemployment where coordinated bargaining (high *CWB*) spreads public-sector-led (high *S*) settlements across the economy and conservative monetary authorities (high *CBI*) do not accommodate the inflationary consequences. Specifically, consider first the top section (low *S*). Here, higher public shares affect unemployment beneficially at high *CWB* and low *CBI* (top right) because traded-sector workers still dominate the coordinated

bargains and monetary authorities tolerate any inflationary effects that do accrue. At high *CWB* and *CBI* (bottom right), however, higher public shares affect unemployment detrimentally because the monetary constriction to combat even the small inflation effect dominates. At low *CWB* and *CBI* in this range (top left), higher public shares also worsen unemployment, here because the large traded sector especially feels the effects of being unable to restrain the public sector within a coordinated bargain and/or by conservative monetary reactions. At low *CWB* and high *CBI* in this range (bottom left), however, higher public shares actually reduce unemployment, probably because public workers have few rights and less power in these cases, so their hiring adds to total employment without much effect on bargaining aggregates. At high public-to-traded shares (bottom section), conversely, further increases in public share always raise unemployment. When *CWB* is high (right-most column), the public lack of restraint is coordinated across the economy and this has especially costly unemployment effects where monetary conservatism is high. (As elaborated later, this particular result helps explain some of the controversies in the emerging *CBI-CWB* interactions literature.) Lastly, at lower *CWB* (left three columns), public hiring also raises unemployment but monetary conservatism here tends to reduce that cost, again, likely due to the inability of public-sector workers to bargain in these cases. Thus, as governments shifted toward antiinflationary monetary policies following the seventies, those political economies where public-sector employment had come to dominate bargaining in aggregate, especially to dominate coordinated bargaining, would have experienced high real (e.g., unemployment) costs in reducing inflation by those policies.

4.5. Discussion, Conclusions, and Implications

4.5.1. Discussion and Conclusions

Broadly, the theory and evidence offered here demonstrate that political-economic regulation of unemployment and inflation depends on the network of institutions and the structural setting within which wage-price bargainers and monetary policy makers interact (echoing Pontusson's [1995b] advice to "put interests in their place and take structure seriously"). More specifically, the theory and evidence show that monetary authority credibility and conservatism interacts with wage-price-bargaining coordination and sectoral structure (traded, sheltered, public) to determine the terms on which policy makers can trade unemployment for inflation. Consider the contributions this represents to *CBI* and *CWB* theory.

First, contrary to neoclassical *CBI* theory, central bank conservatism and autonomy do have real effects on average, and their manifestation depends on the institutions and structure of wage-price bargaining. The real effects of monetary policy stances depend on their credibility, as stressed there, but also on wage-price bargainers' incentives and capacity to respond appropriately to monetary threats. Monetary conservatism, even if credible, buys reduced inflation at high real costs when bargaining is uncoordinated or coordinated but public-sector-dominated. Conversely, lower real costs, or even real benefits, accrue to credible monetary conservatism when bargaining is traded-sector-led and coordinated.[48] These are complementary relations. Second, adding to previous *CBI* work, the theory and evidence here show that credible delegation of monetary authority to conservative central bankers lowers inflation by lesser amounts where the wider institutional-structural configuration of the political economy induces noninflationary policies and wage-price settlements by itself, and vice versa. These are substitute relations. Third, the present theory and evidence resolve previous anomalies in the actions and statements of monetary policy makers. The Bundesbank speaks differently to different entities than the Fed because their audiences are differently structured institutionally, and both contract in response to strong real economies (*incipient inflationary pressures*) because such strength weakens bargainers' incentives to exercise restraint, especially with low or public-sector-led coordination.

These points imply that where government shifts toward conservative monetary policy since the seventies had greater antiinflationary bite, they also, generally speaking, had higher real costs; more favorable trade-offs were possible only where *other* institutional and structural conditions

---

[48] Summarizing existing evidence, Alesina and Summers (1993) find negative correlations of *CBI* and inflation but no correlation of *CBI* with any real variables (e.g., output, employment, real interest rates). The present arguments suggest that such results emerge because previous theories ignore the incentives and capacity of differently organized and structured bargainers to respond to monetary authorities strategically and because previous empirical specifications simply did not allow such effects. As in Figure 4.2, simple linear models of postwar average unemployment regressed on *CBI* find no significant relationship. Allow the effect of *CBI* to depend on bargaining coordination or its sectoral composition, though, and the effects become statistically obvious. See also notes 1, 36, and Franzese 2000a.

favored employment and growth and *thereby* held inflation down. Recall that, with growing unemployment subsidies and other labor market rigidities and burgeoning debt diminishing fiscal maneuverability and efficacy, democratic governments shifted toward monetary policy, grasping at this new conservative monetary orthodoxy that claimed that antiinflation needed only be credible to be costless, in seeking to reconstitute broad electoral coalitions behind macroeconomic management for putative efficiency. However, these monetary-policy and institutional "reforms," as now clarified and shown, retain strong *real* distributional implications whatever their academic and policy-making proponents may have claimed. Thus, as with debt and transfers, democratic contestation over monetary institutions was always much less about "efficiency" and much more about the long-familiar distributional concerns of left and right (Hibbs 1987; Iversen 1999a). Moreover, policy makers soon followed these monetary-policy and institution shifts with other institutional-structural "reforms" intended to spur productivity growth: the best macroeconomic outcome behind which to build broad electoral support, and also the only way to reduce inflation without very large real costs. In these "reforms," the aims of left and right took a strong and more-obvious partisan hue. The left sought to deploy public resources, more heavily funded by taxation of the wealthy, to raise productivity, settling on a strategy of public investment in physical and, especially, human capital, always with an eye to distributional equity. The right, contrarily, sought to reduce public economic activity, taxation, and other political barriers to free-market operations, relying on Adam Smith's invisible hand to direct private investment to raising productivity, wealth, and growth, with less concern for equity (see Boix 1998).[49]

CWB theory, meanwhile, has not usually considered monetary responses to wage-price settlements or the sectorally differentiated incentives of bargainers to exercise restraint and respond to expected monetary threats. This theory and evidence show, contrarily, that both nominal and real impacts of *CWB* depend critically on its sectoral composition and on the credibility and conservatism of the monetary authority. *CWB* most reduces unemployment when the traded sector dominates the public sector, especially where credibly autonomous and conservative monetary authorities reinforce their restraint. *CWB* least reduces unemployment, or even increases it, when the public sector dominates the traded sector,

[49] Boix (1998) more fully elaborates and explores these partisan microeconomic strategies of left and right, and their electoral underpinnings.

especially where a conservative monetary authority will not accommodate their failed restraint. Conversely, *CWB* generally reduces inflation, more so when the traded sector dominates the public sector, and autonomous conservative monetary authorities dampen that impact because they would secure low inflation regardless. As will be discussed further, this suggests that, as public employment grew, eventually coming to dominate the traded sector in the bargaining systems of some of the most coordinated economies, the antiinflation and pro-employment effects of coordination would have diminished noticeably, likely undermining political support for coordinated-bargaining institutions.

Finally, the brief review of previous synthetic work considering *CBI-CWB* interactions found a growing empirical literature highlighting particular *single* interactions between some two of *CBI*, *CWB*, and sectoral structure (see notes 1, 36). The theory and evidence offered here reveals that, as the political-economy cycle framework would suggest (Figure 1.22), the impact of *each* of these political-economic factors tends to depend on *all* of the others. That review also noted one important point of contention to which these concluding remarks now turn before exploring the implications of the theory and evidence in this chapter for monetary regulation of the European economy under a single credibly conservative central bank, for the recent collapse of coordinated bargaining in some countries, and for the continuing viability and utility of the democratic policy commitments.

Contrary to previous findings (see note 36), Iversen (1994, 1996b, 1998a,c) found that credible monetary conservatism had beneficial unemployment effects at intermediate *centralization*, detrimental effects at highest, and little effect at lowest. Cukierman and Lippi (1999) found monetary conservatism had greatest unemployment cost where *coordination* was low, and roughly equally beneficial effects where it was moderate or high. Others found *CBI* had uniformly lower costs as *coordination* increased. The italicized difference notwithstanding, these results seem radically and disturbingly different. The theory and evidence here, however, show coordination to interact beneficially with credible monetary conservatism (*CBI*) where traded sectors dominate public sectors but that this relation reverses where public sectors dominate, which suggests that the increasingly adverse sectoral structure of the most-coordinated economies might explain these differences.

In Iversen's model, wage bargainers seek wage equality and centralized bargaining helps achieve it. The adverse effects of monetary conservatism at high centralization occur therein because conservative monetary policy makers will not allow differential (and inflationary) "wage creep," which is the process by which the relative gains of more-productive or high productivity-growth bargaining units are eroded to produce greater equality. The more disparate the productivity (growth) of those brought under more-centralized settlements, the more wage creep is necessary, and so the more costly the monetary reaction to it.[50]

Note that economies universally became more service-oriented as they advanced, and that productivity growth in services typically lags that in industry. Wage equalization across these sectors thus makes private-sector service-provision increasingly costly in growing economies whose bargaining institutions foster wage equality. With private sectors "priced out" of service-provision, public service-provision must rise or growth and employment suffers (Iversen and Wren 1998). Therefore, centralized or coordinated bargaining *with wage equalization* induces democratic governments in growing economies to raise public-sector employment. But, as shown here, rising public employment also weakens the ability of coordination to produce beneficial nominal and real outcomes. The choice for governments in this situation thus becomes increasingly one of high inflation and low unemployment without monetary conservatism (see, e.g., Calmfors 1993b) or low inflation and high unemployment with it. Thus, considerably less controversy exists between Iversen's arguments and findings and this and previous works than first appears. In fact, they are complementary; together they suggest that coordination might be inherently unstable in the long run, if accompanied by wage equalization, because coordination on equalization induces public-sector growth, which saps the ability of coordination to produce wage-price restraint.

4.5.2. Specific Implications for Current Issues in Europe

4.5.2.1. An Autonomous and Conservative European Central Bank
With rising transfers (Chapter 2), debts (Chapter 3), and trade and financial exposure (e.g., Garrett 1998a) having sapped fiscal maneuverability and efficacy, democratic governments turned to monetary policy to rebuild their postwar coalitions behind macroeconomic management. With wide academic support and much theory and evidence suggesting clear advan-

---

[50] Why the relatively advantaged are oblivious to this erosion, and why "wage creep" is the preferred means of fostering wage equality are not clear.

tages of credible monetary conservatism (Section 4.2.1), and perhaps noting the simultaneous unemployment and inflation success of the "Teutonic Three" (Germany, Austria, and Switzerland),[51] the governments of the European Community (EC) endowed a European Central Bank (ECB) with considerable autonomy and conservatism to direct monetary policy for the single European currency. Theory and evidence here suggest, however, that the Teutonic Three's success in combining low unemployment and inflation derived not only from their credibly autonomous and conservative monetary authorities, but from that combined with their coordinated wage-price-bargaining led by traded sectors. This suggests that, regarding its interactions with wage-price bargainers, the likely costs of delegating to the autonomous, conservative ECB will differ from hopes and expectations.[52]

From the perspective of a European economy, national bargaining units are small, numerous, and uncoordinated. This alone suggests that a highly conservative ECB will be more costly than equally conservative national central banks have been in these three individually.[53] The empirical analysis here allows a crude estimate of these costs that incorporates sectoral-structure considerations. In 1990, the countries then composing the EC had a mean public-to-traded employment ratio (S) of .8±, and a European economy would have an aggregate CWB of perhaps .25. At these values, the estimates indicate that a country with *domestic CWB* = .25 and S = .8 (e.g., Italy) would find long-run[54] unemployment higher by +.5±% and inflation lower by −.8±% for each +.1 increment in credible conservatism (CBI) represented by the shift from their national central bank to the ECB. For countries like Germany, with domestically higher and more traded-sector-led CWB and higher CBI, delegation to the ECB would involve little change in antiinflation, but large adverse changes in the propensity of the newly relevant set of wage-price bargainers to interact beneficially with the new monetary authority.

---

[51] (*Pace* French- and Italian-speaking Swiss.) Admittedly, the monetary policy of Switzerland and, especially (with its pegs), Austria, given their trade and financial integration with Germany, has been dominated by that in their larger neighbor (Franzese 1999a).

[52] Clearly, many other economic and political effects will derive from monetary-policy delegation to one European, autonomous, conservative authority and from a single currency (see, e.g., Eichengreen 1990, 1992, 1994, 1996; Eichengreen and Frieden 1997). The text exclusively stresses wage-price-bargaining interactions.

[53] Hall (1994), Hall and Franzese (1998), Franzese and Hall (2000), and Franzese (2000a) elaborate similar arguments (see also notes 1, 36).

[54] Long-run effects incorporate the dynamic structure of the estimated equations.

Whether these trade-offs are acceptable depends on the relative value given inflation and unemployment, but there *is* a trade-off and its terms depend on the institutional and sectoral structure countries would be exchanging for Europe's institutional and sectoral structure by delegating to the ECB. Within countries, moreover, those constituencies more hurt by unemployment will typically suffer while those more harmed by inflation would generally gain, though, again, both the pains and gains depend on the domestic institutional structure exchanged for the European. Still, that trade-off is likely to be generally steeper for most polities than the popular historical examples (and previous theory) suggested because the institutional and sectoral structure of Europe would interact much less favorably with the ECB than the institutional and sectoral structures of Germany, Austria, and Switzerland have with their banks in the past, unless Europe managed to replicate the traded-sector-led bargaining coordination of those countries.

Therefore, the choice for much of Europe along the monetary-policy axis, at least regarding monetary policy maker interactions with wage-price bargainers, broadly remains the familiar and painful one: inflation or unemployment. *If* lower inflation is chosen, a credible monetary authority can best pursue it, as previously stressed. Even if so, whether domestic autonomous, conservative central banks or a European one is preferable depends on domestic institutional structures relative to the European. Desirable in any case is to foster traded-sector dominance of public in coordinated bargaining. Soskice and Iversen (1998, 2000) suggest, for example, that Europe might manage to replicate the German system of traded-sector-led coordination interacting with a conservative monetary authority (Hall and Franzese 1998) by allowing the German system to lead European bargaining, having the ECB react to its settlements and other bargainers follow its lead. This would reduce the real costs of purchasing ECB-led low inflation, but that outcome is highly unlikely because bargaining coordination is much less easily engineered (see, e.g., Regini 1984) than credible European monetary conservatism, although the latter also requires continued agreement among national governments to maintain and bolster the ECB independence. Perhaps easiest is to alter the structural composition of wage-price bargaining; governments need only (continue) to reduce public-sector employment and raise international exposure. Instituting coordinated bargaining within that structure, however, would require the continued efforts and agreement of many national bargaining agents and so seems much less likely to occur.

4.5.2.2. The Collapse of Corporatism Noting the collapse of coordinated bargaining in Sweden and Denmark, scholars had begun to discuss the general decline of corporatism. However, recent work (Golden et al. 1995a,b) documented that this decline was not then so general as was believed. Centralized wage-price bargaining had indeed declined in Denmark and Sweden.[55] In Denmark, decline began around 1980; in Sweden, hiccups of low centralization in 1984 and 1988 preceded an apparently permanent decline in 1991. Norwegian bargaining centralization also saw great turbulence at least through 1987, but remained fairly high at last documentation. Contrarily, in Austria, Finland, and Germany, there was some decline in the early 1970s, but centralization had not declined further after. Among employer-led-bargaining systems, Japanese concentration is rising, and the authors mention no decline in Switzerland, though comparable data are unavailable.

Scholars attributed these *collapses* of centralized bargaining to new (*post-Fordist*) production techniques, rising capital mobility, or shifting political power from labor to employers in these economies (see, e.g., Pontusson 1992a,b, 1995a; Pontusson and Swenson 1993, 1996). Such arguments are hard to sustain on their own, however, if the decline occurred in some countries, like Sweden, Denmark, and possibly Norway, but not (or not yet) in others. Capital is likely no less mobile in Austria, Finland, Germany, Japan, and Switzerland than in those three. Nor are *post-Fordist* production techniques likely more predominant there than elsewhere among high-coordination countries. A political power-shift has possibly occurred – certainly conservative monetary orthodoxy now reins – and capital mobility and new production techniques may have supported or even caused this shift. Observed right-partisan and pro-employer power-shifts alone, however, do not explain why employers and allied skilled labor have become coordination's enemies when they were previously instrumental in instituting and maintaining it (Pontusson 1992a; Swenson 1989, 1991). Sectoral shifts suggest an explanation.

Figure 4.5 reveals that public sectors have increasingly dominated traded sectors in coordinated economies ($CWB \in \{.75,1\}$). The trend is OECD-wide, but by the mid- to late 1980s, Denmark, Norway, and Sweden had government-to-manufacturing employment-ratios over 1.5.

---

[55] Again, centralization and coordination are not quite identical as pattern-setting bargaining typical of Germany and Japan attest. However, their correlation may suffice here, in contrast to previous sections, because comparison is only within countries over time rather than both across countries and over time.

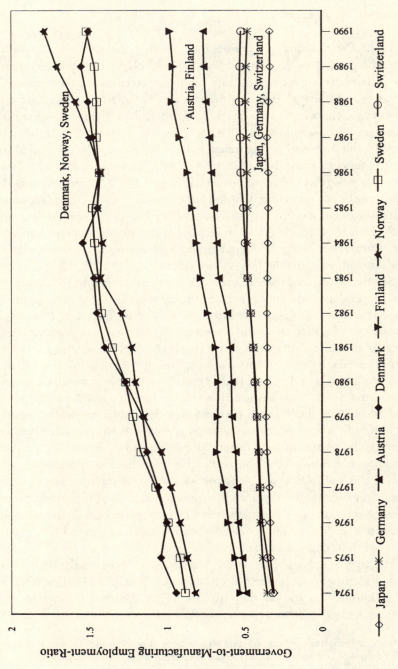

Figure 4.5 Rising Public-to-Traded-Sector Employment Ratios in Coordinated Economies

Only Canada's 1.25 comes close; a few others, including Austria and Finland, now have ratios near 1, whereas most of the sample remained below .75 most of the period. As demonstrated here, this exceptional relative rise in government employment implies that the output and unemployment costs of monetary control of inflation rose dramatically in Sweden, Denmark, and Norway while they rose less in other high-*CWB* economies.

The rise of public-to-traded-sector ratios within the coordinated bargaining systems significantly sapped *CWB*'s ability to induce restraint.[56] As Sweden and Norway lacked autonomous and conservative central banks, governments did not particularly seek to combat inflation monetarily, so rising public-sector influence within coordinated bargaining led to growing inflation and frequent decisions to allow currency depreciation (Calmfors 1993b). Depreciations, which alleviated real impacts of the lack of wage-price restraint, prevented a coalition of employers (especially traded-sector) and traded-sector workers (high-skill-and-productivity-growth) from coalescing against coordinated bargaining. However, this solution grew more difficult to maintain as sectoral trends continued and these increasingly service-oriented economies sought to maintain wage equality. As inflationary pressures mounted, eventually, as when Sweden pegged to the Deutschmark more firmly since the late 1980s, the growing antiinflation coalition won. The tighter money then brought the delayed real costs with a vengeance, which solidified the nascent anticoordination coalition of employers and (skilled) traded-sector workers against the sheltered and especially public sector. A similar process has periodically flared in Norway, but oil resources there have enabled a somewhat weaker commitment to hard currency to persist, yielding a fitful oscillation of bargaining centralization. Denmark, with its more autonomous and conservative central bank, made the commitment to hard currency earlier and more firmly. Accordingly, the real costs of controlling inflation monetarily in the face of rising public-sector influence within coordinated bargaining were felt sooner and more directly. The anticoordination coalition thus solidified and won sooner. In short, in all three countries, the increasing inability of *CWB* to provide wage-price restraint was central to employer and, later, skilled or traded labor

---

[56] Golden et al. (1995a), Iversen 1993a,b, 1994, and Garrett and Way (1995b) provide further relevant evidence; Pontusson (1992a,b), and Pontusson and Swenson (1993, 1996) make related arguments.

disillusionment with coordination and its eventual collapse. If similar sectoral trends continue in other high *CWB* political economies, they can only follow.

An anecdote illustrates just how unlikely wage restraint is to come from the public sector and how damaging such public-sector-led coordination can be to the real economy when conservative monetary authorities respond.[57] Germany has a national bargaining system in which one lead bargain each year is understood by bargainers in that negotiation and economy-wide to set the pattern for wage-price settlements elsewhere.[58] The large, traded-sector metalworkers union and firm confederations, IG Metal and Gesamptmetal, usually conduct the lead bargain, to beneficial effect as shown here. However, in January 1974, IG Metal ceded leadership for the first time to ÖTV, the large public-sector-workers union. ÖTV immediately demanded 15% to 20% wage increases, massively exceeding productivity growth (especially in the public sector) plus forecasted inflation. The Bundesbank publicly admonished, implicitly and then explicitly threatened monetary reactions, and strongly advised the government to resist ÖTV's demands. The government, a relatively weak coalition at the time, eventually granted most of the increase, well over productivity growth plus inflation (expected or realized). Subsequent wage settlements, as typical in Germany, followed suit. In response, the Bundesbank implemented its promised strong monetary contraction, dampening investment and triggering real-exchange appreciation. The results were painful, much more so, not coincidentally, for the traded than public sector.[59] Interestingly, the one decline in German bargaining centralization noted by Lange et al. (1995) and Golden et al. (1995) ensued. Perhaps the lesson was not lost on Nordic employers and definitely not on IG Metal and Gesamptmetal. IG Metal never allowed ÖTV to lead labor in wage negotiations again, and centralization has since been stable.

---

[57] The account summarizes and builds from Kennedy 1991.

[58] See, e.g., Hall and Franzese 1998 and Franzese and Hall 2000. Students of the U.S. automobile industry may recognize such pattern-setting bargaining. The United Auto Workers (UAW) likewise coordinates bargaining within that industry, choosing one of the big three (General Motors, Ford, Chrysler) as its target. Negotiations begin with that firm, and are understood by all in the industry not only to pattern blue-collar settlements at the other two but also to set a base line for white-collar contracting in the industry.

[59] The year 1975 saw an OECD-wide recession; the contention is that Germany's was worse than it could have been because ÖTV led the bargains instead of IG Metal.

4.5.3. Further Implications for Democratic Management of the Economy

As noted in Chapter 1, the main detrimental economic effect attributed to public-sector employment growth is to reduce productivity growth. Nothing here disputes that; indeed, a simple regression can suffice to establish it directly:[60]

$$\Delta Y = \ldots - 0.0125G \ldots$$
$$(0.0040) \quad \bar{R}^2 = .5854; \quad s.e.e. = 0.1207; \quad N = 84 \quad (25)$$

ΔY is the change in natural log of decade-average real GDP per capita (i.e., real growth), used here to proxy productivity growth, and G is government share of total employment, to proxy public-sector employment. Equation (25) indicates that each 1% more public employment-share slows productivity growth per decade by 1.25±%. Thus, 10% higher government employment, a not unusual movement as seen from Figure 1.10, induces 12.5±% lower productivity-growth (strictly, −12.5% GDP per capita growth) over a decade. As Chapter 3 showed, such retardation of growth was a key impetus toward debt accumulation, and, as Chapter 2 showed, employment growth, which only productivity growth can reconcile with real-wage growth, was essential for expanding social-insurance generosity not to produce massive rises in transfers and public spending. Thus, while rising transfers spurred increasing labor market rigidity, limiting fiscal-policy efficacy, and debt growth increasingly constrained fiscal-policy maneuverability, public-employment growth dampened productivity and income growth, exacerbating both difficulties.

Thus, with fiscal policy increasingly ineffective and constrained by these developments, and by growing internationalization, governments logically turned toward monetary policy, once the Bretton Woods collapse removed fixed-exchange requirements, to fulfill their commitments to macroeconomic management, and specifically to redress the OPEC-triggered inflation of the 1970s. However, as shown here, another important and neglected impact of rising public employment was the growing constituency it created that is largely immune to international or even

---

[60] OLS estimation in *decade*-frequency data, with decade indicators and Newey-West autocorrelation and heteroskedasticity-consistent standard errors. The coefficient on G is substantively and statistically significantly negative regardless of whether one instead includes lagged growth or drops the time dummies, etc.

domestic competition and ill-disposed to provide wage-price restraint on its own or to respond well to monetary threats intended to induce such. Meanwhile, with the rest of the economy increasingly exposed to competition, governments' monetary efforts to restrain public-sector bargains created large real costs for the aggregate economy, which fell especially heavily on the expanding traded sector.

This view also helps explain why public-private cleavages have grown so prominent in developed democracies: large public-sector strikes in France, Italy, and elsewhere across the OECD; U.S. government shut-down and lockout in winter–spring 1996; similar troubles in Canada, especially Ontario, in 1995–6, etc. The proximate causes vary: a French proposal to reduce pension eligibility; failure to conclude a budget in the United States;[61] recurring budget crises in Ontario. More such cases of public and private workers airing their differences through their governments can be expected if public work-forces continue to grow, adding to the roles this same sharpening cleavage played in monetary-union debates and coordinated-bargaining collapses as discussed earlier.

In short, in public employment, as in transfers and in public debt, democratic governments have tended to become overcommitted. Over the past 30 years, until fairly recently in most cases, developed democracies have steadily increased their public payrolls, hindering not only produc- tivity and employment growth, but also the effectiveness of both their wage-price bargaining institutions and their monetary policy in regulating the wage-price bargain. In doing so, they have altered the structure of interests in society, exacerbating public-private cleavages, and, in some cases, undermining what was a very successful system of institutions involving an autonomous and conservative central bank interacting with coordinated bargainers that have the capabilities and the incentives to respond effectively to monetary policies.

Thus, as democratic governments turned from the fiscal policies of the Keynesian welfare state to new-orthodox monetary policies and in- stitutional "reforms" in attempting to rebuild their broad postwar coali- tions behind public management of the macroeconomy, they hardly displaced familiar left-right battle lines. Hibbs's (1977, 1987) analysis of left-right partisan politics and democratic governments' management

---

[61] Counterproductively from this view, the workers were paid for the time they were de facto locked out. The popular grumbling about public workers being paid for jobs "we hardly noticed them not doing" is also informative for this: exactly a manifestation of the rising salience of the cleavage in question.

of the Keynes-Phillips macroeconomy applies equally, with but little translation, to modern *institutional-reform* and *supply-side* policy debates. Hibbs's right versus left entailed relatively skilled workers and capitalists versus unskilled workers, who relatively disfavor or favor government involvement in the economy and relatively dislike unemployment less or more than inflation. These same groups align on similarly opposing sides of debates over how and whether to restrain public employment, or to sustain coordinated bargaining, or to institutionalize the policy shift toward monetary conservatism. The theory and evidence of this chapter have shown that, on each front, the relatively unskilled have more to lose and less to gain on their sides of each debate and the relatively skilled and capital-rich more to lose and less to gain on theirs (see Boix 1998).[62]

[62] Boix (1998) well and extensively analyzes this transformation of what might be called *traditional Keynesian partisan macro political-economy* into *modern partisan macro institutional political-economy*. He underemphasizes, however, that even as the locus and terminology of the debate may be changing, the sides and issues of the disputes remain wholly familiar.

5

Comparative Democratic Political-Economy and Macroeconomic Policy Making

This comparative, historical study of the democratic political economy of macroeconomic policy making offered both three separate studies of the transfers, debt, and monetary policies that underlay governments' postwar commitments to political regulation of the economy and a broader set of arguments on the politics and economics of governments' evolving attempts to fulfill those commitments. This concluding chapter also follows these two paths. First, it coordinates some of the findings that emerged repeatedly in various forms throughout Chapters 2–4, commenting on their collective implications for comparative-historical study of the democratic political-economy of macroeconomic policy making. Second, after summarizing the book's results, it returns to the larger questions raised in Chapter 1 to consider very tentatively some potential implications of those results for the continued viability and utility of the democratic commitments.

5.1. Concluding Themes

Four motifs in Chapters 2–4 merit reemphasis; in order of increasing generality and brevity of their treatment here: strategic electoral and partisan policy making, the highly interactive effects of institutions and structure on such strategic actors, the varying information available across those actors for their expectations formation that undergirds such strategic actions, and the centrality of theoretically informed measurement and specification to theoretically informing empirical work.

256

5.1.1. *Strategic Electoral and Partisan Policy Making*

Theories of electoral and partisan effects on economic policy have long, venerable intellectual histories, perhaps representing the cornerstones of modern macro political-economy. The arguments and evidence here have shown that, despite rising fiscal, and international and domestic structural and institutional constraints, electioneering and partisanship remain important sources of policy variation across countries and over time, and the interesting, strategic nature of the partisan and electoral policy making uncovered should rekindle interest among political economists in revisiting and revising them.

5.1.1.1. *Strategic Electioneering Governments* Nordhaus (1975) and Tufte (1978) founded the study of electoral policy and outcome cycles with what has proved an enduringly powerful argument. At its well-known core: democratic policy makers are popularly elected officials and would generally like to remain so; they also have policy instruments employable to manipulate the economic outcomes perceived by voters; voters have short memories and tend to reward (punish) with votes those policy makers deemed responsible for recent positive (negative) economic outcomes; therefore, democratic policy makers will try to engineer positive economic experiences for voters leading up to an election.

Since Nordhaus and Tufte, however, empirical support for electoral cycles has been scarce (e.g., Alesina, Cohen, and Roubini 1992; Alesina and Roubini 1992; Alesina et al. 1997); yet, given the enduring intuitive appeal of the argument, researchers continued to explore them, focusing on what could have gone wrong with the argument at its four foundational points. Few question that democratic politicians seek reelection, but the next two points have received considerable scrutiny.

Rational-expectations theory led economists to question whether electoral policy cycles, being so regular and predictable, could actually alter real economic conditions and whether voters with rational expectations would actually reward incumbents for actions already taken. Rogoff and Sibert (1988) and Rogoff (1990), for example, argue that voters will reward electoral policy cycles, and so elected policy makers will produce them, only if preelectoral policies signal something, incumbents' competence in their model, about likely postelection outcomes. However, evidence from aggregate U.S. political-economic data is mixed. Alesina et al. (1993) found that voters do not reward incumbents for strong past economic outcomes in a manner consistent with their having inferred from that past that incumbents could sustain stronger future performance than challengers. MacKuen et al. (1992), contrarily, found that presidential approval responds more to voters' expectations of future economic performance than their evaluation of past.

Political scientists have taken a different tack. Schultz (1995) argued that for incumbents to manipulate or to be seen to manipulate the economy is likely costly for them, risking negative voter reactions to such opportunism and limiting economic-policy use for other purposes. Therefore, incumbents will manipulate policy for electoral purposes only when benefits outweigh those costs, that is, when the marginal votes that such electioneering might buy are most needed, that is, when they expect forthcoming elections to be close. Using U.K. transfers data and preelectoral forecasts of the race, he found strong support for this argument. Others stressed institutional and structural constraints on incumbent ability to manipulate policy. Monetary policy, for example, is less available to incumbent manipulation where governments have effectively delegated it to authorities less interested in domestic electoral outcomes: autonomous and conservative central banks or, via fixed exchange rates with capital mobility, foreign monetary authorities (Chapter 4; Clark et al. 1998; Clark and Hallerberg 1999; Franzese 1999a,b; Oatley 1999).

Thus, recent advances draw attention to voters' and private economic-actors' rationality, costs of (being seen to be) manipulating policy, and varying degrees of incumbent control over policy instruments: all important advances. Private-sector rationality, for example, suggests that predictable macroeconomic, especially monetary, policies have little real effect, reducing the utility of fiscal and, especially, monetary policy relative to more-direct actions, like transfers, as instruments for preelectoral manipulation. Thus, Tufte's emphasis on transfers seems well founded. Forward-looking voters underscore the role of (credible) campaign promises (signaling), which Tufte also emphasized (and Alt 1985 evidenced). The opportunity costs of electoral manipulation highlight that the value, and so the degree, of incumbent manipulation will vary across elections. And incumbents' abilities and incentives to manipulate policy will likewise vary across country-times and also over different policy instruments depending on the set of institutions and structures that determine (a) the identity and composition of incumbents (unified or fractionalized, uni- or bicameralism, parliamentary or presidential, unitary or federal, etc.), (b) their relative access to different policies (central bank autonomy, international exposure, etc.), and (c) the relative efficacy of available policies in improving voters' perceptions of performance (direct versus indirect policies, the institutional and sectoral structure of the economy, etc.).

Add to these considerations strong evidence in Chapters 2–4 of pre- *and post*electoral surges in transfers, deficits, and (less strong) inflation.[1] First, note that electoral transfers cycles were substantively and statistically strongest, which supports Tufte's emphasis on transfers as particularly useful in engineering preelectoral payoffs for voters because their benefits are more certainly felt, time-able, and targetable, and confer more-appropriate political credit than other policies' benefits. Much previous literature neglected this, expecting as-notable electoral effects on other policies and outcomes. Four other issues arise from these results. First, electoral transfers-surges typically reach only certain segments of the polity: those already eligible and perhaps some, not too obvious, increment in that group. Second, evidence supports both pre- and postelectoral surges in transfers, deficit, and inflation. Third, in fact, the data show statistically and substantively stronger post- than preelectoral surges. Finally, the very sluggish fiscal (but not monetary) policy-adjustment rates found imply that cyclical electoral surges accumulate, ratchetlike, into long-run increases in fiscal levels (but not inflation).

The first and second points underscore that governments (partly) control many policy instruments and, with evidence of electoral cycles in each chapter, that they do indeed use multiple instruments for electioneering.[2] Future work, therefore, should move toward estimating systems of equations that jointly model multiple instruments, exploring electioneering in policy, rather than in particular individual policies. Combining this consideration with others raised before, begins to sketch such a model. Incumbents seek reelection and have policy instruments that might differently aid their reelection bids; their need for votes and the costs of manipulating policies to attain them vary; and they are variably institutionally and structurally constrained from using them. Also, marginal returns are likely

---

[1] One suppressed result in Table 4.1 was a mildly significant ($p \approx 06$) positive coefficient on a lag of *ELE*, which indicates a postelection year.

[2] Estimated deficit cycles were too large relative to those estimated in transfers for the finding in Chapter 2's conclusion that spending was 25% to 50% deficit-financed to explain fully, so governments seem to manipulate deficits per se.

decreasing and marginal costs likely increasing in each instrument because larger surges yield decreasingly larger utility for those receiving, but are increasingly noticeable to those opposing, them. *Strategic* policy makers will, therefore, use all available policies (the Ramsey rule) to obtain their desired electioneering surges, more when expecting close elections, when opportunity costs of electioneering policy are low (e.g., when voters perceive other economic-policy needs as low), and when institutional-structural constraints on incumbent manipulation are low. They will use particular policies more that, relative to other policies, are less institutionally structurally constrained, have lower opportunity costs in terms of other goals, and bring larger and clearer net benefits more directly to forward-looking voters and are less noticeable to, or have less-organized, opponents.

The third point, that postelectoral surges are at least as strong as preelectoral, suggests another neglected line of research. Most important, scholars have forgotten that the identity of the policy maker may change with the election. The implications for inferences regarding the existence of electoral manipulation are subtle but critical. Empirically, because previous studies compared preelectoral years to all others, including post-election years that have even stronger surges, they likely underestimated electioneering.[3] Theoretically, postelectoral surges are possible for three reasons of increasing plausibility and intellectual interest.[4]

First, the apparent postelectoral surges may simply reflect mismatch of calendar-year preelectoral indicators and fiscal-year policies. This cannot explain, however, why postelectoral appeared stronger than preelectoral surges because, with exceedingly rare exception in these samples, calendar and fiscal years *more than half* overlap.[5] Second, the sluggish policy adjustment repeatedly and strongly found throughout the book suggests that implementation of preelectoral policies or their effects may be delayed or persist beyond the preelectoral year. However, for "slow electioneering adjustment" to explain the significance of both pre- and postelectoral indicators, election-year surges must adjust slower than do other policies because these models already control for a common policy-adjustment

---

[3] The size and significance of indicator i's coefficient, β_i, reveals the difference between conditional averages where $i = 1$, $\bar{x}_1$, and $i = 0$, $\bar{x}_0$. Including postelection surges in $\bar{x}_0$ thus yields smaller and less significant $\beta_i = \bar{x}_1 - \bar{x}_0$, ceteris paribus.

[4] One unsustainable explanation is that two-year congressional cycles in the United States explain the finding. Recall that the *ELE* measure cycles appropriately in the United States, [.0491, .2843, .1145, .6633], with the last the presidential-election year.

[5] The care in allocating *ELE* correctly over calendar-years allows such precision.

rate via lagged policy variables.[6] Therefore, the more likely explanation of postelectoral surges surrounds the role, wholly neglected in the literature since Tufte (1978), of strategic interactions between incumbents *and challengers*.

Both candidates make promises during election campaigns, and, while only incumbents can back their promises with policies during the campaign, the election may change the identity of the postelectoral policy makers. This strategic campaigning of both incumbents and challengers and the possible changing of the guard postelection can explain both the existence and the greater strength of postelectoral surges. Tufte (1978) argued that campaigns might induce rising electoral manipulation. As challengers promise, with some (nonzero) degree of credibility, to deliver more with less, the incumbent must follow with increasing promises of her own. Incumbents also likely must move toward fulfilling their promises to maintain credibility because they can act and voters know that. Indeed, most systematic evidence strongly suggests that democratic policy makers actually do generally fulfill their electoral and partisan promises,[7] popular cynicism to the contrary notwithstanding. Thus, transfers (promises and provision of more) and deficits (promises and provision of more with less) rise during campaigns.

To see why postelectoral surges are likely larger yet, compare random samples of policy makers before and after elections. Generous promises must raise candidates' (re)election chances or they would not make them, so postelectoral policy maker samples should contain higher proportions of those who had made larger promises. Conversely, preelectoral samples will include some incumbents who made weaker promises or acted inadequately on them and so more likely lost. Thus, postelectoral effects will more uniformly reflect the fulfillment of large campaign promises by challengers or incumbents, while preelectoral effects will reflect some averaging of sufficient and insufficient incumbent promises and actions. Accordingly, estimated postelectoral effects will be larger and more statistically certain. Indeed, Chapter 2 (3) estimates postelectoral transfer (deficit) surges $2\pm$ times ($15\pm\%$) larger and $4\pm$ ($2.5\pm$) times more significant than preelectoral. Thus, strategic incumbents and election winners,

---

[6] Note that if the last was a preelection, then this is a postelection year. Thus, ELE_{t-1} is the postelection indicator. Again, the care taken to allocate the ELE indicator over the calendar-year makes such precision possible.

[7] Gallagher et al. (1995: ch. 13) summarize the broadly favorable evidence.

competing with strategic challengers and facing rational voters' demand for credibility (i.e., promise fulfillment), create preelectoral *and* larger and more-certain postelectoral policy manipulation.

The ratcheting of electoral surges found in transfers and in debts, but not in inflation, underscores another obvious but neglected point. Electoral surges will accumulate to higher long-run levels in policies that adjust more slowly in polities that hold elections more frequently. That is, through electoral *frequency*, electoral *cycles* have long-run effects. The implications for future work are two.

First, greater care must be taken to specify the dynamics of electioneering. The care taken here in measuring *ELE* and in specifying dynamic empirical models are only limited first steps. The election-year indicator allocated its 1 *ELE* unit to near precisely the calendar year preceding exact election dates and it also incorporated differing election dates across parts of the government (presidents and legislators). While that facilitated many of the preceding insights, other potentially fruitful *details* were ignored. For example, the foreseeability and expected closeness of elections were not incorporated and could have produced more insights (see Chapter 2, note 31). Theories about the distribution of policy influence within government and its determinants could also be explored if less-arbitrary assumptions guided *ELE* measurement. To explore these, policies with strong election cycles could serve as dependent variables in models including separate election-year measures for each government-part.[8] Similarly, dynamic specifications here were informed by theory (especially in Chapter 3) as well as the substance and the stochastic features of the dependent and independent variables, and that bore the fruit, for example, that electoral frequency has long-run effects, but still more attention to theory could go further. This relatively neglected role of measurement and specification in the process from theory building to empirical evaluation and back is elaborated later.

Second, electoral frequency depends on constitutional provisions defining maximum or fixed interelection periods, the conditions under which incumbents may or must call early elections, and party-systemic and other political-economic factors that influence strategic democratic governments' recourse to allowed early elections. Thus, the long-run effects of electoral politics will vary over time across democracies according to the

---

[8] Obviously, empirical leverage in such a model on these theoretical questions would derive only from country-times where the parts had differing election dates.

incentives for strategic policy makers created from the set of constitutional, electoral, and executive-legislative institutions in their polity: exactly the sort of complex institutional interactions broadly stressed throughout this book, and an interesting specific venue for their further exploration.

Thus, electoral policy-manipulation is a reopened and important issue; "rumors of its empirical demise have been greatly exaggerated." To put it starkly, hoping to rekindle debate: Tufte (1978), read correctly and directly rather than in later summary misreadings, was right all along. Strategic competing challengers and incumbents produce electoral manipulation – new here: both preelectoral and, even more, postelectoral – (a) in proportion to the relative importance policy makers attach to a few more votes in that particular election, (b) allocated across multiple policy instruments to the degrees to which (c) international and domestic institutions and structures allow governments to control that instrument and (d) that instrument is easily directed clearly to voters for maximal vote-buying effect. Apparent previous empirical failings condemn more the match between the statistical tests conducted and these arguments than they do election-cycle theory.

5.1.1.2. Strategic Partisan Governments

Partisan-theory intellectual history is also long and illustrious, and, here, partisan policy differences are usually easily found empirically. Controversy regards more outcomes than policies. A core example: to the degree the political and economic decisions of private actors reflect rational expectations, the real effects of partisan macroeconomic policy will be short-term and proportional to the "surprise" from their preelection forecasts of policy to actual postelection-outcome policy. Hibbs (1977, 1987) argued for longer-term effects, and Hibbs et al. (1996) seemed to support. Alesina (1988b) argued for shorter, and Alesina et al. (1993) and Alesina et al. (1997) seemed to support. Likely, something intermediate holds because private actors and public policy makers are probably partly forward-looking but also less than fully informed and rational. The analyses in Chapters 2–4 stressed a different aspect of strategic partisan policy making – how incumbents look forward in the political-economic cycle and manipulate policies to alter the policies and outcomes of future cycles – but some of the same issues surface.

Summarizing the evidence, partisan deficit-cycles were typically small but could be large in the intuitive direction if incumbents face considerable risk of replacement by governments ideologically far from them.

Contrary to some strategic arguments, however, governments act as standard partisan theory predicts, with left or right deficits higher or lower, *only* when facing such replacement risk. When reasonably secure in office, the left amasses surpluses and the right deficits, opposite both partisan theory and some recent strategic extensions. Data more directly support standard partisan theory for transfers, mildly, and for inflation, strongly. The implications for future partisan-theory research are similar to those for electoral manipulation. Scholars have paid too little attention to which policies strategic policy makers could best manipulate for partisan purposes, and to what degree under differing international and domestic institutional structures, and have underestimated the importance of the dynamic properties of different policies.

In jumping to asking when partisan policy-manipulation should have real effects, the current central debate mentioned earlier, scholars skipped several prior questions. First, which policies have greater partisan effects? Evidence in Chapter 3 showed that public debt generally reduced unemployment and raised inflation, distributional effects, but had little impact on growth (efficiency). Thus, left and right governments should strongly differ over debt-related policies. Chapter 4 showed that monetary policy (even if credible) also has opposite unemployment and inflation effects and so should likewise differ strongly under left and right governments. Transfers, instead, go to the old, poor, and unemployed but induce labor market rigidity (inefficiency). Partisans would clearly trade some efficiency for unemployment and welfare benefits at different rates, but retirement benefits are less likely to divide along partisan lines. Thus, transfers produced stronger evidence for electoral than partisan manipulation compared with debts and inflation. This leaves the seemingly odd nature of partisan debt-effects to explain.

Joining nicely to Schultz's (1995) argument and finding that incumbents attempt electoral manipulation only when expecting close elections, these results indicate that only when right and left governments face stiff partisan competition do they employ deficits as their core constituencies would desire. Facing lesser opposition ideological and electoral threat, they are less solicitous and perhaps more cavalier about economic efficiency. Powell (1982: ch. 5) argued similarly that partisan policy-differences will only appear with regular left-right alternations in government. Thus, again, electoral institutions and party-systemic conditions determine what partisan effects to expect and where. Partisan manipulation, like electoral, has opportunity costs, so *strategic* left and right governments will not simply offer their constituents deficits or surpluses under all conditions, even if international exposure and domestic debt levels would not have constrained them from it. Strategic partisan governments have differing *debt* than *deficit* interests.

Alesina and Tabellini (1990) argued that strategic incumbents might amass debt to constrain the fiscal options of expected replacements who are ideologically far from, and would therefore spend quite differently than, themselves. Persson and Svensson (1989) argued that a strategic right might amass debt to constrain the left's desired high spending and a strategic left would retire debt to remove constraints from the right. Aghion and Bolton (1990), Milesi-Ferretti (1995), and Milesi-Ferretti and Spolaore (1993, 1994) argued that, if voters believe the left more (inflationary) default-prone, the right can issue (nominal) debt to increase the amount voters hold and so decrease electoral support for the left, while the left can reduce (nominal) debt to alleviate the electorates' default-risk concerns about it. Unfortunately, these models (a) insufficiently explored the conditions under which such counterintuitive debt incentives of left and right would dominate the more familiar deficit incentives of standard partisan theory, (b) seemed to have underestimated the sluggishness of debt adjustment, and (c) ignored the logical connection between replacement risk and the frequency of partisan oscillation.

Given glacial debt-adjustment, incumbents who expect more-frequent oscillation in office with their oppositions will be less willing to amass debt to constrain future governments because they expect to regain office soon when most of that debt will still constrain them. Moreover, only relatively secure right (left) governments can afford to mortgage some current support to run current deficits (surpluses), risking core-constituency ire to amass (retire) voter-held debt to augment (alleviate) the electorate's inflation and default aversion and so alter voters' partisan preferences to favor them in future elections. Plus, when the left expects to hold office durably, it will want to retain more fiscal maneuverability precisely because its core partisan interests favor deficit responsiveness. Thus, when both are reasonably secure, the left may be less likely to tolerate structural deficits (i.e., to amass debt) than the right; and, when the right and left face strong replacement risk, they will address current deficit-policy to their core constituencies. The results in Chapter 3 support this replacement-risk-augmented partisan-budget-cycle theory, and also accord with Sweden's long-secure left having kept debt relatively low while Italy's equally long-secure center-right tolerated unrestrained structural deficits, and with the greater association of left and right with deficits and surpluses in democracies like the United Kingdom where left-right oscillation occurs with greater regularity. Future theoretical development and empirical models, therefore, need to address the opportunity costs of both strategic-debt and standard-partisan-deficit policy, with greater awareness of debt's slow adjustment-rate and of the logical connection of replacement risk to the frequency of partisan oscillation.

5.1.2. Multiple Institutional-Structural Interactions and the Incentives of Strategic Policy Makers

Another recurrent theme is the importance of multiple interaction effects, especially those among and between institutional and interest structures. Chapter 2 showed voter participation and income distribution each moderate the other's transfers effect. Chapter 3 demonstrated that governments' partisan debt policies depend on their replacement risk, and that fractionalized governments retard fiscal adjustment, magnifying the long-run debt-impacts of all other factors. Chapter 4 found that the unemployment and inflation effects of credible monetary conservatism depend on the degree of coordination in wage-price bargaining and its sectoral composition and, vice versa, those of the coordination and structure of bargaining depend on the monetary stance. Each of these either directly reflects the political-economic structure of interests (e.g., income distribution, sectoral structure) or of institutions (e.g., monetary or bargaining institutions) or is largely institutionally determined (e.g., participation, replacement risk, fractionalization). At least two broad implications for comparative democratic political economy follow.

First, returning to first principles illustrated in Figure 1.22, institutions and structure modify the incentives of political-economic actors because they determine their organizational and other strategic capacities and/or because they condition the relationship between particular actions and outcomes. They do *not*, as sometimes suggested, alter actors' underlying preferences, that is, the arguments to their utility functions; rather, they modify what actions will optimally pursue those goals. The issue seems merely nomothetic, but, practically, theory can be built and evaluated more effectively when appearances that institutional structures change preferences are taken to suggest (a) that theory oversimplified or otherwise misspecified actors' utility functions and (b) that the solution is to specify utilities in less reduced forms closer to their priors that allow institutional structure to vary the optimal actions for obtaining fixed preferences. Chapter 4, for example, revealed that neoclassical models of monetary policy making oversimplified private actors' preferences as being fully encompassed by rational expectations, which in that case was to assume perfect competition and thereby zero strategic-capacity, which are not generally applicable descriptions of the institutional structure of developed democracies. The applied solution returned closer to priors in specifying the utility functions of wage-price bargainers (firms' profits, unions' real consumption and employment) and allowed institutional-structural variables within the model (credible monetary conservatism, bargaining coordination, sectoral structure) to alter the relations between bargainers' actions and their *constant* underlying aims of profits, real wages, and employment. In this way, one can explore the effects of varying parameters of interest, like monetary conservatism (threat size), to derive positive implications *within the model*. If institutional structure alters preferences, contrarily, comparative statics derive from changes *of* the models and so cannot be analyzed *within one* but rather emerge from extramodel assumptions.

Second, such interactive views, as in several results here, underscore that actors' incentives generally depend on the broad configuration of domestic and international political-economic institutions and structures in their environment (see, e.g., Hall and Soskice 2000). Of course, scholars cannot hope to understand, much less to model, the entire sets of possible relevant interactions, but the book demonstrated two broad approaches to this problem that bore fruit.

First, the cycle-of-political-economy framework can guide research to the most prominent institutional interactions. For example, in Chapter 2, the effects of the income distribution on policy makers' incentives to redistribute were seen to depend most directly on the electoral processes that produce representatives from that distribution of interests, especially, how electoral institutions foster or hinder voter participation from across the polity. Similarly, because monetary policy and wage-price settlements jointly produce real wages and outcomes from nominal wages, prices, and money, the incentives of monetary policy makers and wage-price bargainers most directly depend on interactions of institutional structures in those two venues: central bank independence, exchange-rate regimes, bargaining organizations, and sectoral differences in their exposure to competition. The book demonstrated throughout that analyzing one institutional structure exclusively can seriously mislead, so more-encompassing analyses that consider many interactions of institutions and structure are generally preferable, ceteris paribus. Usually, though, such generality can be purchased only with greater complexity and/or abstraction, but, in this respect, doors open to truly cumulative research. Advances made at lower generality or higher abstraction, which could only be made with the clear focus facilitated by such analyses, may later be combined to allow more-encompassing analysis. A positivist's test of what constitutes an advance in this joint effort is the generality and concreteness gained against the parsimony lost.

The second approach to combining multiple interactions parsimoniously and fruitfully is to push harder on theories to specify the nature of the interactions involved, that is, the functional form of the empirical models used to evaluate them.

Chapters 3 and 4 provide two simple examples. In Chapter 3, government fractionalization emerged as a key political-economic factor in explaining wide and expanding differences in public debt across democracies, especially since the 1970s. Theory suggested that weaker governments with many veto actors could adjust less swiftly than more-unified ones to *any* political-economic shock, such as, but not only, the 1970s oil crises. Slower adjustment implies that the long-run effects of *all* other factors depend on fractionalization and, vice versa, that of fractionalization depends on *all* other factors. Commonly, to model interactions like this, scholars would multiply fractionalization by all k other variables and add those k new terms linearly. That consumes k additional degrees of freedom and induces tremendous colinearity among the now $2k + 1$ variables, leaving no hope of meaningful empirical evaluation. Prior empirical research on debt stabilization, recognizing this, ignored its interactive implications, but that misspecified the theory and induced highly sample-dependent – and, as it happened, conflicting – results because fractionalization effects depend on many other factors, whose values will vary across samples. Simply controlling for those other factors will not suffice, but Chapter 3 demonstrated that the theoretical implications were more precise than the common approach realizes, enabling very compact modeling of the many implied interactions. Veto actors retard fiscal-adjustment rates. Adjustment rates, in turn, are modeled by the lagged dependent-variable, and so a single term, multiplying fractionalization by the lagged dependent variable, captures all the theoretically implied interactions. The results were highly statistically significant, robust to permutations of sample and controls, and also highly substantively revealing, highlighting, for example, that fractionalization-slowed adjustment has opposite debt-effects depending on the status quo fiscal situation being debt accumulation or reduction (e.g., post- and pre-1970s). Note that similar arguments should apply to any political-economic consideration that privileges the status quo, and so, many implicitly interactive hypotheses are not currently recognized as such, and even those recognized are not modeled as such in the mistaken belief that to do so would insurmountably compromise empirical leverage on and/or substantive evaluation of the theory.

Similarly, Chapter 4 demonstrated that the inflation effects of monetary delegation to central banks depend on *all* political-economic factors to which autonomous, conservative central banks and responsive, democratic governments would respond differently, and vice versa those of all k such factors depend on the bank's autonomy and conservatism (Franzese 1999b; 1999a shows this extends logically to monetary delegation via exchange-rate pegs to foreign authorities). The implication is again highly interactive and requires $2k + 1$ additional terms as commonly modeled. Chapter 4, however, showed that the implied interactions derive from the convex-combinatorial form (assumed simply a linear-weighted average) of realized inflation, requiring just one additional parameter to model. Again, results were quite significant, robust, and substantively revealing.

Notice, moreover, that any situation of shared policy-making control virtually implies that realized policies will be convex combinations, although not necessarily simple linear-weighted averages. For example, principal-agent situations involve principals who would behave according to $f(X)$ when in full control, agents who would follow $g(Z)$ when fully uninfluenced by principals, and some set of (usually institutional) factors, I, that affect enforcement and monitoring costs, etc., and so determine the degrees, $h(I) \in \{0 \ldots 1\}$, to which principals manage to drive agents to act as desired. $h(I)$ can be quite complicated, but such situations imply that policy, Y, will be: $Y = h(I) \cdot f(X) + (1 - h(I)) \cdot g(Z)$. Thus, all elements of X, Z, and I generally interact to determine Y, but, if $h(I)$, $f(X)$, and $g(Z)$ can be modeled compactly, so can these highly interactive hypotheses. For example, Chapter 4's principals and agents are governments and central banks. $g(Z)$ is a constant, π_c, because the standard theory assumes banks would produce constant low-inflation if they had full and direct inflation control. Inflation under full and direct government control is assumed to respond linearly to some political-economic factors, X. Lastly, the degree of bank control, $b(I)$, is exactly what "central bank independence," C, indices claim to measure. Thus, $\pi = C \cdot \pi_c + (1 - C) \cdot f(X)$ captures all the implied interactions.

These examples show that institutions in general typically have multiple interactive effects and also that multiple institutional interactions can often be modeled more compactly, and so substantively-intuitively and theoretically- and empirically-powerfully, than commonly recognized. Institutions tend to process structures of interests and other conditions into effective pressures on policy makers and other political-economic actors (as in how electoral institutions alter income-disparity effects or governmental structure alters responses to policy determinants), or to apportion the relative abilities of multiple potentially relevant actors to implement policies and affect outcome (as in how monetary institutions allocate inflation-policy control). Institutions thus typically moderate the impacts of several other factors in a common way, that is, proportionally; and, whenever one variable alters the impact of several others proportionally, one term, namely that proportionality, suffices to encompass multiple interactions.

The standard linear-interactive approach instead allows a separate coefficient for each interaction of, for example, fractionalization with another variable, which entertains a possibility that fractionalization can alter the impact of each differently, which demands too much of the data. Theory here implies rather that veto actors retard adjustment. Because this should be no more or less so for parts of debt induced by some factors than others – indeed, more usually, the nature of institutional impacts is that all other factors' impacts will be similarly conditioned – only one coefficient is needed to reflect that *common* impact of fractionalization on the adjustment of all debt, however induced: which asks much less of the data. This expands the scope and sophistication of the multiple institutional interactions scholars can explore. To give a new example, "governments" are usually made of many actors with some partial control of public policy. In the United States, for example, presidents, each house of Congress, and sometimes bureaucracies and state and local authorities jointly control or affect particular policies or outcomes. If theory can specify how the policies of each actor when in full control would respond to the others and to other factors, then convex-combinatorial specifications could allow a single estimation of these responses, uncovering the many implied interactions with just $N - 1$ (N = number of actors) additional factors of proportionality (see, e.g., Franzese 1999a). Further research could then begin to explore theories purporting to explain the actors' relative influence under different conditions by modeling these factors of proportionality.

In sum, political-economic actors' incentives, thus policies and outcomes, depend on interactions of the many international and domestic political-economic institutions and structures in their environment. Especially important interactions were found here between (a) institutions that influence electoral participation and the political-economy's income distribution in determining effective democratic demand for redistribution, (b) government fractionalization and other political-economic conditions that induce debt in determining fiscal adjustments, and (c) monetary-policy-making institutions and wage-price-bargaining institutions and structures in determining unemployment, and (d) monetary institutions and many other political-economic factors in determining inflation. The book demonstrated that such multiple, complex interactions implied by modern institutional political economy can be modeled statistically compactly and substantively fruitfully.

5.1.3. Expectations and Strategic Policy Making in Developed Democracies

Evidence of strategic democratic policy making also recurred throughout, and strategic behavior implies forward-looking political-economic actors. For example, electioneering follows a strategic dynamic wherein voters, incumbents, and challengers each respond to their expectations of the others' promises and actions. Likewise, incumbent partisan governments respond strategically to their expectations of future governments' characteristics and actions, with voters acting on their expectations of, as informed by their experiences under, each. Monetary policy makers and wage-price bargainers also responded strategically to their expectations of the other. Such strategic political-economic behavior rests on actors' expectations of future conditions and actions, their own and others.

Strategic behavior implies *forward-looking* expectations, but this need not mean *fully informed* and *rational*. Chapter 3, for example, found substantively and statistically strong relations between fiscal complexity and public debt, which could not arise if voters were fully informed and rational. Chapter 4 found (and reviewed many others who found) very strong evidence for real economic costs of an institution that previous rational-expectations theory expected had none (these real effects do not depend on any absence of rationality; see Chapter 4, note 1, and Chapter 4, note

36). The weight of these results plus those as weightily demonstrating strategic behavior suggests that political economists take greater care to specify the *degrees* to which different actors will be rational and fully informed in different settings.

Note, first, that *rational* expectations is a misnomer.[9] Lucas's (1976) path-setting article argued that assuming, as had earlier econometric forecasting, that political-economic actors would not alter their current behavior in response to expected policy-changes could badly misinform policy prescriptions. Political-economic actors are reasoning human beings, capable of thinking about how future policies should alter their current choices: *forward-looking* expectations. *Rational*-expectations models of policies and outcomes assume all the model's actors know the model's structure (though they may have uncertainty about some parameters) and form their expectations according to it, or they form expectations and behave as if they knew the model (Friedman 1953), using the *as if* assumption to approximate a more elaborate learning and selection process. Thus, a better name than rational expectations would be *model-consistent* expectations. The only other option, proponents argue, is to apply ad hoc assumptions about expectations formation, the most common of which are purely *adaptive expectations* that assume that political-economic actors only learn from experience (i.e., the past) and do not reason forward to how policies should alter their own behaviors. Both extremes seem implausible,[10] and scholars likely intend either as only an approximation. *Positive* political economists, in asking what policies and outcomes *will* rather than *ought* to occur,[11] must however consider the degrees to which particular actors will manage to become fully informed and react optimally to that information and to which they will instead adopt simplifying heuristics such as adaptive expectations.

---

[9] This paragraph owes much to a lecture by Ben Friedman in his course on macroeconomic theory and policy, spring 1991, Harvard University.

[10] To confirm the implausibility of pure model-consistent expectations, note that some of these models are original research, implying they were not previously known. Thus, they could only be *as if* approximations. To confirm implausibility of pure adaptive expectations, note that actors with large stakes in certain outcomes expend great efforts to discover political-economic models. The only reason for anyone but a political economist to do so is to reason forward and alter one's actions before one must learn through potentially painful experience.

[11] Actually, normative political economists do not escape so easily. If empirical relations between variables depend on the degree of fully informed rationality, then so do any normative pronouncements regarding optimal policies.

Near one extreme, for example, Buchanan and Wagner (1977) argued that voters generally exhibit great fiscal illusion and so democracy induces deficits; near the other, Barro (1974, 1979) argued that political-economic actors fully internalize the long-run debt implications of current budgets, giving no reason for democracy to produce deficits (indeed, public debt would be real-wealth neutral). In studying the debt effects of tax structure complexity, Chapter 3 implicitly asks the degree to which each extreme approximates democratic debt-policy making. Policy makers (or their aides and advisors) certainly have great incentives (and the capability) to understand these relationships, but voters generally will have little such incentives because one vote, informed or uninformed, is unlikely to affect election outcomes and so policy (Downs 1957). Some will nonetheless attempt to become informed out of civic duty or for some other subjective or objective benefit the information will bring them, but more-complicated fiscal systems are more likely to outweigh these benefits (Downs 1960; Buchanan and Wagner 1977). Thus, strategic policy-makers have incentives to complicate or simplify certain policies to raise or lower other actors' abilities to assess fully and properly their costs and benefits, which suggests some hypotheses for future research. For example, Olson (1982) notes that policy makers may complicate tax codes to raise voters' costs of uncovering special-interest loopholes within them. Similarly, Chapter 3's result that fiscal complexity facilitates deficit financing of public economic activities suggests that interests favoring such activities have incentives also to increase such complexity.

In sum, the results suggested that political-economic actors look forward strategically but that they do not all possess equal incentives and abilities to inform those looks. *Model-consistent* and *adaptive* expectations are merely simplifying, equally implausible, ends of a continuum in modeling expectations-formation, and that raises possibilities for future research into what determines where on that continuum key political-economic actors lie. One such investigation that bore fruit here explored varying degrees of fiscal illusion.

5.1.4. Relating Theory to Measurement and Specification to Evidence and Back Again

The final theme emerging from Chapters 2–4 was the crucial value of maintaining close relationship from theory through measurement and specification to empirical evaluation. For example, careful measures of (multiple) election(s) timing, government partisanship, and replacement risk to reflect their theories, in conjunction with modeling the latter pair's interaction to allow the data to adjudicate on three alternative hypotheses, produced many of the inferences on strategic electoral and partisan policy discussed in Section 5.1.1. Likewise, the mapping of competing *influence-* and *veto-actor* theoretical-conceptions of polarization and fractionalization into distinct measures allowed the data to distinguish them unequivocally (favoring the latter). As discussed in Section 5.1.3, closer translation of theoretical predictions of multiple institutional-structural interactions into their empirical specifications allows meaningful statistical and substantive inference from limited comparative-historical evidence available. This subsection's heading clearly summarizes the inference drawn from the emergence of this theme.

Comparative, historical evidence informs understandings of the empirical world, comprises the only database available to political economists with which to evaluate their theories,[12] and, at least as important, provides insights on where and how theories purporting to explain those data may need revision. However, between theory building and empirical evaluation and inference lay the equally critical issues of measurement to represent theoretical concepts and specification to reflect theoretically predicted relationships, through which the limited evidence available will provide the empirical leverage for the evaluations that can inform theoretical refinement. Simply: results can only be as theoretically *informing* as the specification and measurement are theoretically *informed*. This book's relative successes (and failures) no doubt illustrated that mantra (more than) sufficiently.

On a related concluding note, for replication purposes (see, e.g., *PS* 1995), and for future researchers to capitalize on the theoretical refinements informed by these efforts in measurement, specification, and inference, all data employed here (and many supplemental analyses, tables, and figures) are currently available at <http://www-personal.umich.edu/~franzese>.[13]

5.2. *A Prospective Overview*

The book's arguments and findings also sum to relate the comparative evolution of democratic management of the macroeconomy. Condensing that

---

[12] This includes surveys, which are no less historical, but excludes experimental data, which have their own advantages and limitations.

[13] Responsibility for academic propriety (i.e., citation, etc.), and for copyright and intellectual-property law adherence rests fully with the user.

comparative, historical tale to a paragraph:[14] postwar governments in developed democracies committed themselves to some degree of social-insurance, public-good, and macroeconomic-management provision. This democratic class-compromise and postwar-settlement on the Keynesian welfare state had two often conflicting goals:[15] to foster capitalist development and to alleviate its distributional consequences. However, democracy and capitalism distribute political influence and economic resources differently, so governments in these capitalist democracies faced political-economic pressures that induced different trade-offs between these goals than apolitical economic theory predicts. Universal pressures deriving from these differing distributions of political and economic resources, and from shared exposure to common international and domestic political-economic conditions broadly explain the similarities observed in (typically growing) public economic-activity. However, while commonalities in these policy and outcome experiences were notable, variation was as noteworthy. The responses of these similarly democratic governments to similar underlying pressures and challenges differed across countries over time because the domestic and international political-economic institutions and structures of interest of their environments interacted to shape their policy-making incentives differently. Lastly, as their expanding commitments and rising exposure increasingly narrowed fiscal-policy efficacy and maneuverability, democratic governments turned to monetary policy and then monetary and other institutional and structural "reforms," aiming to rebuild the broad postwar coalitions behind their active roles in the economy. But these "reforms," however couched in terms of efficiency, retained important distributional consequences, so long-familiar left-right, equity-efficiency conflicts over these policies were more replicated than replaced by modern political battles over "reforms" of the institutions and structures within which democratic contestation over the public role in fulfilling these commitments will continue.

What, then, may be concluded about the prospects for continued political-economic viability and utility of the policy commitments? Room for more growth certainly seems exhausted on many fronts. Aging populations have already begun to tax the capacity of public-pension systems

---

[14] The web appendix (<http://www-personal.umich.edu/~franzese>) offers a convenient summary outline.

[15] "Keynesian" is meant here to cover aggregate macroeconomic-management policies, fiscal and monetary; "welfare" to refer to redistribution and other equity-intentioned policies; and "state" to imply democratic.

to continue at past rates. Higher and more-persistent unemployment, to which transfers growth itself contributed, also increasingly strain social-welfare-and-insurance systems. In less participatory democracies especially, rising demand for retrenchment of the latter has already made large inroads. Rising debt, resulting in sizable interest premia, constrains fiscal-policy use and further exacerbates the strain on the fisc, especially in more-fractionalized democracies. Governments in most developed democracies are increasingly left with only monetary and "supply-side" policies to try to fulfill their dual commitments to spur capitalist development and ease its distributional consequences. Rising public-sector employment, however, has made monetary regulation of the macroeconomy an increasingly costly option, especially in highly coordinated political-economies. It has also been a severe drag on productivity growth, which may be the only long-run solution to the conflicting growth and distributional goals in capitalist democracy. Thus, modern democratic debate over institutional and structural "reform" of the Keynesian welfare state within which governments attempt to manage the macroeconomy still surrounds very familiar left-right conflicts, the left favoring actived government involvement in spurring growth and equality through public investment in physical and especially human capital, the right favoring reduced government roles to free efficient private allocation of consumption and investment resources (Boix 1998).

Shifting more tentatively toward a prospective view, likely public activity cannot continue to expand to absorb these conflicting interests and goals, and hard decisions about what must and what cannot be cut will come increasingly to the fore. Democratic governments and citizens seem already to be renegotiating the postwar settlement; the classes are making new democratic compromises; and, in "reforming" their policy commitments, capitalist democracies are rediscovering Smith's free hand, Ricardo's free trade, and Schumpeter's creative destruction (competition). The certainty is that the democratic resolution of these political battles will have huge distributional consequences; their efficiency implications are what remain in doubt. Perhaps one might conjecture, though, that the less participatory, less fractionalized, and less coordinated political economies already retreated at least sufficiently from the purported efficiency-dampening side effects of overcommitment. There, the danger may lie in forgetting Marx and Keynes completely. As Offe (1984) reminds us, capitalist development depends to some degree on reducing its volatility (Keynes) and on bringing its working class with it (Marx). Furthermore, Hibbs (1987: ch. 1) showed, the postwar era of growth in government documented, explained, and explored here, coincided with a dramatic postwar rise in average growth and declines in unemployment and growth-volatility relative to the previous 50 years when governments last embraced the "new" conservative orthodoxy of tight money, little public activity, and less social insurance. Furthermore, the increasing (sometimes dramatically increasing) inequality that accompanied public retrenchment in these countries also cannot be viewed with equanimity.[16] The converse conjecture is that the more participatory, more fractionalized, and more coordinated political economies can further rediscover Smith, Ricardo, and Schumpeter with less fear as the greater worries in these political economies may still surround the slower output and employment growth that has plagued them for more than a decade. There, Offe's (1984) other admonition may still be appropriate: only strong growth can continue to fund the alleviation of capitalist inequities.

In advocating differing "reforms" of the institutions and structures within which future policy makers will conduct policy, strategic policy makers in capitalist democracies continue to debate the appropriate trade-offs between distributional and growth goals. Voters, in supporting alternative "reforms," continue to debate the appropriate economic roles of these governments and the trade-offs they prefer. And what strategic governments and voters prefer in these struggles depends on multiple interactions among the international and domestic political-economic institutions and structures that determine the purported efficiency and distribution impacts. The "reforms" chosen will thus reflect less a question of jointly arriving on an unambiguous optimum and more voter and policy maker evaluations of *which* institutional biases to accept in those trade-offs, which of course will depend on whose interests those biases serve, and the choices will continue to differ across countries and over time according to multiple interactions among their international and domestic, political and economic, institutional and structural setting. But

---

[16] The late-1990s U.S.-led growth is notable, especially from a view like Boix's. Productivity growth clearly drove this expansion, and, consistent with the view of partisan policies here and especially that in Boix 1998, it contrasted sharply with the mid-1980s U.S. expansion in that inequality eventually declined in the late-1990s but generally rose through the 1980s.

all this is wholly as it should be. That is precisely what democracy does best and what it should do. It resolves such starkly differing interests by the electoral competition of alternative ideas and ideologies on the peaceful campaign battlefield. One need not look hard to observe how much worse nondemocratic contestation over the economy can be.

References

Achen, C. 1983. "Toward Theories of Data: The State of Political Methodology." In A. Finifter, ed., *Political Science: The State of the Discipline*, 69–93. Washington, D.C.: APSA.

Agell, J., and B.-C. Ysander. 1993. "Should Governments Learn to Live with Inflation? Comment." *American Economic Review* 83 (1): 305–11.

Aghion, P., and P. Bolton. 1990. "Government Debt and the Risk of Default: A Political Economic Model of the Strategic Role of Debt." In R. Dornbusch and M. Draghi, eds., *Public Debt Management: Theory and Practice*, 315–45. Cambridge: Cambridge University Press.

Akerloff, G. A., and J. L. Yellen. 1985. "A Near-Rational Model of the Business Cycle with Wage and Price Inertia." *Quarterly Journal of Economics* 100 (suppl.): 823–38.

Aldrich, J. 1983a. "A Downsian Spatial Model with Party Activism." *American Political Science Review* 77 (4): 1974–90.

1983b. "A Spatial Model with Party Activists: Implications for Electoral Dynamics." *Public Choice* 41: 63–100.

1995. *Why Parties? The Origin and Transformation of Political Parties in America*, 163–93. Chicago: University of Chicago Press.

Aldrich, J., and M. McGinnis. 1989. "A Model of Party Constraints on Candidate Positions." *Mathematical and Computer Modeling* 12: 437–50.

Alesina, A. 1988a. "The End of Large Public Debts." In F. Giavazzi and L. Spaventa, eds., *High Public Debt: The Italian Experience*, 34–79. Cambridge: Cambridge University Press.

1988b. "Macroeconomics and Politics." *NBER Macroeconomics Annual* 3: 13–61.

1989. "Politics and Business Cycles in Industrial Democracies." *Economic Policy* 8: 55–98.

Alesina, A., G. Cohen, and N. Roubini. 1992. "Macroeconomic Policies and Elections in OECD Democracies." *Economics and Politics* 4 (1): 1–30.

Alesina, A., M. DeBroeck, A. Prati, and G. Tabellini. 1992. "Default Risk on Government Debt in OECD Countries." Innocenzo Gasparini Institute for Economic Research Working Paper no. 16. University Bocconi, Milan.

Alesina, A., and A. Drazen. 1991. "Why Are Stabilizations Delayed?" *American Economic Review* 82 (4): 1170–88.

Alesina, A., and R. Gatti. 1995. "Independent Central Banks: Low Inflation at No Cost?" *American Economic Review* 85 (2): 196–200.

Alesina, A., V. Grilli, and G.-M. Milesi-Ferretti. 1994. "The Political Economy of Capital Controls." In L. Leiderman and A. Rozin, eds., *Capital Mobility: The Impact on Consumption, Investment, and Growth*, 289–321. Cambridge University Press.

Alesina, A., J. Londregan, and H. Rosenthal. 1993. "A Model of the Political Economy or the United States." *American Political Science Review* 87 (1): 12–33.

Alesina, A., and R. Perotti. 1994. "The Political Economy of Budget Deficits." NBER Working Paper no. 4637. Cambridge, Mass.

1995a. "Budget Deficits and Budget Institutions." Harvard University and Columbia University. Typescript.

1995b. "Fiscal Expansions and Adjustments in OECD Countries." *Economic Policy* 21: 207–48.

Alesina, A., and D. Rodrik. 1994. "Distributive Politics and Economic Growth." *Quarterly Journal of Economics* 109 (2): 465–90.

Alesina, A., and N. Roubini. 1992. "Political Cycles in OECD Economies." *Review of Economic Studies* 59 (4): 663–88.

Alesina, A., N. Roubini, with G. Cohen. 1997. *Political Cycles and the Macroeconomy*. Cambridge, Mass.: MIT Press.

Alesina, A., and L. Summers. 1993. "Central Bank Independence and Macroeconomic Performance: Some Comparative Evidence." *Journal of Money, Credit, and Banking* 25 (2): 151–63.

Alesina, A., and G. Tabellini. 1987. "Rules and Discretion with Non-Coordinated Monetary and Fiscal Policies." *Economic Inquiry* 25 (4): 619–30.

1989. "External Debt, Capital Flight, and Political Risk." *Journal of International Economics* 27 (3–4): 199–220.

1990. "A Positive Theory of Budget Deficits and Government Debt." *Review of Economic Studies* 57 (3): 403–14.

1992. "Positive and Normative Theories of Public Debt and Inflation in an Historical Perspective." *European Economic Review* 36 (2): 337–44.

Al Marhubi, F., and T. Willett. 1995. "The Antiinflationary Influence of Corporatist Structures and Central Bank Independence: The Importance of the Hump-Shaped Hypothesis." *Public Choice* 84 (1): 153–62.

Alogoskoufis, G. S., and A. Manning. 1988. "On the Persistence of Unemployment." *Economic Policy* 7: 427–69.

Alt, J. 1983. "The Evolution of Tax Structures." *Public Choice* 41: 181–222.

1985. "Political Parties, World Demand, and Unemployment: Domestic and International Sources of Economic Activity." *American Political Science Review* 79 (4): 1016–40.

1987. "Crude Politics: Oil and the Political Economy of Unemployment in Britain and Norway, 1970–85." *British Journal of Political Science* 17 (2): 149–99.

References

Alt, J., and A. Alesina. 1996. "Political Economy: An Overview." In R. E. Goodin and H.-D. Klingemann, eds., *A New Handbook of Political Science*, 645–69. Oxford: Oxford University Press.

Alt, J., and A. Crystal. 1983. *Political Economics*. Berkeley: University of California Press.

Alt, J., and R. Lowry. 1994. "Divided Government, Fiscal Institutions, and Budget Deficits: Evidence from the States." *American Political Science Review* 88 (4): 811–28.

Alvarez, R. M., G. Garrett, and P. Lange. 1991. "Government Partisanship, Labor Organization, and Macroeconomic Performance." *American Political Science Review* 85 (2): 539–56.

Atkinson, A., L. Rainwater, and T. Smeeding. 1995. *Income Distribution in OECD Countries: The Evidence from the Luxembourg Income Study (LIS)*. Social Policy Studies no. 18. Paris: OECD.

Axelrod, R. 1970. *Conflict of Interest*. Chicago: Markham.

1984. *The Evolution of Cooperation*. New York: Basic Books.

Bade, R., and M. Parkin. 1982. "Central Bank Laws and Monetary Policy." Department of Economics, University of Western Ontario. Typescript.

Ball, L., and D. Romer. 1990. "Real Rigidities and the Nonneutrality of Money." *Review of Economic Studies* 57 (2): 183–203.

Baron, D. 1991. "Majoritarian Incentives, Pork-Barrel Programs and Procedural Control." *American Journal of Political Science* 35 (1): 57–90.

Baron, D., and J. Ferejohn. 1989. "Bargaining in Legislatures." *American Political Science Review* 83 (4): 1181–206.

Barro, R. 1974. "Are Government Bonds Net Wealth?" *Journal of Political Economy* 82 (6): 1095–117.

1979. "On the Determination of Public Debt." *Journal of Political Economy* 87 (5): 940–7.

1985. "Government Spending, Interest Rates, Prices, and Budget Deficits in the United Kingdom, 1730–1918." University of Rochester Working Paper. Rochester, N.Y.

1986. "U.S. Deficits since World War I." *Scandinavian Journal of Economics* 88 (1): 193–222.

1990. "Government Spending in a Simple Model of Economic Growth." *Journal of Political Economy* 98 (5), pt. 2: S103–26.

Barro, R., and R. Gordon. 1983a. "Rules, Discretion, and Reputation in a Model of Monetary Policy." *Journal of Monetary Economics* 12 (1): 101–22.

1983b. "A Positive Theory of Monetary Policy in a Natural Rate Model." *Journal of Political Economy* 91 (4): 589–610.

Bartels, L. 1991. "Instrumental and 'Quasi-Instrumental' Variables." *American Journal of Political Science* 35 (3): 777–800.

Beck, N. 1984. "Domestic Political Sources of American Monetary Policy." *Journal of Politics* 46 (3): 786–814.

1992. "Comparing Dynamic Specifications: The Case of Presidential Approval." *Political Analysis* 3: 51–87.

Beck, N., and J. Katz. 1993. "Model Assessment and Choice via Cross-Validation." University of California, San Diego. Typescript.

    1995. "What To Do (and Not to Do) with Time-Series-Cross-Section Data in Comparative Politics." *American Political Science Review* 89 (3): 634–47.

    1997. "Nuisance or Substance: Specifying and Estimating Time-Series-Cross-Section Models." *Political Analysis* 6: 1–36.

Beck, N., J. Katz, R. Alvarez, G. Garrett, and P. Lange. 1993. "Government Partisanship, Labor Organization, and Macroeconomic Performance: A Corrigendum." *American Political Science Review* 87 (4): 945–8.

Berger, S., ed. 1981. *Organizing Interests in Western Europe*. Cambridge: Cambridge University Press.

Bergstrom, T., and R. Goodman. 1973. "Private Demands for Public Goods." *American Economic Review* 63: 280–96.

Berry, W., and R. Lowery. 1987. "Explaining the Size of the Public Sector: Responsive and Excessive Government Interpretations." *Journal of Politics* 49 (2): 401–40.

Blair, A. 1984. "The Emerging Spanish Party System: Is There a Model?" *West European Politics* 7 (4): 120–55.

Blais, A., D. Blake, and S. Dion. 1993. "Do Parties Make a Difference? Parties and the Size of Government in Liberal Democracies." *American Journal of Political Science* 37 (1): 40–62.

    1996. "Do Parties Make a Difference? A Reappraisal." *American Journal of Political Science* 40 (2): 514–20.

Blanchard, O. J. 1989. "A Traditional Interpretation of Macroeconomic Fluctuations." *American Economic Review* 79 (5): 1146–64.

Blanchard, O. J., and M. Watson. 1986. "Are Business Cycles All Alike?" In R. Gordon, ed., *The American Business Cycle: Continuity and Change*, 123–56. Boston and Chicago: NBER and University of Chicago Press.

Bleaney, M. 1996. "Central Bank Independence, Wage-Bargaining Structure, and Macroeconomic Performance in OECD Countries." *Oxford Economic Papers* 48 (1): 20–38.

Boix, C. 1998. *Political Parties, Growth and Equality: Conservative and Social Democratic Economic Strategies in the World Economy*. Cambridge: Cambridge University Press.

Borrelli, S., and T. Royed. 1995. "Government 'Strength' and Budget Deficits in Advanced Democracies." *European Journal of Political Research* 28 (2): 225–60.

Browne, E. C., and J. Dreijmanis, eds. 1982. *Government Coalitions in Western Democracies*. New York: Longman.

Bruneau, T., and A. MacCleod. 1986. *Politics in Contemporary Portugal: Parties and the Consolidation of Democracy*. Boulder, Colo.: Lynne Rienner.

Bruno, M., and J. Sachs. 1987. *The Economics of Worldwide Stagflation*. Cambridge, Mass.: Harvard University Press.

Buchanan, J., and R. Wagner. 1977. *Democracy in Deficit: The Political Legacy of Lard Keynes*. New York: Academic Press.

Calmfors, L., ed. 1990. *Wage Formation and Macroeconomic Policy in the Nordic Countries*. Uppsala: SNS Forlag.

References

1993a. *Centralization of Wage Bargaining and Macroeconomic Performance – A Survey*. Seminar Paper no. 536. Stockholm: Institute for International Economic Studies.

1993b. "Lessons from the Macroeconomic Experience of Sweden." *European Journal of Political Economy* 9 (1): 25–72.

1998. "Macroeconomic Policy, Wage Setting, and Employment – What Difference Does the EMU Make?" *Oxford Review of Economic Policy* 14 (3): 125–51.

Calmfors, L., and J. Driffill. 1988. "Centralisation of Wage Bargaining and Macroeconomic Performance." *Economic Policy* 6: 13–61.

Calvo, G. A., and P. E. Guidotti. 1990. "Indexation and Maturity of Government Bonds: An Exploratory Model." In R. Dornbusch and M. Draghi, eds., *Public Debt Management: Theory and History*, 52–93. Cambridge: Cambridge University Press.

Calvo, G. A., P. E. Guidotti, and Leonardo Leiderman. 1991. "Optimal Maturity of Nominal Government Debt: The First Tests." *Economics Letters* 35 (4): 415–21.

Cameron, D. 1978. "The Expansion of the Public Economy: A Comparative Analysis." *American Political Science Review* 72 (4): 1243–61.

1984. "Social Democracy, Corporatism, Labor Quiescence, and the Representation of Economic Interest in Advanced Capitalist Society." In J. H. Goldthorpe, ed., *Order and Conflict in Contemporary Capitalism*, 143–78. New York: Oxford University Press.

Cameron, D., and K. McDermott. 1995. "Expansion and Contraction of the Public Economy, 1960–1992." Yale University. Typescript.

Carlin, W., and D. Soskice. 1990. *Macroeconomics and the Wage Bargain: A Modern Approach to Employment, Inflation and the Exchange Rate*. Oxford: Oxford University Press.

Castles, F., ed. 1982. *The Impact of Parties: Politics and Policies in Democratic Capitalistic States*. London: Sage.

Castles, F., and P. Mair. 1984. "Left-Right Political Scales: Some 'Expert' Judgements." *European Journal of Political Research* 12 (1): 83–8.

Clark, W. 2000. *Capitalism Not Globalism: Capital Mobility, Central Bank Independence, and the Political Control of the Economy*. Ann Arbor: University of Michigan Press.

Clark, W., and M. Hallerberg. 1999. "Strategic Interaction between Monetary and Fiscal Actors under Full Capital Mobility." New York University and University of Pittsburgh. Typescript.

Clark, W., and U. Reichert, with S. Lomas and K. Parker. 1998. "International and Domestic Constraints on Political Business Cycles in OECD Economies." *International Organization* 52 (1): 87–120.

Coder, J., L. Rainwater, and T. Smeeding. 1989. "Inequality among Children and Elderly in Ten Modern Nations: The United States in an International Context." *American Economic Review* 79 (2): 320–4.

Conway, M. 1985. *Political Participation in the United States*. Washington, D.C.: Congressional Quarterly Press.

Crouch, C. 1985. "Conditions for Trade Union Wage Restraint." In Leon Lindberg and Charles Mair, eds., *The Politics of Inflation and Economic Stagnation*, 105–39. Washington, D.C.: Brookings Institution.

Cubitt, R. 1989. *Precommitment and the Macroeconomic Policy Game*. D.Phil. thesis, Oxford University.

    1992. "Monetary Policy Games and Private Sector Precommitment." *Oxford Economic Papers* 44 (3): 513–30.

    1995. "Corporatism, Monetary Policy and Macroeconomic Performance: A Simple Game Theoretic Analysis." *Scandinavian Journal of Economics* 97 (2): 245–59.

Cukierman, A. 1992. *Central Bank Strategy, Credibility, and Independence: Theory and Evidence*. Cambridge, Mass.: MIT Press.

    1996. "The Economics of Central Banking," Working Paper no. 36–96. Stackler Institute for Economic Studies, Tel-Aviv University.

Cukierman, A., and F. Lippi. 1999. "Central Bank Independence, Centralization of Wage Bargaining, Inflation and Unemployment – Theory and Some Evidence." *European Economic Review* 43 (7): 1395–1434.

Cukierman, A., and A. Meltzer. 1989. "A Political Theory of Government Debt and Deficits in a Neo-Ricardian Framework." *American Economic Review* 79 (4): 713–33.

Cukierman, A., S. Webb, and B. Neyapti. 1992. "Measuring the Independence of Central Banks and Its Effect on Policy Outcomes." *World Bank Economic Review* 6 (3): 353–98.

Danziger, S., and P. Gottschalk. 1995. *America Unequal*. Cambridge, Mass.: Harvard University Press.

Danziger, S., and D. Weinberg. 1994. "The Historical Record: Trends in Family Income, Inequality, and Poverty." In S. Danziger, G. Sandefur, and D. Weinberg, eds., *Confronting Poverty: Prescriptions for Change*, 18–50. Cambridge: Harvard University Press.

Davidson, R., and J. MacKinnon. 1981. "Several Tests for Model Specification in the Presence of Alternative Hypotheses." *Econometrica* 49 (3): 781–93.

De Haan, J. 1999. "Endogenizing the Bias." University of Groningen, the Netherlands. Typescript.

De Haan, J., W. Moessen, and B. Volkerink. 1997. "Budgetary Procedures: Aspects and Changes. New Evidence for Some European Countries." University of Groningen, the Netherlands. Unpublished Manuscript.

De Haan, J., and J.-E. Sturm. 1994. "Political and Institutional Determinants of Fiscal Policy in the European Community." *Public Choice* 80: 157–72.

    1997. "Political and Economic Determinants of OECD Budget Deficits and Government Expenditures: A Reinvestigation." *European Journal of Political Economy* 13 (4): 739–50.

De Haan, J., J.-E. Sturm, and G. Beekhuis. 1999. "The Weak Government Thesis: Some New Evidence." *Public Choice* 101: 163–76.

DeLury, G., ed. 1987. *World Encyclopedia of Political Systems and Parties*. 2nd ed. New York: Facts on File.

References

DeSwaan, A. 1973. *Coalition Theories and Cabinet Formation: A Study of Formal Theories of Coalition Formation Applied to Nine European Parliaments after 1918.* Amsterdam: Elsevier.

Diermeier, D., and R. Stevenson. 1994. "Censoring, Competing Risks, and Cabinet Duration." Paper presented at the annual meeting of the Political Methodology Section of the American Political Science Association, Madison, July.

Dodd, L. C. 1976. *Coalitions in Parliamentary Government.* Princeton: Princeton University Press.

Downs, A. 1957. *An Economic Theory of Democracy.* New York: Harper and Row.

——— 1960. "Why the Government's Budget Is Too Small in a Democracy." *World Politics* 12: 541–63.

Drazen, A., and V. Grilli. 1993. "The Benefit of Crises for Economic Reform." *American Economic Review* 83 (2): 588–608.

Dye, T. 1979. "Politics versus Economics: The Development of the Literature on Policy Determination." *Policy Studies Journal* 7: 652–62.

Eckstein, H. 1966. *Division and Cohesion in Democracy: A Study of Norway.* Princeton: Princeton University Press.

Edin, P.-A., and H. Ohlsson. 1991. "Political Determinants of Budget Deficits: Coalition Effects versus Minority Effects." *European Economic Review* 35 (8): 1597–603.

Eichengreen, B. 1990. "One Money for Europe? Lessons from the U.S. Currency and Customs Union." *Economic Policy* 10: 117–87.

——— 1992. *Should the Maastricht Treaty Be Saved?* Princeton Studies in International Finance no. 74, Princeton.

——— 1994. *International Monetary Arrangements for the 21st Century.* Washington, D.C.: Brookings Institution.

——— 1996. "European Monetary Unification and International Monetary Cooperation." Council on Foreign Relations Study Group on Transatlantic Economic Relations. Typescript.

Eichengreen, B., and J. Frieden, eds. 1997. *The Political Economy of European Integration.* Ann Arbor: University of Michigan Press.

Eijffinger, S., and J. De Haan. 1996. *The Political Economy of Central Bank Independence.* Special Papers in International Economics no. 19, May. Department of Economics, International Finance Section, Princeton University.

Esping-Andersen, G. 1985. *Politics against Markets.* Princeton: Princeton University Press.

——— 1990. *The Three Worlds of Welfare Capitalism.* Princeton: Princeton University Press.

Eulau, H., and M. S. Lewis-Beck, eds. 1985. *Economic Conditions and Electoral Outcomes: The US and Western Europe.* New York: Agathon Press.

European Journal of Political Research. 1992–1998. Political Data Annuals.

Fair, R. 1988. "Sources of Economic Fluctuations in the United States." *Quarterly Journal of Economics* 103: 313–32.

Ferejohn, J., M. Fiorina, and R. McKelvey. 1987. "Sophisticated Voting and Agenda Independence in the Distributive Policy Setting." *American Journal of Political Science* 31 (1): 167–93.

Ferejohn, J., and K. Krehbiel. 1987. "The Budget Process and the Size of the Budget." *American Journal of Political Science* 31 (1): 169–93.

Flanagan, S., 1973. "Models and Methods of Analysis." In G. Almond, S. Flanagan, and R. Mandt, eds., *Crisis, Choice, and Change: Historical Studies in Political Development*, 43–102. Boston: Little, Brown.

Forteza, A. 1998. "The Wage Bargaining Structure and the Inflationary Bias." *Journal of Macroeconomics* 20 (3): 599–614.

Franklin, M. 1996. "Electoral Participation." In L. LeDuc, R. Niemi, and P. Norris, eds., *Comparing Democracies: Elections and Voting in Global Perspective*, 216–35. London: Sage.

Franzese, R. 1994. "Central Bank Independence, Sectoral Interest, and the Wage Bargain." Harvard Center for European Studies Working Paper no. 56. Reprint, no. 5-1, 1995. Cambridge, Mass.

1996a. "A Gauss Procedure to Estimate Panel-Corrected Standard-Errors with Non-Rectangular and/or Missing Data." *Political Methodologist* 7 (2): 2–3.

1996b. "The Political Economy of Over-Commitment: A Comparative Study of Democratic Management of the Keynesian Welfare State." Ph.D. diss., Harvard University.

1998a. "The Political Economy of Public Debt: An Empirical Examination of the OECD Post-War Experience." Paper presented at the Rochester-Northwestern Wallis Conference on Political Economy, Evanston, Ill., November.

1998b. "Political Participation, Income Distribution, and Public Transfers in Developed Democracies." Paper presented at the annual meetings of the American Political Science Association, Boston, September.

1999a. "Exchange-Rate Regimes and Inflation in the Open and Institutionalized Economy." Paper presented at the annual meetings of the American Political Science Association, Atlanta, September.

1999b. "Partially Independent Central Banks, Politically Responsive Governments, and Inflation." *American Journal of Political Science* 43 (3): 681–706.

2000a. "Credibly Conservative Monetary Policy and Labor-/Goods-Market Organization: A Review with Implications for ECB-Led Monetary Policy in Europe." In J. de Haan, ed., *Fifty Years of the Bundesbank: Lessons for the European Central Bank*, 97–124. London: Routledge.

2000b. "Electoral and Partisan Manipulation of Public Debt in Developed Democracies, 1956–1990." In R. Strauch and J. Von Hagen, eds., *Institutions, Politics, and Fiscal Policy*, 61–83. Boston: Kluwer.

2000c. Review of *Political Cycles and the Macroeconomy*, by Alberto Alesina and Nouriel Roubini with Gerald Cohen. *Journal of Policy Analysis and Management* 19 (3): 501–9.

2000d. Review of *Political Parties, Growth and Equality: Conservative and Social Democratic Economic Strategies in the World Economy*, by Carles Boix. *Comparative Political Studies* 33 (5): 686–90.

References

2001. "Monetary Policy and Wage-Price Bargaining: Macro-Institutional Interactions in the Traded, Public, and Sheltered Sectors." In P. Hall and D. Soskice, eds., *Varieties of Capitalism: The Institutional Foundations of Comparative Advantage*. Cambridge: Cambridge University Press.

Franzese, R., and P. Hall. 2000. "The Institutional Interaction of Wage-Bargaining and Monetary Policy." In T. Iversen, J. Pontusson, and D. Soskice, eds., *Unions, Employers, and Central Banks: Macroeconomic Coordination and Institutional Change in Social Market Economies*, ch. 6. Cambridge: Cambridge University Press.

Franzese, R., C. Kam, and A. Jamal. 1999. "Modeling and Interpreting Interactive Hypotheses in Regression Analysis." Paper presented at the annual meetings of the American Political Science Association, Atlanta, September.

Franzese, R., and I. Nooruddin. 1999. "Geographic and Partisan Bases of Representation: Distributive Politics and the Effective Number of Constituencies." Paper presented at the annual meetings of the American Political Science Association, Atlanta, September.

Freeman, J., D. Houser, P. Kellstedt, and J. T. Williams. 1996. "Unit Roots and Causal Inference in Political Science." Paper presented at the annual meetings of the Political Methodology Section of the American Political Science Association, Ann Arbor, Mich., July.

Friedman, M. 1953. "The Methodology of Positive Economics." In M. Friedman, ed., *Essays in Positive Economics*, 3–43. Chicago: University of Chicago Press.

Gali, J. 1992. "How Well Does the IS-LM Model Fit Postwar US Data?" *Quarterly Journal of Economics* 107 (2): 709–38.

Gallagher, M., M. Laver, and P. Mair. 1995. *Representative Government in Modern Europe*. 2nd ed. New York: McGraw-Hill.

Garrett, G. 1992. "The Political Consequences of Thatcherism." *Political Behavior* 14 (4): 361–82.

1993. "The Politics of Structural Change: Swedish Social Democracy and Thatcherism in Comparative Perspective." *Comparative Political Studies* 25 (1): 521–47.

1994. "Popular Capitalism: The Electoral Legacy of Thatcherism." In Anthony Heath, R. Jowell, and B. Taylor, eds., *Labour's Last Chance? The 1992 Election and Beyond*, 107–23. Aldershot: Dartmouth.

1995. "Capital Mobility, Trade, and the Domestic Politics of Economic Policy." *International Organization* 49 (4): 657–87.

1998a. *Partisan Politics in the Global Economy*. Cambridge: Cambridge University Press.

1998b. "Global Markets and National Politics: Collision Course or Virtuous Circle?" *International Organization* 52 (4): 787–824.

1998c. "Shrinking States? Globalization and Policy Autonomy in the OECD." *Oxford Development Studies* 26 (1): 71–98.

1998d. "The Transition to Economic and Monetary Union." In B. Eichengreen and J. Frieden, eds., *Forging an Integrated Europe*, 21–48. Ann Arbor: University of Michigan Press.

2000. "Capital Mobility, Exchange Rates, and Fiscal Policy in the Gobal Economy." *Review of International Political Economy* 7 (1): 153–72.

Garrett, G., and A. Heath. 1991. "The Extension of Popular Capitalism." In A. Heath, R. Jowell, J. Curtice, G. Evans, J. Field, and S. Witherspoon, eds., *Understanding Political Change: The British Voter, 1964–1987*, 120–35. London: Pergamon Press.

Garrett, G., and P. Lange. 1986. "Performance in a Hostile World: Economic Growth in Capitalist Democracies, 1974–1982." *World Politics* 38 (4): 517–45.

1989. "Government Partisanship and Economic Performance: When and How Does 'Who Governs' Matter?" *Journal of Politics* 51 (3): 676–93.

1991. "Political Responses to Interdependence: What's 'Left' for the Left?" *International Organization* 45 (4): 539–64.

1995. "Internationalization, Institutions, and Political Change." *International Organization* 49 (4): 627–55.

Garrett, G., and D. Mitchell. 1999. "International Risk and Domestic Compensation." Yale University. Typescript.

Garrett, G., and C. Way. 1995a. "Labor Market Institutions and the Economic Consequences of Central Bank Independence." Paper presented at the annual meetings of the American Political Science Association, Chicago, September.

1995b. "The Sectoral Composition of Trade Unions, Corporatism and Economic Performance." In B. Eichengreen, J. Frieden, and J. Von Hagen, eds., *Monetary and Fiscal Policy in an Integrated Europe*, 38–61. New York: Springer-Verlag.

1999a. "The Rise of Public Sector Unions, Corporatism, and Macroeconomic Performance." *Comparative Political Studies* 32 (4): 411–34.

1999b. "Public Sector Unions and Wage Determination." In T. Iversen, J. Pontusson, and D. Soskice, eds., *Unions, Employers, and Central Banks*, ch. 9. Cambridge: Cambridge University Press.

Golden, M. 1993. "The Dynamics of Trade Unionism and National Economic Performance." *American Political Science Review* 87 (2): 439–54.

Golden, M., P. Lange, and M. Wallerstein. 1995a. "The End of Corporatism? Wage Setting in the Nordic and Germanic Countries." In S. Jacoby, ed., *Workers of Nations: Industrial Relations in a Global Economy*, 76–100. New York: Oxford University Press.

1995b. "Trade Union Organization and Industrial Relations in the Post-War Era in 16 Nations." Paper presented at the annual meetings of the Midwest Political Science Association, Chicago, September.

Goldthorpe, J. H., ed. 1984. *Order and Conflict in Contemporary Capitalism*. New York: Oxford University Press.

Goodman, J. 1992. *Monetary Sovereignty: The Politics of Central Banking in Western Europe*. Ithaca: Cornell University Press.

Gottschalk, P., and T. Smeeding. 1997. "Cross-National Comparisons of Earnings and Income Inequality." *Journal of Economic Literature* 35 (2): 633–87.

Gourevitch, P. 1986. *Politics in Hard Times: Comparative Responses to International Economic Crises*. Ithaca: Cornell University Press.

288

References

Grilli, V., D. Masciandaro, and G. Tabellini. 1991. "Political and Monetary Institutions and Public Financial Policies in the Industrial Countries." *Economic Policy* 13: 341–92.

Grüner, H. P., and C. Hefeker. 1999. "How Will EMU Affect Inflation and Unemployment in Europe?" *Scandinavian Journal of Economics* 101 (1): 33–47.

Gylfason, T., and A. Lindbeck. 1994. "The Interaction of Monetary Policy and Wages." *Public Choice* 79: 33–46.

Hall, P. 1986. *Governing the Economy: The Politics of State Intervention in Britain and France*. New York: Oxford University Press.

——— ed. 1989. *The Political Power of Economic Ideas: Keynesianism across Nations*. Princeton: Princeton University Press.

——— 1994. "Central Bank Independence and Coordinated Wage Bargaining: Their Interaction in Germany and Europe." *German Politics and Society* (Autumn): 1–23.

Hall, P., and R. Franzese. 1998. "Mixed Signals: Central Bank Independence, Coordinated Wage-Bargaining, and European Monetary Union." *International Organization* 52 (3): 505–35.

Hall, P., and D. Soskice. 2001. *Varieties of Capitalism: The Institutional Foundations of Comparative Advantage*. Cambridge: Cambridge University Press.

Hallerberg, M., and J. Von Hagen. 1999. "Electoral Institutions, Cabinet Negotiations, and Budget Deficits within the European Union." In J. Poterba and J. Von Hagen, eds., *Fiscal Institutions and Fiscal Performance*, 209–32. Chicago: University of Chicago Press.

Harmel, R., K. Janda, and A. Tan. 1995. "Substance vs. Packaging: An Empirical Analysis of Parties' Manifesto Emphases." Paper presented at the annual meetings of the American Political Science Association, Chicago, September.

Harrop, M., and W. Miller. 1987. *Elections and Voters: A Comparative Introduction*. London: Macmillan.

Havrilesky, T., and J. Granato. 1992. "Determinants of Inflationary Performance: Corporatist Structures vs. Central Bank Autonomy." *Public Choice* 76 (3): 249–61.

Headey, B. 1970. "Trade Unions and National Wage Policies." *Journal of Politics* 32: 407–29.

Heclo, H. 1974. *Modern Social Policies in Britain and Sweden*. New Haven: Yale University Press.

Heller, W. 1998. "Divided Legislatures: The Budgetary Effect of Intercameral Partisan Differences in Bicameral Parliaments." University of Nebraska, Lincoln. Unpublished Manuscript.

Hibbs, D. 1977. "Political Parties and Macroeconomic Policy." *American Political Science Review* 71 (4): 1467–87.

——— 1986. "Political Parties and Macroeconomic Policies and Outcomes in the United States." *American Economic Review* 76 (1): 66–70.

——— 1987. *The Americal Political Economy: Macroeconomics and Electoral Politics*. Cambridge, Mass.: Harvard University Press.

1992. "Partisan Theory after Fifteen Years." *European Journal of Political Economy* 8 (2): 361–73.

1994. "The Partisan Model and Macroeconomic Cycles: More Theory and Evidence from the United States." *Economics and Politics* 6 (1): 1–24.

Hibbs, D., F. Carlsen, and E. Pedersen. 1996. "Electoral Uncertainty and Partisan Output Cycles." Paper presented to the Research Training Group in Positive Political Economy, Harvard University.

Hicks, A., and D. Swank. 1984. "On the Political Economy of Welfare Expansion." *Comparative Political Studies* 17 (1): 81–119.

1992. "Policies, Institutions, and Welfare Spending in Industrialized Democracies, 1960–1982." *American Political Science Review* 86 (3): 658–74.

Hicks, A., D. Swank, and M. Ambuhl. 1989. "Welfare Expansion Revisited: Policy Routines and Their Mediation by Party, Class, and Crises, 1957–1982." *European Journal of Political Research* 17 (4): 401–30.

Hirsch, F., and J. Goldthorpe, eds. 1978. *The Political Economy of Inflation*. Cambridge, Mass.: Harvard University Press.

Inglehart, R. 1971. "The Silent Revolution in Europe." *American Political Science Review* 65 (4): 991–1017.

1977. *The Silent Revolution: Changing Values and Political Styles*. Princeton: Princeton University Press.

1990. *Culture Shift in Advance Industrial Society*. Princeton: Princeton University Press.

Inglehart, R., and H.-D. Klingemann. 1987. "Party Identification, Ideological Preference, and the Left-Right Dimensions among Western Mass Publics." In I. Budge, D. Robertson, and D. Hearl, eds., *Ideology, Strategy, and Party Change*, 234–76. Cambridge: Cambridge University Press.

International Monetary Fund (IMF). *International Financial Statistics*. 6/96 CD-ROM, various magnetic tape editions, and various print editions.

Iversen, T. 1993a. "European Monetary Integration and the Politics of Designing Wage Bargaining Institutions: A Comparative Analysis of Germany, Sweden, and Denmark." Paper presented at the conference on Production Regimes in an Integrating Europe, Wissenschaftszentrum, Berlin, July 23–5.

1993b. "National Regimes of Collective Wage Bargaining and Macroeconomic Policies: Lessons from Austria, Denmark, Germany and Sweden." Harvard University. Typescript.

1994. "Wage Bargaining, Monetary Regimes, and Economic Performance in Organized Market Economies: Theory and Evidence." Paper presented at the annual meetings of the American Political Science Association, New York, September.

1996a. "Power, Flexibility and the Breakdown of Centralized Wage Bargaining: The Cases of Denmark and Sweden in Comparative Perspective," *Comparative Politics* 28 (3): 399–436.

1996b. "The Real Effects of Money. An Institutional Model of the Effects of Wage Bargaining and Monetary Policies on Unemployment." Center for German and European Studies Working Paper no. 1.40. University of California, Berkeley.

References

1998a. "Wage Bargaining, Central Bank Independence and the Real Effects of Money." *International Organization* 52 (3): 469–504.

1998b. "Hard Choices for Scandinavian Social Democracy in Comparative Perspective." *Oxford Review of Economic Policy* 14 (2): 59–75.

1998c. "Wage Bargaining, Hard Money and Economic Performance: Theory and Evidence for Organized Market Economies." *British Journal of Political Science* 28 (1): 31–61.

1999a. *Contested Economic Institutions: The Politics of Macroeconomics and Wage Bargaining in Advanced Democracies*. Cambridge: Cambridge University Press.

1999b. "The Political Economy of Inflation: Bargaining Structure or Central Bank Independence?" *Public Choice* 99 (2): 237–58.

2000a. "Decentralization, Monetarism, and the Social-Democratic Welfare State in the 1980s and 90s." In T. Iversen, J. Pontusson, and D. Soskice, eds., *Unions, Employers and Central Banks: Macroeconomic Coordination and Institutional Change in Social Market Economies*, 205–31. Cambridge: Cambridge University Press.

2000b. "The Dynamics of Welfare State Expansion: Trade Openness, De-Industrialization and Partisan Politics." In P. Pierson, ed., *The New Politics of the Welfare State*, ch. 2. Oxford: Oxford University Press.

Forthcoming. "National Regimes of Collective Wage Bargaining and Macro-Economic Policies: Lessons from Austria, Denmark, Germany and Sweden." In R. Locke and K. Thelen, *The Shifting Boundaries of Labor Politics*. Cambridge, Mass.: MIT University Press.

Iversen, T., and T. Cusack. 1998. "The Causes of Welfare State Expansion: De-industrialization or Globalization?" Paper presented at the annual meetings of the American Political Science Association, Atlanta, September.

Iversen, T., and B. Eichengreen. 1999. "Institutions and Economic Performance in the 20th Century: Evidence from the Labor Market." *Oxford Review of Economic Policy* 15 (4): 121–38.

Iversen, T., J. Pontusson, and D. Soskice, eds. 2000. *Unions, Employers and Central Banks: Macroeconomic Coordination and Institutional Change in Social Market Economies*. Cambridge: Cambridge University Press.

Iversen, T., and D. Soskice. 1999. "The Political Economy of Macroeconomic Coordination in an Integrating Europe." Paper presented at the annual meetings of the American Political Association, Atlanta, September.

Iversen, T., and A. Wren. 1998. "Equality, Employment, and Budgetary Restraint: The Trilemma of the Service Economy." *World Politics* 50 (4): 507–46.

1997. "Choosing Paths: Explaining Distributional Outcomes in the Post-Industrial Economy." Paper presented at the annual meetings of the American Political Science Association, Washington, D.C., September.

Jackman, R., and R. Miller. 1995. "Voter Turnout in the Industrial Democracies during the 1980s." *Comparative Political Studies* 27 (4): 467–92.

Janda, K. 1980. *Political Parties Data Handbook*. New York: United Nations.

Jensen, H. 1997. "Monetary Policy Coordination May Not Be Counterproductive." *Scandinavian Journal of Economics* 99 (1): 73–80.

Jonsson, G. 1995. "Institutions and Macroeconomic Outcomes – the Empirical Evidence." *Swedish Economic Policy Review* 2 (1): 181–212.

Kamerman, S., and A. Kahn. 1997. "Investing in Children: Government Expenditure for Children and Their Families in Western Industrialized Countries." In G. Cornia and S. Danziger, eds., *Child Poverty and Deprivation in the Industrialized Countries, 1945–1995*, ch. 4. New York: Oxford University Press.

Katzenstein, P. 1985. *Small States in World Markets: Industrial Policy in Europe*. Ithaca: Cornell University Press.

Keech, W., and H. Lee. 1995. "On a Theory of Voting in Partisan Models of Macroeconomic Policy." Paper presented at the annual meetings of the American Political Science Association, Chicago, September.

Kennedy, E. 1991. *The Bundesbank: Germany's Central Bank in the International Monetary System*. London: Pinter.

Kerr, H. 1987. "The Swiss Party Systems: Steadfast and Changing." In H. Daalder, ed., *Party Systems in Denmark, Austria, Switzerland, The Netherlands, and Belgium*, 107–92. London: Pinter.

King, G., J. Alt, N. Burns, and M. Laver. 1990. "A Unified Model of Cabinet Dissolution in Parliamentary Democracies." *American Journal of Political Science* 34 (3): 847–71.

Kitschelt, H. 1994. *The Transformation of European Social Democracy*. Cambridge: Cambridge University Press.

Klingemann, H.-D., R. I. Hofferbert, and I. Budge. 1995. *The Comparative Manifestos Project*. Wissenschaftszentrum, Berlin.

Klingemann, H.-D., R. I. Hofferbert, I. Budge, with H. Keman et al. 1994. *Parties, Policies, and Democracy*. Boulder, Colo.: Westview Press.

Koole, R., and P. Mair. 1994. "Political Data in 1993." Introduction to *European Journal of Political Research*, special issue: *Political Data Yearbook*. 26 (3–4): 221–30.

Korpi, W. 1980. "Social Policy and Distributional Conflict in the Capitalist Democracies: A Preliminary Comparative Framework." *West European Politics* 3 (3): 296–316.

——— 1983. *The Democratic Class Struggle*. London: Routledge.

Kramer, G. 1983. "Is There a Demand for Progressivity?" *Public Choice* 41: 223–38.

Kreps, D. 1990. "Corporate Culture and Economic Theory." In J. Alt and K. Shepsle, eds., *Perspectives on Positive Political Economy*, 90–143. Cambridge: Cambridge University Press.

Kydland, F. E., and E. C. Prescott. 1977. "Rules Rather Than Discretion: The Inconsistency of Optimal Plans." *Journal of Political Economy* 85 (3): 473–92.

Lambertini, L. 1999. "Are Budgets Used Strategically?" University of California, Los Angeles. Typescript.

Lane, J.-E., and S. Ersson. 1994. *Politics and Society in Western Europe*. London: Sage.

Lane, J.-E., D. McKay, and K. Newton. 1991. *Political Data Handbook: OECD Countries*. New York: Oxford University Press.

References

Lange, P. 1984. "Unions, Workers, and Wage Regulation: The Rational Bases of Consent." In J. Goldthorpe, ed., *Order and Conflict in Contemporary Capitalism*, 98–123. New York: Oxford University Press.

Lange, P., and G. Garrett. 1985. "The Politics of Growth: Strategic Interaction and Economic Performance in the Advanced Industrial Democracies, 1974–1980." *Journal of Politics* 47: 792–827.

1987. "The Politics of Growth Reconsidered." *Journal of Politics* 49 (1).

Larkey, P., C. Stolp, and M. Winer. 1981. "Theorizing about the Growth of Government: A Research Assessment." *Journal of Public Policy* 1 (2): 157–220.

Laver, M., and I. Budge, eds. 1991. *Party and Coalition Policy in Western Europe*. Cambridge: Cambridge University Press.

Laver, M., and W. Hunt. 1992. *Policy and Party Competition*. New York: Routledge.

Laver, M., and N. Schofield. 1991. *Multiparty Government: The Politics of Coalition in Europe*. New York: Oxford University Press.

Laver, M., and K. Shepsle, eds. 1994. *Cabinet Ministers and Parliamentary Government*. Cambridge: Cambridge University Press.

1996. *Making and Breaking Governments: Cabinets and Legislatures in Parliamentary Democracies*. Cambridge: Cambridge University Press.

Layard, R., S. Nickell, and R. Jackman. 1991. *Unemployment: Macroeconomic Performance and the Labour Market*. New York: Oxford University Press.

Lehmbruch, G., and P. Schmitter, eds. 1982. *Patterns of Corporatist Policy-Making*. London: Sage.

Lewis-Beck, M. S. 1990. *Economics and Elections: The Major Western Democracies*. Ann Arbor: University of Michigan Press.

Lijphart, A. 1994. *Electoral Systems and Party Systems: A Study of Twenty-Seven Democracies, 1945–1990*. Oxford: Oxford University Press.

Lin, M. 1999. "Veto Actors and Welfare-Responsiveness of Democratic Governments." University of California, Los Angeles. Typescript.

Lindberg, L., and C. Maier, eds. 1985. *The Politics of Inflation and Economic Stagnation*. Washington, D.C.: Brookings.

Lindblom, C. 1977. *Politics and Markets*. New York: Basic Books.

Lohmann, S. 1992. "Optimal Commitment in Monetary Policy Credibility versus Flexibility." *American Economic Review* 82 (1): 273–86.

Lucas, R. 1976. "Econometric Policy Evaluation: A Critique." In K. Brunner and A. Meltzer, eds., *The Phillips Curve and Labor Markets*, 19–46. Carnegie-Rochester Conference Series on Public Policy, vol. 1. Amsterdam: North-Holland. Reprinted in R. Lucas, *Studies in Business-Cycle Theory*, 104–30. Cambridge, Mass.: MIT Press, 1981.

1981. *Studies in Business-Cycle Theory*. Cambridge, Mass.: MIT Press.

Lucas, R., and L. A. Rapping. 1969. "Real Wages, Employment, and Inflation." *Journal of Political Economy* 77 (3): 721–54. Reprinted in R. Lucas, *Studies in Business-Cycle Theory*, 19–58. Cambridge, Mass.: MIT Press, 1981.

Lucas, R., and N. Stokey. 1983. "Optimal Fiscal and Monetary Policy in an Economy without Capital." *Journal of Monetary Economics* 12 (1): 55–94.

Lupia, A., and K. Strom. 1995. "Coalition Termination and the Strategic Timing of Parliamentary Elections." *American Political Science Review* 89 (3): 648–65.

Mackie, T., and R. Rose. 1991. *The International Almanac of Electoral History*. Washington, D.C.: Congressional Quarterly.

MacKuen, M., R. Erikson, and J. Stimson. 1992. "Peasants or Bankers?" *American Political Science Review* 86 (3): 597–611.

Mankiw, N. G. 1985. "Small Menu Costs and Large Business Cycles: A Macroeconomic Model of Monopoly." *Quarterly Journal of Economics* 100 (2): 529–37.

Marmor, T., T. Smeeding, and V. Greene, eds. 1994. *Economic Security and Intergenerational Justice a Look at North America*. Washington, D.C.: Urban Institute Press.

Martin, L., and R. Stevenson. 1995. "A Unified Approach to Cabinet Formation and Survival in Parliamentary Democracies." Paper presented at the annual meetings of the Midwest Political Science Association, Chicago, September.

Mavgordatos, G. 1984. "The Greek Party System: A Case of Limited but Polarized Pluralism." *West European Politics* 7 (4): 156–69.

Mayer, T., ed. 1990. *The Political Economy of American Monetary Policy*. Cambridge: Cambridge University Press.

Meltzer, A., and S. Richard. 1978. "Why Government Grows (and Grows) in a Democracy." *Public Interest* 52 (summer): 111–18.

——— 1981. "A Rational Theory of the Size of Government." *Journal of Political Economy* 89 (5): 914–27.

Meyer, B. 1995. "Lessons from the U.S. Unemployment Insurance Experiments." *Journal of Economic Literature* 33 (1): 91–131.

——— 1990. "Unemployment Insurance and Unemployment Spells." *Econometrica* 58 (4): 757–82.

Milesi-Ferretti, G.-M. 1995. "The Disadvantage of Tying Their Hands: On the Political Economy of Policy Commitments." *Economic Journal* 105 (433): 1381–1403.

Milesi-Ferretti, G.-M., and E. Spolaore. 1993. "Strategic Policy: A General Framework." Harvard University. Typescript.

——— 1999. "How Cyclical Can an Incumbent Be? Strategic Policy in a Model of Government Spending." *Journal of Public Economics* 55 (1): 121–40.

Milner, H. 1997. *Interests, Institutions, and Information: Domestic Politics and International Relations*. Princeton: Princeton University Press.

Missale, A., and O. J. Blanchard. 1992. "The Debt Burden and Debt Maturity." Massachusetts Institute of Technology. Typescript.

Morgan, M.-J. 1976. "The Modeling of Government Coalition Formation: A Policy-Based Approach with Interval Measurement." Ph.D. diss., University of Michigan, Ann Arbor.

Mosher, J., and R. Franzese. 1999. "*Comparative* Advantage in National Institutional Structures." Paper presented at the German-American Academic Council, SSRC, Center for Advanced Behavioral Studies, Stanford University, July.

Nagel, J. H. 1987. *Participation*. Englewood Cliffs, N.J.: Prentice-Hall.

References

Nordhaus, W. 1975. "The Political Business Cycle." *Review of Economic Studies* 42 (1): 169–90.

Norpoth, H., M. S. Lewis-Beck, and J.-D. LaFay. 1991. *Economics and Politics: The Calculus of Support*. Ann Arbor: University of Michigan Press.

Oatley, T. 1997. *Monetary Politics: Exchange Rate Cooperation in the European Union*. Ann Arbor: University of Michigan Press.

———. 1999. "How Constraining Is Capital Mobility? The Partisan Hypothesis in an Open Economy." *American Journal of Political Science* 43 (4): 1003–27.

Offe, C. 1984. *Contradictions of the Welfare State*. London: Hutchinson.

Olson, M. 1965. *The Logic of Collective Action: Public Goods and the Theory of Groups*. Cambridge: Harvard University Press.

———. 1982. *The Rise and Decline of Nations: Economic Growth, Stagflation, and Social Rigidities*. New Haven: Yale University Press.

Organization of Economic Cooperation and Development (OECD). *Economic Outlook and Reference Supplement* no. 62. 1998 disk.

———. *Economic Outlook, Historical Statistics*. 6/97 disk, extended from print editions.

———. *Labor Force Statistics*. Various print editions.

———. *National Accounts*, Vol. 2: *Detailed Tables*. 1996 1.44MB disk edition, extended by various print editions.

Ozkan, F., A. Sibert, and A. Sutherland. 1998. "Monetary Union, Entry Conditions, and Economic Reform." University of Durham. Typescript.

Pampel, F., and J. Williamson. 1988. "Welfare Spending in Advanced Industrial Democracies, 1950–1980." *American Journal of Sociology* 93 (6): 1424–56.

Penn World Tables. 1995. V. 5.6 by A. Heston and R. Summers. V. 5.x, described in "The Penn World Table (Mark 5): An Expanded Set of International Comparisons, 1950–1988," *Quarterly Journal of Economics* (May 1991): 327–68.

Persson, T., and L. Svensson. 1989. "Why a Stubborn Conservative Would Run a Deficit: Policy with Time Inconsistent Preferences." *Quarterly Journal of Economics* 104: 325–46.

Persson, T., and G. Tabellini, eds. 1994. *Monetary and Fiscal Policy*. Cambridge, Mass.: MIT Press.

Peterson, P. E. 1990. *Welfare Magnets: A New Case for a National Standard*. Washington, D.C.: Brookings Institution.

Pontusson, J. 1992a. "At the End of the Third Road." *Politics and Society* 20 (2): 305–32.

———. 1992b. "The Role of Economic-Structural Change in the Decline of European Social Democracy." Paper presented at the annual meetings of the American Political Science Association, Chicago, September.

———. 1995a. "Explaining the Decline of European Social Democracy." *World Politics* 47 (3): 495–533.

———. 1995b. "From Comparative Public Policy to Political Economy: Putting Political Institutions in Their Place and Taking Interests Seriously." *Comparative Political Studies* 28 (1): 117–48.

Pontusson, J., and P. Swenson. 1993. "Employers on the Offensive: Wage Bargaining, Pay Practices and New Production Strategies in Sweden." Cornell University. Typescript.

1996. "Labor Markets, Production Strategies, and Wage Bargaining Institutions." *Comparative Political Studies* 29 (1): 37–66.

Posen, A. 1998. "Central Bank Independence and Disinflationary Credibility: A Missing Link?" *Oxford Economic Papers* 50 (3): 335–9.

1995b. "Declarations Are Not Enough: Financial Sector Sources of Central Bank Independence." *NBER Macroeconomics Annual* 10: 253–74.

Powell, G. B. 1982. *Contemporary Democracies: Participation, Stability, and Violence.* Cambridge, Mass.: Harvard University Press.

Powell, G. B., and G. Whitten. 1993. "A Cross-National Analysis of Economic Voting." *American Journal of Political Science* 37 (2): 391–414.

Primus, W. 1996. "The Safety Net Delivers: The Effects of Government Benefit Programs in Reducing Poverty." Center on Budget and Policy Priorities ⟨http://www.cbpp.org/sndsum.htm⟩.

1998. "Strengths of the Safety Net: How the EITC, Social Security, and Other Government Programs Affect Poverty." Center on Budget and Policy Priorities ⟨http://www.cbpp.org/snd98.htm⟩.

PS. 1995. "Contributions to the Debate on 'Verification/Replication,'" 28 (3).

Rae, D. 1967. *The Political Consequences of Electoral Laws.* New Haven: Yale University Press.

Rae, D., and M. Taylor. 1970. *The Analysis of Political Cleavages.* New Haven: Yale University Press.

Rama, M. 1994. "Bargaining Structure and Economic Performance in the Open Economy." *European Economic Review* 38: 403–15.

Regini, M. 1984. "The Conditions for Political Exchange: How Concertation Emerged and Collapsed in Italy and Great Britain." In J. H. Goldthorpe, ed., *Order and Conflict in Contemporary Capitalism*, 124–42. New York: Oxford University Press.

Riker, W. 1962. *The Theory of Political Coalitions.* New Haven: Yale University Press.

Rodríguez, F. 1999. "Does Distributional Skewness Lead to Redistribution? Evidence from the United States." *Economics and Politics* 11 (2): 171–200.

Rodrik, D. 1998. "Why Do More Open Economies Have Bigger Governments?" *Journal of Political Economy* 106 (5): 997–1032.

Rogoff, K. 1985. "The Optimal Degree of Commitment to an Intermediate Monetary Target." *Quarterly Journal of Economics* 100 (4): 1169–90.

1989. "Reputation, Coordination, and Monetary Policy." In R. Barro, ed., *Modern Business Cycle Theory*, 236–64. Cambridge, Mass.: Harvard University Press.

1990. "Equilibrium Political Budget Cycles." *American Economic Review* 80 (1): 21–36.

Rogoff, K., and A. Sibert. 1988. "Elections and Macroeconomic Policy Cycles." *Review of Economic Studies* 55 (1): 1–16.

Romer, T. 1975. "Individual Welfare, Majority Voting, and the Properties of a Linear Income Tax." *Journal of Public Economics* 14 (1): 163–85.

Romer, T., and H. Rosenthal. 1978. "Political Resource Allocation." *Public Choice* 33: 27–43.

References

Rose, R. 1984. *Understanding BIG Government: The Programme Approach*. London: Sage.

Rosenstone, S. J., and J. M. Hansen. 1993. *Mobilization, Participation, and Democracy in America*. New York: Macmillan.

Roubini, N., and J. Sachs. 1989a. "Political and Economic Determinants of Budget Deficits in the Industrial Democracies." *European Economic Review* 33 (2): 903–33.

——— 1989b. "Government Spending and Budget Deficits in the Industrialized Countries." *Economic Policy* 8: 99–132.

Rubinstein, A. 1982. "Perfect Equilibrium in a Bargaining Model." *Econometrica* 50 (1): 97–109.

Sani, G., and G. Sartori. 1983. "Polarization, Fragmentation, and Competition in Western Democracies." In H. Daalder and P. Mair, eds., *Western European Party Systems*, 307–40. London: Sage.

Scharpf, F. 1984. "Economic and Institutional Constraints of Full-Employment Strategies: Sweden, Austria, and West Germany, 1973–82." In J. H. Goldthorpe, ed., *Order and Conflict in Contemporary Capitalism*, 257–90. New York: Oxford University Press.

——— 1987. "Game-Theoretical Interpretations of Inflation and Unemployment in Western Europe." *Journal of Public Policy* 7 (3): 227–57.

——— 1991. *Crisis and Choice in European Social Democracy*. Ithaca: Cornell University Press.

Schmitter, P. 1981. "Interest Intermediation and Regime Governability in Contemporary Western Europe and North America." In S. Berger, ed., *Organizing Interests in Western Europe*, 285–327. Cambridge: Cambridge University Press.

Schultz, K. 1995. "The Politics of the Political Business Cycle." *British Journal of Political Science* 25 (1): 79–100.

Sharpe, L. 1988. "The Growth and Decentralization of the Modern Democratic State." *European Journal of Political Research* 16 (4): 365–80.

Shonfield, A. 1965. *Modern Capitalism*. Oxford: Oxford University Press.

Sibert, A. 1999. "Monetary Integration and Economic Reform." *Economic Journal* 109 (1): 78–92.

Sibert, A., and A. Sutherland. 1998. "Monetary Regimes and Labor Market Reform." CEPR Discussion Paper no. 1731. Center for Economic Policy Research, London.

Sims, C. 1992. "Interpreting the Macroeconomic Time Series Facts: The Effects of Monetary Policy." *European Economic Review* 36 (3): 975–1011.

Simmons, B. 1994. *Who Adjusts? Domestic Sources of Foreign Economic Policy during the Interwar Years*. Princeton: Princeton University Press.

Skott, P. 1997. "Stagflationary Consequences of Prudent Monetary Policy in a Unionized Economy." *Oxford Economic Papers* 49 (4): 609–22.

Smeeding, T., M. O' Higgins, and L. Rainwater, with A. B. Atkinson, eds. 1990. *Poverty, Inequality and Income Distribution in Comparative Perspective: The Luxembourg Income Study (LIS)*. New York: Harvester Wheatsheaf.

Smeeding, T., and D. Sullivan. 1998. "Generations and the Distribution of Economic Well-Being: A Cross-National View." *American Economic Review* 88 (2): 254–8.

Soskice, D. 1990. "Wage Determination: The Changing Role of Institutions in Advanced Industrialized Countries." *Oxford Review of Economic Policy* 6 (4): 36–61.

Soskice, D., and T. Iversen. 1998. "Multiple Wage Bargaining Systems in the Single European Currency Area." *Oxford Review of Economic Policy* 14 (3): 110–24.

——— 2000. "The Non-Neutrality of Monetary Policy with Large Price or Wage Setters." *Quarterly Journal of Economics* 115 (1): 265–84.

Spolaore, E. 1993. "Policy-Making Systems and Economic Inefficiency: Coalition Governments versus Majority Governments." Ph. D. diss., Harvard University.

Stevenson, R. 1994a. "Electoral Rules and Intra-Party Organization." Paper presented at the annual meetings of the American Political Science Association, New York, September.

——— 1994b. "Minority Governments and Divided Legislatures." Paper presented at the annual meetings of the Midwest Political Science Association, New York, September.

——— 1997. "Cabinet Formation, Electoral Performance and Economic Voting in Parliamentary Democracies," Paper presented at the annual meetings of the American Political Science Association, Washington, D.C., September.

Strom, K. 1984. "Minority Governments in Parliamentary Democracies: The Rationality of Nonwinning Cabinet Solutions." *Comparative Political Studies* 17 (2): 199–227.

——— 1985. "Party Goals and Government Performance in Parliamentary Democracies." *American Political Science Review* 79 (3): 738–54.

——— 1988. "Contending Models of Cabinet Stability." *American Political Science Review* 82 (3): 923–30.

——— 1990a. *Minority Government and Majority Rule*. Cambridge: Cambridge University Press.

——— 1990b. "A Behavioral Theory of Competitive Political Parties." *American Journal of Political Science* 34 (2): 565–98.

Strom, K., I. Budge, and M. Laver. 1994. "Constraints on Cabinet Formation in Parliamentary Democracies." *American Journal of Political Science* 38 (2): 303–35.

Swenson, P. 1989. *Fair Shares: Unions, Pay, and Politics in Sweden and West Germany*. Ithaca: Cornell University Press.

——— 1991. "Bringing Capital Back In, or Social Democracy Reconsidered: Employer Power, Cross-Class Alliances, and Centralization of Industrial Relations in Denmark and Sweden." *World Politics* 43 (4): 513–45.

Taagepera, R., and M. Shugart. 1989. *Seats and Votes: The Effects and Determinants of Electoral Systems*. New Haven: Yale University Press.

Tabellini, G. 1991. "The Politics of Intergenerational Redistribution." *Journal of Political Economy* 99 (2): 335–57.

References

Tabellini, G., and A. Alesina. 1990. "Voting on the Budget Deficit." *American Economic Review* 80 (1): 37–49.

Taylor, M., and M. Laver. 1973. "Government Coalitions in Western Europe." *European Journal of Political Research* 1 (3): 205–48.

Thelen, K. 1994. "Beyond Corporatism: Toward a New Framework for the Study of Labor in Advanced Capitalism." *Comparative Politics* 27 (1): 107–25.

Tsebelis, G. 1995. "Decision Making in Political Systems: Veto Players in Presidentialism, Parliamentarism, Multicameralism and Multipartism." *British Journal of Political Science* 25 (3): 289–326.

Tufte, E. 1978. *Political Control of the Economy*. Princeton: Princeton University Press.

United Nations (UN). *Age and Sex Demographics*. Various print editions.
Demographic Yearbook. Various print editions.

Velasco, A. 1997. "The Common Property Approach to Fiscal Policy." In M. Tommasi and F. Sturzen egger, eds., *The Political Economy of Reform*. Cambridge, Mass.: MIT Press.

Velasco, A., and V. Guzzo. 1999. "The Case for a Populist Central Banker." *European Economic Review* 43 (7): 1317–44.

Verba, S., N. Nie, and J. Kim. 1978. *Participation and Political Equality: A Seven-Nation Comparison*. Chicago: University of Chicago Press.

Verba, S., K. Schlozman, and H. Brady. 1995. *Voice and Equality: Civic Voluntarism in American Politics*. Cambridge, Mass.: Harvard University Press.

Von Hagen, J. 1992. "Budgeting Procedures and Fiscal Performance in the European Communities." Commission of the European Communities, DG II Economics Papers no. 96. Luxemburg.

Von Hagen, J., and I. Harden. 1995. "Budgeting Processes and Commitment to Fiscal Discipline." *European Economic Review* 39 (3): 771–9.

Warwick, P. 1992a. "Economic Trends and Government Survival in West European Parliamentary Democracies." *American Political Science Review* 86 (4): 875–87.

1992b. "Ideological Diversity and Government Survival in Western European Parliamentary Democracies." *Comparative Political Studies* 25 (2): 332–61.

1992c. "Rising Hazards: An Underlying Dynamic of Parliamentary Government." *American Journal of Political Science* 36 (4): 857–76.

1994. *Government Survival in Parliamentary Democracies*. Cambridge: Cambridge University Press.

1996. "Coalition Government Membership in West European Parliamentary Democracies." *British Journal of Political Science* 26 (3): 471–99.

Warwick, P., and S. Easton. 1992. "The Cabinet Stability Controversy: New Perspectives on a Classic Problem." *American Journal of Political Science* 36 (1): 122–46.

Weingast, B., and W. Marshall. 1988. "The Industrial Organization of Congress: Or, Why Legislatures, Like Firms, Are Not Organized Like Markets." *Journal of Political Economy* 96 (1): 132–63.

Weingast, B., K. Shepsle, and C. Johnsen. 1981. "The Political Economy of Costs and Benefits." *Journal of Political Economy* 89 (41): 642–64.

Wildavsky, A. 1986. *Budgeting: A Comparative Theory of Budgetary Processes*. New Brunswick, N.J.: Transaction Books.

Wilensky, H. 1975. *The Welfare State and Equality*. Berkeley: University of California Press.

———. 1981. "Leftism, Catholicism, and Democratic Corporatism: The Role of Political Parties in Recent Welfare State Development." In P. Flora and A. Heidenheimer, eds., *The Development of Welfare States in Europe and America*, 345–82. London: Transaction Books.

Woldendorp, J., H. Keman, and I. Budge. 1994. "Party Government in 20 Democracies." In *Political Data, 1945–90. European Journal of Political Research*, special issue, 24 (1).

———. 1998. "Party Government in 20 Democracies: An Update (1990–1995)." *European Journal of Political Research* 33 (1): 125–64.

Wolfinger, R., and S. Rosenstone. 1980. *Who Votes?* New Haven: Yale University Press.

Woolley, J. 1984. *Monetary Politics: The Federal Reserve and the Politics of Monetary Policy*. Cambridge: Cambridge University Press.

———. 1985. "Central Banks and Inflation." In L. N. Lindberg and C. S. Maier, eds., *The Politics of Inflation and Economic Stagnation*, 318–48. Washington, D.C.: Brookings.

Yashiv, E. 1989. "Inflation and the Role of Money under Discretion and Rules." Working Paper no. 8–89, PSIE, MIT, November.

Zervoyianni, A. 1997. "Monetary Policy Games and Coalitions in a Two-Country Model with Unionised Wage-Setting." *Oxford Economic Papers* 49 (1): 57–76.

Index

Index

broad (multiple), multicolinearity and, 233n

broad (multiple), "varieties of capitalism" approach and, 58–9

central banks with governments and broader political-economic structure, 3–4, 27, 31, 35, 45–6, 52, 55–6, 58, 197–8, 204–5, 205n, 217–18, 224–8, 226n, 230–1, 233–8, 243, 268–70

domestic with foreign monetary policy makers via exchange-rate regimes, 35–8, 45–6, 54–6, 228, 238, 268–70

electoral and partisan cycles and (*see also* replacement risk), 43–7, 47n, 55–7, 181–5, 257–9, 262–6, 274

electoral institutions and inequality (*see* participation and inequality)

interaction terms (linear), estimation of, inference from, (*see also* nonlinear interactive models; conditional serial-correlation parameters), 4, 82, 103–7, 103n, 149, 152, 152n, 173n, 231–3, 243n, 268–9

international exposure and, 56–7, 260–2, 265, 268–9, 275

labor- and goods-market institutional-structural organization and, 212

monetary policy makers with wage-price bargainers, 3, 27, 31, 35, 52, 55–6, 197–8, 198n, 207, 209, 209n, 216–18, 223n, 224–8, 230–43, 245–6, 249–52, 266, 269–70

monetary policy with debt-determinants via policy-adjustment rates, 25–7, 35, 157, 164–7, 189–90, 223, 275

multicolinearity, interaction terms and, 233n

participation (institutions of) and income distribution, 3–4, 21–2, 43, 55, 71–5, 78–9, 103–8, 116, 266–7, 269–70, 276

partisan cycles and, 46, 264–5

substitute and complement relations in, 198, 225, 226, 236, 240, 243

veto actors (institutions of) and policy-adjustment rates, 3–4, 13, 26–7, 45, 45n, 47–8, 85, 127–8, 132–4, 144–7, 147n, 151, 157–8, 164–6, 175–8, 186–7, 190, 266, 269–70

wage-price bargainers, among sectors of, 3, 30–1, 35, 43, 52–3, 55–6, 197–8, 216–17, 223–30, 233–42, 245–6, 246n, 249–52, 268–9, 276

interest rates (real growth-interest rate-differential, expected, actual) (*see also* inflation; public debt), 26, 130–1, 157, 162–7, 188–90, 223–4, 275

international exposure (*see also* interactions; monetary policy; policy efficacy and maneuverability), 46, 56–7, 77, 77n, 91n, 91–2, 108–16, 129–31, 160–2, 162n, 188, 196, 214–15, 222, 228, 230, 241–2, 246–7, 247n, 249, 253–4, 258–62, 265, 268–9, 275

J-tests (*see* non-nested-model tests)

Keynesianism, Keynesian welfare state "crises" in, 10, 13, 31, 53

monetary threats, Keynes-Phillips tradeoffs and, 222

postwar commitments, neoclassical (Keynesian-welfare-state) view of, 7, 8, 11–13, 275

tension between Keynesian policy and redistribution, 10, 275

victim of its own success, 10–11

labor organization/union density (*see also* wage-price bargaining), 21, 77, 77n, 92–4, 108–16, 230

macroeconomic policy, broad/total public fiscal activity (*see also* specific policies), 13–17, 22, 57, 76–7, 77n, 228, 253

measurement and operationalization (*see also* specification; *and individual entries by variable*), 273–4

measurement-error reduction by averaging, 147n, 229

misspecification and underestimation in electoral-cycles studies, 260n

median-voter models of inequality and transfers (*see also* income distribution; interactions, participation; time horizons), 64–9, 71–2, 80, 99, 101–3, 108–16

monetary policy (*see also* antiinflationary shift; central banks; exchange-rate regimes; inflation; interactions; interest rates; monetary threats; policy-adjustment rates; "reform"; wage-price bargaining), 1–3, 5, 13, 25–7, 31, 35–8, 53–6, 58–9, 157, 164–7, 189–90, 196–200, 200n, 202, 204–6, 216–28, 230–47, 249–52, 254–5, 268, 275–6

monetary threats, interactive model of central banks and bargainers and, 205–6, 219–23, 240–3, 267

multicolinearity (*see* interactions, multicolinearity and)

multiple constituencies (*see* distributive politics)

Index

of monetary-policymaking (central banking), 31, 53–5, 58, 196–7, 204, 223, 244, 254–5

popular and academic calls for, 9–10, 13, 18, 41, 122

of public-debt (fiscal) policy, 27, 53–4, 58, 193–5

of public employment, 31, 53–4, 58, 245

of transfer systems, 22, 54, 58, 122–5

of wage-price-bargaining system, 31, 53–4, 58, 249–52

replacement risk (*see also* partisan cycles), 26, 46–7, 49, 53, 56, 132–5, 135n, 147–51, 151n, 154, 156, 181–5, 188–9, 194, 264–5

replication, 274

Ricardian equivalence (*see also* expectations, rational; fiscal illusion), 128–30, 130n, 190–2, 192n, 195n, 273

serially correlated residuals (*see also* dynamic-models specification), 84n, 150–1n

shadow of the future (*see* time horizons)

spatial correlation, in model systematic-components, 84, 84n, 150, 150–1n, 230, 230n

special interests, 8, 12

specification (*see also* measurement; vector autoregression; *and specific policies and outcomes*)

centrality of theoretically informed models, 2, 4, 42, 59, 228, 256, 262, 266–9, 273–4

of debt model, 151–2

of inflation model, 230–1, 230n

of productivity (growth) model, 253, 253n

of transfers model, 81–5

of unemployment model, 230–1, 230n

stagflation and stagnation (*see also* antiinflationary shift; inflation; interest rates; monetary policy; public debt; real GDP; "reform"; transfer systems; unemployment; veto actors), 3, 10, 16, 21, 23, 26–7, 31, 33, 35, 38, 48, 54–5, 63, 127, 157, 159–60, 163–7, 178, 189–90, 223, 253, 268, 275

systems of equations, 259–60

tax-smoothing (economic conditions), theory of public debt, 127–35, 151, 153–4, 157–67, 188–90

tax-structure complexity (*see* fiscal illusion)

tensions, broader goals of postwar policy commitments, 3, 5, 12, 54, 275

Keynesian policy versus redistribution, 10, 275

Keynesian welfare state, victim of success, 10–11

tensions, liberal democracy and free-market capitalism

capitalism, productive and distributional effects, 9

classical (Aristotle, Mill, Marx, Tocqueville, Hamilton) views of, 8, 276–7

political and economic influence, differing allocation of, 2, 3, 5, 11–12, 12–13n, 18, 21, 31, 54, 59, 64–5, 125, 275

terms of trade (*see* international exposure)

"Teutonic Three," 247–8

time horizons

government's, 70, 80, 80n, 99, 102–3, 108–16, 129n

median voter's, 68–70, 80, 99, 101–3, 108–16

time inconsistency

government duration and, 69–70

income-distribution volatility and, 69–70

mitigation of, by partisan representative democracy, 70

monetary policy and, 199, 202

transfer systems and, 69–70, 102, 102–3n

time-period (year) dummy variables (*see* fixed effects)

"tit-for-tat" strategy in repeated games (*see also* prisoner's dilemma), 140

trade openness (exposure) (*see* international exposure)

trade policy (*see also* exchange-rate regimes; international exposure), 12, 12–13n

transfer systems (*see also* other macroeconomic policies and outcomes; age distribution; antiinflationary shift; income distribution; interactions; macroeconomic policy; median-voter models; participation; "reform"; time horizons; unemployment), 1, 5, 10, 18–22, 38, 43–6, 49–50, 52–5, 62–78, 78n, 80, 85–94, 97–9, 101–25, 129n, 195–6, 223, 244, 253, 275–6

trembling-hand credibility, 221

turnout (*see* participation)

two-stage least-squares (*see* endogeneity, modeling and "testing")

UAW, 252n

unemployment, 6, 21–2, 27, 31–5, 51–2, 76, 85–7, 108–19, 130, 157, 159–60, 188, 191, 193, 229–31, 235, 276

305